COUNCIL FOR EMERGING NATIONAL SECURITY AFFAIRS

American Strategy and Purpose

Reflections on Foreign Policy and National Security in an Era Change

```
I0441176
```

Edited by

William H. Natter, III

Jason Brooks

CENSA

COUNCIL FOR EMERGING NATIONAL SECURITY AFFAIRS

Published in the United States of America
By the Council for Emerging National Security Affairs

Copyright © 2014

Council for Emerging National Security Affairs
20 Walnut Street
Lexington, MA 02421
http://www.censa.net

Library of Congress Control Number:

Library of Congress Cataloging0in-Publication Data
American Strategy and Purpose: Reflections on Foreign Policy and
National Security Strategy in an Era of Change
Edited by William H. Natter, III and Jason Brooks
Includes bibliographical references

ISBN 13: 978-1505516203
ISBN 10: 150551620X

1. National Security Strategy. 2. Foreign Policy I. Title. II. William H.
Natter, III and Jason Brooks

Printed and bound in the United States of America

1 2 3 4 5 6 7 8 9

Cover Art: Diesel + Dust Brand Imaging

CONTENTS

Part III: Potential Policies and Consequences

Dedicated to the memory of Isaac 'Ike' Newton Skelton IV
(1931-2013)
Chairman, Panel on Military Education (1987-1989)
Chairman, House Armed Services Committee (2007-2011)
Member of Congress (1977-2011)
A gentleman and true patriot.

Acknowledgements

This book begins with a dedication to the memory of the late Ike Skelton, a former Member of the United States Congress from the State of Missouri. A lawyer, politician, husband, and father, Skelton not only enjoyed reading history as a personal pastime but also believed in promoting its lessons as a way to address various public policy issues — especially those involving foreign affairs, national defense, and strategy. Inspired by this love of history, Skelton worked tirelessly throughout his career to improve America's professional military education system in an effort to develop a cadre of national security specialists that would be second to none. In recognition of his efforts, the Joint Forces Staff College and the U.S. Army Command and General Staff College each host a library named in his honor. The editors of this volume share the same affinity for the discipline of history and strategic studies, and have directly and indirectly benefited from many of the Skelton-inspired improvements executed throughout the national security community. They are thus appreciative of his labors and are the better for them, and note that this book is partly motivated by his example.

This product would not have come together without the efforts of a number of other individuals, whose inputs were certainly more direct in nature. Mrs. Janis Williams provided essential editing services and indispensable advice for each and every essay. The editors are, therefore, forever in her debt. CENSA interns Alexandra Bellows and Harrison Johnson also provided assistance, either in shaping the initial concept and vision of the original "Call to Authors" statement or by commenting on various essays. Their contributions are appreciated. And CENSA's Board of Directors displayed an uncommon amount of patience with the project even after significant delays occurred for one reason or another. Without their collective authorization, patience, and support, this book would never have made it to publication.

And last but certainly not least, the editors would like to acknowledge each of the contributors for taking the time to submit their respective work and for their patience as questions and revisions were presented during several rounds of edits. Some essays were revised more significantly than others during these iterations; and a few were revamped to include entirely new themes and arguments, a result of questions raised during the editing process. Thus, with respect to the contributors: without *their* patience, understanding, and willingness to adjust, this volume could not have been produced in its final form. For this, the editors also remain grateful.

Foreword

Congressman Mac Thornberry (R-TX), Vice Chairman,
House Armed Services Committee

Director of National Intelligence, retired General James Clapper, testified before Congress that in his 50 years in intelligence,

> "I don't recall a more complex and interdependent array of challenges than we face today.... Never before has the intelligence community been called upon to match such complexity on so many issues, and in a resource-constrained environment."[1]

This "complex and interdependent array of challenges" will test us in various ways. Some test our patience and endurance; others put our values to the test. Many will test the adaptability of our organizations and processes and even our thinking.

When considering our nation's security in the years ahead, we can be fairly certain about two things. One is that we will have to deal with the unexpected. The second is that we will have to meet all of our challenges within tight budgets.

Applying limited resources to essentially unlimited problems is a matter of strategy. And a wide stream of thought convincingly argues that the United States has not done strategy very well in recent years. Thus, there is a real need for serious thinking and insights, such as those offered in

---

[1] http://www.dni.gov/files/documents/Newsroom/
Testimonies/20110310_testimony_clapper.pdf.

this volume, just at the time when we need to address these issues most acutely.

We can start with the threats we face today, and it is a full complement. But they are compounded by worrisome signs that point toward even more difficult times ahead.

For example, we can be reasonably assured that terrorism will remain with us beyond the life of Al Qaeda's core leadership, spreading to other parts of the globe and perhaps evolving to include chemical, biological, or radiological weapons. Serious difficulties with Iran or North Korea may erupt unexpectedly. The collapse of a nuclear state, such as Pakistan, is one of the world's nightmare scenarios. And the growing sophistication of non-state actors like drug cartels and international organized crime adds new complexities to fighting crime, illicit trafficking, and terrorism. Of course, all the while, China and Russia put greater emphasis on key military capabilities designed to offset or neutralize U.S. strengths.

And if that were not enough, we face a new domain of espionage, theft, terrorism, and military operations in cyberspace, which presents a host of difficult problems in law and policy. It is a domain where geography is largely irrelevant, attribution of attacks sometimes impossible, the relationship between government and the private sector undeveloped, and perceived threats to personal privacy crippling. Yet, it is a domain that is a fundamental backbone of modern society.

But, as daunting as those challenges are, we can also be certain that we will have national security threats that we do not predict. In fact, the editors of the book, *America's First Battles*, note that our record in predicting the next war is not good:

> The record of Americans' ability to predict the nature
> of the next war (not to mention its causes, location, time,
> adversary or adversaries, and allies) has been uniformly

dismal.... But the myopia of the past in no way lessens the need to prepare. Quite the contrary. Preparations of the most certain sort possible are required for a most uncertain future.[2]

Accurate predictions will be even harder to make as we contend with such a wide range of challenges, from the individual, lone wolf terrorist using fertilizer-based bombs to kill innocents to the sophisticated nation states threatening us in space and in cyberspace.

We know from our daily lives that the pace of change is accelerating. A cursory review of the national security challenges of the past decade also reminds us that the world can change rapidly and that the unexpected can and does occur. When considering that future military engagements may literally take place at the speed of light, it is clear that our ponderous, industrial age bureaucracies must be reformed.

And yet, this vast array of national security challenges and an unpredictable future will have to be met with limited resources. America has placed itself into a precarious financial position. We have had tremendous growth in government spending, especially in entitlement programs and most especially in those accounts related to health care. Although defense has shrunk from about half of the federal budget in 1960 to less than 20 percent today, no federal program, including defense, will escape the belt-tightening that is necessary for the foreseeable future.

Of course there may be more than monetary constraints placed on our national security options. Modern media and technology bring more information (and perhaps less context) into our living rooms than ever before. We have already seen adversaries who lack the full extent of our sophisticated technology but are able to use media and communications

---

[2] Charles E. Heller and William A. Stofft, eds., *America's First Battles, 1776-1965* (Lawrence: University Press of Kansas, 1986), xii.

tactics against us in quite a sophisticated way. And just as the pace of change is accelerating, our expectations of achieving success quickly are also accelerating. All of these trends may well mean that policy makers will have to operate within the limits of the American people's patience and willingness to engage.

The approach we take to meeting a vast number of security challenges within limited resources involves strategy. Since the end of the Cold War, it seems that our strategy has primarily been to have no strategy at all—to react to the events forced upon us. In fact, some say we have to reach back to the Eisenhower Administration and its Solarium project to find a good example of systemic strategic planning within the U.S. government.

There have, of course, been a number of documents issued by various administrations that were labeled "strategy" but, at least in recent years, these have consisted primarily of a series of vague statements and aspirational goals. Calling a slick-papered publication a "strategy" does not make it one.

As Dr. Richard Rumelt, noted business professor and consultant, writes,

> The core of strategic work is always the same: discovering the critical factors in a situation and designing a way of coordinating and focusing actions to deal with those factors.
>
> A leader's most important responsibility is identifying the biggest challenges to forward progress and devising a coherent approach to overcoming them. In contexts ranging from corporate direction to national security, strategy matters. Yet we have become so accustomed to strategy as exhortation that we hardly blink an eye when a leader spouts slogans and announces high-sounding goals, calling the mixture a 'strategy.'[3]

---

[3] Richard P. Rumelt, *Good Strategy, Bad Strategy: The Difference and Why It Matters* (New York: Crown Publishing Group, 2011), 2.

There is evidence that other countries are, as part of their strategy, pursuing certain technologies, such as anti-access weapons, anti-space weapons, and cyber weapons to offset or deny any American advantage.

We should be quite clear that meeting the broad array of challenges with limited resources makes defense reform a necessity. We must find a way to improve our acquisition process, contracting procedures, and personnel policies, among others—all to get more out of each dollar we spend.

But first, we must have a real national security strategy. Our present situation calls to mind the well-known paraphrase from renowned Victorian author, Lewis Carroll, "If you don't know where you're going, any road'll take you there."

Some attributes of an appropriate strategy seem clear. In an era of rapid change and not a lot of money to spend, any strategy must emphasize innovation and flexibility. It ought to be based on knowledge and understanding, which is different from information. It must facilitate making use of all our instruments of national power and influence.

General notions of the desirable attributes and the goals of a strategy may help shape it but do not provide the clarity that can only be provided through a systematic strategic process.

And while Congress cannot formulate or implement national security strategy, it should be a partner in both. Congress shares some of the responsibility, not only for the problems we face but also for the solutions. Just as any successful strategy will require interagency effectiveness, it will also require integrated effort across the branches of the U.S. government.

So, for example, to implement a strategy there must be predictable funding. There must be a way to achieve the necessary oversight with accountability for the programs that seek to implement the national strategy. When there is a problem, Congress must not overreact with micromanagement or new layers of bureaucracy.

In analyzing national leadership in times of war, Eliot Cohen in *Supreme Command* found that, "It is, indeed, in his ability to adapt, and not in the capacity for grand design, that a war statesman finds his largest test."[4]

So, it is with us as a nation. We must have a strategy, and at the same time, we must understand that any strategy is inadequate. As President Eisenhower said, "Plans are worthless, but planning is everything." Our ability to adapt to new challenges and changing circumstance is our greatest and most important test.

Washington, DC
Fall 2012

---

[4] Eliot A. Cohen, *Supreme Command: Soldiers, Statesmen, and Leadership in Wartime* (New York: The Free Press, 2002), 32.

Preface

Major General Paul D. Eaton USA (Ret)

The essays that follow provide a full spectrum assessment of the threats and challenges that face the United States and the international system, and they shed light on national strategies that can aid American policy makers as they navigate relentless change.

The United States' primary twentieth century challenger and only true existential threat, the Soviet Union, folded its colors over twenty-five years ago ushering in a period of profound national security adjustments, and non-state actors have since evolved to challenge the notion of statehood codified in the Treaty of Westphalia. Where once only national armies, air forces, and navies challenged the control of the global commons, transnational non-state actors have proven capable of undermining free transit, security, and domestic governance.

Compounding the complexity of change are not only the evolving pressures and "geopolitical realities" of resource, technology, and social competition, but also the recent arrival of two new common mediums: space and cyber. Not only must the United States now maintain forces to ensure unimpeded access to the air and sea commons, it must also ensure that such a dependence on the mediums of space and cyber do not become an unacceptable vulnerability. Indeed, the asymmetrical possibilities in space and in the cyber world appear to be even more profound and potentially devastating.

True, the nation-state remains the basic organizational unit of the international system. But in an increasingly connected and competitive world, the nature of challenges and potential threats has transcended lines on the map and is further challenging traditional ways of understanding. To keep pace with such change, the United States must better align its foreign policy and security goals and practices with an improved sense of vital national interests. Without question, the art of defining and identifying such interests is the most important endeavor facing the leaders in Washington.

Managing change and adapting to new operational environments is the primary responsibility of leadership, and it is especially important to the sustainability of American global leadership. The adjustment to the 'rise of the rest', in particular the *BRIC* nations – Brazil, Russia, India and China – but also the general economic improvement throughout nearly all countries (as measured in *gross domestic product)*, should not be lightly or recklessly considered. The same can be said for dealings with Iran, as that country, too, marches along a path of regional ascendancy. For Washington, therefore, adaptation to transnational threats and the proliferation of greater geopolitical competition appears to be the best course of action, one requiring careful deliberation. Such is the journey embarked on in the pages that follow.

With this as a contextual backdrop, America does not need to create new enemies nor, to paraphrase John Quincy Adams, go "abroad in search of monsters to destroy." With respect to Iran, this volume rightly suggests that Washington and Tehran should consider the outline of a grand bargain based on mutually acceptable interests. With respect to China, this volume suggests Washington should remain confident in its relative geopolitical position and continue to manage the spirit of the relationship started by President Nixon in 1972 – even if contemporary circumstances have produced considerable levels of tension and reasons for rivalry. With respect to Latin America, this volume calls for, among other things, improvements in immigration laws and policy. And with respect to al Qaeda and other affiliated terrorist groups, the contributors to this volume call for not only greater clarity and understanding about the threat, but greater conviction in the execution of the response.

As America capitalizes on its departure from Iraq, drives to the end of combat in Afghanistan, and redeploys the bulk of its combat forces, it would be wise for its leadership to seek greater clarity and understanding about the new and unique characteristics of the international security environment. To be sure, the potential for armed conflict remains. But other challenges – old and new – are both significant and many, and the impulse to react imprudently all too great. Strategic promise, on the other hand, can be found in the art and skill of thoughtful and deliberate action, especially if it encourages reciprocal and reassuring behavior in potential adversaries. Such has been the policy of the State Department in its pursuit of "strategic reassurance" for U.S.-China relations and aptly described by former Deputy Secretary of State James Steinberg: "Just as we and our allies must make clear that we are prepared to welcome China's 'arrival'...as a prosperous and successful power, China must reassure the rest of the world that its development and growing global role will not come at the expense of [the] security and well-being of others."[1]

Americans have always been enthralled with the concept of "*exceptionalism*" in the world of human affairs, a sense of self that has influenced or governed the nation's policies and approach to global challenges. This sense of uniqueness coincides with America's founding as a Republic, as shown by

---

[1] Steinberg, President George W. Bush's Deputy Secretary of State, cited in Andrew Nathan and Andrew Scobell, "How China Sees America," *Foreign Affairs*, Volume 91, No. 5 (September/October 2012), p. 44.

Robert R. Tomes in the first essay of this book. America's constitutional tradition, too, has profoundly affected the nation's behavior during interactions with other members of the global community. This fundamental characteristic is fully evident throughout the thinking of the American Founding Fathers and brought to life in the essay provided by David C. Hendrickson.

But understanding the nature of the American character is not enough for U.S. policymakers to meet the unique challenges of tomorrow. To meet these challenges, a greater understanding of the *world* is needed to improve the respective disciplines of policy formulation and strategy. These are the topics and disciplines addressed during the rest of the book, culminating with John Arquilla's impressive essay describing and critiquing the strategic choices made throughout history by many of the world's great powers.

As a whole, the collection of essays contained in the following pages attempt to assist both current and future American policy makers in their search for enlightened leadership. Some of these topics and disciplines are addressed in the subsequent chapters of this book.

Introduction

William H. Natter, III

Post-Cold War Sentiment and American Ascendancy

The post-Cold War euphoria of the 1990s produced a rich conversation about the United States' ascendant position and role in the world. More than two decades hence, many of the same arguments and themes continue, despite the occurrence of a profound shift in America's overall security posture sparked by the events on 9/11.

Several books published during the post-9/11 period are illustrative. One, by Dennis Ross, is optimistically entitled, *Statecraft: And How to Restore America's Standing in the World*; another, by Anne-Marie Slaughter, is entitled, *The Idea That Is America*; and a third, by Joseph S. Nye, Jr., explores *The Future of Power*. Two additional publications deserve special notice due to the differences in their perspective and tone with respect to America's future influence. The first of this group is a confident and hopeful book by Robert Kagan, entitled, *The World America Made*, a marked contrast to Andrew J. Bacevich's, *The Limits of Power: The End of American Exceptionalism*.

This sampling of post-9/11 literature represents a genre that stands on the scholarly foundations of—and in many respects echoes themes found within—similar works published during the 1990s; the sampling also reveals a number of scholars that have maintained influence and relevance despite shifting circumstances. Nye is an excellent example of an author that has transcended the two eras, publishing perhaps his most notable work in 1990: *Bound to Lead: The Changing Nature of American Power*. Another remarkable '90s publication is *The End of History and the Last Man*, in which author Francis Fukuyama predicted the primacy of Western liberal democracy. And in 1996 Donald W. White put forth, *The American Century: The Rise and Decline of the United States as a World Power*, a narrative consonant with a growing feeling at the time that America could not possibly enjoy the same amount of influence in the 21st century as it had experienced during the twentieth.

In addition to nurturing provocative thoughts about social and political trends, the 1990s produced a renaissance of sorts in U.S. strategic theory, yielding a thematic form of discourse that for the most part still shapes the post-9/11 conversation. Barry R. Posen and Andrew L. Ross summarized the debate of the period with an article in 1996 entitled, "Competing Visions for U.S. Grand Strategy." Reflecting on the disintegration of the Soviet Union and American ascendancy — or the "unipolar" moment — Posen and Ross forwarded neo-isolationism and primacy as two viable yet diametrically opposed strategies for guiding U.S. action. While neo-isolationists "embraced a constricted view of U.S. national interests that renders internationalism not only unnecessary but counterproductive,"[1] primacy enthusiasts asserted that "only a preponderance of U.S. power ensures peace."[2]

A form of this strategic debate continues today with "off-shore balancing" standing in opposition to the concept of "deep engagement." "Deep engagement" advocates fully imbibe the idea of establishing an extensive network of forward basing and security commitments abroad in

---

[1] Barry R. Posen and Andrew L. Ross, "Competing Visions for U.S. Grand Strategy," *International Security*, Volume 21, No. 3 (Winter 1996/97): 9.
[2] Ibid., 32.

combination with efforts to protect the "global commons" for navigation and commerce. In contrast, proponents of "off-shore balancing"—a variation of neo-isolationism or retrenchment—see such a commitment as too taxing on a nation in need of a more sound economic footing. The off-shore-*ists* "argue that the United States should scale back its security commitments, share or shed the burdens of maintaining global order, and join with foreign nations to preserve local power balances only when those nations demonstrate that they cannot do so alone."[3]

America's post-9/11 security posture and approach to the world thus occurs against a rich intellectual backdrop. And scholars, strategists, and policymakers alike continue to search for a greater understanding about global affairs, for America's position and role in them, and for an updated philosophical polestar to guide American action in the twenty first century. Yet just beneath the surface of this inspired quest is an American disposition tempered by the weighty experience of war, and weary from the burdens of leadership. This tension should bring to the fore several important questions for American leaders to consider: What is the nature of the moment within which America currently finds itself? What historical and social trends underlie its existence? What political forces and ideals (at home and abroad) shape its thinking and actions? What political, cultural, technological, and militant challenges currently exist around the globe? And

---

[3] Evan Braden Montgomery, "Contested Primacy in the Western Pacific: China's Rise and the Future of U.S. Power Projection," *International Security*, Volume 38, No. 4 (Spring 2014): 120. For an updated discussion of the 1990s debate see Barry R. Posen, "Pull Back: The Case for a Less Activist Foreign Policy," *Foreign Affairs*, Volume 92, No. 1 (January/February 2013): 116-128. In the same volume see the essay on pages 130-142, entitled "Lean Forward: In Defense of American Engagement" by Stephen G. Brooks, G. John Ikenberry, and William C. Wohlforth.

finally, with respect to formulating a response and potential course of action: what is the art of the possible?

Historical Shifts and the Current Strategic Context

The collapse of the Soviet Union and the end of the Cold War precipitated a profound and remarkable global political transformation. And in 1993 historian John Lukacs emphatically trumpeted: "the twentieth century ended with the events of 1989."[4] Policy makers and other interested parties spent the remainder of the decade attempting to understand the meaning and implications of these events, and then the world suddenly changed again in the year 2001. The sudden terrorist strikes on 9/11 triggered yet another form of global geo-political transformation, forcing America to move well beyond philosophical deliberations and debate.

The United States chose to put the primacy theory into practice immediately after 9/11, subsequently engaging in two major overseas contingencies: *Operation Enduring Freedom* and *Operation Iraqi Freedom.* This choice and consequent experience elsewhere (i.e., the Arabian Peninsula, the African continent, and Southeast Asia) led Secretary of Defense Donald Rumsfeld to announce that Washington had committed the U.S. to "The Long War"—an ill-defined and open-ended commitment, possibly requiring the American nation to adopt a permanent war-fighting posture.

The world has changed for Americans in other (and perhaps still indeterminate) ways. In the immediate aftermath of 9/11, leaders in Washington authorized and appropriated billions of dollars' worth of initiatives designed to neutralize or destroy "monsters abroad." An unprecedented number of these activities have been—rightly or wrongly, effectively or

---

[4] John Lukacs, *The End of the Twentieth Century and the End of the Modern Age* (New York: Ticknor and Fields, 1993), 280.

not—extended and expanded, requiring several hundred billion (arguably trillions!) more. And yet, with the second term of the Obama Administration well established, an American "reset" has possibly begun to take root, setting a new approach—wisely or not—for how America engages in foreign affairs, even as turmoil in Iraq and elsewhere flares up again and *Operation Enduring Freedom* winds to a close. Meanwhile, concerns continue to mount about a perceived disconnect between the input and output—or relative effectiveness—of U.S. national security initiatives across the board. Indeed, the impetus for this book began in response to such concerns.

Although the strategic concepts of primacy and retrenchment are neither analyzed nor directly addressed in the following pages, they provide, at a minimum, a critical and necessary backdrop as well as proper context. At least one essay, written by Anna Simons, calls for a retrenchment of sorts as she defends an earlier book she co-authored, entitled *The Sovereignty Solution*, against a critique written by James Hasik. Another, provided by Oriana Skylar Mastro, tackles challenges to U.S. primacy and deep engagement initiatives in the far reaches of the western Pacific, specifically as it pertains to China's "anti-access/area denial," or "A2/AD" strategy. And John Arquilla offers an essay entitled, "Thinking Three Dimensionally About American Defense," in which he creates an x, y, and z theoretical construct for understanding and drawing lessons from the strategic force planning decisions of great military powers in prior eras. Arquilla's essay concludes with an appeal to U.S. strategists and Pentagon force planners to heed such lessons and then includes a suggestion of his own.

Other essays are equally impressive in their own right with respect to airing out the possibilities of policy options for addressing present circumstances: Keith W. Mines combines an assessment of political, technological, and socio-economic transnational trends with his own practical policy recommendations in "The Fall of the House of Westphalia;" with his essay, Brian Mazanec examines the evolution of cyber warfare and draws parallels to the examples of previous technological innovations and their impact on social norms; Guermantes Lailari and Aaron Eitan Meyer combine forces to describe both the challenge and potential consequences of "Lawfare," an emerging "non-kinetic" tool in international competition and conflict;   Tom Carter reviews America's approach to Latin America and probes the issue of immigration reform; and Jason Brooks digs into the realities and nuances of global energy resource competition.

The works of several authors fall more squarely into the strategic realm: Sebastian L. v. Gorka calls for the establishment of several new guiding strategic principles in the fight against al Qaeda; Glenn E. Robinson lays out a case for U.S.-Iranian relations, describing for decision makers the choice between confrontation and a grand political bargain; John J. Klein offers a superb assessment of current U.S. nuclear posture and presents a new vision for the existence and role of nuclear weapons; and Amy Zalman explores public diplomacy and strategic messaging—indeed, the "battle of ideas"—a vitally important topic in this era of independent information sources.

Three contributors—Pruett, Miska, and Kollars—provide solid offerings from the perspective of the practitioner, with each adding recommendations on the practical aspects of—or the "how to" for—bringing into effect the vision and policy goals of senior U.S. leaders. Jesse Pruett advocates effectively for greater support of interagency expeditionary teams in overseas contingencies. Steve Miska provides moral arguments in favor of more extensive authority for the use of the Special Immigrant VISA program and cites the mixed experience in Iraq and Afghanistan. With her contribution, Nina A. Kollars tackles an aspect of the popular "innovation debate" currently raging throughout the Department of Defense, arguing that the user (i.e., the soldier, sailor, airman, or Marine) should be better integrated into—and more accommodated by—weapons systems' design teams. Kollars' piece adroitly addresses the effectiveness part of the innovation debate and implies a path forward for achieving greater efficiencies across the department. Given the reality of declining budgets, defense planners would do well to place greater weight on her observations, as at some point effectiveness begins to achieve a level of efficiency of its own making.

Finally, the opening section of *American Strategy and Purpose* consists of three essays focused on both the character and current strategic position of the United States in world affairs. The first two, offered by Robert R. Tomes and David C. Hendrickson, focus on the American character and political tradition. Tomes explores the concept of "American Exceptionalism," its origin and meaning. Hendrickson provides a link between the debates and policies of today and the original vision of the American Founding Fathers— suggesting strongly that these revolutionaries would be alarmed at, if not appalled by, the rise, extent, and nature of the modern national security establishment (because of its consequential effects on the nature of the Republic itself). The third essay of the opening section, provided by Ali Wyne, addresses the declinist debate about the United States' position in the world, especially as it relates to America's nearest peer strategic competitor active in the Pacific theater: China. Refreshingly, his essay provides a healthy tonic for tempering the alarmist thinking about China's rise and for placing declinist thinking in its proper context. For Wyne, the Chinese are not "ten feet tall" and America is not destined to falter and join the ranks of former great powers of bygone eras.

When the Berlin Wall fell and the Soviet Union disintegrated, scholars Graham Allison and Gregory F. Treverton described post-Cold War United States as existing in yet another "moment of re-creation" — at least its third or fourth opportunity during a century that also involved America's true emergence as a global leader for the first time, a withdrawal, and its participation in two major wars around the globe.[5] Tony Smith soon followed the Allison-Treverton description by publishing *America's Mission*, in which he recalled Woodrow Wilson's desire "to make the world safe for democracy."[6] Coincidentally, historian John Lukacs had declared a victory on this point just a year before, stating in 1993 that the "triumph of democracy has become worldwide."[7] But as we know, history marched on differently and did not heel: the 9/11 attacks instead undermined the validity of Lukacs' assertion, and thrust upon America yet another transitional moment. Ultimately, 9/11 provided an opportunity for America to re-create itself — an opportunity that remains a work in progress, indeed a plight with an uncertain future.

For decision makers, students of American power, and for potential public aspirants keen on harnessing its promise, the scholarly and literary work produced over the past two decades offers ample intellectual fodder for consumption and consideration. If nothing else, its combined effect implores these interested parties to consider the complexity of the

---

[5] Graham Allison and Gregory F. Treverton, eds., *Rethinking America's Security: Beyond Cold War to New World Order* (New York: W.W. Norton and Company, 1992), 13.

[6] Tony Smith, *America's Mission: The United States and the Worldwide Struggle for Democracy in the Twentieth Century* (Princeton: Princeton University Press, 1994), 3-4.

[7] Lukacs, 285.

world in accordance with fairly conventional strategic and foreign policy principles and themes, with some immensely shaped by America's own self-image. The hard and bitter post-9/11 experience, however, should alternately pull the American psyche in a more non-traditional direction, almost as if many of these time-honored world views are — while still relevant — satisfactory no more. Ideally and not so ideally, experience influences outlook and impacts judgment. In short, experience matters.

American Strategy and Purpose is thus offered in the hopes of mapping a more comprehensive picture of America's position and role in the world, one that includes an exploration of America's self-image. It is an effort to bridge the traditional with the non-traditional, to challenge the theoretical with the practical, and to recognize the disciplines of policy, strategy, history, military affairs, economics, and political science as part of a multi-dimensional, interrelated whole. To be sure — and to paraphrase yet another timeless observation offered by historian John Lukacs — the character and elements of world historical development should underlay all calculations of global strategy and political power.[8] Perhaps, after reading this book, readers will agree.

---

[8] Lukacs, 274.

Part I: American Character, Purpose, and Position

American Exceptionalism in the 21st Century

Robert R. Tomes

Introduction

Exceptionalist thinking is on the rise in American politics. Concepts and beliefs associated with the term "American exceptionalism" figured prominently in the 2012 U.S. Presidential election, bringing the term from relatively obscure academic writings to mainstream political discourse. *The Atlantic's* Terrence McCoy found that the term "American Exceptionalism" appeared in national publications in the United States 457 times from 1980 through 2000, expanded to 2,558 times during the 2000s, and then exploded to 4,172 times from 2010 through 2012.[1]

In the run-up to the 2012 election, American exceptionalism became a central part of the debate over which candidate had the better vision for restoring American economic vitality, for preserving America's role in world affairs, and for reawakening the American dream. The *Washington Post* observed that questions about American exceptionalism were a "front," or major battleground, "in the ongoing culture wars" during the election.[2] For Stefen Harper

---

[1] Terrence McCoy, "How Joseph Stalin Invented 'American Exceptionalism'" in *The Atlantic* online accessed November 20, 2012 at www.atlantic.com/politics/archive/2012/03/ho-joseph-stalin-invented-american-exceptionalism/254534/.

[2] Clinton cited in John A. Gans, Jr., "American Exceptionalism and the Politics of Foreign Policy," *The Atlantic* online accessed November 23,

and Jonathan Clarke, American exceptionalism is "the mother of the nation's Big Ideas," those fundamental ideas, concepts, and narratives that recur in our political culture and underwrite foreign policy doctrines, party platforms, and our strategic culture.[3]

However, exceptionalism is not just an idea. It is not just one concept or argument; instead, it's an interwoven bundle of ideas that, together, represent an American creed or ideology. American exceptionalism implies a belief that the United States is unique among nations—for some, even superior. According to a Gallup poll published in December 2010, eighty percent of Americans asked whether "the U.S. has a unique character that makes it the greatest country in the world" responded "yes."[4] A second strain of exceptionalism holds that America has a special or pre-ordained role to play in world affairs, and that role requires America to lead. Exceptionalist thinking also influences the character of global leadership in the form of American unilateralism, an aversion to subordinating American troops to international organizations, and low interest among American voters for strengthening foreign partnerships as a priority in foreign policy. For some, American exceptionalism is about a mission or duty; for others it is a cover for imperialism.

Exceptionalist thinking runs deep in American political culture. It is an ethos tied to an American creed of individuality, liberalism, progressivism, and pragmatism. It is a teleological construct that impels American expansion,

---

1012 at
http:/www.theatlantic.com/international/print/2011/11/American-exceptionalism-and-the-poltics-of-foreign-policy/248779/.

[3] Stefen Halper and Jonathan Clarke, *The Silence of the Rational Center: Why American Foreign Policy is Failing* (New York: Basic Books, 2007), 22.

[4] Jeffrey M. Jones, "Americans See U.S. as Exceptional; 37% Doubt Obama Does" (Gallup online, December 22, 2010) accessed November 23, 2012, at http://www.gallup.com/poll/145358/american-doubt-obama.

leadership, and interventionism to promote, export, and defend that ethos. In its most assertive form, exceptionalist thinking underwrote the George W. Bush Administration's 2002 preemption strategy and 2003 invasion of Iraq.

Exceptionalist thinking heavily influences American foreign policy decision-making, including how leaders and diplomats portray the United States and frame decisions in the context of America's role in the world. In his acceptance speech for the Nobel Peace Prize in 2009, President Barack Obama framed post-Cold War American foreign policy in exceptionalist terms, stating that "the United States has helped underwrite global security for more than six decades with the blood of our citizens and the strength of our arms."[5]

The exceptionalist narrative is more than a rhetorical device to appeal to voters or to market policy decisions to the public. The exceptionalist narrative also resonates overseas, where U.S. policies wrapped in exceptionalist rhetoric can either rally support for American positions or lead to conflict over the implied vision for American leadership, power, or influence. "Nothing is more vexing to foreigners," Andrew Kohut and Bruce Stokes found in their research for *America Against the World*, "than Americans' belief that America is a shining city on a hill—a place apart, where a better way of life exists, on to which all people should aspire."[6]

This article explores the meaning of American exceptionalism, past and present, reviewing the evolution of

5 Obama cited in John A. Gans, Jr., "American Exceptionalism and the Politics of Foreign Policy," *The Atlantic* online accessed November 23, 2012, at
   http:/www.theatlantic.com/international/print/2011/11/American-exceptionalism-and-the-poltics-of-foreign-policy/248779/.
6 Andrew Kohut and Bruce Stokes, "The Problem With American Exceptionalism" (Pew Global Attitudes Project) released May 9, 2006, accessed January 10, 2013, www.pewglobal.org/2006/05/09/the-problem-of-american-exceptionalism.

thinking about it to understand how exceptionalist thinking in American foreign policy shapes domestic and foreign thinking about security affairs. American exceptionalism stands apart from other countries' nationalism and feelings of national pride specifically because American exceptionalism evolved as an ideology.

Roots of Exceptionalism: Forging an American Identity

The origins of exceptionalism rest in America's Puritan roots and the idea that America was founded as a promised land — that is, a new type of republic dedicated to a popular form of government designed to empower individuals and enable them to improve their lives with minimal interference from the state, to achieve an unprecedented level of social mobility (a meritocracy), and to live free of religious persecution or prejudice. Puritans also believed that God sometimes acts through the faithful, or through chosen agents, providing divine guidance and direction to influence history. This strain of Puritan thinking was particularly strong among those who founded colonies and believed that the new Republic was serving a larger, divinely ordained, mission.

Histories of American exceptionalism usually start with Massachusetts Governor John Winthrop's famous 1630 statement in which he envisioned America as a "city on a hill," a sentiment restated by Ronald Reagan as a "shining city on a hill."

Winthrop probably made the statement on the ship *Arbela* on the way to the new world, or in port as part of a Massachusetts Bay Company mission to colonize America. The phrase, adapted from Jesus's Sermon on the Mount, reflected the settlers' belief that they were founding a colony that would be a model for future Pilgrims, one that provided freedom of religion and an environment where prosperity was not tied to—or constrained by—religious affiliation or family origins.

But the sentiment was not focused on the founding of a new republic destined to break from England, and thus Winthrop is not a father of current exceptionalist thinking. Rather, his thinking, directed at a European audience, focused on the example the new colony could provide to other colonists. It implied no vision for a United States as a new nation. Winthrop preached his words to a people who did not anticipate, much less foment, a revolution.

The Founders who did cement revolutionary American thought were influenced by natural law and enlightenment philosophy, resulting in a vision for a new nation based on progress, individual freedoms, a weak executive branch constrained by a legislative body, and a national purpose based on reasoned pursuit of prosperity. The essayist Thomas Paine figured prominently in the founding vision for the new republic. His widely read 1776 pamphlet, *Common Sense*, accurately characterized thinking at the time about the opportunity being offered by the founding of America, observing: "We have it in our power to begin the world over again," and opining that the "birthday of a new world is at hand." With his pen, the image of an exceptionalist, revolutionary nation was given voice.

The Founders believed that humans are inherently flawed yet able to create just and harmonious societies by applying the principles of natural law and Enlightenment-inspired liberalism. They also believed that a "new order of the ages" was upon them, one that opened the way for a society capable of sustaining a peaceful, stable, socially and politically just polity that found strength by embracing diversity. The uniqueness of the new nation included a sense that America would need to chart its own position in global affairs, particularly when it came to trade with the European powers. When George Washington uttered his famous farewell address warning "to steer clear of permanent alliances," later changed to avoiding "entangling alliances," he warned against treaties or agreements that would lock the nation into an alliance with one power over another. Doing so could drag America into war or limit the new nation's flexibility in developing trade and commerce abroad.

At the time of Washington's farewell address, the dilemma facing the nation was whether to align with Britain, which America was trying to break free of, or with France, which was experiencing its own revolutionary violence. The argument was not in favor of, or against, alliances at all, but for preventing the new nation from being constrained in its actions because of a binding agreement. Later strains of exceptionalist thinking transformed the warning against entangling alliances into a recommendation for isolationism, but the real message was an appeal for unilateralism and independence from any outside influence.

The roots of exceptionalist sentiment lie, for social scientist Seymour Martin Lipset, in the founding days of the nation and the evolution of a uniquely American ideology or creed that persists today:

> Born out of revolution, the United States is a country organized around an ideology which includes a set of dogmas about the nature of a good society. Americanism, as different people have pointed out, is an "ism" or ideology in the same way that communism or fascism or liberalism are isms. [T]he nation's ideology can be described in five words: liberty, egalitarianism, individualism, populism, and laissez-faire. The revolutionary ideology which became the American Creed is liberalism in its eighteenth- and nineteenth-century meanings, as distinct from conservative Toryism, statist

communitarianism, mercantilism, and noblesse oblige dominant in monarchical, state-church-formed cultures.[7]

English philosopher G. K. Chesterton adds that, "America is the only nation in the world that is founded on a creed. That creed is set forth with dogmatic and even theological lucidity in the Declaration of Independence."[8] For Lipset, exceptionalist thinking serves both positive and negative impulses in American culture. "The American Creed," he concludes, "is something of a double-edged sword: it fosters a high sense of personal responsibility, independent initiative, and voluntarism even as it also encourages self-serving behavior, atomism, and a disregard for communal good."[9]

Jefferson: Exceptionalism as Restraint

Thomas Jefferson's approach to foreign affairs is often associated with recurring themes or traditions in U.S. foreign policy. His extension of the United States to the Pacific, for example, is associated with an "expansionist" impulse in U.S. foreign policy, and with the mystique of an expanding "frontier"; his deployment of Marines to battle Barbary pirates in Tripoli is often associated with unilateralism and with militarism; his reluctance to build stronger diplomatic ties to Europe is sometimes associated with isolationism; and his attempts to create an international commercial system favorable to U.S. commerce is associated with liberal internationalism.

Many of these associations with foreign policy traditions are contested. Few, however, deny Jefferson's association with the most basic of the themes to emerge from the Founding

---

[7] Seymour Martin Lipset, *American Exceptionalism: A Double-Edged Sword* (New York: W. W. Norton & Company, 1996), 31

[8] Chesterton cited in Lispet, *American Exceptionalism*, 31.

[9] Lipset, *American Exceptionalism*, 268.

Fathers' debates over foreign affairs and America's role in world politics: the notion of American exceptionalism, the belief that by virtue of its form of government, commitment to liberty, and vibrant society, America would serve as an example for others.

Jefferson's approach was premised on an inwardly-focused vision of exceptionalism. The United States should set an example at home, but not attempt to impose an American model of government on others. In a letter to Jefferson, John Adams articulated the underlying rationale for avoiding an outwardly-directed, active form of exceptionalism, asserting that "power always thinks it has a great soul and vast views, beyond the comprehension of the weak; and that it is doing God's service when [in fact] it is in violation of all His laws."[10]

Walter Russell Mead argues that adherents to Jefferson's approach to foreign affairs remain reluctant to export or impose an American form of democracy on other governments. Indeed, Jeffersonians believe that establishing and sustaining "democracy in one country is enough challenge" because "democracy is a fragile plant — difficult to grow, [and] harder to propagate." Although his vision of exceptionalism was inwardly focused, Jefferson did believe that the freer a nation's citizens were, the more restraint that nation would exhibit in foreign affairs. Jeffersonians, however, remain "both skeptical about the prospects for revolutionary victory abroad and concerned about the dangers to the domestic Revolution that might result from excessive entanglements in foreign affairs."[11]

---

[10] Adams cited in Richard J. Payne, *The Clash with Distant Cultures: Values, Interests, and Force in American Foreign Policy* (Albany: State University of New York Press, 1985), 38.

[11] Walter Russell Mead, *Special Providence: American Foreign Policy and How It Changed the World* (New York: Knopf, 2001), 181.

A comparison of Jefferson's writings and statements on foreign engagement with his actual policies also illustrates a recurring tension in American political culture. On the one hand, people attribute to Jefferson a strategy based on limiting entanglements abroad, in order to preserve the flexibility to act unilaterally and shift alliances. On the other, some argue that Jefferson viewed diplomatic agreements and alignments as critical to furthering American interests.

Exceptionalist Thinking in the Nineteenth Century

If Jefferson provided tension for today's exceptionalists about the domestic-international balance in American foreign policy, John Quincy Adams provided a breaking point. Serving as President Monroe's Secretary of State, Adams contended with European intervention in South America, especially Spain's attempt to re-establish a position in the Western Hemisphere. In 1821, when many Americans called for intervention in South America, Adams countered that ideological support for independence movements did not require physical or military support, famously stating that America "does not go abroad in search of monsters to destroy." While the intent was to avoid intervention, in 1823, Adams authored what became known as the Monroe Doctrine, which placed European powers on notice that the United States would view further interference in the Americas as aggression.

Another contribution to the evolution of exceptionalist thinking in the nineteenth century, one also based on the American frontier experience, was presented in 1893 by Frederick Jackson Turner. Turner's thoughts on how the frontier experience had shaped American culture later influenced generations of Americans vis-à-vis popular textbooks and academic curricula. His key contributions to exceptionalist thinking included a dual belief in rugged individualism and egalitarianism, with achievement and social mobility based on hard work, dedication, and idealization of the self-made man or entrepreneur. He combined the American frontier tradition with a powerful set of images and beliefs about how conquering and expanding America established cultural traits that were distinctly American. His later writings led to a Pulitzer Prize, which in turn assured his arguments a place in exceptionalist thinking and amplified the belief that America was distinct from European nations.

One of the most frequently cited expressions of exceptionalism during this period comes from the French writer Alexis de Tocqueville, who, in 1835 and 1840, published two volumes entitled *Democracy in America*. A myth has arisen around his use of the term exceptionalism to describe the United States as being distinct from other nations. In fact, de Tocqueville only used the term once, and not with the meaning often ascribed to him. Observing that American history contained no experience with European feudalism and was dominated by hardship and a struggle to forge a new nation and expand into the newly acquired West, he commented that "the situation of the Americans is therefore entirely exceptional, and it is to be believed that no other democratic people will ever be placed in it."[12] But he was not referring to American democracy or foreign policy. Rather, he was commenting on the lack of unique American art, literature, and scientific achievements.

De Tocqueville did influence the evolution of exceptionalist thinking, not in the use of the term itself, but in his insightful analysis of the uniqueness of American democracy and political culture. Indeed, his analysis showed

---

[12] Alexis de Tocqueville, *Democracy in America* translated by Harvey Mansfield and Delba Winthrop (Chicago: University of Chicago Press, 2002), 420.

how American society evolved without a tradition of aristocracy and nobility, enabling a political system much different from other democracies in the 1830s. He provided both an analysis and endorsement of the American form of liberal democracy that directly influenced how the narrative of exceptionalist thinking evolved through the nineteenth and twentieth centuries. [13]

Soon after the second volume of *Democracy in America* was published, the editor of the *Democratic Review*, John L. O'Sullivan, coined the term Manifest Destiny. In an 1845 essay advocating the annexation of Texas, O'Sullivan set forth the opinion that it was the nation's destiny to expand across a continent that had been provided by "Providence" to assure ample room for new generations of Americans.

By the end of the nineteenth century, exceptionalist thinking had evolved significantly. The Monroe Doctrine established American influence in the Western Hemisphere and blocked European expansion or interference in regional affairs. This established a precedent for believing the U.S. could have a sphere of influence elsewhere. The U.S. further projected influence abroad by liberating and bringing democracy to the oppressed or uncivilized masses, an extension of the civilizing duty or mission that Turner believed was central to America's frontier experience. This sense of duty, or mission, would eventually evolve as an open-door approach to foreign affairs. The open-door approach had two aims: promoting and expanding the American governance model (republican democracy and liberalism), and expanding the global system of trade and commerce in order to secure access to foreign markets for American goods.

---

[13] See Tony Smith, *Americas Mission: The United States and the Worldwide Struggle for Democracy in the Twentieth Century* (Princeton: Princeton University Press, 1994), 16-17.

The idea of Manifest Destiny thus evolved first into a justification for expansion across the continent and then into a mandate to expand abroad. America was, in this view of exceptionalism, a chosen nation acting out God's plan. This religious thread of exceptionalism persisted through the Spanish-American War, until it was muted in favor of a more pragmatic sense of mission and duty to bring order and stability around the globe. In sum, the missionary thread of American exceptionalism began with Puritan thinking at the founding of the republic, ran through the American Revolution to the expansion across North America, was amplified by Manifest Destiny and the promotion of liberalism and free trade, and remains part of American strategic culture in the form of interventionism.

The American Century

Exceptionalist thinking was refined and amplified in the twentieth century, taking on a more assertive tone that emphasized the missionary or interventionist aspect of America's role in world affairs. This was already evident in 1900, when U.S. Secretary of State Richard Olney asserted that "the mission of this country" was to "act" and to seize any "fitting opportunity to further the progress of civilization."[14]

President Theodore Roosevelt refined exceptionalist thinking by stating that the nation's usefulness to the world rested in its ability artfully to balance its growing power with a higher purpose. For a brief period Roosevelt saw the balancing of power and purpose as legitimizing an American form of imperialism that justified further overseas expansion. In 1904, the Roosevelt corollary to the Monroe Doctrine

---

[14] Olney, President Cleveland's Secretary of State, cited in Frank Ninkovich, *The Wilsonian Century* (Chicago: University of Chicago Press, 1999), 24.

expanded the essence of the Monroe Doctrine from merely blocking new European colonization or expansion of European influence in the Americas to actual U.S. intervention in Latin and South America to reduce or otherwise limit European influence anywhere—even in existing or former colonies. This led to a period of increased American military intervention in the Western Hemisphere. U.S. Marines engaged so often in the region that some writers dubbed them the State Department's police force.

After he was awarded a Nobel Peace Prize in 1905 for negotiating an end to the Russo-Japanese War, Roosevelt moderated his desire for overseas territory and increased his appeal to a missionary foreign policy that balanced exceptionalist thinking with a renewed emphasis on trade relations and expanding American commerce.

Jeffersonian views of exceptionalism were largely swept aside in the twentieth century, in favor of expanding American engagement abroad, American leadership in a new self-defense Alliance that committed the nation to the defense of European powers, and more assertive promotion of American views of democracy and liberalism. The change in American exceptionalism in the twentieth century began with President Woodrow Wilson, whose views and arguments defined a version of American foreign policy still dubbed Wilsonianism.

After unsuccessfully trying to keep America out of World War I, Wilson's "Fourteen Points Speech" articulated a post-World War I vision of international relations defined by democracy, self-determination, free trade, and open agreements. Wilson believed that international security affairs and threats to American interests had fundamentally changed, requiring more active and assertive American involvement in global affairs and a new leadership role. His vision for an international organization grounded in agreements that would codify international law to shape norms, expectations, and behavior regarding war and warfare eventually led, after World War II, to the formation of the United Nations.

Also after World War II, Wilsonianism blended with a new American outlook on global affairs, one that included two fundamental analogies: no more Pearl Harbors and no Munich "appeasement" deals. After the Second World War, Americans vowed to forever avoid attacks on the homeland, and supported efforts to neutralize potential threats at their source and at the time of their origin.

Wilson's version of American exceptionalism looked outward, professing a sense of American responsibility to wield its growing power to bring democracy to the world and the belief that America should build strong, enduring alliances and institutions that could check potential flashpoints and conflict. During the Cold War this approach morphed into alliances and partnerships with those nations opposed to Communism. Today, a new form of Wilson's assertive liberalism has expanded fundamental freedoms to the Internet, where the U.S. has extended its version of freedom of speech, worship, want, and fear to cyberspace in the form of an "Internet freedom" policy focused on promoting openness and free speech while reducing censorship.

The impulse to project American power abroad, in the form of a mission or duty to maintain a leadership role, remains a strong theme in American perceptions about the U.S. role in global affairs. Secretary of State Madeleine Albright, for example, demonstrated this when she opined during the Clinton Administration that America was the "indispensible nation" and that the United Sates was justified in its use of force abroad because it could "see further into the future" and by implication would be vindicated in its actions. Albright and others expressing similar sentiment are in many ways merely repeating a cultural meme that runs deep in American political culture, one President Lincoln himself helped shape in his 1862 annual message to Congress, stating that America "was the last best hope of man on earth."

American Exceptionalism During the Cold War: Liberal Institution Building

American exceptionalism changed dramatically after World War II (WWII). America emerged from that war as the most powerful nation, militarily, economically, and politically. While the economically-focused Marshall Plan for rebuilding post-WWII Europe was presented as an unselfish act in the spirit of the wartime Lend-Lease program, it actually evolved as part of a larger agenda to shape the international economic regime and to cement political ties and influence on the continent. Postwar American strategy focused on building an interlocking set of international plans and protocols that founded a new global order covering international trade, international law, international air travel, international communications, and a host of other areas. Collective security arrangements and regional cooperation forums were also formed through American and Western leadership.

The United Nations was created as an international organization that could prevent additional world wars. The Bretton Woods and Dumbarton Oaks conferences sought to create a postwar order aligned to American interests in the critical area of commerce and trade. From the American perspective, the U.S. had saved Europe twice and wanted to create a system of political and economic institutions in its image that, moving forward, would secure a new open-door model whereby American political ideals (liberty, democracy, progressivism) and economic ideals (free markets) could expand with the new postwar order.

Cold War exceptionalist thinking had two fundamental objectives. First was the expansion of the American vision for democracy. In reality, this objective has manifested itself as a negative, meaning that the real threat to American exceptionalism would be the existence of any alternative political order or system that challenged the American vision for international affairs. For this reason, America has often opposed any ideological system that presents an alternative to the expansion of the exceptionalist mission to bring American-style, liberal democracy to other nations. A corollary to this was the objection to any economic order that erected barriers to American trade relations, thus becoming the second fundamental objective of exceptionalist thought. At times, the promotion of free trade or the stability of commerce has trumped the mandate to expand democracy, but the two objectives remain at the core of the postwar international order.

President John F. Kennedy invoked exceptionalism in his first inaugural address, stating that the "revolutionary beliefs for which our forebearers fought are still at issue around the globe – the belief that the rights of man come not from the generosity of the state but from the hand of God. We dare not forget today that we are the heirs of that first revolution." Kennedy inspired a generation of Americans to join causes, from government to the Peace Corps, to volunteer organizations engaging in missionary work abroad. At the end of his address, he reminded Americans that they must do more than merely protect liberty at home. Indeed, they were also charged with a mission to bring liberty to other nations and "truly light the world."

The concept of American exceptionalism was extended and constantly revised during the second half of the twentieth century. Key themes remained, including a "belief that the United States is unique and morally superior to other nations, was rejuvenated, and a stark simplicity of confrontation between good and evil was accepted by most Americans."[15]

Ronald Reagan was among the most successful presidents to combine a sense of American exceptionalism with a duty to lead. Addressing a 1984 meeting of the American Legion, Reagan revised the essence of American exceptionalism: "Americans cannot turn our backs on what history has asked of us. Keeping alive the hope of human freedom is America's mission, and we cannot shrink from the task or falter in the call of duty."[16] On January 14, 1989, in his final radio address to the nation, Reagan intoned: "Whether we seek it or not, whether we like it or not, we Americans are keepers of the miracles. We are asked to be the guardians of a place to come to, a place to start again, a place to live in the dignity God meant for his children."[17] This is the strain of exceptionalism that dominated American thinking through the end of the Cold War.

America Unbound

President Bill Clinton evoked the leadership theme in the exceptionalist narrative in 1995, calling on the nation to "assume the burden of leadership." As "the world's most indispensable nation," Clinton argued, "we must act and we must lead," because if we don't lead, "the job will not get

---

[15] Richard J. Payne, *The Clash with Distant Cultures: Values, Interests, and Force in American Foreign Policy* (Albany: State University of New York Press, 1985), 13.

[16] Ronald Reagan, "Remarks at the Annual Convention of the American Legion in Salt Lake City, Utah, September 4, 1984," *Public Papers of the Presidents of the United States: Ronald Reagan, Book II* (Washington, D.C.: U.S. Government Printing Office, 1991), 1230.

[17] Ronald Reagan, "Final Radio Address to the Nation, January 14, 1989), *Public Papers of the Presidents of the United States: Ronald Reagan, Book II* (Washington, D.C.: U.S. Government Printing Office, 1987), p. 1736.

---

done. We must continue to stand up for the proposition that all people, without regard to their nationality, their race, their ethnic group, their religion or their gender, should have a chance to make the most of their own lives[, and] to taste both freedom and opportunity."[18] In the late 1990s, in the face of stalled diplomatic initiatives, the Clinton administration began a trend that would be amplified by the Bush administration in the aftermath of the 9/11 attacks: a tendency toward military solutions to diplomatic problems.

Halper and Clarke contend that "what began as a technological and tactical transformation" in American military thought in the early 1990s "morphed into a compelling idea: America's technological superiority enables its military to impose solutions more rapidly and effectively than can be achieved through diplomacy."[19]

For President George W. Bush, however, the burden of leading the world into a new era would be shouldered by the United States alone, with Allies reluctantly in tow. It was, as Daalder and Lindsay termed it, a vision of American foreign policy "unbound," in which several revolutionary policy objectives were simultaneously pursued,. These objectives include a shift from reluctant to forceful intervention and interdiction, a declared strategy of preemption, rejection of multilateralism and withdrawal from several international treaties; a reduction in diplomacy, a shift from accommodation with old Europe, a firm belief that America should use its power more broadly and forcefully to shape world affairs, a belief that if the U.S. acted firmly and decisively, other nations would follow, and a myopic view of

---

[18] "Remarks by the President in Freedom House Speech," Washington, October 6, 1995, http://www.clintonfoundation.org/legacy/100695-speech-by-president-in-freedom-house-speech.htm.
[19] Halper and Clarke, *The Silence of the Rational Center*, 153.

long-term consequences of a general approach to foreign affairs.[20]

Several of these traditions came together in the promulgation of what became known as the Bush Doctrine, which featured a strategy of preemption that underwrote the 2003 invasion of Iraq. The Bush Doctrine was first unveiled during West Point's year-long bicentennial celebration, a time of reflection on the institution's creation and on the President, Thomas Jefferson, who supported it. The West Point speech was hardly a celebration of the Jeffersonian tradition, and it actually expanded on the global leadership theme in a direction Jefferson would likely object to, when Bush stated:

> In the world we have entered, the only path to safety s the path of action. And this nation will act. We are in a conflict between good and evil, and America will call evil by its name. By confronting evil and lawless regimes, we do not create a problem, we reveal a problem. And we will lead the world in opposing it.

In a sharp reversal from pre-9/11 thinking, Bush administration officials, in 2002 and 2003, advocated a view that U.S. power must be exercised more forcefully. They further believed that America stood at a critical time in world history, in which American influence could be used to shape regional affairs, including bringing about a political revolution in the Persian Gulf.

Because Bush Administration officials generally viewed diplomatic processes and negotiations as unproductive, and because they believed other nations would rally behind an American-led mission to spread democracy, only minimal efforts were made to engage diplomatically to secure a broad coalition, as Bush's father had done in the first Gulf War.

---

[20] Ivo H. Daalder and James M. Lindsay, *America Unbound: The Bush Revolution in Foreign Policy*, Revised Edition (New Jersey: Wiley, 2005), 2, 13.

Administration officials seemingly adhered to overly optimistic—some would say unrealistic—assessments of how a war in Iraq would evolve. For some, the Bush approach encouraged "American idealism" to "harden into ideology" and then centered a particular ideological position in policy.[21] Part of this ideological bent seems to have been a particular view of the utility and appropriateness of military force as a foreign policy tool, ultimately codified in a new *National Security Strategy* published in late 2002.[22]

Bush's foreign policy, Daalder and Lindsay quip, "turned John Quincy Adams on his head and argued that the United States should aggressively go abroad in search of monsters to destroy."[23] What some refer to as a muscular, or anti-Wilsonian, approach amplified the interventionist tendency in the Wilson school of foreign policy while downplaying its liberal, multilateral corollaries. Indeed, rather than project humility and cultivate coalitions, Bush "pursued with a vengeance" policies and foreign policy objectives opposite to his campaign stances as a soft internationalist. "Now he was reborn as a crusading internationalist who had embraced Woodrow Wilson's vision of a democratic world and who was willing to use American military might to make it happen."[24]

Instead of a reluctant hegemon adhering to a version of American exceptionalism that practiced restraint, the Bush administration practiced exceptionalism with a vengeance and caused a break with the post-World War II tradition of promoting American security through liberal international regimes based on cooperation and collective security arrangements.

---

[21] Halper and Clarke, *The Silence of the Rational Center* 16.
[22] Ibid., 255.
[23] Daalder and Lindsay, *America Unbound,* 13.
[24] Ibid., 78.

By the end of the George W. Bush Administration, it appeared that the American tradition of exceptionalism favored during the Cold War had been turned on its head. Long gone, it seemed, was the tradition that prevented Kennedy from striking Soviet missiles in Cuba, because doing so would be a "Pearl Harbor in reverse." Kennedy did not want the United States to wage preemptive war, or to be perceived as an imperial power.

American Exceptionalism in the Twenty-First Century

There are many themes and narratives embedded in the concept of exceptionalism. What is of particular interest to students of strategic culture is how themes embedded in American political culture, including foreign policy traditions such as exceptionalism, are evoked and associated with other political values both to describe and to proscribe policy initiatives.

Walter A. McDougall suggests that eight multifaceted but distinct American foreign policy traditions compete for dominance within American strategic culture. The two most relevant here are American liberalism — or the idea of the United States as an exceptional democracy — and what he terms global meliorism, which "assumes that the United States alone possess the power, prestige, technology, wealth, and altruism needed to reform whole nations" and that the American public wants its government to undertake such reforms.[25]

The other six foreign policy traditions, arguably, are closely related to these two; unilateralism (sometimes called isolationism) which reserves freedom of action for American foreign policy decisions, the American system of defending

---

[25] Walter A. McDougall, *Promised Land, Crusader State: The American Encounter with the World Since 1776* (Boston: Mariner Books, 1977), 208.

U.S. interests in the Western Hemisphere (associated with the Monroe Doctrine) and the expansion of this view to other regions; progressive imperialism (which dominated American foreign policy for a brief period in the early twentieth century), liberal internationalism or Wilsonianism, which remains a complicated and integral tradition in American policy due to its grand design for American leadership in the world and the enduring relevance of his concepts, and containment (which in practice has meant containing ideological challenges to the post-World War II, largely American approach to global political and economic affairs).

A mix of these and other foreign policy traditions encompass American strategic thinking about foreign policy at any one time and form a complex narrative used by politicians and public intellectuals to define and describe American policy, and to sell foreign policy decisions to the American public. One of the most important reasons that we need to understand the origins and continued influence of exceptionalist thinking is that the idea of exceptionalism maintains resonance in the American body politic.

In its current form, American foreign policy continues to be shaped by exceptionalist thinking, with the missionary impulse to lead and shape events reflecting a strong sense of global meliorism. The general view is that American power should be leveraged to intervene in and shape global affairs, despite varying degrees of differences across party lines, generations, and other cleavages about what such intervention means or how it may manifest (i.e., diplomatic, military, unilateral action, building coalitions).

Moving forward in the twenty-first century, two essential themes in exceptionalist thinking will continue to shape how foreign policy decisions are made, how they are described or presented, and how decisions are linked to images or values that resonate in American culture.

The first theme is that the United States leads by example or, through its actions, becomes an exemplar. American actions demonstrate to other nations how a republic founded on and governed by basic qualities of liberty, equality, and justice leads to stability, prosperity, and individual achievement. This theme manifests in different forms, from a virulent strain of nationalism to a more reserved sense of being a role model others can emulate, if they so choose. Indeed, Americans carry this sentiment in their wallets every day. Since 1955, the great seal of the United States is printed on the back of every dollar bill with the Latin phrase *Novus Ordo Secorum*—"New Order of the Ages."

The second theme is that America has a mission and, for some, a duty, to bring to others those same basic qualities that make America unique. Exceptionalist thinking in this form embodies a spectrum of beliefs that, over time, have established a range of cultural norms, values, and foreign policy traditions that policy makers are influenced by, and which they use to sell policies domestically and internationally. Leading by example, when it comes to foreign policy, covers a broad range of behaviors, from building collective security regimes intended to moderate unilateral intervention to legitimizing American unilateralism in violation of international norms that undermine those same security regimes upheld as critical to international stability.

Conclusion

The prevailing notion of American exceptionalism is changing. A 2009 Pew research survey, for example, found that, for the first time since World War II, forty-nine percent of Americans believed the United States should "mind its own business and let other countries get along the best they can." In April 2010, a similar question had forty-six percent believing the U.S. should "let other countries deal with their own problems."[26]

Despite these views of American assertiveness in world affairs, a majority of Americans consistently believe that the United States is unique and stands apart from other nations as the greatest country in the world. Americans fundamentally believe their nation is exceptional.[27] But views of American cultural superiority, a component of exceptionalist thinking that emerged during the Cold War, is now split generationally. Another Pew research effort conducted in 2011 found that sixty percent of Americans fifty or older believed that the United States is culturally superior to other nations, and thirty-seven percent of respondents under the age of thirty agreed.[28]

A number of systemic challenges to the post-World War II international order require a new approach to building security partnerships and liberal institutions similar to those erected during the Cold War that helped the United States exert its leadership. One of the most significant challenges is poverty and the increasing disparity in wealth and opportunity that prevents American visions of freedom, progress, justice, and liberalism from taking hold in a growing number of nations. With over one-sixth of the world's

---

[26] http://people-press.org/question-search/?qid=1765375&pid=51&ccid=50

[27] On the changing nature of exceptionalism see John A. Gans, Jr., "American Exceptionalism and the Politics of Foreign Policy," *The Atlantic*, 2011. Available at: http:/www.theatlantic.com/international/print/2011/11/American-exceptionalism-and-the-poltics-of-foreign-policy/248779/. Last accessed November 23, 2012.

[28] Stephanie Condon, "Americans Split on American Exceptionalism, poll shows," CBS News online November 18, 2011. Available at: http://wwwcbsnews.com/8301-503544_162-57327537-503544/americans-split-on-america-exceptionalism-poll-shows/. Last accessed November 23, 2012.

population living near or below the poverty line, individual or human security challenges create endemic pockets of insecurity that prevent the evolution of liberal democracies. The only route toward stability and opportunity in these areas is long-term international commitments to fundamental political and economic reform, a process that will take decades. At home, this requires America to put its own house in order and reinvigorate a stagnant middle class that, for the first time in modern memory, will see a new generation of Americans unable to realize greater prosperity than did their parents.

Exceptionalist thinking is likely influenced by both real and perceived beliefs about America's relative position as a great power. Indeed, this is likely the view President Obama takes, in contrast to his predecessor, in terms of the need for partnerships. Partnerships are certainly important when it comes to European affairs and when addressing perpetual crises in the Middle East and Persian Gulf regions. In these areas, the United States has diminished capacity for additional interventions, especially unilateral actions. As foreign policy and defense policy shift to Asia as part of the so-called "strategic pivot" or "re-balance" of forces to the Pacific Basin, the United States will best be served by returning to a long-term strategy based on partnerships, collective security regimes, and international institutions that moderate attempts by any power to dominate regional affairs. In dealing with a rising China, this means reinforcing economic organizations, trade regimes, environmental security regimes, and other regional security organizations.

Americans are still more likely than others to claim that their culture is superior to others, and this attitude can cause friction as well as an additional challenge. Other nations perceive exceptionalist thinking as an expression of American superiority and perhaps, in the years since the invasion of Iraq, as imperialism. Such reactions confound many

Americans because, as stated earlier, Americans believe that the United States is indeed an exceptional nation, despite debates about how exceptionalism should be manifest in the future.

Foreign reactions to exceptionalist thinking are especially pronounced when it comes to military intervention, which is too often thinly veiled as American magnanimity. While explaining and defending interventions — including those in Korea, Lebanon, Vietnam, Grenada, Panama, Haiti, Somalia, Kosovo, Afghanistan, and Iraq — U.S. presidents have relied on familiar metaphors and an appeal to shared values to gain domestic support for military activities abroad, while selling such interventions externally as part of some sacred mission — or moral duty — for the United States to lead.

A growing number of Americans do not think the United States should pursue the unilateral, assertive nationalist agenda of the 2000s, preferring that the United States instead lead coalitions, or assume a more moderate role in global affairs. Americans also generally support American involvement in global affairs, although fewer support a leadership role than in the past. According to a 2011 Gallup World Affairs survey, sixty-six percent of Americans believe the U.S. should retain a leadership role in world affairs (down from seventy-five percent in 2009), with fifty percent favoring an active role for the United States. Only sixteen percent favor a leading role. Isolationist sentiment rose from twenty-three to thirty-two percent between 2009 and 2011.[29] It seems that support for an assertive variant of exceptionalism is on the wane, or that the American public is changing its views on American foreign policy after a decade of war.

---

[29] Stephanie Condon, "Americans Split on American Exceptionalism, poll shows," CBS News online November 18, 2011 accessed online November 23, 2012 at http://wwwcbsnews.com/8301-503544_162-57327537-503544/americans-split-on-america-exceptionalism-poll-shows/.

Despite the fact that the tone of exceptionalist thinking is shifting away from the missionary, or assertive, approach that dominated much of the last century, the belief in American exceptionalism remains central to our political culture and shapes how we think about American power and influence. Because exceptionalist thinking is central to American political culture but is often perceived abroad as arrogance, we must continue to understand how exceptionalist thinking has evolved, how it shapes policy, and how it affects our ability to influence global affairs. While acknowledging the uniqueness of exceptional thinking in public discourse, political scientist Stephen Walt laments that it nevertheless makes it "harder for Americans to understand why other" nations become "alarmed by U.S. policies," and that American interests abroad would be better served "if Americans were less convinced of their own unique virtues and less eager to proclaim them."[30]

Exceptionalist thinking will continue to influence American foreign policy decision-making and it will continue to define how Americans view the nation's role in global affairs. Our long-term foreign policy interests will be furthered by emphasizing the uniqueness of American ideals and culture, and by moderating the temptation to project missionary and assertive narratives that place our Allies and partners on the defensive.

---

[30] Stephen M. Walt, "The Myth of American Exceptionalism" in *Foreign Policy* (November 2011). Available at: at http://www.foreignpolicy.com/articles/2011/10/11/the_myth_of_american_exceptionalism. Last accessed January 10, 2013.

Making Peace with War: The National Security Complex and the American Purpose

David C. Hendrickson

Introduction

An aversion to standing armies was long part of the American heritage. "On the smallest scale," observed James Madison, a standing force "has its inconveniences. On an extensive scale, its consequences may be fatal. On any scale it is an object of laudable circumspection and precaution."[1] The experience of World War II and then the Cold War made the United States throw such precautions to the winds. A large and permanent military establishment became part of the accepted order of things. Though the dreadful experience of the Vietnam War checked the growth of the military establishment, this effect was temporary. Given renewed impetus by the Reagan administration, Congress lavished funds on a revitalized military in the 1980s. The end of the Cold War left the United States without a "peer competitor," with U.S. military spending reaching to nearly half of total military spending worldwide. The terrorist attacks on September 11, 2001 then gave a powerful boost to the growth of the military establishment and the national security state.

---

[1] *Federalist* No. 41, Alexander Hamilton, James Madison, and John Jay, *The Federalist Papers*, ed. Clinton Rossiter (New York: Mentor, 1961 [1787-1788]), 257.

It is difficult not to feel ambivalence both toward the entrenchment of the national security complex and toward the emergence of the United States as the dominant military power in the world. The American-led world order, as international orders go, is more peaceful and prosperous than any other in world history.[2] From isolated pockets in the international system, liberal democracy has expanded to encompass large sections of the globe. Variants of market capitalism prevail almost everywhere. A set of ideas concerning human rights and democracy has demonstrated worldwide appeal. And yet the price of this expansion has also been substantial. As America has transformed into a warfare state, its institutions have undergone a degree of militarization that is alarming when considered in relation to traditional conceptions of the American purpose. Its international behavior, especially during the last decade, has been reckless to a degree unparalleled since the creation of the post-World War II national security state.

These developments point to a profound predicament with respect to the American role in the world: on the one hand, American military power, when defensively arrayed, has made an important contribution to the creation and maintenance of this relatively peaceful international order; on the other hand, the abuses to which it has been subject have made it hazardous to maintain large forces that constitute a perpetual temptation to employ them in war. The predicament is that there is no apparent way to resolve the question—that is, to provide the benefits of the defensive array without making the nation vulnerable to offensive uses, in effect hitching what might otherwise be a perfectly reasonable aim with what are patently illegitimate objects.

---

[2] See Steven Pinker, *The Better Angels of Our Nature: Why Violence Has Declined* (New York: Viking, 2011).

Conceived in Peace

In distant days, it was thought that a central purpose of America was to seek "by appeals to reason and by its liberal examples to infuse into the law which governs the civilized world a spirit which may diminish the frequency or circumscribe the calamities of war, and meliorate the social and beneficent relations of peace."[3] Among the most commonly expressed ideas of the late eighteenth century was one that saw a close connection between despotic governments and war. As a free constitutional republic, America was to chart a different course.

The Founding generation had great experience in war, and gave extensive consideration to the issues raised by armed conflict. None of the founders was a true pacifist, preferring peace to war in every instance. In their view, the American Revolution was the paradigmatic case of the just and defensive war. At the same time, the philosophy of civil freedom they articulated and even, in some instances, invented, was one heavily imbued with skepticism about the justifications often given, and utilities forecast, for the decision to resort to force. While accepting that war would sometimes be necessary, and that a universal and perpetual peace was an unrealizable dream of philosophers, the Founders also understood that war inescapably poses a threat to fundamental republican values and often involved its authors in unexpected calamities. The history of the European state system was replete with instances in which war had strengthened the monarch against popular power. That Europe had precious few republics — and much warfare — had a causal rather than merely contingent relation. James

---

[3] James Madison, Eighth Annual Message, December 3, 1816, *A Compilation of the Messages and Papers of the Presidents of the United States, 1789-1897* (Washington, D.C.: Government Printing Office, 1900), 1: 580.

Madison explored that theme in many places, but most succinctly in his *Political Observations* of 1795:

> Of all the enemies to public liberty, war is, perhaps, the most to be dreaded, because it comprises and develops the germ of every other. War is the parent of armies; from these proceed debts and taxes; and armies, and debts, and taxes are the known instruments for bringing the many under the domination of the few. In war, too, the discretionary power of the Executive is extended; its influence in dealing out offices, honors, and emoluments is multiplied; and all the means of seducing the minds are added to those of subduing the force of the people. The same malignant aspect in republicanism may be traced in the inequality of fortunes and the opportunities of fraud growing out of a state of war, and in the degeneracy of manners and of morals engendered by both. No nation could preserve its freedom in the midst of continual warfare.[4]

Madison believed that the propensity toward war was strongly heightened by certain internal institutions — monarchy, aristocracy, "funding systems" — that created a profound disjunction between those who gained, and those who lost, from war. Republics, he argued, would be far less bellicose than monarchies, but would not themselves be immune to that tendency because they could borrow money for warlike enterprises. "Each generation," Madison proclaimed, "should be made to bear the burden of its own wars, instead of carrying them on, at the expence of other generations." Then the people would proceed more cautiously. "Were a nation to impose such restraints upon itself, avarice would be sure to calculate the expenses of ambition." [5]

---

[4] James Madison, "Political Observations," *Selected Writings of James Madison*, ed. Ralph Ketcham (Indianapolis: Hacket, 2006), 236.

[5] James Madison, "Universal Peace," *James Madison: Writings*, ed. Jack N. Rakove (New York: Library of America, 1999), 506-07.

"Independence and Union" was the motto of early American statecraft. Though America was separated from the European system by the Atlantic Ocean, the seas were in those days both a barrier and a highway, and in fact the larger experience of the non-European world in the eighteenth and nineteenth centuries was domination by European powers. The United States was determined to avoid that fate, and thus "independence" entered its lexicon as a key concern and value. At the same time, however, the manifest differences among the states and sections suggested that North Americans could easily slide into war amongst themselves. Indeed, what really drove constitutional thought in this era was the fear that there would develop in North America, in the absence of union, a war system that would mirror Europe's own. To avoid that fate was the great problem faced by the Philadelphia Convention. It was brilliantly articulated by Alexander Hamilton, John Jay, and James Madison in the *Federalist*, as they enumerated the potential sources of conflict among the states in the absence of a strengthened union. The American Constitution was, in fact, a kind of peace pact, whose fundamental rationale and purpose was to discover the institutions that would make possible the peaceful reconciliation of disputes. Now at last, claimed James Wilson in his celebrated defense of the Constitution, "is accomplished, what the great mind of Henry IV of France had in contemplation, a system of government, for large and respectable dominions, united and bound together in peace, under a superintending head, by which all their differences may be accommodated, without the destruction of the human race!"[6]

---

[6] James Wilson's Summation and Final Rebuttal, *The Debate on the Constitution*, ed. Bernard Bailyn (New York: Library of America, 1993), 1: 866. See discussion in David C. Hendrickson, *Peace Pact: The Lost World of the American Founding* (Lawrence: University Press of Kansas, 2003).

When he became president, Thomas Jefferson warned that "sound principles" would not justify taxing "the industry of our fellow citizens to accumulate treasure for wars to happen we know not when, and which might not perhaps happen but from the temptations offered by that treasure."[7] Experience showed, however, that professions of peace had to be tempered by a willingness to respond to aggression. Jefferson lamented in 1806 that "The love of peace which we sincerely feel and profess, has begun to produce an opinion in Europe that our government is entirely in Quaker principles, and will turn the left cheek when the right has been smitten. This opinion must be corrected when just occasion arises, or we shall become the plunder of all nations."[8] Jefferson did not want war, and in fact he sought, even when refusing to turn the other cheek, to retaliate through economic sanctions rather than armed force, finding in that method "another umpire than arms" for the disputes among the nations.

Jefferson's great opponent, Alexander Hamilton, never had much use for such ideas, believing that a war of commercial retaliations with Great Britain would ultimately end with a real war. He was an advocate of military preparedness, while ever seeking to "combine energy with moderation." He did not think republics were especially peaceful, noting that there had been almost as many popular as kingly wars. But he, too, feared the domestic consequences of a resort to war. Were the United States to slide into war with one of the European powers, he warned, "in the fermentation of certain wild opinions, those wise, just, and temperate maxims which will forever constitute the true security and felicity of a state

---

[7] Thomas Jefferson, "First Annual Message," *A Compilation of the Messages and Papers of the Presidents of the United States, 1789-1897* (Washington, D.C.: Government Printing Office, 1900), 1: 328.

[8] Cited in Reginald C. Stuart, *The Half-way Pacifist: Thomas Jefferson's View of War* (Toronto: University of Toronto Press, 1978), 35.

would be overruled and that a war upon credit, eventually upon property and upon the general principles of public order, might aggravate and embitter the ordinary calamities of foreign war."[9] Like the Jeffersonians, Hamilton saw peril to the nation's basic institutions as ensuing from the resort to war. He, too, was astonished "with how much precipitance and levity nations still rush to arms against each other...after the experience of its having deluged the world with calamities for so many ages."[10] George Washington agreed: for the sake of humanity, Washington noted, it was "devoutly to be wished, that the manly employment of agriculture and the humanizing benefits of commerce, would supersede the waste of war and the rage of conquest; that the swords might be turned into plough-shares, the spears into pruning hooks, and, as the Scripture expresses it, 'the nations learn war no more.'"[11]

In the generation that followed the Founding, American leaders continued to put forth a view of the Constitution that stressed its anti-militaristic features. Protesting the incursion of General Andrew Jackson into Spanish-held Florida in 1818 without executive or congressional authorization, Henry Clay said that the members of the "immortal Convention" had seen "that nations are often precipitated into ruinous war, from folly, from pride, from ambition, and from the desire of military fame." By "expressly and exclusively" granting the war power to Congress, the hope was to spare the United States "from the mad wars that have afflicted, and desolated,

---

[9] Alexander Hamilton, "The Defense No. 18," *The Papers of Alexander Hamilton*, ed. Harold Syrett et al 26 vols. (New York: Columbia University Press, 1961-79), 19: 300.

[10] Alexander Hamilton, "Defense of the Funding System," *Hamilton Papers*, 19: 56.

[11] George Washington, "Washington to Marquis de Chastellux," *George Washington: Writings*, ed. John Rhodehamel (New York: Library of America, 1997), 675.

and ruined other countries."[12] Were the United States to take up the cause of liberty and independence in other countries, wrote John Quincy Adams, "the fundamental maxims of her policy would insensibly change from *liberty* to *force.*" Such a policy would involve the United States "in all the wars of interest and intrigue, of individual avarice, envy and ambition, which assume the colors and usurp the standard of freedom."[13] Peace was celebrated as the "true policy of this Republic" and "the animating genius" of American institutions.[14] As William Seward summarized the case in 1844: "The first want of every nation is peace, the last is peace. It wants peace always. So our forefathers understood the philosophy of government; for they established a system which dispensed with even the forces necessary for perfect defence, rather than cumber it with such as might tempt it to unnecessary collision with other states."[15]

Made by War

While conceived in peace, it is undoubtedly also true that the United States has been made by war. The impact of war explains much of "who we are." It has profoundly shaped the development of American institutions. Its undeniable salience rises up like a specter to disturb the pacific professions of our leaders. This was true enough in the nineteenth century, when

---

[12] Henry Clay, "On the Seminole War," *The Works of Henry Clay*, ed., Calvin Colton et al, 10 vols. (New York: G.P. Putnam's Sons, 1904), 6: 197.

[13] John Quincy Adams, *An Address Delivered . . . on the Occasion of Reading the Declaration of Independence* (Washington, D.C., 1821), 29.

[14] Robert Stockton, cited in David C. Hendrickson, *Union, Nation, or Empire: The American Debate over International Relations* (Lawrence: University Press of Kansas, 2009), 187.

[15] William Seward, Speech at a Whig Mass Meeting, *The Works of William H. Seward*, ed. George E. Baker, 5 vols. (New York: Redfield, 1853-84), 1: 267.

the Mexican War vastly expanded the boundaries of the United States and the Civil War recast the federal union into an indissoluble national state. But it has been yet more dramatically true over the past seventy years. The Second World War, and then the ensuing Cold War with global communism, created a far greater standing complex of military forces than had existed at any previous time in American history, one that was further entrenched by the American response to the terrorist attacks of September 11, 2001.

Among the central justifications for the military establishment is the contribution it has made to global security. For more than six decades, said President Obama in his Nobel Prize acceptance speech, the United States "has helped underwrite global security . . . with the blood of our citizens and the strength of our arms."[16] Obama was merely restating a consensus already well entrenched, giving an overall perspective hardly different from the pronouncements of the first President Bush and President Bill Clinton in the 1990s. Obama was reticent to say so, but others have insisted that the United States has emerged as the world's *de facto* government—providing an array of public goods that the nations would have been incapable of securing on their own.[17] We have been, apparently, the inspiration, midwife, architect, and practical builder of this secure and peaceful world.

How convincing is this judgment? There are partisans on either side of the ideological wars who would answer this question wholly in the positive, or wholly in the negative, but neither position is convincing. The picture is mixed. It surely

---

[16] Remarks by the President at his Acceptance of the Nobel Peace Prize, White House Press Office, December 10, 2009.

[17] Michael Mandelbaum, *The Case for Goliath: How America Acts As the World's Government in the 21st Century* (New York: Public Affairs, 2005).

cannot be denied that the American-led world order has positive accomplishments to its credit. The post-World War II reconstruction of Europe, to which the United States made a vital contribution, was undoubtedly the grandest achievement. In Asia, especially in the years since the end of the Vietnam War, the willingness of the United States to open its market to exports has resolved what would otherwise have been an impossible dilemma for Japan and the neo-mercantilist developing countries that followed in Japan's wake. In both regions, American power created the space within which Germany and Japan marginalized a once dominant military sector. As far as the pacification of Europe and East Asia is concerned, the positive accomplishments of the post-World War II and Cold War eras continued into the post-Cold War period. The existence, since 1990, of what has been a significant measure of military unipolarity has made a state-led challenge to the order a dangerous enterprise for competitors to contemplate, much less directly undertake.

But although there have been positive accomplishments, there have also been grave drawbacks in American conduct. The Vietnam War was the most dramatic illustration of failures from the Cold War period, but a litany of other dubious enterprises scarred by hubris and accompanied by the inveterate tendency to exaggerate the dangers of the Communist menace. The military unipolarity that fell to the United States after the collapse of the Soviet Union then created an imbalance of power in the world political system and resulted, for us, in a series of imperial temptations. The victory of the United States over Saddam Hussein's Iraq in the first Gulf War in 1991 is invariably celebrated as a "good war," but the extremity of force employed in the war helped spawn the terrorist attacks of 9/11. The blowback was yet more severe for its being unrecognized—to bow to this particular reality was to put oneself in the "blame America first" camp.

Undoubtedly, the most egregious use of force over the past two decades was the 2003 Iraq War launched by President George W. Bush. The 2003 Iraq War struck directly at the prohibition against preventive war that had been the centerpiece of the twentieth century movement to outlaw war. In word and deed, we were far from the sentiments with which the American century was launched: that aggressive war was the crime of crimes. On the contrary, we seemed to have imbibed the spirit of revolutionary France, which, as Alexander Hamilton wrote two hundred years ago, had "betrayed a spirit of universal domination; an opinion that she had a right to be the legislatrix of nations; that they are all bound to submit to her mandates, to take from her their moral, political, and religious creeds; that her plastic and regenerating hand is to mould them into whatever shape she thinks fit; and that her interest is to be the sole measure of the rights of the rest of the world."[18] That spirit has moderated from its high watermark under the first term of the George W. Bush administration, but it has not disappeared.

Culturally, too, Americans made their peace with war. They have grown comfortable with war in ways that would have shocked the sensibility of earlier generations.[19] Brought up on a diet of video games and Hollywood spectacle, our young people—especially those attracted to military service—are saturated with violent imagery from an early age. Skill in the application of violence seems, according to sportscasters, celebrities, and politicians, to be at the pinnacle of human striving. Our soldiers, we are repeatedly told, "represent what

---

[18] Americus, "The Warning I," *Works of Alexander Hamilton*, ed. Henry Cabot Lodge (New York, G.P. Putnam, 1974), 6: 233-34.

[19] The best study remains Andrew Bacevich, *The New American Militarism: How Americans Are Seduced by War* (New York: Oxford University Press, 2005).

is best in America." They are "a generation of heroes."[20] Everything they do, it seems, they do for freedom. In public ritual, patriotism has become identified almost exclusively with service to the national security state, no matter how remote the connection between our imperial wars and the preservation of our liberty—no matter, indeed, that imperial wars and the national security state threaten rather than preserve domestic liberty. We are to honor their sacrifice by reinforcing the very traits that got them killed.

The ugly effects of war are readily ignored. These effects are to be seen not only in the toll of the victims, measured in the anodyne term "collateral damage," but also among the agents of destruction—not only, that is, among those who are killed, but also among those who do the killing.[21] Perhaps the hyperbolic praise is a function, in part, of the unspoken knowledge that military service often results in awful psychological consequences for those who serve, making this over-the-top rhetoric a guilty expiation for the dehumanizing sins we ask soldiers to commit in the name of patriotism. Whatever the source, we are well along a road similar to that which Hamilton described, by which war leads to frequent infringements on the rights of the people, a condition that in turn weakens "their sense of those rights" and leads them "to consider the soldiery not only as their protectors, but as their superiors."[22]

In classical republican thinking, the danger of standing military establishments was that they would disorder republican institutions, leading to the usurpation of civilian rule. The step from considering the military as superiors to

---

[20] President Obama, cited in Stacy A. Anderson, "Obama July 4th Speech," *Huffington Post*, July 4, 2012.

[21] See David Philipps, *Lethal Warriors: When the New Band of Brothers Came Home* (New York: Palgrave Macmillan, 2010).

[22] *Federalist* No. 8, Rossiter, 70.

thinking of them as masters, as Hamilton wrote, was "neither remote nor difficult." President Dwight Eisenhower was thinking in these classical terms when he warned of the acquisition of unwarranted influence by the military-industrial complex. "The potential for the disastrous rise of misplaced power," he observed, "exists and will persist." Military officers, it is true, are not more bellicose than their civilian superiors in our democracy, and sometimes they exercise (as with the prospect of a preventive war with Iran) an institutional restraint against the initiation of war, though their influence also seems to work towards the perpetuation of war once it has been launched. America's militarization also does not conform to the classic fears of a "garrison state," which featured a mobilized and regimented population. Instead of being enveloped by military norms and discipline, civilians live apart—and are increasingly separate—from the military, while elevating those who serve into icons. But if the militarization we have experienced does not exactly conform to older fears, it is no less a form of militarization. Instead of a mobilized population, we have gotten both the Surveillance State and the Emergency State.[23] Instead of a military caste hungering for military solutions to international problems, we have civilian elites who have hungered for those solutions, for whom the military has proved a dutiful servant.

There is much that is artificial and unbalanced about the U.S. role in the world. It goes to the very definition of

---

[23] See Shane Harris, *The Watchers: The Rise of America's Surveillance State* (New York: Penguin, 2011) and David C. Unger, *The Emergency State: America's Pursuit of Absolute Security at All Costs* (New York: Penguin, 2012). The development confirms Hamilton's prediction that even "nations the most attached to liberty" would, if threatened by continual war, "resort for repose and security to institutions which have a tendency to destroy their civil and political rights. To be more safe, they at length become willing to run the risk of being less free." *Federalist* No. 7, Rossiter, 67.

republican government that such a regime should embody a governing apparatus of countervailing powers,[24] but there is no international equivalent to the separation of powers, judicial review, popular representation, and all the other devices that the Founders erected to preserve a balanced republican regime in the United States. From a republican standpoint, the assumption by one power of a "world government" role is scarcely justifiable; at a minimum, it holds out clear dangers. The mantra of U.S. leaders is that other powers should have a voice, but not a veto, over U.S. decisions regarding the use of force, even uses of force that otherwise would be illegal, whereas the essence of constitutional government is that it should provide not only for the use of power but also for its effective limitation and constraint. Keeping "all options on the table," as the United States has so often done, legitimizes offensive war in a fashion far removed from classic ideas of constitutional government. The rhetorical U.S. emphasis on partnership and cooperation with other liberal democracies, though appealing to what must be considered as virtues, has frequently not operated as a serious constraint on the use of force and has more than once emboldened "allies" to take provocative stances in the expectation of U.S. support. Georgia did it in 2008, with its invasion of South Ossetia. Britain and France did it in 2011 by agitating for intervention in Libya. China's neighbors do it over disputed territorial waters. Israel does it repeatedly.[25]

---

[24] See Scott Gordon, *Controlling the State: Constitutionalism from Ancient Athens to Today* (Cambridge, MA: Harvard University Press), and Daniel H. Deudney, *Bounding Power: Republican Security Theory from the Polis to the Global Village* (Princeton: Princeton University Press, 2007).

[25] See especially G. John Ikenberry, *Liberal Leviathan: The Origins, Crisis, and Transformation of the American World Order* (Princeton: Princeton University Press, 2011), and the critical review of Richard K. Betts, "Institutional Imperialism," *The National Interest*, no. 113 (May/June 2011): 85-96.

The Expansion of Force

The past two decades have also witnessed a dramatic expansion of the accepted justifications for the use of force. In the first half of the twentieth century, and even well beyond into the Cold War, the U.S. role was focused on the illegality of aggression. American leaders accepted the framework of a society of states that allowed for a plurality of regime types, and that united states in a framework of law that defended the idea of their mutual independence. Such was the central idea informing the U.N. Charter, and it is one that has been seriously weakened. It was essentially injured by the acceptance of preventive war against Iraq. The war on terrorism, too, has loosened, if not obliterated, these constraints. As a war with no apparent end, the war on terrorism has acquired a near-permanent character, making enemies of the state the object of drone strikes in a substantial number of countries, including Pakistan, Afghanistan, Yemen, and Somalia. Sometimes these secret operations occur with the consent of the concerned states, sometimes not, but there is no mistaking the development of a permanent apparatus for the waging of secret war. It is based on a primitive calculus that virtually ignores the rage produced in societies that are the recipient of such strikes. Like the drug war, to which it bears many disturbing parallels, it purports to be the remedy for things of which it is itself the cause.

The expansion in justifications for the use of force can also be seen in the idea, heartily embraced by the George W. Bush administration, that force is a legitimate instrument for spreading democratic institutions. In his second Inaugural, President Bush declared that "the policy of the United States [is] to seek and support the growth of democratic movements and institutions in every nation and culture, with the ultimate goal of ending tyranny in our world." Both the wars in Iraq and Afghanistan had this as one of their purposes. Though the Obama administration has drawn back from such a crusade, the Bush Doctrine continues to find contemporary supporters. There are, however, no supporters to be found among the Founders for this project. It is not that the doctrine was unknown; on the contrary, the example of the French Revolution that soon followed, with its promise to "accord fraternity and assistance to all peoples who shall wish to recover their liberty," gave the issue unusual prominence, and both sides of the party debate during the immediate post-Constitution period rejected the underlying idea as an offense against the law of nations. Alexander Hamilton considered the French project repugnant to "the general rights of Nations [and] to the true principles of liberty." Thomas Jefferson, who, unlike Hamilton, strongly sympathized with the French Revolution, nevertheless acknowledged that "the French have been guilty of great errors in their conduct towards other nations, not only in insulting uselessly all crowned heads, but [in] endeavoring to force liberty on their neighbors in their own form."[26] Jefferson's view was that the first violation of the non-intervention principle had been made by the crowned heads of Europe, not the French revolutionaries. While the Founders did believe that the United States stood for a form of government that had universal relevance and that the political truths embodied in the Constitution were open, in principle, to all peoples, this belief existed happily alongside the idea that the United States had neither a right nor a duty to bring others to an appreciation of these truths through force. Rather than being contradictory, these ideas originated in the same school of thought. Like religious intolerance, the denial of legitimacy to other forms of government was seen to cause

---

[26] Hamilton and Jefferson are cited in Robert W. Tucker and David C. Hendrickson, *Empire of Liberty: The Statecraft of Thomas Jefferson* (New York: Oxford University Press, 1990), 51.

perpetual war, and such a condition made for an international environment hostile to the spread of free institutions.

Yet another development that has expanded justifications for the use of force has been the growing acceptance in recent decades of a "responsibility to protect." Whereas preventive war was advanced almost furtively as a justification for U.S. intervention, disguised under the label of "preemption," the idea of intervention to protect imperiled populations has acquired much greater international legitimacy.[27] A 2005 U.N. General Assembly document recognizing a responsibility to protect was adopted unanimously, though with the proviso that any military action must take place under the auspices of the U.N. Security Council. It is safe to say that the American public is distinctly out of sympathy with intervention for this reason, but it remains as a potential justification for the use of U.S. military forces and it was the main justification for the 2011 intervention in Libya.

Genocide, war crimes, ethnic cleansing, and crimes against humanity are evil deeds, and it is proper that the international community should look for ways to mitigate their reach or, in extreme cases, to put an end to them. At the same time, there are strong reasons for questioning the capacity to undertake and sustain interventions that satisfy the principle of proportionality—wherein the good done, or evil averted, by the use of force is greater than the evil produced by such use. One must also look with suspicion on the elasticity with which these humanitarian criteria are sometimes invoked, opening a potentially large wedge in justification of offensive uses of force. As a practical matter, it surely deserves notice that the humanitarian interventions most recently urged upon

---

[27] Gareth Evans and Mohamed Sahnoun, co-chairs, *The Responsibility to Protect: Report of the International Commission on Intervention and State Sovereignty* (Ottawa, Canada: International Development Research Centre, 2001).

us — Libya, Syria, Sudan — are those that have arisen within or on the fringes of the Islamic world and are thus connected in subtle ways with the ongoing "war on terror" and an unspoken clash of civilizations. The record of western intervention does not, in some instances, lack plausible connections with resource imperialism. We may foreswear such selfish connections in theory, but in practice they often seem to govern official decisions.

Acceptance of a duty of humanitarian intervention also lends a patina of moral justification for the existence of a large and enduring military establishment, which has been and is likely to be employed for other purposes. If widely accepted, it would carry the nearly inevitable consequence of encouraging rebellion in the expectation of outside support, a consequence the more deeply to be feared insofar as uses of force *in anticipation of* humanitarian disaster are authorized. [28] While U.N. and regional peacekeeping operations, in which troops are dispatched to preserve a peace already made, have proved their utility in some instances over the last generation, humanitarian interventions that lead with the sword are far more dubious. The older rule forbidding such interventions, which embodied this traditional skepticism about the capacity of outsiders to resolve civil wars successfully, is of greater weight. Given the opposing considerations on either side — the felt need to "do something" in the face of humanitarian crisis, the no less imperative lesson of the disutility and unanticipated consequences of outside military intervention — perhaps it is inevitable that we should err. If so, it appears better to this observer to err on the side of caution.

Of all the expansions in justification for the use of force, the adoption of a preventive war rationale is the least tenable. The legal and moral norm against it arose from hard and bitter experience over the consequences produced by the aggressive

---

[28] Evans and Sahnoun, *The Responsibility to Protect*, 33.

use of force in the twentieth century, of which the two world wars were the ultimate symbol; the wisdom of that norm was once again confirmed by the results of the Iraq War. The preventive war rationale rests on images of the enemy that are fed by relentless propaganda and that, as also happened during the Cold War, read those enemies out of the human race. Only a public opinion that, through the miracles of modern military technology, imagines that it has been able essentially to immunize itself from the consequences of war would so easily entertain such ideas. The ease with which it is considered in the United States today testifies to the dangers of the enormous military establishment we have created. It virtually invites irresponsibility in the use of force.

A Way Out?

When the United States assumed its world leadership in the 1940s, no other power was better equipped, by dint of constitutional tradition and pacific bearing, to lead the world toward peace. Its Founders considered peace as the essential purpose and framework of America's basic institutions. Those "present at the creation" of the sweeping reorganization of world order after 1945 also saw the creation of institutions that would preserve international peace as their most pressing concern. They "rejected the idea of peace by universal empire or by the diplomatic juggle of the balance of power," adopting instead "the ideal of the cooperative peace — the ideal which is the great contribution of the Americas to world thought."[29] But while the United States did play a vital role in the creation and maintenance of the relatively peaceful order that arose out of the Second World War, that role has come at a high

---

[29] The expression is that of A.A. Berle, Jr., Assistant Secretary of State in the Franklin Roosevelt administration, "No, Says Berle," *The New York Times*, January 14, 1940.

cost. Our institutions have been militarized to an inordinate degree, certainly to an extent that would have alarmed the Founders of the United States. Our political culture celebrates war and warriors in unseemly fashion, and pushes out of sight and out of mind the wastage brought by our own uses of force. Our criteria for waging war has expanded broadly; considered alone, some of these expansions are not without justification — nothing in matters of war and peace is simple — but the multitude should strike us with alarm. The insensible shift in our maxims against which John Quincy Adams warned — from liberty to force — has taken place. We have become habituated to empire.

There is no easy solution to the predicament in which we find ourselves. The military establishment and national security state are facts of life; they are not going away. Contrary to the expectations of the Founders, Congress has proved a willing abettor of wars of folly. The economic crisis spawned by the 2008 financial crash, from which recovery has been anemic, has deepened the fatigue felt by the American people over the unexpected costs and failed objects of the wars in Iraq and Afghanistan, but there has been little reconsideration of the overall place of the United States in the world and whether a different strategy could achieve essential national goals at far lesser cost. Avarice has not been made to calculate the expenses of ambition. The inability to pay for what we want, and to want only what we are willing to pay for — symbolized by trillion dollar budget deficits — has deepened since the Great Recession but this has not produced a serious push to reduce the overall size of the national security complex.[30] Indeed, in some respects, ambitions have expanded: the United States has become more vocal in opposition to China's territorial claims in its eastern and

---

[30] The formulation is drawn from Walter Lippmann, *U.S. Foreign Policy: Shield of the Republic* (Boston: Little, Brown, 1943), 8.

southern seas, and the U.S. clearly intends to build up its presence in Asia. Progress was recorded by former Secretary of Defense Robert Gates, when he observed that anyone who contemplates sending "a big American land army into Asia or into the Middle East or Africa should 'have his head examined,'" but an air and naval war in those places is not so self-evidently foreclosed.[31] It is very much "on the table" with regard to Iran, as reputed voices of sanity within both the Bush and Obama administrations have insisted. We may hope that the civilian leaders of the military establishment will confine themselves to defensive purposes and rein in the extravagant justifications for the use of force to which we have become accustomed. However, experience suggests that we are far from finished with such temptations.

For a free state, the maximization of power is a fatal objective for foreign policy. Constitutional democracies may be less subject to the abuse of power than other states, but they are hardly exempt from the frailties incident to human nature. The people of America, as Hamilton warned in *The Federalist*, are "remote from the happy empire of perfect wisdom and perfect virtue."[32] So they remain. Moreover, constitutional democracies have reason to fear not only threats from abroad, but also overly centralized power at home. In the long history of reflection on the security predicaments of free states, domestic hierarchy or tyranny is as significant a problem as international anarchy or conquest. That crucial theme, though missing from much contemporary academic writing on international politics, and missing, too, from the conduct of recent American statecraft, was at the core of the republican security theory to which America's Founding

---

[31] Speech at West Point, quoted in Thom Shanker, "Warning Against Wars Like Iraq and Afghanistan," *New York Times*, February 25, 2011.
[32] *Federalist* No. 6, Rossiter, 59.

Fathers made such distinguished contributions.[33] That theory is far more sophisticated and relevant than contemporary ideas of domination and superiority, because it places the preservation of free institutions and the control of power at the core of its concern. We would do well to return to that insight.

---

[33] See Deudney, *Bounding Power.*

American Power and Influence in the New Century: Taking Stock and Looking Forward

Ali Wyne

Introduction

In this essay, I will try to take stock of where the United States finds itself a little over a decade after the attacks of September 11, 2001. President Barack Obama began his second term in office at a time when Americans' concerns about their country's global role may be more acute than at any point since the Cold War, perhaps even since the Second World War. Indeed, "America is in decline" is increasingly offered as a statement of fact rather than a point of contention.[1]

As during previous declinist cycles, some of this anxiety is overwrought. Few would deny, of course, that the years since 9/11 have exacted a steep toll on U.S. power and influence. Begin with the wars in Iraq and Afghanistan: beyond costing more than $1.4 trillion to date—roughly 9% of America's gross domestic product (GDP) in 2011—these wars prevented the

---

[1] In "America's 'Que Sera' Declinism," *Zócalo Public Square*, April 1, 2010, available at
http://www.zocalopublicsquare.org/2012/04/01/americas-que-sera-declinism/ideas/nexus/, I consider why Americans seem to be responding differently to today's declinism than they did to prior waves; and in "What Does It Mean to Argue that 'America Is in Decline'?" *Big Think*, June 9, 2012, available at http://bigthink.com/power-games/what-does-it-mean-to-argue-that-america-is-in-decline, I argue that the quoted phrase is not as clear as it sounds.

U.S. from re-balancing to the Asia-Pacific until this decade.[2] Gross federal debt increased from 57.3% of GDP in 2000 to 98.7% in 2011.[3] From 2000 to 2007, the U.S. averaged 2.6% real growth annually; from 2007 to 2011, less than 0.25% annually.[4] Based on seven indicators—GDP, consumption, stock-market performance, wages, house prices, wealth, and unemployment—The Economist calculates that the U.S. "has lost almost a decade of [economic] progress to the financial

---

[2] According to the homepage of the National Priorities Project's website, http://costofwar.com/, the former figure was $1.41 trillion as of the end of 2012. According to the Bureau of Economic Analysis, "Table 1.1.5—Gross Domestic Product" (accessed July 27, 2012), at http://www.bea.gov/iTable/iTable.cfm?ReqID=9&step=1, U.S. GDP at the end of 2011 was $15.3 trillion.

The U.S. should arguably have rebalanced to the Asia-Pacific region at the turn of the century, if not in the mid-1990s, when policymakers began to focus on the rise of China in earnest. See the Department of Defense's February 1995 report, *United States Security Strategy for the East Asia-Pacific Region*:

Although China's leaders insist their military build-up is defensive and commensurate with China's overall economic growth, others in the region cannot be certain of China's intentions...Absent a better understanding of China's plans, capabilities and intentions, other Asian nations may feel a need to respond to China's growing military power...The United States and China's neighbors would welcome greater transparency in China's defense programs, strategy and doctrine.

[3] Office of Management and Budget, "Table 7.1—Federal Debt at the End of the Year: 1940-2017," accessed February 13, 2012, at http://www.whitehouse.gov/sites/default/files/omb/budget/fy2013/assets/hist07z1.xls.

[4] Bureau of Economic Analysis, "Gross Domestic Product—Percent change from preceding period," accessed July 27, 2012, at http://www.bea.gov/national/xls/gdpchg.xls.

---

crisis."[5] Furthermore, more than a decade of attacking Al Qaeda and its affiliates has limited the dynamism of U.S. foreign policy at a time when the global balance is, arguably, in greater flux than at any time in the past 70 years.

The Good News

While this list of sobering headlines could be extended, one should not neglect the other side of the ledger. The point of calling for a balanced appraisal of this sort — taking stock not only of what is going wrong in the U.S., but also of what is going right — is not to deny the number, severity, and, in some cases, novelty, of the challenges that the U.S. confronts, at home and abroad. The declinist debate would be more constructive, however, if it appreciated that self-examination need not devolve into self-flagellation (just as nuanced analysis need not lapse into wishful thinking). Too many assessments that find the U.S. to be in decline compare its weaknesses against the strengths of other countries; the "balance sheet" for a given country, however, should include both its strengths and its weaknesses, as well as plausible trajectories for each.

The principal blows to U.S. power and influence in recent years have been self-inflicted.

While it may seem odd to frame such a conclusion favorably, it is reassuring that America's trajectory is, in considerable measure, a function of decisions that its leaders make or do not make, rather than a function of phenomena external to its leaders' control. America's decision to invade Iraq in 2003 is one that most observers judge, in retrospect, to

---

[5] "Rolling back the years," *The Economist* online, February 23, 2012, http://www.economist.com/blogs/graphicdetail/2012/02/daily-chart-15.

have been misguided. The downgrading of America's triple-A credit rating in 2011 resulted from misguided spending and taxation policies, along with partisan infighting that nearly led the U.S. to default on its debt.[6]

Those who argue that the U.S. is in decline often discuss such choices alongside concerns about aging infrastructure, an educational system that fails to provide students the practical skills they need to excel in today's global economy, and a political model that penalizes compromise. Importantly, however, the latter are not new challenges; they have evolved over decades and, however serious, they are the types of problems that virtually every country struggles to address. Furthermore, they did not prevent America's ascent to great-power and, subsequently, superpower, status.

Two plausible outcomes have not materialized.

First, while the global financial crisis dealt an appropriate, and likely irreversible, blow to highly financialized capitalism, it does not appear to have mainstreamed the "Beijing Consensus" or invalidated the judgment that capitalism remains the single best system for generating sustained gains in prosperity. *China 2030*, a joint report of the World Bank and China's Development Research Center, warns that a Chinese "attempt to sustain the past growth model for an extended period could lead to a forced change in course as China finally reaches some of the limits of economic, social, environmental, or external sustainability." It also notes that "over time, the government's strong role...has contributed to ever more serious economic imbalances and social disharmonies"; and concludes that the growth of state-owned enterprises "will likely further crowd out private sector activity, dampen

---

[6] For those who argue that the debt poses an insoluble challenge, recall that in February 2000, then-Chairman of the Federal Reserve Alan Greenspan expressed concerns about continuing budget *surpluses*.

competition, and conflict with efforts to build sound foundations for a market-based economy."[7] Kishore Mahbubani concludes that "[c]apitalism itself is not in crisis, but [W]estern capitalism is....For all its flaws and defects, capitalism remains the best system to improve human welfare. This is why the whole world (barring North Korea) has accepted it, in one form or another."[8]

What ongoing economic turmoil has done is stimulate an overdue conversation on varieties of capitalism. "The real question," argues Niall Ferguson, "is which countries' laws and institutions are best, not only at achieving rapid economic growth but also, equally importantly, at distributing the fruits of growth in a way that citizens deem to be just."[9]

Second, the "soft balancing" that has long been occurring against U.S. foreign policy has yet to yield the countervailing coalitions that many observers feared would emerge, particularly in response to the Bush administration's *2002 National Security Strategy*.[10] While that document represented less of a substantive departure from prior U.S. national-security policy than was suggested at the time, it was unusually explicit in justifying unilateral action in pursuit of a

---

[7] *China 2030: Building a Modern, Harmonious, and Creative High-Income Society* (Washington, D.C.: World Bank and Development Research Center of the Chinese State Council, February 2012): 80, 83, and 26.

[8] Kishore Mahbubani, "Western capitalism has much to learn from Asia," *Financial Times* online, February 7, 2012, blogs.ft.com/the-a-list/2012/02/07/western-capitalism-has-much-to-learn-from-asia/.

[9] Niall Ferguson, "We're All State Capitalists Now," *Foreign Policy* online, February 9, 2012, www.foreignpolicy.com/articles/2012/02/09/we_re_all_state_capitalists_now.

[10] According to Robert A. Pape, "soft balancing" encompasses "actions that do not directly challenge U.S. military preponderance, but that use nonmilitary tools to delay, frustrate, and undermine aggressive unilateral U.S. military policies." See Pape, "Soft Balancing Against the United States," *International Security*, 30:1 (Summer 2005): 10.

unipolar order: it called on the U.S. to develop "forces [that] will be strong enough to dissuade potential adversaries from pursuing a military build-up in hopes of surpassing, or equaling, the power of the United States...[and] be prepared to act apart [from our friends and partners] when our interests and unique responsibilities require."[11] Summarizing much of the U.S. policy establishment's concern about such prescriptions, John Ikenberry warned in September 2002 that "[t]he major states may not have much leverage in directly restraining American military policy, but they can make the United States pay a price in other areas." Therefore, he concludes, "the neoimperial grand strategy...steps into the oldest trap of powerful imperial states: self-encirclement."[12] Despite that concern, the BRIC countries (Brazil, Russia, India, and China) seem unlikely to develop into a coherent bloc; and the Shanghai Cooperation Organization seems unlikely to become a counterbalance to the North Atlantic Treaty Organization. The countries with which the U.S. has adversarial relationships are not great powers: consider Iran and North Korea. Robert Kaplan and Stephen Kaplan note that in Britain, Canada, and Australia, the U.S. has a "bulwark of allies" that "finds no equivalent in its competitor nations' strategic arsenals."[13]

Important phenomena favor America's strategic position going forward.

While current commentary about the approaching of U.S. energy independence may be exaggerated, declining oil

---

[11] George W. Bush, *The National Security Strategy of the United States of America* (Washington, DC: White House, September 2002): 30-31.

[12] G. John Ikenberry, "America's Imperial Ambition," *Foreign Affairs*, Volume 81, No. 5 (September/October 2002): 58.

[13] Robert D. Kaplan and Stephen S. Kaplan, "America Primed," *National Interest*, No. 112 (March/April 2011): 44.

consumption and the development of indigenous reserves of tight oil and shale gas are indeed reducing America's vulnerability to the vagaries of global energy markets at a time when China's is increasing. Over time, this trend could not only make energy a reliable pillar of the U.S. economy, but also allow the U.S. to remold its relationships in the Middle East, the region that arguably has caused it more foreign-policy headaches in recent decades than any other.

Abroad, the U.S. has yet to realize the full potential of free-trade agreements with South Korea, Colombia, and Panama. It is making progress towards establishing a free-trade area with the European Union, and finalizing a Trans-Pacific Partnership (TPP)—the latter of which would include, for now, the U.S., Australia, Brunei, Canada, Chile, Malaysia, Mexico, New Zealand, Peru, Singapore, and Vietnam. According to National Security Adviser Tom Donilion, a TPP "that includes Japan...would represent an annual trading relationship of $1.7 trillion."[14]

Furthermore, while criticisms of U.S. power and influence are unlikely to abate, they increasingly coexist with concern about the consequences of relative U.S. decline. Such anxiety has enabled the U.S. to reinvigorate efforts to restore its leadership in the Asia-Pacific, which is increasingly the nerve center not only of global economics, but also of global geopolitics. Many of China's neighbors are strengthening their diplomatic and military ties with the U.S. and with each other—not because they are trying to realize some organic vision of an Asian community, but because they are uncertain of how China's regional conduct will change as its heft increases.[15]

---

[14] Tom Donilon, "The President's Free-Trade Path to Prosperity," *Wall Street Journal* (April 14, 2013).

[15] America's reorientation towards the region is not without its risks. Because it was formalized in a military context—it was the Department

of Defense that announced that the U.S. would "of necessity rebalance toward the Asia-Pacific region" — it is likely to heighten what Henry Kissinger calls China's "greatest strategic fear": "that an outside power or powers will establish military deployments around China's periphery capable of encroaching on China's territory or meddling in its domestic institutions." See Kissinger, *On China*, reprint edition (New York: Penguin Books, 2012), 540. Furthermore, warns Justin Logan, there is a possibility that China's neighbors "will continue to free-ride on American exertions" if they discern in U.S. foreign policy a more enduring commitment to the Asia-Pacific.

See Logan, "Asia's Free-Riders," *Foreign Policy* online, November 9, 2011, http://www.foreignpolicy.com/articles/2011/11/09/asias_free_riders.

Absent a successful U.S. effort to enlist other countries, primarily China, in sharing the burden of global governance more fully, this free-riding risk could extend well beyond that region. Consider this warning from Eric X. Li, a trenchant observer of U.S. politics:

For a brief period after the Cold War, America was able to be both Leviathan and a national player within the [postwar] system, because its national interests could be seen to coincide with the world's interests. That moment has passed. The attempt to play the dual role of ruler and participant has cost America dearly and could bankrupt the country, economically and socially, if it continues. After just one generation in this role, the United States is deeply in debt; its middle class is crumbling; its industries have been hollowed out; its infrastructure is in disrepair; its education system is badly underfunded; its social contract is in shambles. The weight of free riders is crushing the one participant who would be ruler.

See Li, "Hang on, Leviathan, Hang on," *International Herald Tribune* June 5, 2012).

The challenge will be for the U.S. to convince China that its rebalancing is a multifaceted policy — not a predominantly military one — from which both China's neighbors and China itself stand to benefit. Shawn Brimley and Ely Ratner offer important counsel in this regard:

[Rebalancing] in reality includes economic, diplomatic, and security objectives: strengthening relations with traditional allies; building deeper ties with emerging powers, including China; working with the region's multilateral institutions; diversifying the United States' military

Not long before this book went to press, Ian Bremmer and David Gordon offered the following rebuttal to the declinist case:

> [S]everal economic and political factors are now reviving talk of America the Resilient, both at home and abroad. A technology-driven U.S. energy boom may be the biggest surprise of all....The revolution in production of tight oil and shale gas has fueled U.S. job growth, created conditions for a revival of low-cost U.S. manufacturing, and now offers Washington the chance to use energy — both exports and technology—as a tool of foreign policy. Add a housing market turnaround, and these changes set the stage for a dynamic U.S. recovery....Even as the sequester and its spending cuts weigh on near-term growth, Congress has mostly abandoned the fiscal brinksmanship of the past two years and is on track to pass comprehensive immigration reform in 2013, providing medium- and long-term economic benefits. And despite President Obama's renewed focus on climate change, his "all-of-the-above" energy policy will allow for continued growth of tight oil and shale gas

posture; promoting human rights and democracy; and advancing U.S. trade and business interests...the Obama administration has made clear, both publicly and privately, that a positive and constructive relationship with China is key to the success of its broader strategy in Asia....Although the military aspects of the rebalancing strategy have garnered the most attention in the media, civilian departments and agencies have also begun to shift their priorities and resources to Asia....Congress must do its part by making sure that key agencies and departments have the funds in the first place....Washington should insist that the militaries of countries such as Australia, Japan, Singapore, South Korea, and Thailand contribute to regional security at levels commensurate with their capabilities. It is also critical that the United States continue to coordinate with these countries on diplomatic, development, and defense initiatives to maximize the efficiency and effectiveness of U.S. engagement in the region.

See Brimley and Ratner, "Smart Shift: A Response to the 'The Problem with the Pivot'," *Foreign Affairs*, Volume 92, No. 1 (January/February 2013): 177-81.

production....Asian nations are eager to partner with the United States as an alternative to China, and Europeans are eager for U.S. trade and investment to help lift their economic malaise....The Trans-Pacific Partnership and its nascent trans-Atlantic counterpart have the ability to create a trade, investment and regulatory framework to establish free market principles as the bedrock of 21st-century global economics and get beyond the deadlock of the need for universalism in the World Trade Organization.[16]

The Significance of China's Rise

With 2014 well underway, then, the prognosis for the U.S. is not as grim as much declinist commentary would suggest. Even so, the country's policymakers face a daunting array of challenges going forward, foremost among them, arguably, being the rise (or return, depending on one's perspective) of China. At least at a superficial level, the power transition between the U.S. and China is the latest chapter in the story that has defined history: the rise and fall of great powers.[17] Former Secretary of State Hillary Clinton suggested the magnitude of the challenge that they confront when she stated that "our two nations are trying to do something that has never been done in history, which is to write a new answer to the question of what happens when an established power and a rising power meet."[18]

---

[16] Ian Bremmer and David Gordon, "Powers on the Mend," *International Herald Tribune*, April 11, 2013.

[17] I say "superficial" because the U.S.-China power transition is, in many aspects, unique in the annals of power transitions. I try to expound this proposition in "China May Not Be a U.S. Ally, But It's Also Not an Adversary," *Forbes* online, November 6, 2012 http://www.forbes.com/sites/realspin/2012/11/06/china-may-not-be-a-u-s-ally-but-its-also-not-an-adversary/.

[18] Remarks by Hillary Clinton at The Great Hall of the People, Beijing, September 5, 2012.

The manner in which U.S.-China relations evolve will have an inordinate impact, not only on prospects for global peace and prosperity—the two countries have the world's two largest economies, are the world's top two spenders on national defense, and are the world's top two consumers of energy, among other distinctions—but also on the capacity of global governance. It is difficult to think of a global challenge on which meaningful progress can be made without close cooperation between the U.S. and China. Thus does Graham Allison call the management of their relationship "[t]he defining geopolitical challenge of the next half century."[19]

China's rise figured prominently in the 2012 U.S. presidential contest. In an article explaining how he would respond to growing Chinese power, then-candidate Mitt Romney called for a world "in which [America's] economic and military power is second to none."[20] In October 2011, he argued that "[t]his century must be an American century. In an American century, America has the strongest economy and the strongest military in the world."[21] And in the summer of 2012, he made perhaps his strongest statement in this vein to date: "If you do not want America to be the strongest nation on earth, I am not your president."[22]

President Obama, meanwhile, had to—and continues to—fight the perception that he "accepts" U.S. decline, even though he emphasizes the singular importance of U.S. leadership in international affairs. He observed in the 2010 *National Security Strategy* that "no nation should be better

---

[19] Graham Allison, "The Cuban Missile Crisis at 50: Lessons for U.S. Foreign Policy Today," *Foreign Affairs*, Volume 91, No. 4 (July/August 2012): 15.

[20] Mitt Romney, "How I'll Respond to China's Growing Power," *Wall Street Journal*, February 16, 2012.

[21] Speech by Mitt Romney at The Citadel, Charleston, S.C., October 7, 2011.

[22] Speech by Mitt Romney at the 113th Veterans of Foreign Wars National Convention, Reno, Nevada, July 24, 2012.

positioned to lead in an era of globalization" than the U.S., which he often characterizes as the "indispensable nation in tackling major international problems."[23] He made this case even more forcefully while campaigning for the presidency in late 2007: "The mission of the United States is to provide global leadership."[24] Even so, he was compelled to ratchet up his own rhetoric in the last campaign, avowing that "[i]f anyone tries to tell you...that America is in decline, you tell them this. Like the 20th century, the 21st century will be another great American century. We are Americans, blessed with the greatest form of government ever devised by man."[25]

While this rhetoric can be attributed in part to election-year politics, it also reflects a deep-seated uncertainty about the course of an international system in which America's relative preeminence continues to diminish. After all, the U.S. has been unrivaled for a long time—at least according to the metrics that one intuitively associates with that characterization: it has had the world's largest GDP for roughly a century and a quarter; it has spent the most on

---

[23] Barack Obama, *National Security Strategy* (Washington, D.C.: White House, May 2010): ii; Barack Obama's interview with Fareed Zakaria, *Time*, January 30, 2012.

According to Uri Friedman, associate editor of *Foreign Policy*, "Clinton aide Sidney Blumenthal and historian James Chace coined the term ['indispensable nation'] in 1996 to encapsulate the idea of 'liberal internationalism' in the post-Cold War world." See Friedman, "Democratic platform swaps 'American exceptionalism' for 'indispensable nation'," *Foreign Policy* online, September 4, 2012, http://blog.foreignpolicy.com/posts/2012/09/04/democratic_platform _swaps_american_exceptionalism_for_indispensable_nation.

[24] Barack Obama, "Renewing American Leadership," *Foreign Affairs*, Volume 86, No. 4 (July/August 2007): 4.

[25] Speech by Barack Obama at the 113th Veterans of Foreign Wars National Convention, Reno, Nevada, July 23, 2012.

national defense since at least 1949; and it has been the central anchor of the international system during the postwar era.[26]

On current trend lines, however, China's GDP is likely to overtake America's within the decade, even if its soft landing continues. Further, it's hardly implausible that China's defense spending could overtake America's within a few decades (*The Economist* estimates that it could do so as early as 2035).[27] These transitions are likely to be disconcerting to Americans for several reasons: events are occurring far more rapidly than virtually any observer, including influential members of the Chinese commentariat, would have predicted; the U.S. has grown accustomed to an international system absent a peer competitor; and for now, Chinese governance defies the (weakened, but still powerful) U.S. conviction that authoritarian regimes are incapable of achieving robust long-term economic growth.

The good news is that the U.S. appears to be making a long-overdue transition towards a healthier balance of consumption and exports. As the *Economist* recently explained, "[c]onsumers are now engaged in a long, hard process of shedding debt and learning to live within their means. This is essential, but it has a price: an uncommonly feeble recovery."[28] Completing that transition, realizing the nascent energy revolution's full potential, and commercializing innovations in myriad domains — ranging from nanotechnology to digital printing to synthetic biology — could result in a long-term U.S. economy that, while considerably smaller than China's in overall size, is more

---

[26] The 1949 date comes from this writer's e-mail correspondence with Sam Perlo-Freeman, director of the Program on Military Expenditure and Arms Production at the Stockholm International Peace Research Institute, August 6, 2012.

[27] "The dragon's new teeth," *The Economist,* April 7, 2012.

[28] "Points of Light," *The Economist,* July 14, 2012.

balanced, more capable of self-renewal, and less vulnerable to disruptions in global markets.

Unfortunately, however, these steps are unlikely to revitalize America's economy in the short term. Some observers, including Columbia University economist Joseph Stiglitz, argue that sluggish growth and high unemployment are likely to persist for several years, perhaps even becoming "the new normal" for the U.S. economy over the long term.[29] Accordingly, the decades during which the aforementioned economic and military transitions occur between the U.S. and China will be a central test of America's strategic patience: will the U.S., already fiscally constrained, focus on renewing and reenergizing its economy—thereby laying the foundation for a more sustainable defense posture—or will it become overly fixated on China's growing GDP and defense spending? In any competition, even one that has strong cooperative elements, participants must remain aware of, but not preoccupied with, their competitors' actions.

U.S.-China Relations

Unfortunately (though perhaps inevitably), the overarching driver of current U.S.-China relations is strategic mistrust. Accordingly, there is a limit to how far the relationship can progress if the two countries primarily discuss their current areas of disagreement—and even those in a piecemeal fashion. It behooves both to start at the end and take a bird's-eye view: that is, to imagine international

---

[29] In October 2010, Joseph Stiglitz argued that Western government officials and economists had begun to concede "the dismal picture of the immediate future about which I had warned: a new 'normal' with higher unemployment rates, lower growth, and lower levels of public services in the advanced industrial countries." See Stiglitz, *America, Free Markets, and the Sinking of the World Economy* (New York: W. W. Norton, 2010), 300.

orders of, say, 2050 or 2100, that could sustain continued U.S. leadership and perpetual Chinese ascendance, and to construct pathways for each to get there.[30] Such a discussion should be grounded in a few propositions:

- Neither country will be able to approach, let alone achieve, dominance over the international system;
- A military confrontation between them would be mutually destructive, as would an abrupt economic decoupling;
- The U.S. neither could nor should attempt to contain China's rise; and
- China should accommodate itself to a strong, enduring U.S. presence in the Asia-Pacific.

In addition, both countries should:

- Articulate their vital national interests, identify what they regard as the central threats to those interests, and ask each other to clarify any ambiguities. China, for example, has neither affirmed nor denied speculation that it regards the South China Sea as a "core interest."
- Ask each other tough questions. For one, the U.S., should ask China: where do you hope and expect to be when your leadership assesses that China's "peaceful rise" is complete? What steps are you taking to prevent hackers from stealing U.S. intellectual property? China, for its part, should ask the U.S.: how will you ensure that your strategy of hedging against our rise does not

---

[30] Monographs such as Kenneth Lieberthal and Wang Jisi's *Addressing U.S.-China Strategic Distrust* (Washington, D.C.: Brookings Institution, April 2012) are invaluable not only for being candid, but also for juxtaposing perspectives from leading U.S. strategists and their Chinese counterparts.

evolve into one of *de facto* containment? How will you maintain your stated posture of neutrality as tensions over territorial disputes in the South China Sea continue to increase?

A More Balanced Conception of Power

To manage China's rise, the U.S. needs not only to pursue a longer-term strategy towards China, but also to ensure that it does not underestimate its own power. Whereas overestimating one's power can yield hubris, the reverse can yield defensiveness and even paranoia. It is imperative, then, for the U.S. to adopt a conception of power that takes into account a broader set of metrics and considerations. The size of a country's GDP, after all, is only one component of its economic power; the role of the country's currency in global markets matters, as do the innovativeness of its citizens, the strength of its higher-education system, and the outlook of its demographics.

- Roughly 60% of global allocated foreign-exchange reserves are dollar-denominated; China's currency, the renminbi, is not yet a global reserve currency.[31]
- 47 of the world's 100 most innovative companies are in the U.S.; none are in China.[32]
- 31 of the world's 100 leading universities are in the U.S.; three are in China.[33]
- America's working-age population will have increased

---

[31] International Monetary Fund, "Currency Composition of Foreign-Exchange Reserves," available at http://www.imf.org/external/np/sta/cofer/eng/cofer.pdf . Last accessed December 28, 2012.

[32] http://top100innovators.com/. Last accessed September 1, 2014.

[33] http://www.topuniversities.com/university-rankings/world-university-rankings/2012.

23% by 2050; China's will have decreased 21%.[34]

Similarly, the level of a country's defense spending is only one component of its military power; the composition of that spending matters, as does the reach of the country's capabilities.

- China is developing capabilities that render America's presence in the Asia-Pacific more costly, as well as asymmetric capabilities, especially in cyberspace, that could compromise U.S. national security and interests. Even so, the U.S. remains the only country that can project power globally.

- If and when China's defense spending equals America's, Chas Freeman notes that it "will [all] be concentrated on the defense of China and its periphery." China borders fourteen countries, each of which is concerned about the consequences of China's rise; moreover, that country faces tumult in Xinjiang and greater Tibet, which collectively comprise over two-fifths of its territory.[35]

---

[34]According to the U.S. Census Bureau's International Database, China's working-age population (comprising individuals 15-64) was 983.3 million midway through 2011, and will decrease to 776.3 million by midway through 2050; the corresponding figures for the U.S. are 209 million and 255.2 million.

In considerable measure because of immigration, the U.S. is poised to buck the developed-world phenomenon of population stagnation (and even decline in some countries); according to Ben Wattenberg, its population will reach 400 million by 2050 and 500 million by 2100. See Wattenberg, "Immigrants and 'Comparative Advantage'," *Wall Street Journal*, August 8, 2012 .

[35] Chas Freeman, "The China Bluff," *National Interest* online, available at http://nationalinterest.org/commentary/the-china-bluff-6561. Last accessed December 23, 2012. It is revealing that China spends more on "internal security" than national defense.

A Word on Influence

Then there is influence, or the ability to achieve outcomes with the power at one's disposal. The declinist narrative belies the reality that the U.S. has never been able to dictate geopolitics. Distinguished Harvard professor Joseph Nye reminds us that

> possession of power resources does not always imply that one gets the outcomes one prefers....Consider the situation after World War II. The U.S. accounted for more than one-third of global product and had an overwhelming preponderance in nuclear weapons. Nonetheless, the U.S. was unable to prevent the "loss" of China, "roll back" Communism in Eastern Europe, prevent stalemate in the Korean War, defeat Vietnam's National Liberation Front, or dislodge the Castro regime in Cuba.[36]

Thus does Robert Kagan stress that it is difficult to gauge whether the U.S. is in decline without "a reasonable baseline from which to measure. To compare American influence today with a mythical past of overwhelming dominance can only mislead us."[37] A related misunderstanding is that influence essentially grows in parallel with power, and can do so indefinitely. America's recent difficulties in Iraq and Afghanistan illustrate that even a country that is far and away the most powerful in the international system may struggle to achieve the outcomes that it seeks.

The increasingly common refrain, then, that the U.S. should "choose" leadership over decline is problematic in at

---

[36] Joseph S. Nye, "American Power after Bin Laden," Project Syndicate, available at http://www.project-syndicate.org/commentary/american-power-after-bin-laden .

[37] Robert Kagan, *The World America Made* (New York: Alfred A. Knopf, 2012),): 122.

least two respects. First, it suggests that the U.S. can retain its current share of power and influence simply by trying. It is wrong to argue that the country's path is entirely a function of external phenomena; it is equally wrong, however, to argue that those phenomena have no impact on that path. After all, no level of exertion can indefinitely prevent the rise of other countries or the proliferation of non-state actors.[38] Second, it is not self-evident that accumulating greater power resources would enable the U.S. to make more headway in halting Iran's and North Korea's work on their respective nuclear programs, compelling Pakistan to fight extremists in North Waziristan, defeating the Taliban in Afghanistan, forging a global accord to mitigate climate change, reducing systemic risk in global financial markets, preventing cybertheft, or making progress on any of its other foreign-policy objectives.

These considerations suggest a paradox: on the one hand, America's relative power may continue to decline, and the limitations to its influence may continue to grow; on the other hand, its comprehensive power is unlikely to be surpassed for some time, and it will continue to be looked to for leadership in addressing the world's most urgent challenges. These data suggest, furthermore, that the U.S. needs to develop new mechanisms for converting its prodigious power resources into global leadership. Among the most promising proposals is Anne-Marie Slaughter's notion of "network centrality":

> A state's ability to position itself as close to the center of critical networks as possible and to mobilize, orchestrate and create networks will prove a vital source of power. The United States should thus strive to be the most central node...in the networks that are most important to advancing its interests and that are most

---

[38] Nor is it clear that such an outcome, even if theoretically possible, would advance U.S. interests. Thus while the revival of Western Europe and the Asia-Pacific after World War II diminished America's share of gross global product considerably, it also strengthened U.S. leadership.

connected to other networks....Formulating and implementing this strategy involves a series of steps. First is to...see problems in terms of the connections between the relevant actors and, hence, to see the relevant choke points, switches and sources of influence. The second step is to master the tools of gathering intelligence about relevant networks and mapping them in real time. Third is to build the key relationships that will allow U.S. officials and their allies to use pressure or persuasion at the relevant points in the network. Fourth is to learn which kinds of networks work for which affirmative purposes...and to create the official infrastructure to host and foster those networks. The fifth and final step is to understand how to provide platforms that will encourage and enable U.S. citizens, corporations, organizations and institutions of all kinds to organize themselves effectively to produce and implement solutions to problems that concern them.[39]

Conclusion

Managing China's rise is, of course, only one of many U.S. foreign-policy imperatives. I spotlight it in this essay because, arguably, it has more potential than any other phenomenon to distort America's self-image — how the U.S. understands its own power resources and capacity for shaping the international system — and accordingly prevent it from adopting a sustainable grand strategy. The National Intelligence Council's new report, *Global Trends 2030*, offers a useful corrective to declinism (and to its ever-rarer antithesis, triumphalism):

> Although the United States' (and the West's) relative decline vis-à-vis the rising states is inevitable, its future

---

[39] Anne-Marie Slaughter, "A Grand Strategy of Network Centrality," in Richard Fontaine and Kristin M. Lord (eds.), *America's Path: Grand Strategy for the Next Administration* (Washington, D.C.: Center for a New American Security, May 2012),): 46.

role in the international system is much harder to project...The U.S. most likely will remain 'first among equals' among the other great powers in 2030 because of its preeminence across a range of power dimensions and legacies of its leadership role. More important than just its economic weight, the United States' dominant role in international politics has derived from its preponderance across the board in both hard and soft power....[The U.S. will] have to contend with the growing diffusion of power, which would make it virtually impossible...for any power to act hegemonically....The legacy of U.S. power—as chief architect of the post-WWII order—has a potentially long tail.[40]

For those who imagine that the U.S. once exercised hegemony, this conclusion will surely be disappointing. Objectively, however, its position remains enviable. Numerous trends point to an economic renaissance in the U.S.—a renaissance that most observers believe will be integral to its ability to exercise global leadership, as it has in decades past.[41] In addition, the liberal international order that it underpins abroad (albeit under growing duress) does not yet face a coherent alternative. An economically stronger U.S. will be more persuasive in convincing rising powers—China, in particular—that they should strengthen that system rather than seeking its replacement. These outcomes are hardly guaranteed. It would be a shame, however, if misguided declinism dissuaded the U.S. from even seeking them.

---

[40] *Global Trends 2030: Alternative Worlds* (Washington, D.C.: National Intelligence Council, December 2012),): x and 101.

[41] See, for example, Ruchir Sharma, "Head of the Class," *Foreign Policy* online, available at http://www.foreignpolicy.com/articles/2013/04/08/breakout_nation_sharma_us_economy. Last accessed April 8, 2013.

Part II: Challenges of the Modern World — What to Do?

Lawfare: An Emerging Threat to National Security

Aaron Eitan Meyer and Guermantes Lailari

Introduction

More than a decade ago, Major General Charles Dunlap, USAF (ret) coined the term "lawfare" to denote "the use of the law as a weapon of war." Lawfare applies legal means and processes to attain strategic goals traditionally pursued via the employment of armies. He observed that "'lawfare'...is the most recent feature of twenty-first century combat."[1] And indeed, the historical events of the past two decades have proven him correct, as lawfare has increasingly become a fourth-generation warfare tactic alongside more well-known warfare techniques in information, economics, and cyberspace.

The manifestation of lawfare, or legal warfare, depends on the proponent's goals and capabilities. In this essay, we will demonstrate how a state actor (China) and a non-state actor (the Muslim Brotherhood) each utilize lawfare against the interests of the United States. We will briefly discuss case

---

[1] Dunlap, "Law and Military Interventions: Preserving Humanitarian Values in 21st-Century Conflicts," 5.

* Editor's note: The first section of this essay pertaining to China and its engagement in the practice of Lawfare has been penned by Guermantes Lailari. Aaron Eitan Meyer is responsible for the latter section on the Muslim Brotherhood.

studies to identify an existing gap in American understanding and capabilities.

China's "Three Warfare Strategy"

Since 1997, the U.S. Congress has required the Department of Defense (DoD) to provide both a classified and an unclassified annual report focused on the military power of the People's Republic of China (PRC), entitled the "Military and Security Developments Involving the People's Republic of China" (CMPR). A description and an assessment of the PRC's Three Warfare strategy of 2003 is included in these reports, of which one strategic pillar is legal warfare (or lawfare):

> The Chinese concept of 'three warfares' (*san zhong zhanfa*) refers specifically to psychological warfare, media warfare, and legal warfare... Legal Warfare uses international and domestic law to claim the legal high ground or assert Chinese interests. It can be employed to hamstring an adversary's operational freedom and shape the operational space. Legal warfare is also intended to build international support and manage possible political repercussions of China's military actions. China has attempted to employ legal warfare in the maritime domain and in international airspace in pursuit of a security buffer zone.[2]

Our case study of a non-state actor will focus on the Muslim Brotherhood, a group with a demonstrated dislike for the West vis-à-vis its support of al Qaida, Hamas, the Egyptian Islamic Jihad, and other terrorist organizations. Such support was disclosed in November 2008 during preliminary proceedings leading up to the ruling in U.S. federal court against the leadership of the U.S.-based Holy Land Foundation, or HLF. The verdict found the HLF guilty of

---

[2] Secretary of Defense, "Annual Report to Congress: Military and Security Developments Involving the People's Republic of China 2011," 26.

providing material support to Hamas, a finding subsequently reaffirmed by the Fifth Circuit Court of the United States in December 2011.[3] The case, and the respective documents admitted as evidence, demonstrate how the Muslim Brotherhood not only has supported a designated terrorist organization, but also has actively sought to undermine the U.S. internally, terming the latter effort as part of a "grand Jihad in eliminating and destroying the Western civilization from within..."[4]

We believe that examining the use of the law in these two different scenarios can shed light on why U.S. policy makers and strategists should view the law as a potential weapon — one utilized by the United States, or against it by potential adversaries. Lawfare needs to be assessed and embraced and, ideally, it needs to become a permanent arrow in the quiver in the armamentarium of national power. Unless this capability is integrated into all aspects and levels of statecraft, the United States will continue to exist on the world stage at a political, policy, strategic, operational, and tactical disadvantage.

China's Legal Warfare Strategy (San Zhong Zhanfa – 三种战法)

Whereas the first official use of the term was not sanctioned by the Chinese government until 2003,[5] Chinese sources have been referencing the concept of a legal warfare since 1999, first in a publication entitled *Unrestricted Warfare*. Another reference appeared the following year, this time in

---

[3] "Fifth Circuit Appeals Court Upholds HLF Convictions."

[4] "An Explanatory Memorandum on the General Strategic Goal for the Group In North America," Section 4, subsection 4, on "Understanding the Role of the Muslim Brother in North America."

[5] Secretary of Defense, "Annual Report to Congress: Military and Security Developments Involving the People's Republic of China - 2010," 26.

Science of Military Strategy, with a notation that "war is not only a military struggle, but also a comprehensive contest on [the] fronts of politics, economy, diplomacy, and *law*."[6] In contrast, no official DoD acknowledgement of the term occurred until the 2006 submission of the congressionally-mandated CMPR report. And while each of the subsequent annual reports submitted through 2011 referred to the concept, it mysteriously disappeared from both the 2012 and 2013 editions.[7] This is a surprising omission, since no evidence exists to suggest that the Chinese military has removed legal warfare from its planning or operational use. In fact, the reverse appears to be the case.

Echoing the observations of General Dunlap (noted above), the 2011 submission of the CMPR asserted that the purpose of the Chinese legal warfare and broader "soft warfare" strategy is to "undermine the spirit and ideological commitment of the adversary."[8][9]

Origin of China's Warfare Strategy

The Ancient Era

China's present attention to, and engagement in, lawfare is rooted in various events and doctrinal teachings dating back to the earliest days of its 5,000-year cultural existence. Without attempting to summarize the entirety of Chinese war theory,[10] several key notions of the current Chinese "legal warfare"

---

[6] Secretary of Defense, "Annual Report to Congress: Military Power of the People's Republic of China - 2007," 13.

[7] Secretary of Defense, "Annual Report to Congress: Military and Security Developments Involving the People's Republic of China - 2012."

[8] Dunlap, "The Mottled Legacy of 9/11," 440.

[9] Secretary of Defense, "Annual Report to Congress: Military and Security Developments Involving the People's Republic of China 2011," 26.

[10] Thomas, "The Chinese Strategic Mind-Set," 52.

---

strategy are highlighted here, and their respective origins are discussed.

During the 5th Century, Sun Tzu asserted, in *The Art of War*: "to fight and conquer in all your battles is not supreme excellence; supreme excellence consists in breaking the enemy's resistance without fighting."[11] He also claimed that "[t]he Moral Law causes the people to be in complete accord with their ruler, so that they will follow him regardless of their lives, undismayed by any danger."[12] Thus we see the philosophical underpinnings of non-kinetic competition and the beginnings of the concept of Chinese lawfare. Not only is it a tool to be used against an external adversary, but also in domestic situations to ensure that the people are "in complete accord with their ruler."[13] Sun Tzu further proclaimed that all warfare is based on deception and that "when able to attack, we must seem unable; when using our forces, we must seem inactive; when we are near, we must make the enemy believe we are far away; when far away, we must make him believe we are near."[14] Therefore, the effective use of lawfare against an unaware adversary is a good example of deception.

The Modern Age

Published in 1999 by two Chinese People's Liberation Army Air Force Senior Colonels, Qiao Liang (乔良) and Wang Xiangsui (王湘穗), *Unrestricted Warfare* lists 24 possible types of new warfare and three are highlighted in grey below:[15]

---

[11] Giles, *The Art of War by Sun Tzˇu*, 11.

[12] Ibid., 3.

[13] Ibid., 1.

[14] Ibid., 4.

[15] Liang and Xiangsui, *Unrestricted Warfare*, 146.

Military	Quasi-military	Non-military
Nuclear	Diplomatic	Financial
Conventional	Network	Trade
Bio/Chemical	Intelligence	Resources
Ecological	Psychological	Foreign Assistance
Space	High Tech	Legalistic
Electronic	Smuggling	Embargo
Guerilla	Drug Warfare	Media
Terrorist	Simulated (Intimidation)	Ideological

Figure 1: Possible types of new warfare

Some of these types are described by Liang and Xiangsui in further detail:

> ...**psychological** (spreading rumors to intimidate the enemy and break down his will); smuggling (throwing markets into confusion and attacking economic order); **media** (manipulating what people see and hear in order to lead public opinion along); drug (obtaining sudden and huge illicit profits by spreading disaster in other countries); network (venturing out in secret and concealing one's identity in a type of warfare that is virtually impossible to guard against);...resources (grabbing riches by plundering stores of resources);...economic aid (bestowing favor in the open and contriving to control matters in secret); and **international law** (seizing the earliest opportunity to set up regulations).[16]

Of the list, only the three highlighted above in grey — *psychological, media* (sometimes referred to as public opinion), and *legalistic* (legal warfare) — are formally and publicly

---

[16] Liang and Xiangsui, *Unrestricted Warfare*, 51–55. The translations are not exactly the same.

accepted into Chinese military doctrine/grand strategy, although it seems likely that the incorporation of many of the other types has also taken place.

China's "Soft War" Strategy: Psychological, Media, and Legal Warfare

In December 2003, China's Chinese Communist Party Central Committee (CCP) and the Chinese Central Military Commission (CMC) approved a new strategy[17] to include non-kinetic options under the rubric of the newly-created Three Warfare Strategy (三种战法) or Soft Warfare Strategy, one with a focus on psychological, media (public opinion), and legal objectives.[18] This strategy requires them to pursue such objectives in a mutually supportive and multi-disciplined fashion at all times.

China has since employed and applied a legal warfare strategy in several ways, especially with respect to relations with Taiwan and the enforcement of the U.N. Convention on the Law of the Sea (UNCLOS). With respect to Taiwan, the Secretary of Defense's office previously reported that "China's National People's Congress passed an 'anti-secession law' in March 2005 as a means to pressure the Taiwan leadership, build a *legal foundation to justify a use of force, and form a rhetorical counter to the U.S. Taiwan Relations Act...*" and noted further that, "China's current approach to preventing Taiwan independence combines diplomatic, economic, *legal*,

---

[17] Cheng, "The Chinese People's Liberation Army and Special Operations." This new strategy was published as the *Regulations on Political Work in the People's Liberation Army* or *Chinese People's Liberation Army Political Work Regulations* [zhongguo renmin jiefangjun zhengzhi gongzuo tiaoli] in 2003 and revised 2010.

[18] The references to legal warfare and the Three Warfare Strategy in the regulations fall under wartime political work or political warfare.

psychological, and military instruments to convince Taipei that the price of declaring independence is too high."[19] In 2006, the Secretary of Defense's office fine-tuned this assessment in a section entitled "China's Legal Warfare":

> Chinese military strategists are taking an increasing interest in *international law as an instrument of policy in a conflict.* Some PLA thinkers believe *law can be used as a weapon to deter adversaries prior to combat.* For example, in a Taiwan Strait context, China could launch a concerted *information campaign to portray third-party intervention as illegitimate and outside of international legal norms.*[20]

The 2006 Department of Defense's report to Congress again highlighted strategic moves of China that employed lawfare techniques, this time with respect to UNCLOS, noting:

> China is also pursuing a global effort to shape international opinion on issues related to interpretation and application of the *U.N. Convention on the Law of the Sea.* By a series of scholarly articles and organized symposia, it has sought to shift scholarly opinion and the perspective of national governments *away from interpretations of maritime law that favor freedom of navigation and toward interpretations of increased sovereign authority and control over the full 200 nautical mile Exclusive Economic Zone [EEZ] and the airspace above it.* This is an assertion of claims and rights in the maritime domain that could *enhance the legitimacy of coercive Chinese operations at sea.*[21]

Heritage Foundation scholar Dean Cheng suggests that these actions are designed to follow a general strategy of legal warfare to serve the following purposes:

- To sap U.S. will and raise doubts about the justification of intervention, hopefully retarding U.S. responses;

---

[19] Secretary of Defense, "Annual Report to Congress: The Military Power of the People's Republic of China - 2005," 3 and 39. Lailari's emphasis.

[20] Secretary of Defense, "Annual Report to Congress: The Military Power of the People's Republic of China - 2006," 38. Lailari's emphasis.

[21] Ibid., 36. Lailari's emphasis.

- To attenuate U.S. alliances, thereby affecting access to vital ports and resupply facilities, as well as limiting foreign support for U.S. efforts;
- To reinforce domestic will and sustain the conflict, compelling the U.S. to confront the prospect of a longer war.[22, 23]

"Operationalizing" China's "Legal Warfare": South China Sea and Other Regions

Since 2003, China has operationalized legal warfare in a variety of areas beyond Taiwan and has made great strides in developing an operational capability to support a "soft power" approach to statecraft. The application of the strategy, for instance, has been displayed in both the East and South China Seas (where disputes continue to involve many countries), and it has also been seen applied in contests involving India, Bhutan, Tibet, Nepal, Japan, and South Korea, as well as in domestic situations affecting political factions within China's own Xijing province, according to our analysis and various regional news reports. Furthermore, disputes in functional and non-geographical areas have provided a setting for lawfare strategies to take place, as in the realms of commercial relations and intellectual property, cyberspace, and international law (especially patent law).

With respect to the South China Sea, assertions made by PRC Major General Luo Yuan provide more evidence of China's effort to operationalize legal warfare. In 2012 he stated that China must demonstrate a seriousness in that region in at least five different ways: (1) establish an administration presence in the area "typified by local government and the People's Congress"; *(2) establish a legal presence*; (3) provide for

---

[22] Cheng, "Winning Without Fighting: Chinese Legal Warfare."
[23] Cheng, "China's Active Defense Strategy and Its Regional Impact."

a military presence "which includes the positioning of the military and patrol activities"; (4) create an economic presence "including fishing activities and development activities of natural resources"; and (5) establish a presence within and throughout public opinion "in order to ensure that international society recognizes China's sovereignty."[24]

China's actions have not gone unnoticed by neighboring countries. The Japanese Ministry of Defense flagged the behavior in a 2009 *White Paper* and has continued to do so each subsequent year with an annual update.[25] The growing awareness of Beijing's regional encroachment is also reflected in the work of the Tokyo-based National Institute for Defense Studies, and specifically in a 2012 report on China. The report reveals an expectation of legal warfare as part of Chinese doctrine.[26]

Weaponizing China's Legal Warfare: How is it unique?

The U.S. and other Western nations have applied lawfare methods at times in the past, but the West has not created a doctrine, built a cadre of lawyers, or taken steps to maintain an enduring capability for dealing with such dynamic and challenging issues on a 24/7 basis. In contrast, the Chinese have made significant gains in this area, not only with respect to doctrinal development, but also in terms of building a foundation and a capacity to address strategic, operational, and tactical issues in a comprehensive fashion. Liang and Xiangsui foretold this condition in 1999 and eerily foreshadowed the events of 9/11 in *Unrestricted Warfare:*

---

[24] National Institute for Defense Studies, "China Security Studies Report," 32.

[25] Ministry of Defense, "Annual White Paper."

[26] National Institute for Defense Studies, "China Security Studies Report," 6.

...with the next century having still not yet arrived, the American military has already encountered trouble from insufficient frequency bandwidth... Whether it be the intrusions of hackers, *a major explosion at the World Trade Center, or a bombing attack by bin Laden,* all of these greatly exceed the frequency band widths understood by the American military. The American military is naturally inadequately prepared to deal with this type of enemy psychologically, in terms or measures, and especially as regards military thinking and the methods of operation derived from this. This is because they have never taken into consideration and even refused to consider means that are contrary to tradition and to select measures of operation other than military means.[27]

Beijing has pursued and encouraged the PLA to follow a legal warfare path. In 2003 the PLA amended its *Regulations on the Political Work of the People's Liberation Army* to include legal warfare, and the PLA Air Force also published a chapter in its doctrine entitled "Legal Warfare Operations."[28] In 2004, the *Analysis of 100 Cases of Legal Warfare* was published, offering an examination of historical examples dating back to World War I including descriptions, case analyses, and lessons learned for each instance.[29] Other relevant published works include: *Media Warfare Textbook* (2005),[30] *Under Informatized Conditions: Legal Warfare* (2007),[31] and *Research on Military Soft Power* (2010).[32] Furthermore, Beijing has sanctioned a number of guidebooks to help promote the discipline, to include: "100 Questions & Answers about Media Warfare, Psychological

[27] Liang and Xiangsui, *Unrestricted Warfare*, 144–145. Lailari emphasis.
[28] Zengfu, *Kongjun Junshi Sixiang Gailun [An Introduction to Military Thinking on the Air Force].*
[29] Wensheng, *Analysis of 100 Cases of Legal Warfare (Faluzhan Yibaili Jingdian Anli Pingxi).*
[30] Liu, *Media Warfare Textbook [Yulun Zhan Zhishi Duben].*
[31] Yunxia, *Under Informatized Conditions: Legal Warfare [Xinxihua Tiaojianxia: Falu Zhan].*
[32] Gensheng, *Research on Military Soft Power [Junshi Ruan Shili Yanjiu].*

Warfare and Legal Warfare" and "Basic Questions about Media Warfare, Psychological Warfare and Legal Warfare."[33]

To better understand the differences between China and western nations as they pertain to the application of lawfare, or legal warfare, Dean Cheng offered the following during congressional testimony in 2012:

> What makes the Chinese conception of legal warfare unique is that it is an offensive, rather than defensive, orientation towards the use of the law in times of crisis or conflict. American JAGs are focused on advising American officers on when their actions may violate the law; the case where a JAG advised against firing a missile against Mullah Omar because of the presence of civilians in his convoy is perhaps the best example.

> By contrast, the Chinese conception is to use the law to attack and constrain opponents by seizing the initiative on the legal battlefield and thereby disrupt enemy operations. This includes efforts at legal deterrence or coercion, which would warn an opponent that their every action will be scrutinized for possible violations of international law or the laws of armed conflict, in order to impose self-constraint; legal strikes, which would officially charge the enemy with operational activities that violated the law; and legal counter-attacks, which would highlight enemy efforts at slanting or misrepresenting international law in their favor.[34]

Chinese National Security Legal Warfare

China generally tests its legal warfare methods in domestic situations prior to greater applications in the international arena. In an article about the PLA and space warfare, Larry Wortzel of the American Enterprise Institute references a PLA

---

[33] Chin, "An Investigation into Media Warfare Operations of the PRC."
[34] Testimony before the House Foreign Affairs Committee.

publication entitled *The New Revolution in Military Affairs and Building a Military Legal System*,[35] and notes:

> ...the importance [to the PLA] of ensuring that [it] sets out legal justifications for military actions in advance of any conflict... . . . . as these debates [continue to] take place in China, the General Political Department is developing ways to justify its potential military actions in domestic law. Such activities and actions in domestic law are intended to have a future impact on international law and international opinion. Beijing did this in the 1992 Maritime Law adopted by the National People's Congress, which extended sovereign claims over some three million square miles of the East and South China Seas, marking it as Chinese territory on its maps. The 2005 Anti-Secession Law is another example of how domestic law is used by Beijing to justify potential military action in the future — in this case against Taiwan.[36]

This legal effort ensures maximum maneuvering space for the Beijing leadership in domestic affairs, and it precipitates an ability to create the best legal framework for justifying an action to the international community in a high-minded fashion and in accordance with the principles of "international law." It is a model followed by the PRC in the Korean War (1953), the Sino-Indian War (1962), the Sino-Russian crisis (1969), and the Sino-Vietnam conflict (1979). Again Wortzel provides a worthy observation about past Chinese legal positions: "Chinese diplomats and military leaders carefully staked out their legal positions...this concept of legal warfare has roots in China's diplomatic practice that have been reinforced by the observation of modern war."[37] With respect to China, therefore, U.S. policy makers must view legal warfare as a tool that has potential applications throughout all

---

[35] Jixian and Zheng, *The New Revolution in Military Affairs and Building a Military Legal System [Xin Junshi Geming yu Junshi Fazhi Jianshe]*.
[36] Wortzel, "The Chinese People's Liberation Army and Space Warfare."
[37] Ibid.

phases of peace, conflict, and post-conflict; it is a tool for political warfare as well as for the military.[38]

Military and Legal Warfare

The comprehensive and sustainable nature of Beijing's approach to lawfare is also evident in the effort Beijing has committed to legal doctrine analysis and case study reviews of various military actions and incidents. An excellent analysis of the incidents involving American and Chinese military personnel (at least from the U.S. perspective) is provided by Raul Pedrozo, in the *Chinese Journal of International Law*:

> In the case of the EP-3 [collision incident in 2001], the intercept procedures employed by the [Chinese] F-8 were clearly reckless and irresponsible, [and] were not consistent with the ICAO[39] Rules of the Air and certainly did not demonstrate "due regard" on the part of the Chinese pilot. Similarly, in the case of the USNS Impeccable incident [in 1999], directing Chinese civilian vessels to maneuver within 25 feet of the Impeccable in an attempt to snag the towed-array cable and then intentionally stop in front of Impeccable, thereby forcing the U.S. ship to take emergency action to avoid a collision, was certainly not in compliance with China's obligations under COLREGS[40] and clearly did not demonstrate "due regard" for the right of the U.S. ship to engage in lawful activities in the EEZ.[41]

To the contrary, these incidents demonstrate Beijing's attempt to change the standards under COLREGS, replace them with a different set of acceptable behavior, and assert

---

[38] Scobell, Lai, and Kamhausen, *Chinese Lessons from Other Peoples' Wars*, 185.

[39] International Civil Aviation Organization.

[40] International Regulations for Preventing Collisions at Sea.

[41] Pedrozo, "Responding to Ms. Zhang's Talking Points on the EEZ," 212–213.

sovereignty over the entire EEZ. As evidence of this perspective, Wang Xiangsui, one of the authors of *Unrestricted Warfare*, said, in a 1999 interview:

> We are a weak country, so do we need to fight according to your rules? No. War has rules, but those rules are set by the West. But if you use those rules, then weak countries have no chance. But if you use nontraditional means to fight, like those employed by financiers to bring down financial systems, then you have a chance.[42]

Legal Warfare, the Economy, and Cyberspace

A closer examination into the execution of Beijing's lawfare strategy reveals not only a maritime component but also similar and parallel — if undeclared — campaigns in the domains of economic and cyber warfare. Beijing has persistently claimed jurisdiction, and indeed sovereignty, over an expanded EEZ, one with borders approaching the coasts of Malaysia and Brunei, well past the first chain of islands off the mainland Chinese coast, and one defined in a manner inconsistent with the norms of international law. Consonant with these claims, Beijing has repeatedly attempted to restrict navigation through its EEZ, creating friction with neighboring countries. With its repeated attempts to expand national sovereignty beyond the internationally-recognized 12-mile boundary of territorial waters, China is, in effect, conducting a sea denial strategy as it attempts to force foreign warships to "obtain permission to undertake innocent passage." [43] The figure below[44] shows the conflicting EEZ's between China and her South China Sea neighbors:

---

[42] Pomfret, "China Ponders New Rules of 'Unrestricted War.'"

[43] Kotani, *Freedom of Navigation and the U.S.-Japan Alliance: Addressing the Threat of Legal Warfare*, 2.

[44] O'Rourke, *Maritime Territorial and Exclusive Economic Zone (EEZ) Disputes Involving China: Issues for Congress*, 12.

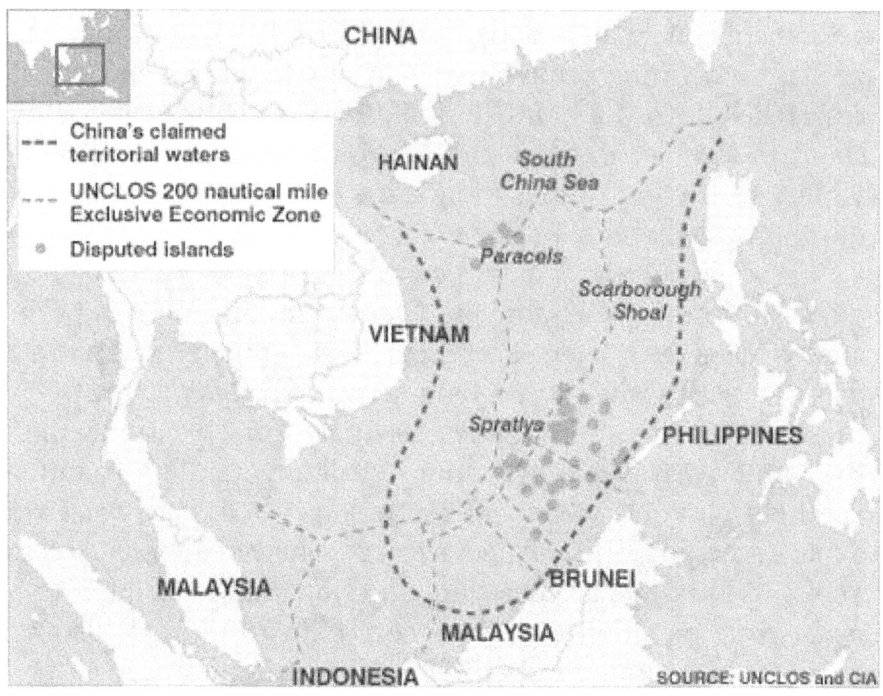

Figure 2: Conflicting EEZs in the South China Sea

Japan is especially vulnerable to any restrictions in global navigation, given that its total trade by volume is 99.7% maritime-based. It must have felt an acute sense of anxiety when learning of recent Chinese efforts to "annex" the East China Sea; and current trend lines do not offer Tokyo much reason to rest easy. In late 2012, Chairman Wang Yilin of the China National Offshore Oil Corporation (CNOOC) declared during the launch of CNOOC's first deep-water rig: "Large-scale deep-water rigs are our mobile national territory and a strategic weapon."[45] This statement suggests that lawfare, as applied in the maritime domain, has combined with a form of economic warfare to create a *fait accompli* territorial expansion in a manner beyond Beijing's practice of directing new

---

[45] Spegele and Ma, "For China Boss, Deep-Water Rigs Are a 'Strategic Weapon.'"

settlements on small islands.[46] In light of these developments, perhaps a defining principle of maritime lawfare is indeed, as researcher Tetsuo Kotani describes, "an attempt by coastal states to increase the waters that are under their jurisdiction, while restricting other maritime powers' freedom of navigation, especially in EEZs."[47]

Chinese behavior has been similarly expansive and offensive in the cyber domain. Chinese involvement in cyber attacks has been well documented for much of the past decade: the so-called Titan Rain series of attacks against U.S. sites in 2003; the Byzantine Hades attacks in 2006 (also called Byzantine Anchor, Byzantine Candor, and Byzantine Foothold), involved "spear-phishing" tactics to gain access to e-mail accounts and related servers. Shady Remote Access Tool (RAT) began in 2006, too, an effort that amounted to a multi-year operation targeting more than 70 individuals and organizations located in 14 different countries.[48]

The year 2009 was especially eventful, as the following occurred: the Night Dragon attacks against petrochemical and energy corporations; the GhostNet attacks against the Dalai Lama; and attacks against U.S. Air Force sites, which elicited sensitive blueprints of the next-generation F-35 fighter aircraft. [49] Moreover, Canadian government servers were attacked in 2011, and as recently as 2013 Chinese assistance was suspected of aiding North Korean hackers during the disruption of commercial interests in South Korea.

The scope and nature of the intellectual property (IP) targeted or stolen during these events is not insignificant, should not be ignored, and conveniently aligns with the

---

[46] Murphy, "Deepwater Oil Rigs as Strategic Weapons."
[47] Kotani, *Freedom of Navigation and the US-Japan Alliance: Addressing the Threat of Legal Warfare*, 3.
[48] Krepinevich, *Cyber Warfare: A "Nuclear Option"?*.
[49] Gorman, Cole, and Dreazen, "Computer Spies Breach Fighter-Jet Project."

following priorities contained in Beijing's Five-Year Economic Plan: clean energy; advanced semiconductors; high-end manufacturing, especially in aerospace and telecommunications; and biotechnology, including drugs and medical devices. [50] The economic consequences, therefore, can be serious. In 2010 alone, the U.S. Federal Bureau of Investigations estimated that IP losses to international hackers amounted to nearly $500 billion, of which a large amount was attributed to China. [51]

The 2010 "Aurora" attack against Google deserves special attention and perhaps offers the most insight into Beijing's interests and motivations. Specifically, Aurora "compromised the Gmail accounts of human rights activists" in China, succeeded in accessing Google "source code repositories," and thereby penetrated the servers of more than a thousand U.S. firms. [52] In response, Google re-routed search methodologies from the mainland site (Google.cn) to its Hong Kong site (Google.com.hk), allowing mainland users unfettered Internet access and thereby riling Chinese government officials intent on enforcing strict censorship policies.[53]

Timothy Thomas argues that the Google case provides an excellent example of how the Chinese employ the Three Warfare strategy and legal warfare techniques, specifically, to counter the West:

> Chinese regulations note that it is the media's job to support a righteous cause, the legal expert's job to justify the cause, and the psychological warfare personnel's job to bolster friendly morale while attacking the enemy's morale. This is how the media can be used to control public opinion and eliminate any chance of China "losing

---

[50] Riley and Walcott, "China-Based Hacking of 760 Companies Shows Cyber Cold War - Bloomberg."

[51] Ibid.

[52] Grow and Hosenball, "Special Report."

[53] Lum, Figliola, and Weed, *China, Internet Freedom, and U.S. Policy*, 9.

face." The "three warfares" [strategy] permit[s] China to enter any fray, whether in peace or war, with a political advantage that can be used to alter public or international opinion.[54]

Muslim Brotherhood's Warfare and Lawfare Strategy

The Muslim Brotherhood (MB) organization, and, more specifically, its Egyptian core, has achieved considerable attention of late. This is generally due to its short-lived post-Mubarak, prominence in Egyptian governance. Though concerned with spreading its religious propaganda since its inception,[55] the "core MB" itself has not been conclusively involved in direct lawfare operations. But its extensive support system, originally established to fund the offshoot group Hamas and to influence public religious and political debates,[56] has made use of a lawfare strategy in the form of maneuvering within Western — and specifically North American – legal systems.

Two preliminary if tentative conclusions can be drawn about MB lawfare-related activities. First, MB's lawfare approach, to date, has been a complementary tactic aimed at insulating itself and associated groups from critique rather

---

[54] Thomas, "Google Confronts China's 'Three Warfares,'" Summer 2010, 105–106.

[55] According to Walter Laqueur, MB founder Hassan al-Banna envisioned the organization's primary goal as being to spread religious propaganda, leaving the means of achieving the same open to interpretation and revision depending on the course of events. See *No End to War: Terrorism in the Twenty-First Century* (New York: Continuum International Publishing Group, 2003), 31.

[56] Lorenzo Vidino, The Muslim Brotherhood in the West *Characteristics, Aims and Policy*, Testimony presented before the House Permanent Select Committee on Intelligence, subcommittee on Terrorism, HUMINT, Analysis, and Counterintelligence on April 13, 2011 http://intelligence.house.gov/sites/intelligence.house.gov/files/documents/SFR20110413Vidino.pdf at 3.

than primarily as an offensive tool. Second, although these attempts have not proven to be as successful as originally intended, the extent of their collective effect on public discourse and media-influenced narratives is cause for considerable concern, consequently creating some level of doubt about the accuracy of open-source intelligence-gathering efforts.

Hamas

While the MB's core Egyptian organization was prevented from developing a military capability, its Palestinian offshoot, Hamas, was not similarly circumscribed. So while Hamas was able to develop political, social, and ideological infrastructure much along the lines of the original MB, it was also able to engage in systemic violence and terrorism against the State of Israel. Hamas's violent opposition to Israel and to the Middle East Peace Plan resulted in its inclusion on the State Department's Foreign Terrorist Organization list in 1995,[57] a status it continues to retain.[58] Its ongoing attempts to undermine Israel's political and legal credibility through "delegitimization" efforts has been termed lawfare as well, although it is important to point out that delegitimization and lawfare are by no means coextensive, and the former often hews considerably more closely to a remarkably effective propaganda campaign than to the use of the law per se.[59]

---

[57] President William J. Clinton, Executive Order 12947 of January 23, 1995, "Prohibiting Transactions With Terrorists Who Threaten To Disrupt the Middle East Peace Process,"
http://www.presidency.ucsb.edu/ws/?pid=51612.
[58] "Foreign Terrorist Organizations," U.S. Department of State, Bureau of Counterterrorism. List updated as of January 27, 2012; last visited August 14, 2012.
http://www.state.gov/j/ct/rls/other/des/123085.htm.
[59] This includes ongoing debates as to the roles of humanitarian and human rights law frameworks, the relative importance of doctrines of

Though it is indisputably an offshoot of MB, Hamas has not always pursued an agenda completely coincident with MB's overall strategy.[60] Irrespective of the operational and strategic differences, the relationship has proven mutually supportive.[61] According to the Israeli Security Agency Shabak, "[a]fter Hamas's formation, the Muslim Brotherhood directed its world-wide chapters to establish so-called 'Palestine Committees' to support Hamas from abroad."[62] Additionally, Hamas assumed control of Islamic charities in the West Bank and Gaza, as well as "Muslim Brotherhood charity funds which operated in the U.S., such as the Holy Land Foundation for Relief and Development (HLF) and Europe since the early 90s."[63]

---

proportionality and military necessity, and related issues. Manipulation of public opinion in derogation of applicable legal principles factors heavily into this type of lawfare, but may be more properly analyzed as effective propaganda utilizing legal terminology rather than lawfare as per the definition cited in the beginning of this chapter. However, this distinction, unfortunately, is ignored by some organizations with vested interests in promulgating institutional definitions of lawfare.

[60] In Dr. Vidino's words, when MB ideology was exported, "in the Palestinian territories, it took a peculiar turn and became Hamas." See FN 2, supra.

[61] Operational independence is in fact a characteristic of the MB model. See, generally, Vidino, supra at FN 2 and "Spotlight on Hamas – Ideology and Involvement in Terror" http://www.shabak.gov.il/SiteCollectionImages/ופרסומים%20סקירות/te rror-portal/docs/english/hamas-sum-en.pdf at 1.

[62] *United States v. Holy Land Foundation*, No. 09-10560, 664 F.3d 467 (5th Cir. December 7, 2011) http://www.ca5.uscourts.gov/opinions/pub/09/09-10560-CR0.wpd.pdf at 9.

[63] "The Union of Good – Analysis and Mapping of Terror Funds Network," The Israeli Security Agency (Shabak), http://www.shabak.gov.il/SiteCollectionImages/english/TerrorInfo/c oalition_en.pdf.

The Holy Land Foundation

The Holy Land Foundation, or HLF, was established in 1988 as the "Occupied Land Fund," and, as the U.S. Department of Justice would later state, "HLF existed to support Hamas" from its very inception, and funneled millions of dollars raised in the United States to the terrorist entity.[64] By the time HLF was shut down by federal authorities in December 2001, it was the largest Islamic charity in the U.S. During the course of the trial, evidence emerged that tied numerous U.S.-based Muslim groups to the MB, though not necessarily to Hamas directly.

Maintaining Operational Flexibility in the U.S.

For purposes of lawfare analysis, one of the most interesting pieces of evidence to emerge in the HLF trial was the recording of a meeting held by members of a domestic "Palestine Committee" held in Philadelphia in 1993. The recording included a founder of the Council on American-Islamic Relations (CAIR), Omar Ahmad, who identified two "dangers" that faced organizations operating in the U.S.,[65] namely "a financial connection or orders," the latter of which he explained further as "if you work for someone overseas and he gives you orders to carry out."[66]

Ahmad continued, "If you cover these two bases, you will find that you, as an American organization, can do whatever you want. This is from [a] legal point of view. As for the media, it is possible that you could be destroyed by the media

---

[64] DOJ Press Release "Federal Judge Hands Downs Sentences in Holy Land Foundation Case: *Holy Land Foundation and Leaders Convicted on Providing Material Support to Hamas Terrorist Organization,*" May 27, 2009. http://www.justice.gov/opa/pr/2009/May/09-nsd-519.html.

[65] He was specifically referring to the Islamic Association for Palestine.

[66] Transcript excerpts are available online at http://www.investigativeproject.org/documents/case_docs/719.pdf.

without the law touching you."[67] While the lack of clear foreign control – whether by the MB, Hamas and/or foreign state actors – provided certain organizational protections against legal sanctions imposed by the government, Ahmad's concern that the media could destroy the organization led to offensive legal operations aimed at influencing critical media attention. This can be said to have led to subsequent attempts to use lawsuits in order to further insulate the organizations from scrutiny and attendant criticism.

Ultimately, between 2003 and 2005, high-profile lawsuits filed by CAIR and its Canadian counterpart, and subsequent threats of similar suits, failed to suppress the publication of articles highly critical of the organizations, and likely drew considerably more attention than did the articles themselves. A defamation suit against then-Representative Cass Ballenger (R-NC), who termed CAIR "the fundraising arm for Hezbollah," failed when federal D.C. District Court ruled that Ballenger was immune from such a suit as a member of Congress,[68] a ruling that was later upheld by the D.C. Circuit Court of Appeals.[69] Similar lawsuits brought in Canada against journalist David Frum and the National Post, and against David B. Harris and CFRA Radio, failed to result in judgments for the organization. Similarly, KinderUSA filed a libel lawsuit against Matthew Levitt and the Washington Institute for Near East Politics over statements that the organization funded Hamas in the book *Hamas: Politics, Charity, and Terrorism in the Service of Jihad*. However, Levitt and the Washington Institute responded by filing an "anti-SLAPP" motion to dismiss the suit on the grounds that it was brought expressly to silence protected free speech activity and

---

[67] Ibid.

[68] *Council on Am. Islamic Rels. Inc. v. Ballenger*, 366 F. Supp. 2d 28 (D.D.C. 2005).

[69] *Council on Am. Islamic Rels. v. Ballenger*, 444 F.3d 659 (D.C. Cir. 2006).

this led to Kinder USA dropping the lawsuit before the judge ruled on the motion.[70]

On the other hand, MB has been active within the United States since the 1960s. The Investigative Project on Terrorism (IPT) has identified "the Muslim Students' Association (MSA) founded in 1963, the North American Islamic Trust (NAIT) 1971, the Islamic Society of North America (ISNA) 1981, the International Institute of Islamic Thought (IIIT) 1981, the Islamic Association for Palestine (IAP) 1981, the United Association for Studies and Research (UASR) 1989, the American Muslim Council (AMC) 1990, the Muslim American Society (MAS) 1992, the Muslim Arab Youth Association (MAYA), the Council on American-Islamic Relations (CAIR) 1994, and others" as MB offshoots.[71] The IPT concluded that "[i]n fact, nearly all prominent Islamic organizations in the United States are rooted in the Muslim Brotherhood."[72] With the notable exception of organizations that have definitively assisted Hamas or other designated Foreign Terrorist Organizations, organizations with MB origins or ties have, by and large, remained relatively free to function.

It is impossible to show definitively how lawfare (including legal intimidation in the form of threatened lawsuits) and its chilling effect on public discourse is directly attributed to MB-affiliated organizations within the U.S. and other Western nations. Organizations not necessarily linked to MB have also utilized similar legal tactics to silence their own

---

[70] Matthew Levitt noted the chilling effect such suits have had in an October 12, 2007, op-ed for the New Republic Online, along with discussion of the outcome of his case. "Chilling Effect" is available on the Washington Institute Web site at http://www.washingtoninstitute.org/policy-analysis/view/chilling-effect.

[71] "The Muslim Brotherhood," http://www.investigativeproject.org/documents/misc/135.pdf.

[72] Ibid.

critics and achieved similar results;[73] and the basic tactic itself can readily be utilized by organizations that have no connection whatsoever to MB or any other Middle East-based group. Moreover, alternative organizations, such as the right-leaning Thomas More Law Center and the Middle East Forum's Legal Project, have been created as a counterbalance in an effort to prevent defamation lawsuits of this sort from effectively winning by default.[74] Still, ample evidence exists to suggest that the lawfare concept has matured, to some extent, even if its previous deployments have not ultimately resulted in success.

The relatively simplistic defamation lawsuits that have proven less than entirely effective do not represent any sort of endpoint in terms of how lawfare may be applied presently or in the future. Insofar as it is rooted in the constantly expanding and evolving field of law, lawfare is an inherently adaptable concept that can readily manifest in varied forms in order to support various goals. The Internet – specifically online publications and other forms of Internet-dependent communication – represents a prime example of an emergent lawfare target, given the current state of ambiguity and flexibility inherent in relevant legal doctrines as they may be applied to this medium. In any event, it would be a significant mistake to assume that unsuccessful attempts to operate within the judicial system to date represent any sort of endpoint in terms of lawfare tactical development or its evolving potential strategic utility. If anything, the failure of these past lawfare attempts will likely lead to more nuanced

---

[73] See, e.g., *Trita Parsi v. Seid Hassan Daioleslam*, 595 F.Supp.2d 99 (D.D.C. 2009); *Global Relief Found. Inc. v. New York Times Co.*, 390 F.3d 973, 974 (7th Cir. 2004); and *Ghafur v. Bernstein*, 131 Cal. App.4th 1230, 1234 (4th Div. 2005) CERTIFIED FOR PARTIAL PUBLICATION. The plaintiffs sued for libel over alleged ties to Iran, Al Qaeda, and al-Fuqra, respectively.

[74] In the interests of disclosure, one of the authors served as assistant director of the Legal Project between 2008 and 2010.

actions that are considerably harder to identify (much less quantify) as lawfare, suggesting even greater challenges and obstacles in the future for mounting an effective response. Policymakers must take concrete action to ensure non-partisan identification of non-state lawfare in its incipient phase both on the policy level and on the operational level.

Conclusions

We strongly urge the U.S. government to look at the threat of legal warfare, or lawfare, as a growing national security threat, especially since both state and non-state actors have demonstrated a fully developed strategy and set of supporting tactics. Lawfare represents a multifaceted threat that may manifest in a form analogous to strategic litigation or diplomacy, for example, and might be thereafter employed in vastly different ways, depending on the operational capabilities and strategic goals of the state and non-state actors involved. Furthermore, if combined with other forms of warfare (i.e., media warfare or psychological warfare) and ignored, the U.S. government runs the further risk of losing ground in the court of public opinion, both globally and domestically. Therefore, based on this initial analysis, we recommend the following:

1) Conduct a comparative strategic analysis, much as Andrew Marshall from the Office of Net Assessment and his team analyzed the strengths and weaknesses of the U.S.S.R. and the U.S. in the 1970s. This analysis should pay particular attention to lawfare and its use by both state and non-state actors such as China and the Muslim Brotherhood;
2) Engage the leading American political parties as well as all three branches of government and the American public, to embrace the resulting strategy and ensure

consistency across electoral transitions, avoiding piecemeal or contradictory policies. In other words, develop a new grand strategy that takes into account both offensive and defensive lawfare. Furthermore, make a concerted effort to improve coordination between the U.S. and its allies, with the specific objective established for developing complementary lawfare-related domestic policies in a way that will enhance bilateral and multilateral agreements. For example, freedom of navigation programs should be enhanced, renewed, or developed in the South and East China Seas.[75] Without confronting such challenges to free trade, and without addressing the expansive claims pertaining to the EEZ, Western leaders would be accepting considerable risk in an area that could become a source for future armed conflict;[76]

3) Apply the right amount of manpower and resources to address identified requirements and gaps necessary for responding to, and fielding, adequate lawfare techniques. Specific attention should be given to the Chinese Three Warfare Strategy and its integration with other aspects of state power. Attention also should be given to non-state actors' use of lawfare in combination with propaganda and other efforts to influence public opinion. Finally, consideration should be given to the development of both a strategy and a doctrine to better inform and prepare military commanders for lawfare; such an effort could be attempted through the expansion of *Joint Publication 1-04, Legal Support to Military Operations,*[77] perhaps

---

[75] Kotani, *Freedom of Navigation and the US-Japan Alliance: Addressing the Threat of Legal Warfare,* 5.
[76] Ibid., 4.
[77] Joint Staff, "Legal Support to Military Operations."

morphing the effort into a *Joint Publication Operations* (3-XX) series document. Admittedly, however, a broader approach may be necessary, given that the issue is not confined solely to the realm of the military, and because Beijing has developed a truly national and international approach to the development of strategy and doctrine;

4) Determine what other strategies and tactics are being used in combination with lawfare. China could be using all or some combination of the 24 types of warfare described in the 1999 publication entitled *Unrestricted Warfare,* and MB might be using the "Grand Jihad" strategy referred to in court documents from the Holy Land Foundation trial;

5) Re-assess and refine the strategy frequently to detect countermoves and adjustments, and to avoid politicization or other forms of ideologically-motivated subjectivism;

6) Re-examine international and domestic laws knowing that China, the Muslim Brotherhood and others are actively using lawfare. Consider ratifying, modifying, or creating new laws with lawfare in mind that would enhance the national security interests of the U.S. while placing in check those of state and non-state actors who exploit loopholes in them. Enforcement of these laws also needs to be addressed. For example, the U.S. should look again at the effect of not ratifying the United Nations Convention on the Law of the Sea (UNCLOS).[78]

7) Examine how nations such as China, Iran, and Russia or non-state actors such as MB use lawfare against *non-state actors* such as international corporations. For

---

[78] Kotani, *Freedom of Navigation and the U.S.-Japan Alliance: Addressing the Threat of Legal Warfare,* 4.

example, Google accused China of conducting an act of economic espionage against its system. In response to these accusations, China employed its Three Warfare Strategy and shifted the discussion by "diverting attention from the real issue under consideration, the probes, and redirected the focus to various legal issues."[79] Chinese penetration into the 2008 political campaign computers of both President-elect Barack Obama and Senator John McCain also portend similar events in the future.[80]

Therefore, lawfare plays an important role as a new weapon in the realm of international affairs, affecting the full spectrum of actions during war and peace. Without learning how to use and respond to it, both defensively and offensively, leaders in Washington run the risk of operating at a disadvantage – a situation that could, to paraphrase Sun Tzu, cause America to collapse, even before the onset of armed hostilities.

---

[79] Thomas, "Google Confronts China's 'Three Warfares,'" Summer 2010, 106.
[80] Ibid., 102.

Bibliography

"2010 Annual Summary Data and Trends in Terrorism," The Israel Security Agency (Shabak). http://www.shabak.gov.il/SiteCollectionImages/english/TerrorInfo/reports/2010summary2-en.pdf.

"An Explanatory Memorandum On the General Strategic Goal for the Group In North America," The Muslim Brotherhood, May 22, 1991. http://www.txnd.uscourts.gov/judges/hlf2.htmlhttp://www.txnd.uscourts.gov/judges/hlf2.htmlhttp://www.txnd.uscourts.gov/judges/hlf2.html.

Cheng, Dean. "China's Active Defense Strategy and Its Regional Impact." *The Heritage Foundation*. Accessed August 26, 2013. http://www.heritage.org/research/testimony/2011/01/chinas-active-defense-strategy-and-its-regional-impact.

— — —. "The Chinese People's Liberation Army and Special Operations." *Special Warfare* no. July-September 2012 (September 2012). http://www.soc.mil/SWCS/SWmag/archive/SW2503/SW2503TheChinesePeoplesLiberationArmy.html.

— — —. "Winning Without Fighting: Chinese Legal Warfare." The Heritage Foundation, May 18, 2012. https://thf_media.s3.amazonaws.com/2012/pdf/bg2692.pdf.

Chin, Ch'en. "An Investigation into Media Warfare Operations of the PRC." *National Defense Magazine* (November 1, 2006). http://www.mnd.gov.tw.

Clinton, President William J. Executive Order 12947: "Prohibiting Transactions With Terrorists Who Threaten To Disrupt the Middle East Peace Process." January 23, 1995 http://www.presidency.ucsb.edu/ws/?pid=51612.

Dunlap, Charles. "Law and Military Interventions: Preserving Humanitarian Values In 21st Century Conflicts." Carr Center for Human Rights Policy, Harvard Kennedy School Program on National Security and Human Rights, 2001. http://www.hks.harvard.edu/cchrp/Web%20Working%20Papers/Use%20of%20Force/Dunlap2001.pdf.

Dunlap, Charles J. "The Mottled Legacy of 9/11: A Few Reflections on the Evolution of the International Law of Armed Conflict." *Yearbook of International Humanitarian Law* 14 (December 2011): 431–442. doi:http://dx.doi.org.mutex.gmu.edu/10.1007/978-90-6704-855-2_17.

"Federal Judge Hands Downs Sentences in Holy Land Foundation Case: Holy Land Foundation and Leaders Convicted on Providing Material Support to Hamas Terrorist Organization." Department of Justice. May 27, 2009.

"Fifth Circuit Appeals Court Upholds HLF Convictions." *Investative Project on Terrorism*, December 7, 2011. http://www.investigativeproject.org/3331/fifth-circuit-appeals-court-upholds-hlf.

"Foreign Terrorist Organizations," US Department of State, Bureau of Counterterrorism. Last updated September 28, 2012. http://www.state.gov/j/ct/rls/other/des/123085.htm.

Gensheng, Ma. *Research on Military Soft Power [Junshi Ruan Shili Yanjiu]*. PLA Press [Jiefangjun Chubanshe], 2010.

Giles, Lionel. *The Art of War by Sun Tz'u*. Pax Librorum Publishing House, 2009. www.paxlibrorum.com/res/downloads/taowde.pdf.

Gorman, Siobhan, August Cole, and Yochi Dreazen. "Computer Spies Breach Fighter-Jet Project." *Wall Street Journal*, April 21, 2009, sec. Technology. http://online.wsj.com/article/SB124027491029837401.html.

Grow, Brian, and Mark Hosenball. "Special Report: In Cyberspy Vs. Cyberspy, China Has the Edge." *Reuters*. April 14, 2011. http://www.reuters.com/article/2011/04/14/us-china-usa-cyberespionage-idUSTRE73D24220110414.

House Foreign Affairs Committee Hearing: "Investigating the Chinese Threat, Part One: Military and Economic Aggression: Testimony of Dean Cheng."[1]. Lanham, United States: Federal Information & News Dispatch, Inc., March 28, 2012. http://search.proquest.com.mutex.gmu.edu/pqrl/docview/963678710/fulltext/1401D358D3F47813648/12?accountid=14541.

Jixian, Liu, and Liu Zheng, eds. *The New Revolution in Military Affairs and Building a Military Legal System [Xin Junshi Geming yu Junshi Fazhi Jianshe]*. Beijing, China: PLA Press [Jiefangjun Chubanshe], 2005. http://www.aei.org/papers/foreign-and-defense-policy/regional/asia/the-chinese-peoples-liberation-army-and-space-warfare/.

Joint Staff. "Legal Support to Military Operations." Department of Defense, August 11, 2011. http://www.dtic.mil/doctrine/new_pubs/jp1_04.pdf.

Kotani, Tetsuo. *Freedom of Navigation and the US-Japan Alliance: Addressing the Threat of Legal Warfare*. US-Japan Papers. Tokyo, Japan: Japan Center for International Exchange, December 2011. http://www.jcie.org/researchpdfs/USJapanPapers/Kotani.pdf.

Krepinevich, Andrew. *Cyber Warfare: A "Nuclear Option"?* Study. Center for Strategic and Budgetary Assessments, August 24, 2012. http://www.csbaonline.org/publications/2012/08/cyber-warfare-a-nuclear-option/.

Laqueur, Walter. *No End to War: Terrorism in the Twenty-First Century*. Continuum NY & London, 2003

Liang, Qiao, and Wang Xiangsui. *Unrestricted Warfare*. Beijing, China: PLA Literature and Arts Publishing House, 1999. http://www.unec.net/of_interest/countries_against_us/Unrestricted_Warfare/unrestricted.pdf.

Liu, Gaoping. *Media Warfare Textbook [Yulun Zhan Zhishi Duben]*. National Defense University Press [Guofang Daxue Chubanshe], 2005.

Lum, Thomas, Patricia Figliola, and Matthew Weed. *China, Internet Freedom, and U.S. Policy*. Library of Congress Congressional Research Service, July 13, 2012. http://www.fas.org/sgp/crs/row/R42601.pdf.

Marantis, Demetrios. "2013 Special 301 Report." Office of the US Trade Representative, May 1, 2013. http://www.ustr.gov/sites/default/files/05012013%202013%20Special%20301%20Report.pdf.

Ministry of Defense. "Annual White Paper." Accessed September 1, 2013. http://www.mod.go.jp/e/publ/w_paper/.

Murphy, Martin. "Deepwater Oil Rigs as Strategic Weapons." *Naval War College Review* 66, no. 2 (Spring 2013): 110–114.

National Institute for Defense Studies. "China Security Studies Report." The National Institute for Defense Studies, 2012. http://www.nids.go.jp/publication/chinareport/pdf/china _report_EN_web_2012_A01.pdf.

O'Rourke, Ronald. *Maritime Territorial and Exclusive Economic Zone (EEZ) Disputes Involving China: Issues for Congress.* Library of Congress Congressional Research Service, August 9, 2013. http://www.fas.org/sgp/crs/row/R42784.pdf.

Pedrozo, Raul (Pete). "Responding to Ms. Zhang's Talking Points on the EEZ." *Chinese Journal of International Law* 10, no. 1 (March 1, 2011): 207–223. doi:10.1093/chinesejil/jmq035.

Pomfret, John. "China Ponders New Rules of 'Unrestricted War'." Newspaper. *Washington Post Froeign Service*, August 8, 1999. http://www.lexisnexis.com.mutex.gmu.edu/hottopics/lnac ademic/.

Riley, Michael, and John Walcott. "China-Based Hacking of 760 Companies Shows Cyber Cold War - Bloomberg." Business News. *Bloomberg.com*, December 14, 2011. http://www.bloomberg.com/news/2011-12-13/china-based-hacking-of-760-companies-reflects-undeclared-global-cyber-war.html.

Scobell, Andrew, David Lai, and Roy Kamhausen, eds. *Chinese Lessons from Other Peoples' Wars.* US Army War College, 2011. http://www.dtic.mil/cgi-bin/GetTRDoc?AD=ADA553490.

Secretary of Defense. "Annual Report to Congress: Military and Security Developments Involving the People's Republic of China - 2010." Department of Defense, 2010. http://www.defense.gov/pubs/pdfs/2010_CMPR_Final.pd f.

— — — "Annual Report to Congress: Military and Security Developments Involving the People's Republic of China - 2012." Department of Defense, 2012.

http://www.defense.gov/pubs/pdfs/2012_CMPR_Final.pd
f.

— — — "Annual Report to Congress: Military and Security
Developments Involving the People's Republic of China -
2013." Department of Defense, 2013.
http://www.defense.gov/pubs/2013_China_Report_FINA
L.pdf.

— — — "Annual Report to Congress: Military and Security
Developments Involving the People's Republic of China
2011." Department of Defense, 2011.
http://www.defense.gov/pubs/pdfs/2011_cmpr_final.pdf.

— — — "Annual Report to Congress: Military Power of the People's
Republic of China - 2007." Department of Defense, May 23,
2007. http://www.defense.gov/pubs/pdfs/070523-china-
military-power-final.pdf.

— — — "Annual Report to Congress: The Military Power of the
People's Republic of China - 2005." Department of Defense,
July 19, 2005.
http://www.defense.gov/news/Jul2005/d20050719china.p
df.

— — — "Annual Report to Congress: The Military Power of the
People's Republic of China - 2006." Department of Defense,
2006.
http://www.defense.gov/pubs/pdfs/China%20Report%20
2006.pdf.

— — — "The Military Power of the People's Republic of China: A
Report to Congress Pursuant to the National Defense
Authorization Act (Fiscal Year 2000)." Department of
Defense, July 2005.
http://www.defense.gov/news/Jul2005/d20050719china.p
df.

Spegele, Brian, and Wayne Ma. "For China Boss, Deep-Water Rigs
Are a 'Strategic Weapon'." *Wall Street Journal*, August 29,
2012, sec. Business.
http://online.wsj.com/article/SB10000872396390444233104
577592890738740290.html.

"The Dating Game." *The Economist*. Accessed August 14, 2012. http://www.economist.com/blogs/dailychart/2010/12/save_date.

"The Union of Good – Analysis and Mapping of Terror Funds Network," The Israeli Security Agency (Shabak). http://www.shabak.gov.il/SiteCollectionImages/english/TerrorInfo/coalition_en.pdf.

Thomas, Timothy. "Google Confronts China's 'Three Warfares'." *Parameters* 40, no. 2 (Summer 2010): 101–113.

— — — "The Chinese Strategic Mind-Set." *Military Review* 2007, no. November-December (December 31, 2007): 47–55.

"U.S. National Debt Clock : Real Time." Accessed August 13, 2012. http://www.usdebtclock.org/.

Vidino, Lorenzo. "The Muslim Brotherhood in the West: *Characteristics, Aims and Policy*." Testimony presented before the House Permanent Select Committee on Intelligence, subcommittee on Terrorism, HUMINT, Analysis, and Counterintelligence on April 13, 2011.

Wensheng, Cong. *Analysis of 100 Cases of Legal Warfare (Faluzhan Yibaili Jingdian Anli Pingxi)*. Beijing: People's Liberation Army Publishing House, 2004.

Wortzel, Larry. "The Chinese People's Liberation Army and Space Warfare." *American Enterprise Institute*, October 17, 2007. http://www.aei.org/papers/foreign-and-defense-policy/regional/asia/the-chinese-peoples-liberation-army-and-space-warfare/.

Yunxia, Song, ed. *Under Informatized Conditions: Legal Warfare [Xinxihua Tiaojianxia: Falu Zhan]*. Military Science Press [Junshi Kexue Chubanshe], 2007.

Zengfu, Min, ed. *Kongjun Junshi Sixiang Gailun [An Introduction to Military Thinking on the Air Force]*. PLA Publishing House [Jiefangjun Chubanshe], 2005.

Court Rulings

Council on American Islamic Relations. Inc. v. Ballenger, 366 F. Supp. 2d 28 (D.D.C. 2005). United States District Court for the District of Columbia.

Council on American Islamic Relations v. Ballenger, 444 F.3d 659 (D.C. Cir. 2006). United States Court of Appeals, District of Columbia Circuit.

Global Relief Foundation Inc. v. New York Times Co., 390 F.3d 973, 974 (7th Cir. 2004). United States Court of Appeals, Seventh Circuit.

Ghafur v. Bernstein, 131 Cal. App.4th 1230 (4th Div. 2005) CERTIFIED FOR PARTIAL PUBLICATION. California Fourth District Court of Appeal.

Trita Parsi v. Seid Hassan Daioleslam, 595 F.Supp.2d 99 (D.D.C. 2009). United States District Court for the District of Columbia.

United States v. Holy Land Foundation, No. 09-10560, 664 F.3d 467 (5th Cir. December 7, 2011). United States Court of Appeals, Seventh Circuit. http://www.ca5.uscourts.gov/opinions/pub/09/09-10560-CR0.wpd.pdf.

China's Anti-access/Area Denial (A2/AD) Capabilities: Is the U.S. Rebalancing Enough?[1]

Oriana Skylar Mastro

Introduction

Over the past two decades, American strategists have become increasingly concerned with the possibility that an adversary could reduce the credibility of United States military power projection by adopting an anti-access/area denial (A2/AD) approach to warfare. No other country has fielded forces with comparable quantity and quality to those of the United States, at least since the fall of the Soviet Union. Given mostly unrestricted U.S. global power projection over the past twenty years, coupled with advances in information technology, the consideration of countermeasure options has naturally gained traction in certain capitals around the world. The United States has also become more vulnerable to the A2/AD threat over time. Due to the atrophy of overseas bases since the end

---

[1] This chapter draws upon testimony the author presented to the U.S.-China Economic and Security Review Commission's hearing on "China's Active Defense Strategy and its Regional Impact," January 27, 2011. Also, a more comprehensive version of this essay is planned to be included in the forthcoming Winter 2014/2015 issue of The Washington Quarterly.

of the Cold War, it is unlikely that the United States will have sufficient forward-deployed bases and forces in the vicinity of a future conflict before it erupts.[2] Such trends further increase the incentives for an opponent to design capabilities that "interfere with the U.S. military's ability to deploy to or operate within overseas theaters of operation."[3]

While countries such as North Korea, Pakistan, Iran, and Syria possess some A2/AD capabilities, the country capable of posing the greatest challenge to the U.S. global reach is the People's Republic of China (PRC).[4] In terms of anti-access, which refers to "the ability to *prevent* an opposing force from entering an area of operations,"[5] China is developing capabilities designed to have "the effect of slowing the deployment of [opposing] forces into a theater, preventing them from operating from certain locations within that theater, or causing them to operate from distances farther from the locus of conflict than they would normally prefer."[6] For example, China has prioritized the advancement of anti-satellite and cyber weapons that could blind the communications networks the United States relies on to deploy and operate its forces.

The objective of area denial, on the other hand, is not prevention, but disruption—to compel the desired behavior by "impos[ing] severe costs on the enemy's freedom of action

---

[2] Roger Cliff et. al., *Entering the Dragon's Lair: Chinese Anti-access Strategies and Their Implications for the United States* (Santa Monica: RAND Corporation, 2007), xiii.

[3] Cliff et al, *Entering the Dragon's Lair*, xiii.

[4] For more on the evolution of China's strategy, as well as its potential impact, see Thomas G. Mahnken, "China's Anti-Access Strategy in Historical and Theoretical Perspective," *Journal of Strategic Studies* 34: 3 (2011): 299-323.

[5] "The China Syndrome," *The Economist*, June 9, 2012, 36.

[6] Cliff et al, *Entering the Dragon's Lair*, xiv.

once it has [gained access]."[7] Chinese integrated air defenses, anti-ship cruise and ballistic missiles, maritime bombers, missile and torpedo-carrying submarines, and fast patrol boats are all designed to inflict prohibitively high costs on any country operating within the first island chain near the China mainland.[8] In short, the cumulative effect of China's increasingly capable layered air defenses, as well as its fighter, ship, and missile assets, could curtail U.S. freedom of maneuver.[9]

On January 5, 2012, Secretary of Defense Leon Panetta issued new strategic guidance for the Department of Defense (DoD) on the priorities that would allow the United States to sustain its role as the preeminent leader on the global stage.[10] The major focus was that "while the U.S. military will continue to contribute to security globally, *[it] will of necessity rebalance toward the Asia-Pacific region.*"[11] Five months later, at the Shangri-La security dialogue in Singapore, Secretary Panetta articulated the following four principles meant to guide the U.S. rebalancing effort: to abide by international rules and order; and to emphasize partnerships, presence, and power projection.[12]

---

[7] "The China Syndrome," *The Economist.*

[8] The first island chain extends from the southern tip of Japan to northern Indonesia, to include Taiwan but not the Philippines. See "The China Syndrome."

[9] R. Jordan Prescott, "AirSea Battle As Presently Conceived," *Small Wars Journal* (January 11, 2012).

[10] For the complete guidance, see "Sustaining U.S. Global Leadership: Priorities for 21st Century Defense," *U.S. Department of Defense,* January 2012, Available at:
http://www.defense.gov/news/Defense_Strategic_Guidance.pdf. Last accessed Feb 6, 2013.

[11] Italics in the original. "Sustaining U.S. Global Leadership," 2.

[12] Leon E. Panetta, "The U.S. Rebalance Towards the Asia-Pacific" (delivered at the Shangri La Security Dialogue, Singapore, June 2, 2012).

What are the major components of China's A2/AD approach and how does the U.S. rebalancing address these challenges? In this chapter, I will lay out a comprehensive characterization of China's active defense strategy – the A2/AD approach in American parlance. I will explore how China is responding to the U.S. declaration that it will rebalance toward Asia. I will then discuss some aspects of the rebalancing strategy manifested to date, their potential effectiveness, and what more could be done. Finally, I will argue that the Obama Administration will need to look beyond hardware responses to the kinetic and geographic components of China's A2/AD strategy in order to appropriately counter those political and deterrent components designed to erode U.S. credibility as a Pacific power. To this end, I present three balancing acts the United States must master in its renewed focus on Asia if it is successfully to counter China's A2/AD strategy at acceptable costs.

China's Active Defense Strategy: A Comprehensive Understanding

China's active defense strategy was first promulgated on January 13, 1993, when Central Military Committee (CMC) chairman Jiang Zemin released the National Military Strategic Guidelines for the New Period (*xin shiqi guojia junshi zhanlue fangzhen*). That document provided the overall principles and guidance to plan and manage the development of the People's Liberation Army (PLA).[13] The operational component of these

---

[13] For more on the history and content of these guidelines, see David M. Finkelstein, "China's National Military Strategy: An Overview of the 'Military Strategic Guidelines,'" in *Right Sizing the People's Liberation Army: Exploring the Contours of China's Military,"* ed. Roy Kamphausen and Andrew Scobell (Carlisle: Strategic Studies Institute, 2007).

guidelines is known as active defense (*jiji fangyu*), which serves as "the highest level of strategic guidance for all PLA military operations during war and preparation for war during peacetime" based partially on "non-linear, non-contact and asymmetric" operations.[14] Consequently, China is now fielding capabilities designed to deter, deny, disrupt, and delay the deployment of U.S. forces into the Chinese theater.

China seeks to capitalize on U.S. weaknesses, specifically the great distances the U.S. needs to travel in order to engage China militarily. For example, China seeks to deny the U.S. military's ability to maneuver physically and engage Chinese forces with mass or precision by targeting U.S. communications and logistical networks, bases throughout East Asia, and U.S. ships and aircraft in the region. Chinese leaders also aim to exploit less physical vulnerabilities, such as a perceived lack of U.S. resolve and casualty aversion.[15] For these reasons, since 2005, U.S. observers and strategists have conceptualized China's active defense strategy as an A2/AD

---

[14] "People's Liberation Navy-Doctrine," *Global Security*, Available at: http://www.globalsecurity.org/military/world/china/plan-doctrine.htm. Last accessed Feb 6, 2013. See also *The Annual Report to Congress: Military and Security Developments Involving the People's Republic of China* (Washington, D.C.: Department of Defense, 2010): 22. Hereafter cited as PRC Power Report 2010. See Andrew S. Erickson, "China's Evolving Anti-Access Approach: 'Where's the Nearest (U.S.) Carrier?'" *China Brief* 10:18 (September 10, 2010). China first recognized a position of dramatic military inferiority relative to the United States during the 1991 Gulf War. Since then, the PLA has focused on adopting asymmetric means to counter U.S. power projection capabilities. See Michael P. Flaherty, "Red Wings Ascendant: The Chinese Air Force Contribution to Antiaccess," *Joint Forces Quarterly* 60 (2011): 96.

[15] For the most comprehensive study on China's anti-access strategies, see Cliff et al, *Entering the Dragon's Lair*.

strategy, though China has never publicly acknowledged adopting such a strategy.[16]

The bottom line is that China's 'active defense' strategy covers a broad range of Chinese strategic thinking designed to raise the costs of military intervention by the United States. Specific aspects of the strategy include preventing the United States from operating from certain bases in theater, forcing U.S. forces to operate at farther distances from the theater of operations than preferred, or delaying U.S. deployment from outside the theater. The various means and objectives of the strategy are often confused. Therefore, I argue that it is best to conceptualize China's A2/AD strategy as encompassing four interrelated pillars:

1) *geographic* (increasing the distance and time required for U.S. forces to arrive in theater from areas of safety before China achieves its political objectives);
2) *kinetic* (degrading the U.S. military's ability to penetrate anti-access environments with an enhanced conventional precision strike system consisting mainly of cruise and ballistic missiles as well as attacks on key enabling capabilities, such as space-based networks that enable C4ISR missions;[17]
3) *political* (exploiting perceived weaknesses in political support and resolve of U.S. allies and friends, thereby keeping the U.S. out, because countries will not allow us to base there); and

---

[16] Flaherty, "Red Wings Ascendant," 96. First mention was in the 2005 PRC power report to Congress.

[17] C4ISR stands for command, control computers, communication, intelligence, surveillance and reconnaissance, which together provide the U.S. with domain awareness.

4) *deterrent* (making involvement so costly that the U.S. opts out of responding, or responds minimally, in a given contingency).

The Geographic Pillar

China has come to understand how dependent the United States is on space products and services for commanding deployed troops, passing intelligence, surveillance and reconnaissance (ISR) data, and enabling precision targeting and engagement. The Chinese believe network attacks or the employment of an anti-satellite (ASAT) weapon could delay the deployment of U.S. military forces by disrupting communications and denying information vital for determining location and the movement of forces. The PLA's ability to disrupt regional airfields, bases, and logistics nodes, as well as naval surface and carrier operations, could exacerbate the geographic challenges of power projection by forcing the United States to operate farther from the theater of conflict. Also, the PLA has moved many of its forces deeper inland in an obvious attempt to create greater geographic dilemmas for U.S. forces.

Investments directed at holding U.S. military forces at risk represent some of the most dramatic aspects of the PRC's rapid militarization modernization program. A2/AD capabilities include advanced and extended-range air defense, air-to-air and precision strike capabilities, C4ISR, and force projection enablers such as aerial refueling, airlift, and logistic capabilities.[18] Though many of the capabilities discussed below, under the kinetic pillar, could be employed to increase the time and distance required for U.S. forces to arrive in theater, the differentiation between the two realms is useful because it better explains how and why certain systems, platforms, or weapons are employed.

---

[18] Flaherty, "Red Wings Ascendant," 99.

The Kinetic Pillar

Aspects of the kinetic pillar of China's active defense have changed as well, especially as regards the extent of China's military reach. The range of aerial refueling capable SU-30MKK fighters deployed in Nanjing and Guangzhou Military Regions already can hold Okinawa at risk, as can H-6 bombers with air-launched cruise missiles that, with engine modifications, can strike as far as Guam.[19] The PLA has terminally-guided anti-ship ballistic missile (ASBM) systems that reportedly can engage adversary surface ships up to 1,000 nautical miles (nm) from the PRC coast, cued by increasingly sophisticated surveillance and attack networks.

The inventory of the PLA Navy includes: conventional and nuclear-powered attack subs; surface combatants such as guided-missile destroyers equipped with long-range anti-ship cruise missiles (ASCMs) and SAM systems, such as the indigenously produced Luzhou and Luyang I/II DDGs, and the Russian procured Sovremenny II-class DDG; as well as maritime strike aircraft.[20] A number of these maritime strike aircraft, in particular the FB-7, FB-7A, B-6G, and the SU-30 MK2, can be armed with ASCMs to target surface combatants.[21] China's conventional and nuclear powered attack submarines — the KILO, SONG, YUAN, and SHANG-classes — also are capable of firing ASCMs.[22] The J-20 stealth

[19] Ibid., 100.

[20] For more, see Oriana Skylar Mastro, "Chinese Ship-Based Air Defense Systems," in *China's Strategy for the Near Seas* (Annapolis, MD: Naval Institute Press, 2013).

[21] Ronald O'Rourke, "China Naval Modernization: Implications for U.S. Navy Capabilities-Background and Issues for Congress," *CRS Report for Congress*, (August 11, 2008): 46.

[22] *The Annual Report to Congress: Military and Security Developments Involving the People's Republic of China* (Washington, D.C.: Department of Defense, 2011): 29. Hereafter cited as *PRC Power Report 2011*.

fighter will increase China's ability to strike regional air bases, logistical facilities, and other ground-based infrastructure. In addition, the air defense component of A2/AD includes surface-to-air-missiles (SAMs): the HQ-9, SA-10, SA-20, and the extended-range SA-20 PMU2. [23]

China's burgeoning military capabilities have been accompanied by an evolution in thinking about where and how to apply the A2/AD approach. Previously, China was focused solely on developing a force that could deter, delay, or degrade U.S. intervention in a conflict involving Taiwan. In the past five years, however, Chinese writings have extended the same logic to potential conflicts in the South or East China Seas. In general, China has been looking beyond Taiwan since at least December 2004, when Hu Jintao put forth the new historic missions for the PLA to ensure China's sovereignty and protect its expanding national interests.[24] Given the right coordination and surveillance networks, China can now strike targets well beyond what Chinese strategists refer to as the first island chain, referenced earlier and defined by a line through the Kurile Islands, Japan, the Ryukyu Islands, Taiwan, the Philippines, and Indonesia (Borneo to Natuna Besar). Indeed, many Chinese capabilities can today range a second island chain, one that runs in a north-south line from the Kuriles through Japan, the Bonins, the Marianas, the Carolines, and Indonesia.[25] In terms of range, the second island chain encompasses maritime areas out to approximately 1,800 nm from China's coast, including most of the East China Sea and East Asian sea lines of communication (SLOCs). Though the full extent of the Chinese anti-ship

---

[23] O'Rourke, "China Naval Modernization," 46.

[24] For more on the new historic missions, see *PRC Power Report 2011*, 16-17.

[25] "People's Liberation Navy-Offshore Defense," Available at: *Globalsecurity.org, http://www.globalsecurity.org/military/world/china/plan-doctrine-offshore.htm*. Last accessed Apr 2, 2013.

ballistic missile capability remains uncertain, China's ability to target U.S. carrier strike groups (CSGs) in the Western Pacific, or threaten to render them operationally ineffective with submunitions, would allow China to achieve its A2/AD goal without risk of further escalation or confrontation.[26]

China also has the world's most active land-based ballistic and cruise missile program, providing Beijing with a real capacity for conventional precision strike at significant range. The Defense Department's annual report to Congress for 2011 on Chinese military and security developments clearly lays out Chinese capabilities to deny U.S. power projection, noting some 1,000-1,200 short-range ballistic missiles (SRBMs) and additional medium-range ballistic missiles (MRBMs) capable of conducting precision strikes against land targets and naval vessels out to the first island chain.[27] China's MRBMs can extend PLA's range to 1,000-3,000 kilometers and other investments allow for even further reach.[28] According to publicly available analyses, the PLA has approximately twenty liquid-fueled limited range CSS-3 intercontinental ballistic missiles (ICBMs), between fifteen and twenty liquid-fueled CSS-2 intermediate range ballistic missiles (IRBMs), and about fifty CSS-5 road mobile, solid-fueled MRBMs, all of which are highly-relevant for regional deterrence missions.[29]

Though the quantity of Chinese SRBMs has not changed significantly in recent years, the quality has. China is fielding advanced variants with improved ranges, accuracies, and

---

[26] ASBM is allegedly based on the DF-21D/CSS-5 solid propellant medium range ballistic missile. See anonymous, "On the Verge of a Game Changer," *Proceedings Magazine* 135, no. 5 (2009).

[27] *PRC Power Report 2011*, 30. Other conventional munitions in China's arsenal include Land-attack cruise missiles such as the YJ-63, KD-88, and DH-10 systems, ground attack munitions, anti-radiation weapons, and artillery-delivered high precision munitions. See Ibid.

[28] *PRC Power Report 2011*, 30.

[29] *PRC Power Report 2010*, 34.

more sophisticated payloads, gradually replacing earlier generations of stocks with those capable of precision strike.[30] These modern variants could be used as terror weapons to convince allies and friends of the United States not to get involved in a particular contingency. Or, they could be used to strike air bases in Taiwan or Japan in such a way that the United States would not be able to generate enough sorties to contest air superiority, even if all countries involved had the will to support such operations.[31]

With its extensive and robust arsenal, China could thus deny the United States access to the region with strikes to runways, aircraft, and other equipment, thereby rendering air bases temporarily unusable. One recent RAND study had dire predictions for the survivability of U.S. air bases in Japan, arguing that China "could damage, destroy or strand 75 percent of aircraft based at Kadena" with just thirty-four missiles armed with submunitions.[32] In addition to the ASBM, long-range cruise missiles such as the DH-10/YJ100, and improved mobile ballistic and air defense missiles such as the HQ-9, could also be used as military impediments to U.S. regional power projection.[33] Moreover, the PRC is developing new platforms and capabilities that will extend its operational reach, possibly as far as the Indian Ocean.[34] Though there are few indications that China's active defense focus has reached this point, the PLA's overall expansion in its military capacity

---

[30] Ibid.

[31] Mahnken, "China's Anti-Access Strategy," 314.

[32] Wendell Minnick, "RAND Study Suggests U.S. Loses War with China," *Defense News*, October 16, 2008. For more on Chinese A2/AD challenges in a Senkaku scenario, see Oriana Skylar Mastro and Mark Stokes, "Air Power Trends in Northeast Asia: Implications for Japan and the U.S.-Japan Alliance," *Project 2049*, July 2011.

[33] General Norton A. Schwartz and Admiral Jonathan W. Greenert, "Air-Sea Battle," *The American Interest Magazine*, February 20, 2012.

[34] *PRC Power Report 2010*, 33.

allows it to plan for a much broader range of contingencies, all of which will likely feature ways to keep U.S. forces at bay.

The Political Pillar

While the kinetic and geographic components of China's approach have received the most attention in Washington policy circles, the more elusive political and deterrent A2/AD pillars can be just as effective, if not more so, in undermining U.S. ability to project power in the region. The political pillar refers to the idea that, in a conflict, China will pressure countries with military threats or economic inducements to limit or deny the United States use of facilities necessary for power projection. As Congressional Research Service naval expert Ronald O'Rourke convincingly argues, "To threaten regional bases and logistics points, China could employ SRBM/MRBMs, land-attack cruise missiles, special operations forces, and computer network attack (CNA). Strike aircraft, when enabled by aerial refueling, could simultaneously engage distant targets using air-launched cruise missiles equipped with a variety of terminal-homing warheads."[35] Even during peacetime, though most countries want the United States to remain in the region, the priority on stability above all else may mean nations throughout the region might pressure the United States to accept a greater degree of parity with China, thereby displacing U.S. influence in the region to a certain degree.

A recent example of such efforts came from Chinese defense strategist and retired senior military officer Song Xiaojun. In an opinion piece published in May 2012, Song warned Australia that it could not reconcile its close economic relationship with China with the fact that it relies on the United States for security and would have to, at some point, choose which country to prioritize in its foreign policy

---

[35] O'Rourke, "China Naval Modernization," 46.

decision making. He argued that "Australia has to find a godfather sooner or later," and whom Canberra chooses "depends on who is more powerful based on the strategic environment."[36] An editorial in a nationalist Chinese state-run newspaper also responded to the news that the United States will station 2,500 Marines in Darwin with the warning that Canberra is risking getting itself "caught in the cross fire" between China and the United States.[37] The first detachment of Marines from the Marine Air-Ground Task Force (MAGTF), whose specialty is rapid response, arrived in April 2012.[38]

The Deterrent Pillar

The deterrent A2/AD pillar—perhaps the most important and most difficult to counter–posits that Washington may opt out of responding in a number of contingencies, given that China's active defense initiatives exceed the political costs for the United States. This could preclude an intervention decision altogether, or involve a Beijing-directed preemptive strike on American forces attempting to deploy to the region, in the hopes of delivering the necessary psychological shock to the United States, its allies, and friends in the region.[39] As noted when discussing the kinetic pillar, Washington's uncertainty with respect to the maturity of the ASBM fleet and the risk it entails, "might deter carrier strike groups from entering the region in the first place."[40] In other words, the possibility of these capabilities may be enough to convince the United States to opt out of a conflict.

---

[36] Philip Wen, "Canberra 'must pick strategic godfather,'" *The Sydney Morning Herald,* May 16, 2012.

[37] Malcolm Moore, "Chinese Anger at U.S. Base in Australia," *The Telegraph,* May 16, 2012.

[38] Panetta, "The U.S. Rebalance Towards the Asia-Pacific."

[39] Cliff et al, *Entering the Dragon's Lair,* 31.

[40] Mahnken, "China's Anti-Access Strategy," 315.

China's public response to the U.S. declaration that it will rebalance toward Asia reflects the beliefs underpinning the deterrent pillar. The main theme found throughout Chinese media sources is that the United States is too weak-willed to carry through its policies, which are in any case ill-advised.[41] The Chinese media further claims that the past ten years at war in Southwest Asia has eroded the U.S. sphere of influence and has seriously affected the state of U.S. regional hegemony in the western Pacific.[42] Chinese writers also note that, while the United States may want, theoretically, to return to being the main force in the Asia-Pacific, its economic dependence on China and its relative depletion of resources imply that it will fail to fulfill its proclamations and promises.[43] In short, so the argument goes, while the United States wants to protect vital interests in the region, its desire to do so at an acceptable cost trumps all other considerations. Concordant with this view, China believes it can increase the real and perceived costs of intervention, and successfully convince the United States to restrain itself. The ultimate result—ironically—is an American-self-imposed, anti-access doctrine.

---

[41] For more on the growing importance of Asia, and China in particular, with respect to the West, see

张茉楠：《警惕美国"平衡中国战美国力图重塑亚太经济合作与贸易格局》，《中国经贸》，2011年3月 and

王鸣鸣：《发挥"领导作用"平衡各方力量美国全力推行"重返亚洲"战略》，《人民日报》2011年1月26日

[42]

阮建平：《经济与安全"再平衡"下的美国对华政策调整》，《东北亚论坛》，2011年1月；and 张茉楠：《警惕美国"平衡中国战略"——美国力图重塑亚太经济合作与贸易格局》，《中国经贸》，2011年3月

[43] 庞中英：《中国也需对美"再平衡"》，《社会观察》，2012年6月；

阮建平：《经济与安全"再平衡"下的美国对华政策调整》，《东北亚论坛》，2011年1月

U.S. Rebalancing and its Implications for the A2/AD Threat

Though not inspired solely by China's growing A2/AD capabilities, U.S. rebalancing toward Asia addresses many aspects of the challenge. This section evaluates recent diplomatic and military changes, made in the first Obama administration, designed to elevate the U.S. role in the region.

Military efforts

The DoD rebalancing strategy is designed to counter the two most concrete pillars of China's A2/AD strategy: the kinetic and geographic components. Forward-deploying more assets in the region, such as the MAGTF Detachment already deployed to Australia and the dedication of 60 percent of U.S. warships to the Asia-Pacific Theater by 2020, addresses the geographic pillar.[44] To mitigate the risks associated with the kinetic pillar, the United States has invested in new aerial-fueling tankers, a new long-range stealthy bomber, advanced maritime patrol and anti-submarine warfare aircraft, and the U.S. "is improving missile defenses, and continuing efforts to enhance the resiliency and effectiveness of critical space-based capabilities."[45]

New operational concepts such as "Air Sea Battle" are meant to guide U.S. efforts to organize, train, and equip its military forces in ways that mitigate challenges posed by all four pillars. Air Sea Battle "relies on highly integrated and tightly coordinated operations across war-fighting domains"[46] in order to "to disrupt and destroy enemy A2-AD networks and their defensive and offensive-guided weapons systems in

---

[44] Panetta, "The U.S. Rebalance Towards the Asia-Pacific." Before, 50 percent of U.S. naval assets were dedicated to the Pacific and 50 percent to the Atlantic.

[45] Italics in the original. "Sustaining U.S. Global Leadership," 4-5.

[46] Schwartz and Greenert, "Air-Sea Battle."

order to enable U.S. freedom of action to conduct concurrent and follow-on operations."[47] In its rebalancing efforts, the DoD has committed itself *"to invest as required to ensure its ability to operate effectively"* to include "implementing the Joint Operational Access Concept (e.g., Air-Sea Battle)."[48]

The current U.S. operational response also relies heavily on investments in and the deployment of antiballistic missiles (ABMs), as well as other counter-strategies designed to evade, confuse, and defend. High-tech investments include a next-generation missile interceptor jointly developed with Japan.[49] To defend ships at sea, the United States continues to invest in Aegis/Standard Missile ABMs and, to defend air bases ashore, in Patriot PAC-3 ABMs. Vulnerabilities at fixed bases have also been identified, although substantial steps to harden and disperse such assets remain immature. But most importantly, American officials recognize the need to present a credible, survivable, crisis-stabilizing force posture, given the enhanced threat environment, and have directed efforts in hardening, dispersal, warning and active defense at U.S. regional facilities. For example, Army Chief of Staff, General Odierno, referenced the option of pre-positioning equipment in the Pacific aboard ships and out of harm's way, available for crisis response or to help train allied militaries in the region.[50]

Diplomatic efforts

Though the military aspects of rebalancing have received the most attention, the State Department has also been directing parallel and complementary diplomatic efforts.

---

[47] Prescott, "Air-Sea Battle As Presently Conceived."

[48] Italics in the original. "Sustaining U.S. Global Leadership," 4-5.

[49] Panetta, "The U.S. Rebalance Towards the Asia-Pacific."

[50] "Army Jockeying for Role in 'Air-Sea Battle,'" *National Defense Magazine,* February 21, 2012.

These efforts are not only "designed to reassure America's Asian allies that it will do whatever is needed to shield them from Chinese bullying,"[51] but also they address the political vulnerabilities of America's Asian presence. U.S. attempts to reduce the American footprint in Okinawa, in order to make the U.S. presence more politically sustainable, while simultaneously developing Guam as a more resilient strategic hub for U.S. military operations in Asia, is one such example.[52] As Secretary of Defense Panetta articulated at Shangri La, strengthening U.S. alliances with Japan, South Korea, Australia, the Philippines and Thailand, as well as partnerships with Indonesia, Malaysia, India, Singapore, Vietnam and New Zealand, are critical to U.S. efforts to increase presence and ensure stabilizing U.S. power projection in the region. The security and defense relationships the United States has with these countries have intensified in recent years. An example of this dynamic is the comprehensive memorandum of understanding the United States signed with Vietnam in 2011.[53]

While all these initiatives are a step in the right direction, to be truly effective the United States needs to, in the words of Assistant Secretary of State for East Asia Kurt Campbell, sustain regular high-level engagement opportunities, not just with treaty allies, but also with other influential countries in the region.[54] To this end, the Obama administration has moved beyond a reliance on the traditional hub-and-spokes network of bilateral alliances, with the United States at its center, to strengthening its multilateral regional participation

---

[51] "China Syndrome," 34.
[52] Panetta, "The U.S. Rebalance Towards the Asia-Pacific."
[53] Ibid.
[54] Dr. Kurt Campbell, "Doing More Without More," (keynote address given at the 2012 annual CNAS conference, Washington, D.C., June 13, 2012). Available at: http://www.cnas.org/node/8439. Last accessed Apr 2, 2013.

as well. President Obama's decision to join the East Asia Summit and personally attend the November 2011 meeting reflects this shift in U.S. priorities.[55] In 2012, Secretary Panetta was the first American Secretary of Defense to meet privately with all defense ministers of the Association of South East Asian Nations (ASEAN). Moreover, former Secretary of State Hillary Clinton regularly attended the ASEAN Regional Forum (ARF), making efforts to elevate the role of the organization.[56] In July 2012, Secretary Clinton embarked on a grand tour of Southeast Asia, attending the ARF, the EAS Foreign Ministers Meeting, and the U.S.-ASEAN Post-Ministerial Conference, in addition to being the first Secretary of State to visit Laos in fifty-seven years.[57] In Laos, Clinton also announced an additional commitment of $50 million to the Lower Mekong Initiative, thereby pledging financial and technical support to Cambodia, Laos, Thailand, and Vietnam to improve infrastructure, health care, education and their ability to manage environmental issues.[58] These examples indicate a clear break with America's historical diplomatic strategy in Asia.

With the establishment of programs, and vis-à-vis routine and regular order, the State Department strives to sustain a high level of operational engagement that spans every aspect of societal engagement to include trade and people-to-people relations in addition to traditional state-to-state engagements.

---

[55] For more on these efforts, see "Fact Sheet: East Asia Summit," *The White House Office of the Press Secretary.* Available at: http://www.whitehouse.gov/the-press-office/2011/11/19/fact-sheet-east-asia-summit. Last accessed Apr 2, 2013.

[56] Panetta, "The U.S. Rebalance Towards the Asia-Pacific." The author would also like to thank Ely Ratner for his input.

[57] "U.S. Secretary of State Hillary Clinton on Historic Laos visit," *BBC News,* July 11, 2012.

[58] Patrick Barta, "Southeast Asia Gets a Boost from Clinton," *The Wall Street Journal,* July 13, 2012.

The ultimate goal is a multipolar system, with the U.S. military the first-among-equals, which would create the stability necessary to allow commerce to flourish as it has the past few decades. U.S. policy in the region needs to give equal weight to the economic dimensions of relationships, because strong economic ties serve as the foundation for political relationships and eventually military cooperation. Because all aspects of U.S. policy in the region are mutually reinforcing, the State Department needs also to create an environment conducive for enhanced U.S. business presence. The Trans-Pacific Partnership (TPP), a proposed multilateral free trade agreement between the United States and countries in the region, is an attempt to liberalize and integrate these economies further.[59] But in Southeast Asia, in particular, where most countries cannot meet the TPP standard, the United States needs to refocus its economic and investment efforts to promote the economic component of its relations. Countries in the Asia-Pacific region prioritize economic development, and as long as the U.S. economic presence diminishes in contrast with that of China, the United States is ceding influence.[60]

What more can be done?

To date, the military components of the rebalancing have received the most attention, primarily because they are highly visible. But when determining which meetings to attend or what platforms to pre-position, considerations should center more intensely on the political and deterrent pillars of A2/AD, because China is willing to accept military setbacks in

---

[59] Participant countries include Australia, Brunei, Chile, Malaysia, New Zealand, Peru, Singapore, and Vietnam. For a solid analysis of TPP, see Brock R. Williams, "Trans-Pacific Partnership (TPP) Countries: Comparative Trade and Economic Analysis," *Congressional Research Service,* May 30, 2012.

[60] For more on this, see Campbell, "Doing More Without More."

a given contingency if overall political objectives are achieved. While the State Department has amplified diplomatic efforts in the region, it remains unclear whether such efforts will lead to enhanced access in these countries "when the balloon goes up" in a crisis.

For desired access to occur, it is logical to assume that U.S. allies need sufficient reassurances that the United States can and will protect and shield them from Chinese military coercion and economic warfare. For these potential allies, the weighing of both short- and long-term consequences of such an allegiance will be paramount. For Washington, alleviating the concerns of allies, and convincing them to join in what may be an indirect conflict against China, will be difficult even if the balance of regional power is still tipped in the U.S. favor. Regardless of such specific and detailed calculations, a coordinated diplomatic strategy designed to signal U.S. resolve and improve American access to regional third parties is a cost-effective and necessary complement to U.S. military strategy.

A Way Forward

China's strategists are betting that not all wars are won by the side with the strongest military. Indeed, China's experience in fighting the Korean War proves that a country willing to sacrifice blood and treasure can overcome a technologically superior opponent. In the next section, I outline three balancing acts that, if mastered, will allow the United States to signal resolve to China and provide reassurance to friends and allies.

The United States needs to learn to accept risk without being reckless. China is masterful at chipping away at U.S. credibility through advancing militarization and the coordination of coercive diplomacy. China often uses limited military action as a signaling tactic to establish the credibility of its determination to set a baseline from which an escalation can take place if its demands are not met. Assertive Chinese activities in the South China Sea in 2012, including Chinese patrol boats attempting to ram a Philippine vessel, Chinese vessels cutting or disabling the cables of Vietnamese survey ships, and detaining 21 Vietnamese fisherman for seven weeks, demonstrate that China elevates risk to slice away at the interests of others—in this case to promote its interpretation of Exclusive Economic Zone (EEZ) rights.[61] The great strategist Thomas Schelling captures this approach when he writes it is "the sheer inability to predict the consequences of our actions and to keep things under control...that can intimidate the enemy."[62] Because China introduces risk for exactly this reason, the U.S. focus on reducing risk of escalation through crisis management, though necessary, is unlikely to produce a marked change in Chinese behavior. Such futility is reinforced by a tendency among the ranks of the U.S. military to focus on worst-case "great battle" scenarios, instead of the less lethal engagements that characterize Chinese coercive diplomacy.

The United States, while promoting stability, must permit the possibility of escalation. To signal to China that the United States will not opt out of a conflict, the Obama Administration must signal willingness to escalate to higher levels of conflict when China is purposely testing U.S. resolve. If countries think the United States cannot (or will not) protect its allies, they may begin to gravitate towards China. For U.S.

---

[61] For a more comprehensive list, see "Key Asian Indicators: A Book of Charts" (Asian Studies Center, The Heritage Foundation, July 2012). For more on Chinese coercive diplomacy in the South China Sea, see Oriana Skylar Mastro, "The Sansha Garrison: China's Deliberate Escalation in the South China Sea," *Center for a New American Security (CNAS)*, Flashpoints Bulletin 5, September 2012.

[62] Thomas C. Schelling, *Arms and Influence* (New Haven: Yale University Press, 1966), 109.

allies, enhancing credibility may mean bolstering allies' capabilities, diversifying basing for aircraft, strengthening passive defenses at air bases, and being prepared to respond in kind if China launches an attack. However, if the United States takes a tough stance, increasing its observable military presence (and thus its vulnerability), China may react strongly by punishing American allies and partners—many of whom count on China as their number one trading partner. General anxiety about the U.S. ability to balance all these competing requirements could reduce U.S. political access to the region, thus increasing the effectiveness of the political dimension of China's anti-access strategy.

The United States must achieve engagement without encirclement. If China feels encircled, it may react in ways that are destabilizing for the region. American strategists must examine their approach to regional basing to ensure that it strengthens America's relationships with its allies and partners, addresses any Chinese concerns of containment, and reliably facilitates the forward deployment and sustainment of American military forces in the region. It is the responsibility of American policymakers to make clear to U.S. allies and partners that it is not necessary to choose between China and the United States. Instead, the United States and its allies should publicly seek a positive and constructive relationship with China, while striving for the maintenance of a robust military edge necessary to guard against potential Chinese aggression and coercion. Strategic distrust is likely to linger because the leadership in Beijing seems convinced that the United States seeks to constrain or even upset China's rise.[63] But in conjunction with prudent changes to American force

---

[63] For a more comprehensive analysis of China's position, see Kenneth Lieberthal and Wang Jisi, "Addressing U.S.-China Strategic Distrust," *Brookings Institution, John L. Thorton China Center Monograph Series*, March 4, 2012.

posture in the region, talks among the top civilian and military leaders of both countries might alleviate such distrust and lead to agreements on modalities to reduce tension in the commons, encourage mutual restraint in the deployment of especially destabilizing new capabilities, and create a better level of mutual understanding about the security situation on the Korean peninsula and Taiwan.[64]

Ultimately, the American objective in the region must be peace and stability at an acceptable cost. Given this, it is critical to understand the four components of China's A2/AD strategy and how best to maintain the U.S. position as a Pacific power. In addition to regularly attending meetings in the region and developing new technology, new platforms, and new operational concepts designed to defeat China's A2/AD strategy, the United States needs to accept risk without being reckless, permit the possibility of escalation while promoting stability, and promote engagement without encirclement. By mastering these three balancing acts, the United States will be able to maintain peace and stability in East Asia without sacrificing American interests.

---

[64] Ibid., xii.

The Fall of the House of Westphalia: National Security Doctrine and Strategy in the Age of Atomized Destructive Power

Keith W. Mines

Introduction

In *The World Set Free*, written thirty-one years before the invention of the atomic bomb, H.G. Wells paints a disturbing picture of a domestic nuclear attack: "All through the nineteenth and twentieth centuries the amount of energy that men were able to command was continually increasing... Destruction was becoming so facile that any little body of malcontents could use it....A man could carry about in a handbag an amount of latent energy sufficient to wreck half a city..."[1]

Wells had a futuristic imagination that was uncanny, and although many of his predictions languish on the sci-fi shelf, this one could walk right off the set of Jack Bauer's "24." What is most chilling in Well's prediction is the collision of technology (atomized destructive devices) and politics (newly empowered malcontents). He may have been the first modern thinker to peer into a frightening new world in which the state was no longer the primary proprietor of the ultimate tools of violence, as by then enshrined in the Westphalian

---

[1] H.G. Wells, *The World Set Free* (London: Macmillan and Co., 1914).

international order for more than three and a half centuries. In his fictional world, sub-national groups, immune to deterrence, could destroy cities.

For more than a decade we have been collectively seized with the specter of nuclear terrorism, something the May 2010 National Security Strategy singles out three times, concluding that "the American people face no greater or more urgent danger."[2] It is a long-shot opaque threat never likely to be imminent. But neither can it be ruled out in a world where destructive energy is ever more tightly packaged, and terrorist groups have increasingly moved from publicity-seeking events to catastrophically destructive events.

Still, we have been loath to build doctrine or strategy around this threat, leaving it on our "to do" list while we focus on more familiar and less messy conventional geopolitical issues — with Asia as the latest example. But the harsh reality is, if we do nothing but contain nuclear and biological terrorism, liberal society will muddle through. If we do not, and if we endure such a strike from within, the course of civilization will be forever diverted. We might largely recover, but we would never be quite the same.

For the next decade, core national security doctrine must center on the geo-political shift from a tight Westphalian cluster of sovereign states interacting in a rough world order, to one of increasingly lethal non-state actors. Such doctrine should be supported by a short-term strategy focused on two key areas. First is strengthening measures to eliminate the possible circulation of weapons and weapons grade material. Second is curtailing the appeal and the operating space of terrorist groups. A parallel longer-term effort should be made to strengthen weak and dysfunctional states, helping them develop the institutions to impose a monopoly over the use of force from their territory. The latter effort will require a full

---

[2] The White House, *U.S. National Security Strategy*, May 2012, 23.

U.S. commitment and leadership, with parallel new and strengthened institutions, notably a Civilian Security Assistance Agency.

Doctrinal and Strategic Drift

In the kind of collaborative analysis among young foreign policy professionals that the Council for Emerging National Security Affairs (CENSA) is particularly well suited for, I conducted a survey in 2007 that posited twenty-one candidates competing for the honor of the post 9/11 Mr. X.[3] Predictably, no consensus candidate emerged, although doctrines centering on state-building and new global architecture edged out proposals for neo-containment or a return to unabashed American primacy. It's disconcerting to note that the two presidential doctrines of the period received almost no support.

If the sweepstakes were replayed today, I suspect the results would again yield no clear winner, something Daniel W. Drezner, writing in *Foreign Affairs* recently thought was fine. He dismissed the need for a clear strategy, as long as our intention and execution are competent, allowing that strategy can be important "as a signaling device."[4] Drezner quotes the National Journal's Michael Hirsch as saying "the real Obama doctrine is to have no doctrine at all. And that's the way it's likely to remain."[5]

---

[3] *The Search for Mr. X: A CENSA Member's Survey on National Security Doctrine After Containment*, Final Results, December 2007, available at: http://www.censa.net/index.php?option=com_content&view=article&id=252:the-search-for-mr-x-a-censa-members-survey-on-national-security-doctrine-after-containment&catid=42:essays&Itemid=146. Last accessed January 2, 2014.

[4] Daniel Drezner, "Does Obama Have a Grand Strategy?" *Foreign Affairs* 90, no. 4 (July-August 2011): 57-68.

[5] Drezner, 64.

Why this aversion to doctrine and strategy, and where does it leave us? Several reasons present themselves. First, if an administration has a doctrine, it is compelled to follow it. When asked in 2003 to confirm his doctrine, President Bush said pre-eminence and pre-emption could be construed as part of the doctrine, but he would not go so far as to affirm them as anything approximating comprehensiveness, apparently seeking the flexibility to retool doctrine as the threat evolved.

Second, a strategic heir to George Kennan has not yet arisen. There is no shortage of great writers, but only a handful combine penetrating analysis with relevant field experience. Two policymakers writing a comprehensive foreign policy treatise actually begin by pointing out that their "political coming-of-age was marked by the fall of the Berlin Wall, not by the Vietnam War."[6] In fact, a lack of experience was considered a badge of honor by some of the young architects of the Iraq War. At the other extreme, some elder statesmen are prisoners of their experience and choose to ignore what is messy in favor of what is familiar. Zbigniew Brzezinski recently wrote that "the United States' central challenge over the next several decades is to revitalize itself, while promoting a larger West and buttressing complex balances in the East that can accommodate China's rising global status."[7] "Kennan, Now More Than Ever" would sum things up nicely.[8]

---

[6] Mona Sutphen and Nina Hachigian, *The Next American Century* (New York: Simon & Schuster, 2010), 1.

[7] Zbigniew Brzezinski, "Balancing the East, Upgrading the West: U.S. Grand Strategy in an Age of Upheaval," *Foreign Affairs* 91, no. 1, (January – February 2012): 97-104.

[8] Unfortunately, the institution that produced Kennan in the first place, the State Department, is still where much of the Kennanesque experience in the world resides, but State has driven all policy prescriptive writing from its ranks by a top-down fear of publishing (one that is not similarly

Third is the familiar lament that we have lost the clarity of a monolithic threat. The May 2010 National Security Strategy speaks of "multiple threats—from nations, non-state actors, and failed states."[9] The Army's 2012 posture statement posits a multiple threat environment when it argues that the U.S. faces "the continuing threat of violent extremism, the proliferation of lethal weapons and materials, the destabilizing behavior of Iran and North Korea, the rise of new powers in Asia and an era of uncertainty in the Middle East."[10] It is, to an extent, a legitimate reading of the world, but a diffusion of threats would seem to argue for more discipline in connecting the threats and seeing the interplay between them, rather than abdicating the intellectual field to a list of bad things in the world.

This theme is brilliantly taken up by Gallagher, Geltzer, and Gorka, who see in "the complexity trap,"[11] a more insidious reason for doctrinal and strategic drift. The authors reject the "cult of complexity," arguing that previous eras during which we somehow developed a coherent strategy were really no less complex, and that we lose the required focus to develop appropriate policies and execute them well if we hide behind the wall of complexity. It is convenient, and can be made to sound compelling, but in the end, such thinking evinces simple slothfulness. Collectively, the three strategists posit that "if complexity...real or perceived, is truly the defining characteristic of the current strategic environment, then we should be witnessing a corresponding renaissance in grand strategy, design and long-term strategic

---

enforced in the military; to the contrary, it is highly encouraged, such that it could easily be Major X, not Mr. X this -round).

[9] National Security Strategy, i.

[10] "2012 Army Posture: The Nation's Force of Decisive Action," 1.

[11] Michael J. Gallagher, Joshua A. Gerltzer, and Sebastian Gorka, "The Complexity Trap," *Parameters*, (Spring 2012): 5-16.

planning," something which is clearly not happening to an effective degree.[12]

Historical and Geo-Political Convergence

It was not always thus. What distinguished Kennan's Long Telegram and, later, Sources of Soviet Conduct was his ability to place the impending U.S.-Soviet rivalry in its cultural and historical context, based on his years of living in Russia and mastering Soviet intentions and limitations. From this he crafted the rudiments of the containment doctrine, in essence that "Soviet pressure against the free institutions of the western world is something that can be contained by the adroit and vigilant application of counter-force at a series of constantly shifting geographical and political points."[13]

When NSC-68 gave policy teeth to the Long Telegram, it was in the wake of the Soviet nuclear proofs that ended the brief U.S. unilateral nuclear age and thrust the world into a bilateral nuclear contest—the centerpiece of the Cold War. This new paradigm reached a sort of stasis as U.S.-Soviet competition became the overriding factor in global statecraft.

But brewing beneath the surface were fundamental changes to the world order that were outgrowing containment, even a new and updated containment. They accelerated dramatically after the fall of the Berlin Wall, unleashing a veritable revolution in geopolitics the likes of which the world had never seen. The 9/11 attacks subsequently provided a window on three trends—all in play before the attacks, all still advancing today. These trends capture not only the socio-political and geo-strategic elements

---

[12] Gallagher et. al., 13.
[13] George Kennan, "The Sources of Soviet Conduct," *Foreign Affairs* 25 (July 1947): 566-582.

of the threat, but also the play of technology, which, as in the Cold War, is a key driver of change.

Three Trends – Weapons, Terrorists, and Urbanization

First, the technological component of our current struggle is the increasing availability of "weapons of atomized destructive power," chemical, biological, radiological, and nuclear weapons that are slipping from tight control by the major powers to loose control by an increasing number of regional powers. These powers are often irrational actors, have ties to terrorist groups, and maintain a tenuous hold on power. Meanwhile, the technology itself, especially for low-end weapons systems such as dirty bombs and biological weapons, is more readily available.

The second trend is the rise of apocalyptic terrorism. For centuries, terrorism had been a tactic that Rand analyst Brian Michael Jenkins aptly refers to as "armed propaganda," a means to influence the behavior of states. It occurred within the state system, with terrorists largely limited in their destructive impulses by a desire to kill for attention, not for killing's sake. Typically, they were rational actors with goals and a political end-state, however unlikely that end-state might have been.

With the rise of recent terrorist groups, however, these earlier assumptions no longer hold. The Aum Shinrikyo Tokyo subway attack in 1995 was perhaps the first terrorist action not tied to an immediate political objective, but simply intended to kill as many people as possible in support of an apocalyptic belief system. According to one reporter "those responsible later told police they were trying to inflict maximum casualties on the station at Kasumigaseki, where most of Japan's central ministries are, as a first blow in a colossal battle with the government that they believed would bring the end of the world."[14]

Al Qaeda, too, possesses an apocalyptic worldview. Dr. Sebestyen Gorka coined the phrase "hyper-terrorism" to refer to attacks by terrorist groups that had irrational, as opposed to limited and achievable, goals. Al Qaeda, he extrapolated, sought as an end-state "the creation of a caliphate, starting with the Middle East and Central Asia, but eventually spreading through a campaign of asymmetric warfare that exploits the very aspects of the liberal democratic system. No political resolution is...possible, given the absolute and transcendentally informed nature of the desired state-of-affairs (a global caliphate) that al Qaeda wishes to achieve."[15] A careful tracking of the statements of Al Qaeda, coupled with what we know about the group's efforts to acquire chemical and nuclear weapons, led Jenkins to conclude that, by 2001, al Qaeda "had an active chemical weapons research program and clearly had continued its interest in acquiring nuclear weapons."[16] Its motive in acquiring these weapons, he suggests, shifted in 2002 from "deterrence to reciprocation."[17] Writing in 2008 Jenkins concluded that "the issue is not [bin Laden's] intentions but the distance between intentions and accomplishments. Osama bin Laden wants a nuclear weapon and probably would use it if he had one."[18]

Where, then, does that leave us, post bin Laden? In March 2010, prior to bin Laden's demise, FBI Director Robert Mueller warned Congress, "Al Qaeda's continued efforts to access

---

[14] Martin Fackler, "Tokyo Gas Attacks Arrest Reawakens National Trauma," *New York Times*, June 7, 2012.

[15] Sebastian Gorka, "International Cooperation as a Tool in Counterterrorism: Then and Now," see chdsnet.org.

[16] Brian Michael Jenkins, *Will Terrorists Go Nuclear?* (Amherst: Prometheus Books, 2008), 255.

[17] Jenkins, *Will Terrorists Go Nuclear?*, 255.

[18] Jenkins, *Will Terrorists Go Nuclear?*, 249.

chemical, biological, radiological, or nuclear materials poses a serious threat to the United States." Since bin Laden's death, as recently as the spring of 2012, the Yemeni branch of Al Qaeda published in its on-line publication *Inspire* a posthumous appeal by Anwar Al-Awlaki to the faithful: "The use of poisons of chemical and biological weapons against population centers is allowed and highly recommended due to the efforts on the enemy."[19] Nothing in the post-bin Laden period would suggest a retraction of apocalyptic ends among hard-cord Al Qaeda operatives.

The third trend is simpler and clearer: the advancing vulnerability of cities. The course of human interaction through the 20th Century was that of increasing centralization in every aspect of life, and urbanization on a large scale. Buildings became taller, transportation networks moved larger numbers of people in smaller devices, food and water supplies emanated from fewer sources, and information was collected and moved with increasing centrality. As perhaps never before in history, modern society is centered on the city as its foundational concept. Absent the ability to populate and peacefully inhabit cities, it is difficult to imagine the continuation of civilization as currently organized.

The Fall of the House of Westphalia, and the Rise of Apocalyptic Terrorism

What, then, is the historical context of these trends? As early as 1974, Brian Jenkins worried that "power, defined in its crudest sense as the capacity to kill, destroy, disrupt, alarm, and oblige us to expend vast resources for security, was descending to smaller and smaller groups—gangs whose

---

[19]*Global Security Newswire Blog,* "Al-Qaeda Magazine Urges Chemical, Biological Strikes Against Foes," blog entry by the National Journal, May, 3 2012.

grievances, real or imaginary, could not always be satisfied. Or, to put it another way, the bands of irreconcilables, fanatics, and lunatics that have existed throughout history were becoming an increasingly potent force."[20]

Is Deterrence Dead?

One recurring issue in all this is deterrence, which, as Ignatieff and Bobbitt point out, is at the heart of the Westphalian system. The nation state system has produced a very rough order that has for long stretches seemed so bloody and so unkempt that seemingly nothing could be worse. In retrospect, however, we see that it could. For all its flaws, the current system offers a rough order among states that, more often than we notice, maintains peaceful coexistence through deterrence, and, when things collapse, a means of rebuilding. William Langewiesche suggests that if nuclear weapons pass into the hands of the new stateless guerrillas, they will offer "none of the retaliatory targets that so far have underlain the nuclear peace—no permanent infrastructure to protect, no capital city, and indeed no country to call home."[21]

Jenkins is less absolute, and believes that "deterrence as a concept need not be abandoned," arguing that "although terrorists cannot be deterred in the same way that the use of nuclear weapons was deterred during the cold war, there are national governments that may provide support to terrorists, terrorist constituencies, and terrorist sympathizers; all of those are vulnerable to direct or retaliatory consequences of a

---

[20] Jenkins, *Will Terrorists Go Nuclear?*, 279.

[21] William Langewiesche, *The Atomic Bazaar: Dispatches from the Underground World of Nuclear Trafficking* (New York: Farrar, Strauss, and Giroux, 2008), 17.

terrorist nuclear attack."[22] Deterrence may not be dead, but it certainly will require different tools to enforce.

Towards a Post-Westphalian Doctrine and Strategy

A statement of doctrine[23] that centers on post-Westphalian threats could be captured as follows:

Certain terrorist groups have moved from traditional motives of influencing states and drawing attention to causes within states, to broader, ill-defined apocalyptic ends in which they seek to kill on the largest scale possible. Their goals could be linked to a broader end-state such as the establishment of a global caliphate, but could also be linked to nothing coherent at all. These groups can form rapidly, are often inspired by a virtual world of grievances and rage, are generally non-hierarchical, and can be very resilient in their structure.

This new motivation by some terrorist groups to kill broadly is occurring at a time when traditional constraints on the development of biological and nuclear weapons are loosening, due to the slow but steady proliferation of the weapons themselves to unstable states, and the increasing availability of the knowledge to produce such weapons. The single most compelling danger the United States and the world will face in the coming decade is the convergence of

---

[22] Jenkins, *Will Terrorists Go Nuclear?*, 372.

[23] One of the more distressing outtakes from the CENSA survey was a lack of agreement on the difference between strategy and doctrine and the relationship between the two; participants were split evenly on whether doctrine derives from strategy or the reverse. For our purposes, I will follow Webster and common practice. The dictionary definition of doctrine is "a statement of fundamental government policy, especially in international relations," while strategy is "the science and art of employing the political, economic, psychological, and military forces of a nation or group of nations to afford the maximum support to adopted policies in peace or war." If doctrine is the statement of policy, and strategy offers support to the policy, doctrine trumps strategy, even grand strategy.

weapons of atomized destructive power and apocalyptic terrorist groups. Keeping the ultimate weapons out of the hands of terrorists is the first priority of our national security institutions.

Decisive measures must be taken in the short-term to continue to eliminate the possible circulation of weapons and weapons-grade material, while curtailing the appeal and the operating space of terrorist groups. In the medium-term, these interests will best be met by strengthening the nation-state system and ensuring that it retains a monopoly on the use of force. From this constellation of stronger individual states, more viable international organizations will be possible, strengthening the Westphalian system broadly. This strengthened system is key to advancing U.S. interests in the world and managing impending threats.[24]

---

[24] For reference, the rough equivalent from NSC-68 reads as follows: "For several centuries it had proved impossible for any one nation to gain such preponderant strength that a coalition of other nations could not in time face it with greater strength. The international scene was marked by recurring periods of violence and war, but a system of sovereign and independent states was maintained, over which no state was able to achieve hegemony. Two complex sets of factors have now basically altered this historical distribution of power. First, the defeat of Germany and Japan and the decline of the British and French Empires have interacted with the development of the United States and the Soviet Union in such a way that power has increasingly gravitated to these two centers. Second, the Soviet Union, unlike previous aspirants to hegemony, is animated by a new fanatic faith, antithetical to our own, and seeks to impose its absolute authority over the rest of the world. Conflict has, therefore, become endemic and is waged, on the part of the Soviet Union, by violent and non-violent methods in accordance with the dictates of expediency. With the development of increasingly terrifying weapons of mass destruction, every individual faces the ever-present possibility of annihilation should the conflict ever enter the phase of total war. . . In summary, we must, by means of a rapid and sustained build-up of the political, economic, and military strength of the free world, and by means of an affirmative program intended to wrest the initiative from the Soviet Union, confront it with convincing evidence of the determination and ability of the free world to frustrate

Reducing the Availability of the Weapons...

An immediate strategy for implementing this doctrine would have two main lines of effort. The first is to reduce the availability of weapons of atomized destructive power. This is hardly an area wanting for attention; it has been the topic of intense congressional scrutiny, several fruitful commissions, and it is near the top of every Administration's "in-box." Graham Allison,[25] Brian Michael Jenkins,[26] and Michael Levi[27] offer road maps, bolstered recently by the work of Mohammed ElBaradei, the head of the International Atomic Energy Agency (IAEA).[28]

These proposals cover a number of areas, each full of subsets, making for a very expansive plan of action overall. They include ways to:

1) Strengthen intelligence capabilities
2) Improve counterterrorism capabilities and strategy
3) Destroy any groups suspected of moving towards nuclear weapons
4) Create a multilayered defense (Bobbitt also advocates "making our infrastructure more slippery, more redundant, more versatile, and more difficult to attack")
5) Reduce nuclear arsenals

---

the Kremlin design of a world dominated by its will." (NSC-68, 4 and 64-65.)

[25] Graham Allison, *Nuclear Terrorism: The Ultimate Preventable Catastrophe* (New York: Times Books, 2004), 15.

[26] Jenkins, *Will Terrorists Go Nuclear?*, 376-377.

[27] Michael Levi, *On Nuclear Terrorism*, (Harvard: Council on Foreign Relations, 2007), 141.

[28] Mohamed ElBaradei, *The Age of Deception: Nuclear Deception in Treacherous Times*, (New York: Metropolitan Books, 2011).

---

6) Improve safeguards of nuclear stocks
7) Strengthen international cooperation and institutions, especially in non-proliferation efforts, and the safeguarding of highly enriched uranium
8) Reinforce state accountability for what emanates from their territory
9) Conduct a humble foreign policy

Most of these thinkers agree with Levi, who believes that "no defense can eliminate nuclear terrorism: as long as we continue to live with nuclear weapons and materials, eradicating nuclear terrorism will not be an option."[29] But they consider choosing and pursuing the right strategy key to reducing our vulnerability and the odds of attack.

...and the Operating Space of Terrorists

The second imperative is to reduce the operating space of terrorists. Any strategy to eliminate terrorist threats must include both hunting down active terrorists, and reducing the breeding ground for new terrorists. The art of counterterrorism is managing these two competing lines of effort so that they support, rather than undermine, each other.

On the first issue, of capturing or destroying the immediate threat, much has been learned over the past decade, and our ability to track, detain, and eliminate terrorists has been vastly enhanced. But the field is ever evolving. A new proposal put forward by Sebestyen Gorka is for a "super-purple" force, in which institutional barriers are eliminated and a more seamless interagency force is built.[30] Until law enforcement, intelligence, operations, and

---

[29] Levi, *On Nuclear Terrorism*, 152.
[30] Gorka, "International Cooperation as a Tool in Counterterrorism."

diplomacy are more closely intertwined, dangerous gaps will remain. Once the U.S. has mastered the concept of "super purple," it should take on the challenge of "international super-purple," and include other friendly services in joint counterterrorism teams.

The second issue centers largely on reducing the rage in the Islamic world or — insofar as possible — ensuring that such rage is channeled away from direct attacks on America and its allies. In *The Crusades Through Arab Eyes*,[31] an insightful work on the clash between Islamic and Christian society that still resonates today, Lebanese author Amin Maloof describes how a series of military campaigns that to the West are but a historical footnote, remain a cultural touchstone in the Islamic world today. Along these same lines, Pascual, Jones, and Stedman believe that Al Qaeda has evolved as a movement defined by its political and cultural anti-Americanism, and "is attracting ever more recruits, not to a central organization, not even to Salafist jihad, but to the cause of standing up for Islam against the United States."[32] Cato's Ivan Eland argues, in his 1998 essay, "The Best Defense is to Give No Offense,"[33] that the way to roll back this rage and reduce American vulnerability to super-terrorism is to curtail America's interventions. Through the interventions in Iraq and Afghanistan — shaded by images of Muslim humiliation and offense in a series of cultural blunders from Abu Ghraib to anti-Mohammed preacher Terry Jones — American neutrality has, for a large part of the globe, been erased. With access to a full range of information, building on centuries of Western

---

[31] Amin Maloof, *The Crusades Through Arab Eyes*, (London: Al Saqi Books, 1985).

[32] Carlos Pascual, Bruce Jones, Stephen John Stedman, *Power and Responsibility: Building International Order in an Era of Transnational Threats*, (Washington, D.C.: Brookings Institution Press, 2009), 210.

[33] Ivan Eland, "Protecting the Homeland: The Best Defense is to Give no Offense," CATO Policy Analysis No. 306, May 5, 1998.

enlightenment, and balanced by first-hand knowledge of Muslim freedoms and success in the West, these negative images can be explained and moderated. But few madrassa-educated young men have these sorts of balancing factors, and so are left only with what they are fed, a theme brilliantly taken up by Ahmed Rashid in his work on the Afghan Taliban.[34]

There is no substitute for taking known terrorist leaders out of the fight, by whatever means available. And there will be a time for liberating, or supporting the liberation of Muslim societies. But occupations, when they are necessary, should be internationally sanctioned, well managed, and brief, such that America does not bear the brunt of the liberated country's frustration.

Back to the State

Over the longer term, what has become clear in the past ten years of conflict is the importance of viable, sovereign states that have the capacity to secure territory and control extremist groups directly, confronting issues such as jihadism within their own cultural context.

The imperative of strong and viable states to control material and ideological threats was one of the core conclusions Michael Ignatieff drew from his observations of the conflict zones of the 1990s: "More than development, more than aid or emergency relief, more than peacekeepers, these societies need states, with professional armies under the command of trained leaders... The police and armies of the

---

[34] Ahmed Rashid treats this topic brilliantly in *Taliban: Military Islam, Oil and Fundamentalism in Central Asia* (London: I.B. Tauris & Co Ltd, 2000), see esp. p. 111. He suggests that the Taliban's policies toward women were largely a product of a generation of young men raised in isolation from their communities, shuttled between Madrassas and war.

nation-state remain the only available institutions we have ever developed with the capacity to control and channel large-scale human violence."[35]

Ashraf Ghani puts it in broader terms: "Security organizations recognize that crumbling states are at the root of ongoing conflicts, terrorism, and expanding networks of criminality that traffic in drugs, arms, and people."[36] And Francis Fukuyama, writing in 2004, concluded that "for the post-September 11 period, the chief issue for global politics will not be how to cut back on stateness but how to build it up." The art of state-building, he writes, "will be a key component of national power, as important as the ability to deploy traditional military force to the maintenance of world order."[37]

The present question for U.S. policymakers is whether, even after accepting that stronger states would be helpful, we are in a position to bring this about. Before 9/11, Americans had a love-hate relationship with state-building, one that stemmed from recent memories of perceived failed attempts, such as in Viet Nam and Somalia. Nonetheless, the premise of helping build institutions in support of a functional state was difficult to ignore immediately after 9/11, as the road followed by the perpetrators of those attacks traveled through a largely dysfunctional Afghanistan. This dialogue was quickly truncated by policymakers such as Eliot Abrams, who circulated a paper "asserting that peacekeeping [as a first step to state-building in a place like Afghanistan] was...a failed

---

[35] Michael Ignatieff, *The Warrior's Honor: Ethnic War and the Modern Conscience*, (New York: Henry Holt and Company, 1997), 159-160.

[36] Ashraf Ghani and Clare Lockhart, *Fixing Failed States: A Framework for Rebuilding a Fractured World*, (Oxford: Oxford University Press, 2008), 4.

[37] Francis Fukuyama, *State-Building: Governance and World Order in the 21st Century*, (Ithaca: Cornell University Press, 2004), 120-121.

concept, one that had been tried and found wanting throughout the 1990s."[38]

After later reversing course and engaging in the two largest state-building efforts in U.S. history, we are currently experiencing yet another visceral negative reaction to the process, as a result of frustration at how things have turned out. Dr. Colin Gray captures this well: "Nations cannot be built...by well-meaning but culturally arrogant foreign social scientists, no matter how well intentioned and methodologically sophisticated... If insurgents, terrorists, or pirates are a serious threat to international order and American national security, they must be neutralized...even if only for a while. Truly lasting societal reconstruction is certainly not a practicable option; we have to settle for what is good enough for today and the near-term future."[39]

This line of thinking, according to *The New Yorker's* Ryan Lizza, is supported by the current ten-year defense budget, which will "shift the Pentagon away from planning for the types of multi-year nation-building exercises that America undertook in Iraq and Afghanistan," focusing instead on less ambitious policies such as "targeted assassination of Al Qaeda leaders by teams of Navy Seals and Predator drones...[while] cooperating closely with Israel to develop stuxnet."[40]

The question is whether this will be adequate in a world where ungoverned territories allow such tremendous opportunities for terrorists. The U.S. National Strategy for Counterterrorism would seem to come down in favor of state-building, declaring, "We will build the will and capacity of states whose weaknesses al-Qa'ida exploits... Our challenge is

---

[38] James F. Dobbins, *After the Taliban: Nation-Building in Afghanistan*, (Washington, D.C.: Potomac Books, 2008), 130.

[39] Colin S. Gray, "Concept Failure," *Prism*, Volume 3, No. 3, (June 2012): 29.

[40] Ryan Lizza, "The Second Term," *The New Yorker*, June 18, 2012, 54-55.

to break this cycle of state failure to constrict the space available to terrorist networks."[41]

This convoluted relationship with state-building will not be solved any time soon, and will likely always be subject to the whims of domestic political debates within the U.S. But we should be careful in such debates not to choose that which is expedient in the short term over that which is crucial in the long term. And we should not confuse things we have done poorly with things that cannot be done at all. Former Special Envoy for Somalia, Haiti, the Balkans and Afghanistan, Ambassador James Dobbins, has produced meticulous work on state-building, in which he points out that the Abrams piece cited above was "entirely counterfactual."

"By 2002," he writes, "tens of millions of people in such places as Namibia, Cambodia, Mozambique, El Salvador, East Timor, Sierra Leone, Albania, Bosnia, Kosovo, and Macedonia were living at peace—and for the most part under freely elected governments—because U.N., NATO, American or European troops had come in, separated combatants, disarmed contending factions, rebuilt the country, held elections, installed new governments, and stayed around long enough to watch them take root." Dobbins' careful analysis shows that viable state-building, if properly planned, resourced, and internationalized with a full commitment, can indeed work.[42]

---

[41] The White House, *National Strategy for Counterterrorism*, June 2011, 9.

[42] See James Dobbins, John G. McGinn, Keith Crane, Seth G. Jones, Rollie Lal, Andrew Rathmell, Rachel M. Swanger, and Anga R. Timilsina. *America's Role in Nation-Building: From German to Iraq*, (Santa Monica, CA: Rand Corporation, 2003). Also James Dobbins, Seth G. Jones, Keith Crane, Andrew Rathmell, Brett Steele, Richard Teltschik, Anga Timilsina, *The UN's Role in Nation-Building: From Congo to Iraq*, (Santa Monica, CA: Rand Corporation, 2005).

And Stronger State Institutions

This is not, however, to say that we simply need to apply ourselves to the task of state-building in order to be successful. We have few standing tools for the mission, and most of the successful cases were conducted in an ad hoc fashion that relied as much on luck as skill. We would benefit from new tools to guide states toward both improved political cohesion and better public administration.

Public administration as a focus for a doctrine countering nuclear terrorism might seem like a stretch. But it is the institutions of governance that help fill the spaces on the map where weapons and terrorists may move and flourish. It is fundamental to success that we get better at implanting good governance. There is a need for trained, organized, and experienced international civil servants to be able to deploy to provide a kind of "shadow government," backing up and mentoring the ranks of the newly appointed civil service of a reconstituting state, until that state can stand on its own. To date, this has been handled in a very ad hoc way, perhaps best exemplified by the reliance on military officers to fill the vast majority of mentoring positions for ministries in Afghanistan, even in areas far afield of the officers' expertise. Institution building should be a standing deployable capacity built on a military model. Also useful would be an International Public Administration Academy, where newly selected civil servants could go for training, as well as a standing capacity to quickly implant such academies within post-conflict states.

Similarly, we do not have a standing capacity to build security institutions, backed up by solid doctrine and organizational responsibility; the recent cost for this void has been catastrophic. After the initial missed opportunity for effectively training and equipping security forces in Iraq and

Afghanistan,[43] we shifted large numbers of personnel to this mission, where progress has been steady if uneven. But all the training institutions we have built to deliver this assistance are one-time organizations that are disbanded when their mission finishes; we still lack the institutional means to rapidly train, equip, and mentor the full gamut of law enforcement, judicial, and security institutions. This systematic failure has led to the current generation of U.S. soldiers being in combat longer than any generation in our history, in places where local security forces could be engaged for $20 a day.

Shifting some of our combat and law enforcement power (and the resources attached to them) to developing a <u>standing capacity</u> to build combat power and establish security forces for new allies, would pay incredible dividends going forward. We need a Civilian Security Assistance Agency, with full time personnel, resources, and facilities to quickly and decisively build law enforcement, judicial, and intelligence institutions in struggling states, alongside a newly empowered Defense Security Assistance Agency, that commands a division worth of trainers and stores of equipment ready to be deployed to build capacity in proxies, allies, and friendly institutions.

Concluding Thoughts

A certain Jason Epstein responded, in a recent *New York Review of Books,* to a review by Christian Caryl of two works on unmanned aerial vehicles (UAVs).[44] Caryl had raised the possibility that "the United States cannot rest on the assumption that it will retain a monopoly over this technology

---

[43] The initial effort to train the Afghan security forces was assigned to a Special Forces B Team, normally reserved to advise a brigade; equipment was solicited from the 1970s stocks of the Warsaw Pact nations.

[44] Christian Caryl, letter to the editor, "Predators and Robots at War," *New York Review of Books,* September 29, 2011.

forever. The day when U.S. forces are attacked by a drone — perhaps even one operated by a terrorist — is not far away."

Epstein goes on to ask, "What if some of these forty-odd countries at work on UAV's were to create swarms of such vehicles, each component armed with a miniaturized nuclear weapon aimed, for example, at the United States or China? Would this not realize the fantasies of infuriated prepubescents to destroy not merely their classmates but all life on earth? Is it wise to entrust our frustrated and easily enraged species with such armaments? Or is it no longer possible to keep these terminal weapons out of our hands? Is the situation like climate change, a once preventable calamity, but now no longer in our control?" I have watched all seven seasons of 24 and think about this sort of thing constantly, but must confess I never entertained drones with nukes. New technologies, supporting unfettered rage, will undoubtedly continue to lead to new and threatening scenarios.

Jonathan Schell's 1982 *New Yorker* essay "The Fate of the Earth"[45] was published as a book by Stanford University Press, just prior to 9/11. Regardless of how one feels about Schell's abolitionist policy prescriptions, the comprehensiveness and passion he brings to the nuclear dialogue is compelling. In a more recent essay, "New Weapons and the Real Twentieth Century,"[46] Schell brings the issue up to date, arguing that the world's relatively recent liberal order is more fragile than many concede. It is fragile because just beneath the surface of this global order is the capacity for nations to exterminate whole cities. Containing the spread of that capacity to sub-national groups could – more than any single issue -- define our ultimate success as a

---

[45] Jonathan Schell, *The Fate of the Earth and The Abolition*, (Redwood City, CA: Stanford University Press, 2000).

[46] Jonathan Schell, *The Unfinished Century and the Crisis of Weapons of Mass Destruction*, (Brooklyn, NY: Verso, 2003).

civilization. Since Norwegian commandos attacked the heavy water plant at Vemork to destroy Hitler's access to enriched uranium, we have been involved in a race to contain the world's worst weapons. It is a race that will never end, and we would do well to pick up the pace.

How to Defeat Al Qaeda[1]

*Sebastian L. v. Gorka**

Introduction

The year 2013 saw the 12th anniversary of the horrendous terrorist attacks of September 11, 2001. Al Qaeda's religiously-motivated murder of almost 3,000 people on that sunny Tuesday morning led directly to military operations in Afghanistan and then Iraq, which together have made up the longest American military engagement since 1776. We are still fighting a war that has already outlasted our combat in Korea, World War II and even Vietnam. While the mastermind behind the September 11th attacks is dead - thanks to the courage and audacity of the U.S. military and intelligence community - the war is not over, and the enemy is not vanquished. At the twelve-year mark of this war, there remain two disturbing truths that the American policy elite has yet to recognize or understand:

---

[1] This article is based in part upon the author's testimony to the House Armed Services Committee, Sub-Committee on Emerging Threats and Capabilities, June 22, 2011. The full testimony can be read at http://armedservices.house.gov/index.cfm/files/serve?File_id=127215 8c-1011-4dcc-aae3-c8002ec14630 and the video is available at http://www.youtube.com/watch?v=gfmN86SlpKY.

* The views here expressed do not necessarily reflect the views of the Department of Defense or any other government agency.

Stunning tactical successes, no matter how numerous, do not necessarily lead to strategic victory.

The second related point is that today, more than a decade after September 11th, America still does not fully understand the nature of the enemy that most threatens U.S. citizens, and thus the United States' strategic response is undermined.

Know the Enemy

One of the more important reasons for the lack of an effective response to al Qaeda is that a clear and overarching strategy for the post-9/11 era is lacking. While we have been given first the Global War on Terror (GWOT) and then the Long War, and now Overseas Contingency Operation, or O.C.O., we are still looking for the new George Kennan, who will write the new version of the Long Telegram which can be used to formulate a strategic doctrine on par with the Cold War's containment policy[2]. Without a strategic-level doctrine, it would be very difficult to execute an effective response to any significant threat.

After World War II (WWII), our ability to effectively communicate what the stakes of the confrontation were, why America had to act, and what we wished to achieve were much improved. There were several reasons for this. Communication is best when it clearly demonstrates values. Thus in the late 1940s, after four years of engagement in a global war against a totalitarian enemy, America's values were clear. In subsequent years, after thirty years of the Soviet Union's existence, the values of the enemy were not obtuse or difficult to grasp. With the Berlin Blockade, the launch of

---

[2] The Council for Emerging National Security Affairs has compiled a survey of national security practitioners and academics judging the various potential doctrines that have already been penned, but have not yet won universal adoption by the Administration. For details see The Search for Mr. X at www.censa.net.

Sputnik and the first Soviet atomic test, it was clear that the game was one of survival, of Them or Us. The enemy was clearly an enemy; we knew what the other side was capable of, what they wanted and, most important of all, the previous four years had shown us who we were. But the post-9/11 period has been different.

During the hazy days of post-Cold War peace dividends, our previous enemy had been vanquished, or rather had become our 'friend.' Therefore, it was more difficult to remember what America and the West stood for. The attack on 9/11 itself came as a huge surprise. Despite the 1993 World Trade Center (WTC) bombing, the USS Cole attack, and the several embassy bombings, we did not appreciate the scale of the threat against us. We didn't comprehend the intention of the enemy, and we underestimated his true capabilities. Even after 9/11 we have been obstructed in our understanding of our foe by the fact that his motivation is not simply political or rational, but is religiously informed and indifferent to the logic of nation-state behavior. It is thanks to this confusion that today when you ask someone anywhere in the world whom they associate with the word 'Caliphate' they will often reply with the name of Osama bin Laden. If you ask the same person which person or country they associate with the words 'democracy' or 'liberty,' the answer might not be the United States. By contrast, not so long ago the word association of 'democracy' or 'liberty' with the United States would almost certainly have been a foregone conclusion

To simplify matters, and given the urgency of the task, we can boil the communications task down into three fundamental questions the United States and its allies must answer if they are to have any chance of building a coherent strategic approach which can delegitimize Al Qaeda. These are:

1) Who is the enemy? The answer to this question should be short and simple.
2) Who are We? What do we believe in and what do we stand for as a nation and what do we require of other nations that hold themselves to be part of the community of peace-loving and freedom-loving countries?
3) What are the core values that inform our behavior and our policies, and which are not negotiable?

Given the weakness of strategic communications, or the clarity of messaging, to date, I would suggest one additional twist. At the moment, it would be a waste to spend significantly more money trying to make the United States or the West look good in the eyes of non-Western audiences. An improved image will come only when we are judged by our actions. Instead, we should focus on making the enemy look 'bad.' Why is it, for example, that since 9/11 al Qaeda has been responsible for the death of far more Muslims than Westerners? This is the type of issue that should be at the heart of our counter-narrative assault on al Qaeda.

There is, however, one more important point, which all the discussion of strategic communications in the last seven years has omitted. While it's true that we were much better at strategic communications (or rather propaganda and political warfare) during the Cold War, there is a very important reason for this. When America established tools such as Voice of America, Radio Liberty and Radio Free Europe, it was targeting a completely different audience from the prospective audience of today. For the most part, citizens of the captive nations behind the Iron Curtain were not staunch Communists who had to be converted through these broadcasts. The people of Hungary, Poland, East Germany, the Baltic states and others believed in democracy, and they longed to be free. They didn't tune into U.S.-funded broadcasts because they wanted to be converted to the American value system. They were already pro-American and simply wanted access to information denied them by their illegitimate masters. This is not the case today. Yesterday the audience was with us, but captive. Today, the audience may be suffering under a less than democratic regime or an authoritarian government but that does not mean they are necessarily on our side. The Cold War may have been about winning "hearts and minds," but today we must win "hearts and souls."

After Abbottabad - America and the Strategic Principles of Counterterrorism

The special operations raid against Osama bin Laden in Abottabad will clearly become the textbook example of how perfectly to execute high-risk military operations in the post-9/11 world. In locating and killing Osama bin Laden on foreign soil, America has again demonstrated its peerless capacity at the tactical and operational level. Nevertheless, as the supreme military thinker Sun Tsu taught, "Tactics without strategy is simply the noise before defeat," and it is my firm conviction that the last ten years of this conflict have lacked the strategic guidance that a threat of the magnitude of transnational terrorism demands.

This can be illustrated with one simple observation. Since the escalation of the Iraqi insurgency in 2004, the subsequent rewriting and rapid application of the U.S. Army/USMC Field Manual 3-24 on Counterinsurgency, and the release of General Stanley McChrystal's report on operations in Afghanistan, Washington has persisted in calling our approach to the threat in theater a "Counterinsurgency Strategy." (In fact, a basic Internet search on the term "Counterinsurgency Strategy" yields more than 300,000 results). This is despite the fact that counterinsurgency has always been, and will always be, a doctrinal approach to irregular warfare, and never a strategic solution to any kind of threat.

In a mechanical sense, Strategy explains how one matches resources and methods to ultimate objectives. But grand strategy must also explain the *why* of war, never simply the operational *how to* of war. The fact that even official bodies can repeatedly make the mistake of blurring this distinction so many years into this fight indicates that we are breaking cardinal rules of how to realize America's national security interests.

With regard to the requirement to understand the enemy, let me share a personal experience. Several years after September 11th, I was invited to address a senior group of Special Operations officers on the last day of a three-day event analyzing progress in the conflict. As I rose to speak on the final day, I told the assembled officers – all of whom had just returned from the theater of operations or were about to deploy there – that I would have to discard my prepared comments. The reason was that for 2½ days I had witnessed brave men risking their lives debate with each other and us, the invited guests, the identity of the enemy and asking whether or not al Qaeda is an organization, a movement, a network, or an ideology. This, I said, would be akin to U.S. officers having debated each other in 1944 over the question of what the Third Reich was, or what Nazism actually represented. The plain fact of the matter is that we have failed, institutionally, to meet our duty to become well-informed about our enemy's strategic and operational approach, or "Threat Doctrine." Without a clear understanding of Enemy Threat Doctrine, victory is likely impossible.

The reasons for our paucity of understanding in this area are many. In the preceding section we discussed functional problems. But most of these stem from two serious and connected obstacles of strategic magnitude. The first is a misguided belief that the religious character of the enemy's ideology should not be discussed, and that we need not address it, but should instead use the phrase "Violent Extremism" to describe our foe, thus avoiding any unnecessary unpleasantness. The second is that, even if we could demonstrate clear-headedness on the issue and accurately recognize the religious ideology of al Qaeda and its associate movements as a form of hybrid totalitarianism, we still drastically lack the institutional ability to analyze and comprehend its worldview and strategic mindset or understand its ultimate objectives.

A careful look at the past can help us grasp the importance of understanding the enemy, and why such an understanding is crucial within the U.S. national security establishment. It is now well recognized that not until 1946, with the writing of George Kennan's classified "Long Telegram" (later republished as The Sources of Soviet Conduct under the pseudonym "X"), did America begin to understand the nature of the Soviet Union (USSR), why it acted the way it did, how the Kremlin thought, and why the USSR was an existential threat to America.[3] Consider now the fact that this document was written three decades after the Russian Revolution, and that despite all the scholarship and analysis available in the United States at the time, it took more than a generation to penetrate the mind of the enemy and come to a point where a counter-strategy could be formulated. Now add to this the fact that today our enemy is not a European secular nation-state, as was the USSR, but a non-European, religiously-informed, non-state terrorist group, and we see the magnitude of the challenge. While initiatives such as the U.S. Army's Human

---

[3] The declassified text of Kennan's original cable can be found at http://www.ntanet.net/KENNAN.html. The pseudonymous article he later wrote for a broader audience in Foreign Affairs is at http://www.historyguide.org/europe/kennan.html.

Terrain System (HTS) and the teams it provides to theater commanders are well-meant efforts in the direction of trying to understand the enemy's nature and environmental context, the initiatives still miss the mark on more than one level.

To begin with, if we rely solely upon anthropologists and social scientists, as the HTS does, it is very difficult, if not impossible, to provide the contextual knowledge we need to understand and defeat our enemy. Today our multi-disciplinary analysis of the enemy and his doctrine equally requires the expertise of the regional historian and the theologian, the specialist who knows when and how Sunni Islam split from Shia Islam and what the difference is between the Meccan and Medinan verses of the Koran. We should ask ourselves, honestly, how many national security practitioners know the answers to these questions, or at least know where to turn, within government, to provide such essential expertise.

Secondly, after nearly a decade of experience and consideration we must take the counsel of the 9/11 Commission seriously in recognizing that the threat environment itself has changed beyond the capacity of our legacy national security structures to deal with it.

In the case of how two of the 9/11 hijackers (Nawaf al-Hamzi and Khalid al-Midhar) were flagged as threats and still permitted to enter the United States legally, we see proof of how our national security structures do not live up to the threat our new enemies represent. This problem is not unique to the United States, but is a product of what the academic world calls the Westphalian system of nation-states and how we are structured to protect ourselves.

For the 350 years since the Treaty of Westphalia that ended the religious wars of Europe, Western nations developed and perfected national security architectures that were predicated on an institutional division of labor and discrete categorization of threats. Internally, we had to maintain constitutionality as well as order. Externally, we had to deal with the threat of aggression by another state. As a result, all our countries divided the national security task-set into separate conceptual and functional baskets: internal versus external, military versus non-military. And this system worked very well for three and half centuries, while nation-states fought other nation-states during the age of so-called 'conventional warfare.' However, as Philip Bobbitt masterfully describes in his book, The Shield of Achilles, that age is behind us. Al Qaeda, Al Shabaab, or even the Muslim Brotherhood cannot be forced into analytic boxes that are military or non-military, or into internal or external threat categories.[4] The leaders of the Western world must recognize the hard truth that the threat environment is no longer primarily defined by the state-actor.

Take, for example, the case of the most successful al Qaeda attack on U.S. soil since 9/11, the massacre at Fort Hood, Texas. On November 5, 2009, a Major serving in the U.S. Army decided that his loyalty lay with his Muslim co-religionists and not his nation, or his branch of service. He was recruited, encouraged, and finally blessed in his actions by Anwar al-Awlaki, a U.S. citizen turned-Muslim cleric hiding out in Yemen. Just before Major Hasan was about to be deployed into theater, he instead chose the path of Holy War against a so-called infidel and slew thirteen and wounded thirty-one of his fellow servicemen, their family members, and colleagues on the largest U.S. Army base in the United States.

How Westphalian was this deadly attack by al Qaeda? What does it have to do with conventional warfare? Was this

---

[4] Philip Bobbitt, *The Shield of Achilles – War, Peace and the Course of History* (New York, N.Y.: Random House, 2002). In "The Age of Irregular Warfare – So What?," *Joint Forces Quarterly*, Issue 58, (3rd Quarter, 2010): 32-38, I take the discussion further and discuss just how different this post-Westphalian threat environment is and how we need to reappraise key Clausewitzian aspects of the analysis of war.

threat external or internal in nature? Was it a military attack or a non-military one? As you can see, the conceptual frameworks and capabilities that served us so well through the last century fail us today. As a result, we must develop new methodologies to analyze the threats to our nation and new ways to bridge the conventional gaps between government and agency departments and their respective mindsets -- gaps that are so deftly exploited by groups such al Qaeda.[5] We must recognize that the master of military strategy, Carl von Clausewitz, wrote his *meisterwerk* in the context of state-on-state war. His trinity of government, people, and military, and the related characteristics or reason, passion, and skill do not obtain in the realm of irregular warfare as they do in conventional war (see Figure 1). Today the enemy is more flexible and is not driven by rational conceptualizations of *raison d'etat*.

The paradox of al Qaeda is that while we have, during the last ten years, been incredibly successful in militarily degrading its operational capacity to do us harm, al Qaeda has become even more powerful in the domain of ideological warfare and other indirect forms of attack. While bin Laden may be dead, the narrative of religiously-motivated global revolution that he embodied is very much alive and growing in popularity.[6] And while we have crippled al Qaeda's

[5] For a discussion of how to bridge these gaps institutionally and conceptually and so be able to defeat the new types of threat we face see the concept "Super-Purple" described in my chapter "International Cooperation as a Tool in Counterterrorism: Super-Purple as a Weapon to Defeat the Nonrational Terrorist," in, Christopher C. Harmon, Andrew N. Pratt and Sebastian L. v. Gorka, eds., *Toward a Grand Strategy Against Terrorism*, (New York, N.Y.: McGraw Hill, 2011), 71-83.

[6] For the rise of Jihadi ideology and what should be done in response, see Sebastian L. v. Gorka: "The Surge that Could Defeat Al Qaeda," ForeignPolicy.Com, August 10, 2009. Available at: http://www.foreignpolicy.com/articles/2009/08/10/the_one_surge_that_could_defeat_al_qaeda.

capacity to execute mass casualty attacks with its own assets on the mainland of the United States, we see that its message holds traction with individuals prepared to take the fight to us individually, as in the incidents involving Major Hasan, Faisal Shahzad, the Times Square attacker, or Umar Farouk Abdulmutallab, the Christmas-Day bomber.

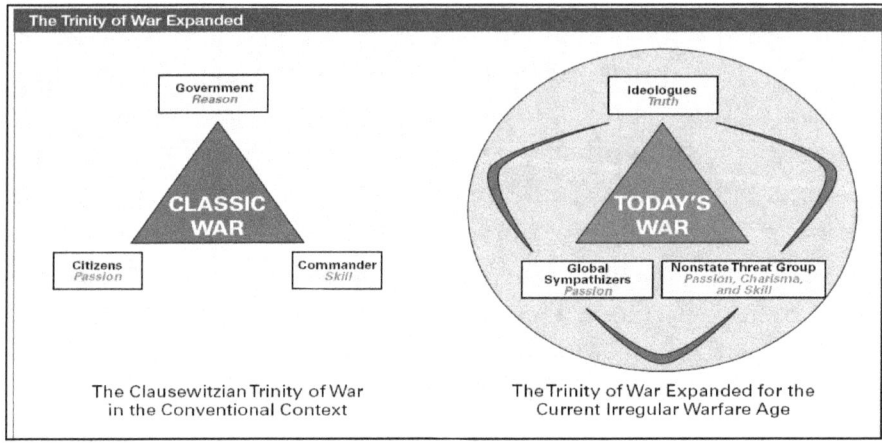

Figure 1: Clausewitz versus Irregular Warfare

Counterterrorism: Beyond the Kinetic

Although we have proven our capacity in the last ten years to engage our enemy kinetically at the operational and tactical level with unsurpassed effectiveness, we have not even begun to take the war to al Qaeda at the strategic level of counter-ideology. To paraphrase Dr. James Kiras of Air University in Alabama, whose views I highly respect, we have denied al Qaeda the capability to conduct complex devastating attacks on the scale of 9/11, but we now need to transition away from concentrating on dismantling and disrupting al Qaeda's network, to undermining its core strategy of ideological attack. We need to employ much more the indirect approach made famous by our community of Special Forces operators: working "by, with, and through" local allies--and moving beyond attacking the enemy directly at the operational and tactical level to attacking it indirectly, at the strategic level.

We need to bankrupt transnational Jihadist terrorism at its most powerful point: its narrative of global religious war. For the majority of the last ten years, the narrative of the conflict has been controlled by our enemy. Just as in the Cold War, the United States must take active measures to arrive at a position where it shapes the agenda and the story of the conflict, where it forces its enemy to be off-balance and perhaps retreat to such an extent that Jihadism would eventually lose all credibility and implode as an ideology. For this to happen, Americans must re-think, from the ground up, the way in which strategic communications and information operations are run across the U.S. government. Additionally, Congress itself will have to work to remove out-dated limitations on our national ability to fight the war of ideas. Such limitations as the Smith-Mundt Act were only effective in an era before the world was connected through modern communications and the Internet.

America's ability to fight al Qaeda and similar transnational terrorist actors will depend upon its capacity to communicate to its citizens and the world what it is fighting for, and exactly what about Jihad ideology is so threatening to the universal values Americans hold so dear. To quote Sun Tsu again, in war it is not enough to know the enemy in order to win. One must first know oneself. During the Cold War, this happened naturally. Given the nature of the Soviet Union and the nuclear threat it clearly posed to the West, every day for four decades—from the first successful Soviet atom-bomb test to the collapse of the USSR in 1991—Americans knew what was at stake and why communism could not be allowed to spread its totalitarian grip beyond the Iron Curtain.

However, with the end of the Cold War and the decade of a so-called peace dividend in the 1990s, America and the West understandably lost clarity about how to guard its way of life, which was precious and worth fighting for. The specter of WWII had been vanquished and the Cold War had been won.

The shock of the September 11th attacks did not, however, automatically return America to a point of clarity. The reasons for this flow from several of the observations I have already made, but also from the fact that its enemy is a religiously-colored one, unlike the secular foe America faced during the Cold War.

Due in part to a misinterpretation of what the Founding Fathers actually meant by "separation of church and state," Americans today have hobbled our capacity to understand and counter this enemy at the strategic level. Based on my experience with military operators stationed abroad, and U.S. law enforcement officers fighting terrorism at home, I submit that many in senior management positions in government have misconstrued the matter to such an extent that religion has become a taboo issue within national threat analysis. This is despite the fact that all those who have brought death to our shores as al Qaeda operatives have done so not out of purely political conviction but because they feel divinely justified and sanctioned by God. If Americans wish to combat the ideology that drives these murderers, we ignore the role of religion at our peril.

The official decision in recent years to use the term "Violent Extremism" to describe the threat is misleading and deleterious to our ability to understand, and defeat, the enemy. America is not at war with all forms of violent extremism. The attacks of September 11th were not the work of a group of terrorists motivated by a generic form of extremism. We are not at war with communists, fascists, or nationalists, but rather with religiously-inspired mass-murderers who consistently misrepresent the Koran in order to justify their actions. Denying this fact simply out of a misguided sensitivity will delay the West's ability to understand the nature of the current conflict and to delegitimize its foe. By analogy, imagine that, in the fight against the Ku Klux Klan, federal law enforcement had been forbidden from describing the group they were trying to neutralize as white supremacists or racists. Imagine that during WWII, for political reasons, we forbade allied forces from understanding the enemy as a Nazi regime fueled and guided by a fascist ideology of racial hatred, but instead insisted on calling the Nazis "violent extremists." We did not do it then and we must not do it now. The safety of America's citizens and our chances of eventual victory depend upon our being able to call the enemy by its proper name: Global Jihadism.[7]

To conclude, the twelve years since September 11, 2001, can be summarized as a vast collection of tactical and operational successes, but the period marks a vacuum in terms of strategic understanding, strategic purpose, and strategic response. To paraphrase a former U.S. Marine who knows the enemy very well (and whom I greatly respect), we have failed to understand the enemy at any more than an operational level and have instead, by default, addressed the enemy solely on the operational plane of engagement. Operationally we have become most proficient at responding to the localized threats caused by al Qaeda, but those localized threats are simply tactical manifestations of what is happening

---

[7] For the best work on understanding the enemy we now face, see Patrick Sookhdeo, *Global Jihad: The Future in the Face of Militant Islam* (McLean, VA: Isaac Publishing, 2007), and the analytic work of Stephen Ulph, including: *Towards a Curriculum for Teaching Jihadist Ideology*, The Jamestown Foundation. Available at: http://www.jamestown.org/single/?no_cache=1&tx_ttnews%5Btt_new s%5D=36999. For an overview of the key thinkers and strategists of Global Jihadi ideology, see Sebastian L. V. Gorka: "Jihadist Ideology: The Core Texts," lecture to the Westminster institute. Audio and transcript available at: http://www.westminster-institute.org/articles/jihadist-ideology-the-core-texts-3/#more-385.

at the strategic level, driven by the ideology of Global Jihad. As a result, by not responding to what al Qaeda has become at the strategic level, we continue to attempt to engage on the wrong battlefield.

The twelfth anniversary of the attacks in Washington, in New York, and in Pennsylvania, afford those in the U.S. government who have sworn to uphold and defend the national interests of this greatest of nations a clear opportunity to recognize what we have accomplished and what needs to be reassessed. All involved must recommit themselves to attacking this deadliest of enemies at the level which it deserves to be, and must be: – the strategic.

Osama bin Laden may be dead, but his ideology of global supremacy through religious war is far more vibrant and sympathetic to audiences around the world than it was on the day before the attacks more than a decade ago. We need to guarantee the conditions by which the executive branch of the U.S. government is able finally to produce a comprehensive understanding of the enemy threat doctrine that is Global Jihadism, a document akin to Kennan's foundational analysis that eventually led to the Truman Doctrine and its exquisite operationalization in Paul Nitze's plan for containment, NSC-68.[8]

After more than a decade into this war, a strategic re-evaluation is justified. I suggest four principles to guide such a reevaluation:[9]

---

[8] The declassified NSC-68, which operationalized George Kennan's enemy threat doctrine analysis of the USSR, is available at:
http://www.airforce-magazine.com/MagazineArchive/Documents/2004/December%202004/1204keeperfull.pdf.

[9] For a lengthier discussion of these principles, see the forthcoming monograph by Gorka, Sloan, and Ishimoto from the Joint Special Operations University, U.S. Special Operations Command.

The United States must suppress the sphere of mobility of al Qaeda and its Associated Movements (AQAM). This war will not end in a neat ceasefire and peace treaty. It must consist of constant pressure against both the will and the capability of Global Jihadists.

The American intelligence and national security communities must invest far greater effort into understanding the historic, economic, social and political factors that AQAM use to mobilize its followers and operators. This is NOT a cause and effect relationship, but a dynamic whereby exploit objective condition through a subject mobilizing religious ideology.

This war is no longer simply about hijacked planes, improvised explosive devices or gun-men. Ten years after 9/11 it is perhaps more non-kinetic than it is physical. America must rediscover and deploy the tools it used so effectively in past ideological wars to build a powerful and globally applicable counter-narrative. This narrative must undermine the legitimacy and attractiveness of the enemy, as well as deter potential allies and recruits. America must drive the global agenda of justice and liberty, as it did during WWII and the Cold War.

The American national security establishment must purge itself of well-intentioned but neutering concepts of political correctness and cultural sensitivity concerned about who the enemy is and what it intends. AQAM uses religion not only to win adherents but also to justify mass murder. We must tackle this reality head-on. The religious nature of our enemy's ideology cannot obstruct us from defining and realizing our national interests.

Only if we have an overarching strategic response will America be able to defeat al Qaeda and its associates before the next significant anniversary of 9/11.

Re-evaluating the Role of Information in National Strategy and Policy Making

Amy Zalman

Introduction

This chapter examines the place of information policy in the toolbox available for the execution of U.S. grand strategy. It makes the argument that, despite some bows in the direction of strategic communication in recent national strategy documents, the discipline remains substantially undervalued and underexploited. By means of case studies, the author further argues that this undervaluation has contributed to the travails of the United States in addressing foreign policy challenges, and to the continuing challenges associated with foreign perceptions of "Brand America." The power of information lies in its ability to help shape and alter people's perceptions of themselves and the world around them. We act on the basis of our perceptions; they constitute our reality. Strategy theorists have long recognized the power that lies in one's ability to influence the perceptions of others. In 1947, Hans Morgenthau defined the ability to "control minds and wills" as the fundamental basis of power in international relations. In the early 1990s, Joseph Nye argued that a version of attractive power that mobilized ideas and public sentiment was in the ascendant.[1] John Arquilla and David Ronfeldt predicted in 1999 that the rising importance of a "still inchoate" information strategy would reshape established arenas of political, economic and military power as "the world is turning anew into a highly charged battleground of ideas" in which "the key to success will likely lie in managing informational capabilities and resources skillfully—i.e., strategically."[2]

Currently, the most prominent articulation of a role for information in U.S. foreign policy may be found in the 2010 National Security Strategy (NSS), which proposes that the United States must "do a better job understanding the attitudes, opinions, grievances and concerns of people," as well as a better job "understanding how our actions will be perceived."[3]

This suggestion is right on target. It is one that should be fundamental to national security strategy. Yet rather than making precisely this argument, the NSS fails to press home the operational point. It merely observes that these forms of understanding should be used in "developing strategic communication." Rather than giving a core priority to this discipline, it entrenches the perception of strategic communication, typically understood as activities executed through the Undersecretary of Public Diplomacy and Public Affairs, the Broadcasting Board of Governors, and via select activities in the military, as, at best, a marginal activity in the exercise of foreign policy. While it would be difficult to denote, statistically, which foreign policy issues and activities

---

[1] Joseph S. Nye, Jr., *Bound to Lead: the Changing Nature of American Power* (New York: Basic Books, 1991).

[2] John Arquilla and David Ronfeldt, *The Emergence of Noopolitik: Toward an American Information Strategy* (Santa Monica, CA: RAND Corporation, 1999), 1.

[3] Office of the President of the United States, *National Security Strategy* (Washington, DC: Government Printing Office, 2010),) 16.

matter most in Washington's collective unconscious, it is acknowledged anecdotally that communications and public diplomacy rank low and are perceived as 'soft,' and this has negative connotations. The minimal resources allocated to these activities suggests as much.

The framers of this section of the NSS appear to be trying to make up for the repeated debacles in understanding foreign cultures and behaviors that characterized the most active years of the Global War on Terror (GWOT). Among other failures, the United States did not understand its potential reception in Iraq, nor the insurgency that followed the U.S. invasion. Poor understanding of local concerns in Afghanistan, Iraq, and elsewhere led to wasted and counterproductive uses of financial aid intended to improve relations.

Various U.S. statements and actions enraged local sensibilities in ways Americans did not always understand. These included culturally insensitive statements, such as calling the war a "crusade," as well as larger actions, such as what came to be perceived as occupations in Iraq and Afghanistan. Institutionally, the United States has a poor sense of how historical memory shapes contemporary viewpoints. In result, it did not understand how the histories of 19th-century Western imperialism and the post-1967 Israeli occupation of Palestinian lands would influence perceptions of an international coalition presence. As even these well-known examples should make clear, the perceptions of foreign publics are central to how international events unfold. Correspondingly, they should be central to foreign policy planning.

In the rest of this paper, I explain why information and perception are of particular importance in the current strategic landscape, and I present two short cases that I hope will illustrate the degree to which information is important in international affairs today.

Public Perceptions, International Politics and the Redistribution of Power

During the early days of the Westphalian nation-state system, national leaders needed only to take into account the perceptions of other foreign leaders. Wider popular opinion counted for little. Only those in leadership positions had the power to act on their perceptions in a way that would change the direction of diplomacy or war.

Over the course of the 19th and 20th centuries, this situation began to change. The Enlightenment generated (and was generated by) new ideas about the natural rights of men (and, later, women). The printing press enabled the spread of newspapers, and public schools empowered more people to read them. Radio and television, like newspapers before them, encouraged a new sensibility among the masses as they embarked on their daily pursuits, connecting them to causes and to one another far beyond their daily geographic reach. The advent of the information age intensified these trends. As their ability to connect across territorial boundaries grew, people began to develop "global," rather than merely local or national, identities.

By the late 1990s, satellite television had begun making inroads into states' hitherto near absolute capacity to control the information flowing into and out of their own countries, and expanding average citizens' view of the world beyond their national borders. The spread of mobile telephony and Internet access have produced more ways for people to influence one another, and have provided the public of many countries with a means to try to shift decision-maker and public opinion to serve political goals they think are important. These changes in the communication environment have empowered individuals and groups who were previously silent on the political stage, or who had less power to spread their views. Individuals, ad-hoc groups, transnational criminal networks, voluntary associations, religious and other non-government organizations (NGOs) now have the same communication tools as do the government and professional media, although these varied groups can differ in their structural power and the consequent effectiveness at wielding them.

As the 2010 National Security Strategy rightly observes, "Individuals, corporations and civil society play an increasingly important role in shaping events around the world."[4] Similarly, the 2010 Quadrennial Diplomacy and Development Review (QDDR) notes that, "the diplomatic landscape of the 21st century features an increasingly varied set of actors who influence international debates: more states capable of acting on their own diplomatic agenda, a variety of U.S. Government agencies operating abroad, transnational networks, corporates [sic], foundations, non-governmental organizations, religious groups and citizens themselves."[5] Some of these actors have become more powerful almost solely *because* of their new powers of communication; others, such as global firms, media conglomerates, states and cities, are the beneficiaries of profound changes in economies and markets prompted by the information and computing revolution.

This changing landscape presents a baffling scenario for the national security strategist, who must be aware of, and be able to prioritize, the views and persuasive capabilities of a ever growing variety of actors. We will have to find new ways to think about how to calibrate the degree to which actors' power to persuade relates to their overall effectiveness, and how perception and influence through perception work in

---

[4] *National Security Strategy*, 8.
[5] U.S. State Department, "Executive Summary," *Leading Through Civilian Power: the First Quadrennial Diplomacy and Development Review* (Washington, D.C.: GPO, 2010),) v.

networks of multiple actors. Some of these new ways will emerge through trial and error in the international system itself, as both crises and enduring problems present themselves with characteristics of this changed environment.

A critical step in this process—and the focal point of this essay – is the need to reframe our understanding of the strategic landscape. The crowded, multi-actor landscape conveyed by the 2010 QDDR is one on which power's currency is information and influence. Yet the current mainstream conception of how international affairs should be conducted does not describe it that way, as strategy documents such as the NSS make clear.

Instead, there are two discussions held in parallel about information and actors on the strategic landscape, when there should be only one. First, there is discourse about the redistribution of power among a widening, diverse group of actors who function at different levels of organization in the international system. These are characterized as active agents "capable of carrying out their own diplomatic agenda." A second, separate discussion concerns strategic communication, centering on information, understanding, communication, perception, and relationships between the United States and what are described as "target audiences" or "target publics." Such audiences are implicitly characterized as the passive recipients of American communications.

In fact, the active agents with their own diplomatic agendas and the passive audiences who are the recipients of strategic communication, who appear as discrete communities in government discourse, are, in the real world, the same people and organizations. The individuals, citizen groups, NGOs, criminal networks, rising states, inhabitants of crowded cities, rural workers and global corporations who are active participants in global politics and who stymie American policy making are both agents in global politics *and* the recipients of American communications, intended and unintended. An accurately holistic model of the international system would clearly demonstrate the dynamically networked relationships and feedback loops between agents and audiences (and how all actors play both roles).

Once we understand that the "target audiences" of strategic communication are fundamentally the same active agents who are participants in the international system, a couple of other observations fall into place. First, the directive to understand the concerns, attitudes, and grievances is more important than it may at first seem. It is important not simply to understand how such actors respond to American initiatives, but also how their worldview and concerns will shape their approach to participating in the political system. Second, it should become clear that the marginalized arena of strategic communications is an inadequate platform for generating national strategy and policy instruments to address a multi-actor international landscape. The two areas under discussion should be transposed. This is not to say that strategic communication is not a crucial activity in the multi-layered, multi-actor environment under description. It is essential that the United States have a sophisticated understanding of the communications environment, and that the U.S. understands how to deploy communications effectively. But "strategic communication" as a discipline has been rendered a subsidiary activity among others, serving the larger enterprise of foreign policy and strategy even as information, communication, and perception have become central characteristics of the strategic environment. Only after strategists fully appreciate this centrality can the United States begin to effectively incorporate it into policy, rather than include it as an afterthought.

Non-traditional actors and information are fundamental elements in both of the two brief cases to follow. One details a traditional strategic context that involves armed conflict; the second describes the untraditional context of global climate change politics.

Case Study 1: Conventional Foreign Policy Issues – Syria Chemical Weapons

Among modern democracies, states must typically influence two parties in order to win a war: the adversary and the home public, whose consent to the war keeps recruits and funding flowing as needed. So it was for the United States in World War II, during which home audiences were offered a steady diet of Hollywood movies and exhortative posters in support of the war, while enemy Nazis were the object of deception campaigns, such as the large scale Operation Bodyguard, which misled the Germans to believe that the Allied landing would be in Pas de Calais, rather than Normandy. Crucial in those events were communication at various levels and the ability of Allied governments to shape perceptions. Today, this same crucial need can be more difficult to achieve because it is more difficult to keep information within particular borders. In the contemporary environment, it would be possible for the whole world to watch, read, and listen to information designed to generate support by Americans for a war effort.

The specter of Syrian chemical weapons – now asserted by the U.S. Administration to have been deployed by the Assad regime – provides an interesting illustration of how strategic communication can be mobilized in support of a policy aim. For various historical reasons, the idea that chemical weapons are more inhumane than conventional weapons has strong resonance in the West. As a result, chemical weapons are a potent symbol in the discursive battle between the Assad government and Free Syrian Army over whether either has used sarin gas. The United Kingdom, France, Israel, a United Nations Commission, and the U.S. intelligence community have all charged that chemical weapons have been used.

The particularly charged symbolism of chemical weapons may have been what led the Obama Administration to identify such weapons as a 'red line' that would provoke a response from the United States. Chemical weapons have a more specific place in the history of U.S.-Syrian relations, as well. This history goes back a quarter of a century, but had its most recent expression when President George W. Bush included Syria under the umbrella of "rogue nations" at the height of an American concern with the confluence of terrorism and weapons of mass destruction (WMD). As the United States made preparations for the 2003 Iraq invasion, it repeatedly warned Syria about chemical weapons. Following the invasion, the issue of chemical weapons and American irritation with Syrian's loose policing of its Iraqi border were often conflated by the president, Secretary of Defense Rumsfeld, and other administration members, such as John Bolton, Under Secretary of State for Arms Control, who reported in September 2003 that Syria was supporting terrorists and manufacturing WMDs.[6]

At present, the chemical weapons information battle — that is, different actors' efforts to gain advantage from having the threat of chemical weapons interpreted in a way that would serve their aims — has no winners, and the Obama Administration, mindful of the way claims about Iraqi WMD helped lead the United States to war in 2003, has refrained from making outsized gestures on the basis of such information. Nevertheless, history demonstrates that information and the perceptions that it helps drive have a life of their own. When information amasses in certain configurations, it can tip perceptions enough to change policy

---

[6] U.S. Department of State Archive, from records of The United States and the Global Coalition against Terrorism, September 2001-December 2003 (Washington DC: office of the Historian); "Syria Denies it Has Chemical Weapons" *Daily Mail Online*, August 30, 2003.

or provoke crises. For example, American perceptions about events in Vietnam, based on television images, helped bring that war to an end. In a nod to the power of such images, the government prohibited media publication of photos of any war-dead lying in coffins. This prohibition continued from 1991 until 2009, when former Secretary of Defense Robert Gates lifted the ban. Like chemical weapons, flag-draped coffins provide both literal information and resonant symbols.

Some American opinion makers active in policy or media circles seem eager to use the issue of Syrian chemical weapons to "regionalize" the conflict and draw Iran into the discursive fray. These opinion makers are interested in driving American actions related to Iran. In the American public opinion space, the suspected use of chemical weapons has raised Americans' previously low interest levels, suggesting the conceptual potency of "chemical weapons." [7] The addition of potent "memes" such as Al Qaeda, Islamist extremists, Hezbollah, or Iran to the formulation of charges could go in unexpected directions that will constrain options for the U.S. government.

As it stands, the Syria chemical weapons case is an example of how access to the means of mass communication by non-state actors, as well as the greater transparency of the global information environment, are changing the expected rules of international affairs. It is not necessary to think of these changed conditions as being more complex than in the past. Rather, a new element that we do not entirely understand has been introduced: average citizens and other non-state actors are playing forceful roles in international politics, by manipulating information *for the purpose of* affecting perceptions. Lawmakers without sophisticated understanding of the regions about which they must make decisions are particularly susceptible to these maneuvers.

---

[7] Pew Research Center, "Chemical Weapons Charges in Syria Draw a Bit More Public Attention," May 3, 2013.

Recall the Kony 2012 video, in which an unknown NGO created such a powerful video sensation that it prompted congressional representatives to respond with new proposed legislation to fund Special Forces to find Ugandan rebel leader Joseph Kony, even when that may not have been the best response.[8]

Greater transparency also means that American actions are more closely and easily scrutinized. President Obama's declaration of a "red line" and his subsequent failure to act in a recognizable way created a credibility problem that influences how the United States is perceived, in ways that may not be evident, ways that may not have national security consequences that are immediately apparent. In Syria, the charge of a Syrian National Council member that Assad's

---

[8] Recall the Kony 2012 video. Invisible Children, Inc. a U.S.-based NGO, garnered over 30 million views of its video within three days of its release in the spring of 2012 . The video's rapid spread helped the group to reach its goal to pressure the U.S. government to engage military forces to locate Joseph Kony, head of Ugandan rebel militia, the Lord's Resistance Army. One lawmaker who responded to the pressure enthused that "the passion that my constituents…have shown on this issue through social media outlets has made a tremendous difference in raising awareness."
As it happened, however, there were multiple problems and inconsistencies both in the work of the group that created the video and in the basis for their claims: Kony, for example, has not been in Uganda for some years and there are existing Ugandan efforts to address the issue, which led to accusations that the film reinforced Western images of Africa as a country in need of being saved by the West. Detailing the issues that the video raised is beyond the scope of this footnote. Suffice it to say that the response to the film by American lawmakers demonstrated a high degree of vulnerability to an information campaign that appealed to pre-existing values and political frameworks. See Scott Wong, "Joseph Kony Captures Congress' Attention," *Politico*, March 22, 2012. Also see the Huffington Post for a short Joseph Kony documentary: http://www.huffingtonpost.com/2012/03/08/joseph-kony-video-stop-kony_n_1332427.html.

forces "are using weapons of mass destruction...while the international community does nothing"[9] does not represent an existential threat to the United States. But it is worth observing that the red-line-credibility issue is being braided into the collective story of the Syrian uprising, and may shape views in ways that will later affect American-Syrian relations.

The chemical weapons situation demonstrates the degree to which information, communication, and perception rest squarely in the center of policy problems. It reveals the fact that decision-makers should consider information, communication, and perceptions more comprehensively, and thus effectively, when they evaluate the costs and benefits of a potential course of action.

Case Study 2: Problem Solving on a Global Stage — Brazil's rainforests

In addition to traditional strategic issues, 21st century governments must address other complex global problems that can threaten national security, including climate change, transnational crime, global terrorism, and epidemic disease. Complex global problems transcend geopolitical boundaries. They are not linear in progression, which is to say that causes may lie far from their ultimate impact — as HIV and SARS did. Paradoxically, issues whose causes lie beyond the territorial reach of a state are precisely those that may require the most attention. As the severity of global challenges rises, governments may find themselves with a "decreased ability . . . to mitigate [such challenges]." In result, "nongovernmental actors become the advocates of the needs, interests and values of the people at large, thus further undermining the role of

---

[9] "Syrian Regime 'Using Chemical Weapons' in Battle for Homs, *Daily Telegraph* Agency, July 7, 2013.

governments...."[10] The National Intelligence Council's *Global Trends 2030* takes for granted that "the increasing number of players needed to solve major transnational challenges will complicate decision making."[11]

These complications are particularly apparent in efforts to shift the direction of global discourse and shape perceptions. Indeed, information is arguably the primary ground on which competition and conflict over global issues is now fought. In the realm of information, small groups lacking other forms of material power have as much access to public opinion as do the largest states, and large NGOs and transnational corporations are formidable competitors, which have more resources than many states.

Brazilian rainforests are a characteristic example of a complex global problem. Brazilian rainforests are central to the world's environmental health. They absorb carbon dioxide and help regulate the earth's climate and, as home to half of the world's animals and plants, they are crucial to global biodiversity. Yet they are a terrestrial feature of a sovereign state and their disposition is a more direct function of domestic interests and politics than of broader international efforts to limit deforestation and promote reforestation.

The fact that rainforests are on the global agenda at all is a result of efforts to use information to shape global perceptions since the mid-1980s, when the Rainforest Action Network and the Rainforest Alliance were founded. At that time, environmentalism was a fringe activity. Mass communication took place through television and radio broadcast or posted mail; NGOs were just beginning to gain a political voice; and

---

10 Manuel Castells, "The New Public Sphere: Global Civil Society, Networks, and Global Governance," *The ANNALS of the American Academy of Political and Social Science* 616, no. 1 (March 1, 2008): 83.

11 National Intelligence Council (U.S.), *Global Trends 2030: Alternative Worlds* (Washington DC: Office of the Director of National Intelligence, 2012), vii.

private corporations were not visibly active in the public domain for most products. To illustrate the distance traversed in the intervening years: in 1986, the Rainforest Action Network sent its membership a newsletter alerting them to the fact that Coca Cola had plans to "convert 50,000 acres of rain forest to frozen orange juice" and urging opposition. (Coca Cola owns Minute Maid and Simply Orange, and oranges are one of the major crops grown on deforested land).[12] Yet in 2011, Cutrale, a subsidiary of Coca Cola sought and was granted certification of its sustainability practices by the Rainforest Alliance. In the space of twenty-five years, the relationship between an NGO and a commercial firm shifted from one of opposition over deforestation to one of cooperation, and allowed for the non-governmental organization to assume a certifying function — a role traditionally reserved for government.

These new forms of power on the part of non-state actors represent both opportunity and challenge, but in order to understand them, it will be important to understand the way these organizations use information and communication. The values of environmentalism took hold largely in public space, and represented the efforts of environmentalist NGOs and others to introduce new values and integrate existing ones into environmental causes. Private firms, understanding that they could link consumption habits to particular values, also participated in this shift. Tropicana partnered with a non-profit called CoolEarth to offer purchasers the opportunity to save rainforests by redeeming points on cartons of juice — the

---

[12] Rainforest Action Network, "Coca Cola to Convert 50,000 Acres of Rainforest to Frozen Orange Juice, *Rainforest Action Network Alert*, May 3, 1986, cited in Mark Pilisuk with Jennifer Achord Rountree, *Who Benefits from Global Violence and War: Uncovering a Destructive System* (Westport, CT: Greenwood Publishing Group, 2008).

more juice a consumer bought, the larger the square footage they saved.[13]

These activities may seem far from the domain of national security. But we can understand them by way of analogy with counterterrorism. We have come to understand that people who turn to terrorism often do so on the basis of their perceptions of the world. For example, they may have unyieldingly Manichean views of the world, as divided into good and evil. In that case, countering terrorism would begin with accurately understanding how individuals arrive at such perceptions, and shaping conditions that would promote new, more productive ways of viewing themselves and the world. Human perception is a complex mix of our material and subjective reality, as earlier noted by Castells, and so seeking to change that cannot be a function of "strategic communications" or message dissemination, but a more substantive activity that might include diplomatic activity; international aid, especially on behalf of education; various forms of communication; and other activities that address the concerns and grievances of would-be terrorists.

Addressing climate change could work along the same lines. Like terrorism, some elements of climate change are a function of human activity, and some — regardless of their source — can be addressed by individuals and institutions through particular action and behavior. Reforestation is only one of many such options, but it is complicated because it will take place only as a voluntary behavior structured through regulations and laws. Moreover, as noted above, different parties have diverse, often conflicting stakes in what happens with the rainforest. But, speaking analogically, just as a would-be terrorist may behave violently on the basis of his or her worldview, so does the would-be environmentalist behave on the basis of his or her worldview. However people behave

---

13 http://www.coolearth.org/tropicana.

around rainforests — whether they support particular rainforest legislation, occupy rainforest land to make a statement, or dismiss climate change altogether (because climate change is, after all, not something that most of us actually experience firsthand) — they do it because of their perceptions. If we are persuaded that climate change will ultimately threaten international stability through extreme weather, dramatically changed agricultural cycles, or political instability arising from those events, we should also recognize that action to reverse trends in that direction is rooted in individuals' worldviews.

And the more that individuals, NGOs, and global businesses help shape policy formation, the more their perceptions and their efforts to shape others' opinions matter. In the case of the Brazilian rainforests, many of the current political pressures on those Brazilian leaders and the powerful agricultural lobby resisting rainforest-friendly legislation comes from groups seeking to change perceptions — spanning from global citizen groups such as Avaaz (a self-described global web movement to "bring people-power to decision-making"), to scientists venturing into the political fray, to environmental NGOs.[14] In the United States, mainstream policy recommendations center on traditional economic incentives and efforts to work primarily through formal diplomatic channels. But to do only that in this Brazilian case is to ignore important, vibrant areas where the final disposition of the rainforests is decided — in competitions over perception among non-traditional actors.

Yet up to this point, the U.S. government has failed to exploit these vibrant areas or to contribute meaningfully to new coalitions emerging on the information age landscape. NGOs, global firms, and citizen environmental groups are not

---

[14] http://phys.org/news/2012-06-scientists-brazil-environmental-leadership.html.

waiting for prompting from the United States to take action on rainforests, nor will traditional economic incentives or diplomatic efforts supersede non-state actions. So the United States would do well to accept new realities and plan at the highest strategic level to develop credible roles for itself within evolving and potential networks of concerned actors.

The first step to developing a more credible role is to assess all of these actors in a new kind of framework that puts states and non-state actors on the same plane. Clearly, different actors wield different kinds of power, with different levels of effectiveness. Citizen activist groups do not and cannot act in the same ways as states.

Yet despite the factors that distinguish states and non-states, *all* stakeholder institutions and groups are alike in that they hold a worldview—a set of guiding perceptions about the world that shape their approach to it—and all have access to some means by which to influence others' perceptions, however different in type and scope these means may be. If U.S. policy planners began their analysis with these comparative factors in mind, they might find the dynamics of power in the information age more clearly revealed. These dynamics comprise a network of actors who are simultaneously agents and recipients of communication designed to shift perceptions and, ultimately, behavior. At present, the United States often appears immobilized over how to proceed when it cannot function as sole global leader, but there are no other leaders stepping forward, either. A map of the actors seeking to influence one another could also be a first step toward positive collaboration in a network.

Recommendation: Incorporate Information and Perception Awareness into Foreign Policy Making

In the abstract, the premise that policy planners should be aware of the role that information and perceptions play in international affairs is not controversial. Seasoned national security professionals clearly do incorporate this layer of understanding into their judgment, often so subconsciously that it is invisibly woven into their broader insights as regards a region or situation. Analysts, academics, and members of think tanks remind us frequently that armed force has less relative effectiveness in the information age, and that publics' demands for transparency and responsiveness from government are more effective than they once were.

Despite this wisdom among practitioners, however, as the above examples from recent foreign engagements show, the United States at the institutional level does not mobilize information as effectively as it could. In some cases, such as Syria, the United States should make sure it is mindful of the potential threat that could flow from the symbolic manipulation of the use of "chemical weapons," whether by American actors with political agendas, Syrian factions in the conflict, or other regional actors. In other situations, such as global problem solving around climate change, the United States could better seize positive opportunities to exploit existing networks and information flows to promote its interests.

The basic problem, however, runs deeper than any particular case. It is that, as a government, the United States views information and perceptions in international politics through the lens of communication, which itself is seen as a lowly activity. Information and perceptions are an afterthought, compared with the list of decisions that traditionally drive the management actions of foreign policy professionals. This list is long, including, at the least: appraisals of military force structure; reviews of legal and judicial culture; estimates on trade and economic trends; judgments about the statutory requirements and governing policies affecting human rights and civil liberties; assessments of responses to diplomatic negotiations or demarches (and their form of delivery), foreign assistance, and/or the introduction of military activity. But these activities only tell one part of the story; full context requires that we add to the list an appraisal of stakeholder efforts to manipulate how foreign policy contexts are perceived.

The existing lens narrows the vision of current U.S. policy makers and causes information-derived or dependent issues — videos that go viral and news items that spread like wildfire in global media space; problems that stem from failures to understand others; or problematic perceptions of leadership decisions — to be viewed as communication issues, rather than as being fundamental. Moreover, this approach fails to fully consider the degree to which government activities in these other, more traditional realms — economic aid, armed force, or diplomatic gesture — are also forms of information that generate new or feed existing perceptions.

The President, Congress, and all senior U.S. policy makers should be concerned about the widespread and deeply embedded bias against — or simple ignorance about — the importance of information management within and throughout all levels of the national security community. As a result of this bias, low- or mid-level policy makers are unlikely to view the international context as the product of perceptions, or international actors as agents of those perceptions. The foreign policy options they design then arrive at the desks of senior leaders without benefit of assessments of the information landscape.

This is no fault of the well-meaning civil servants employed in their respective organizations of the U.S. government, and necessarily consumed with routine and internally focused, day-to-day responsibilities. The personnel system does not reward those who focus on external, worldwide trends, or on the communications environment. Yet this need not be the case. Indeed, the history of executive level interest in information strategy offers meaningful precedents that herald a solution. President Reagan indicated his understanding of information as an element of national power in various National Security Decision Directives (NSDDs). NSDD-130 on U.S. Information Policy, recommended among other actions, that U.S. Government personnel be encouraged to focus on the field of international information, and that all U.S. agencies should develop international information career tracks. Modified and expanded for the current environment, this is a proposal worth pursuit.

A future culture to understand the convergence of international affairs and information issues should be nurtured. Creating this future requires a cultural shift in the way that communication and information are understood in developing policy strategy. The following recommendations are offered as potential starting points for generating an information-astute foreign policy environment. A few are narrow, and tactical, while the rest offer broader suggestions for further contemplation and potential development:

1. *Educate and train for a new culture*. First, the professional military education (PME) institutions should incorporate information as an element of power into their curricula with the same rigor and enthusiasm as its sister elements of the "DIME" construct (i.e. the diplomatic, military and economic instruments). These senior level institutions play a crucial role in developing the culture and normative expectations of senior leaders across government; changes in their curricula are a relatively controlled arena for socializing new ways of conceiving the international system.

By way of example, the National War College (NWC) recently inaugurated the position of "information integration chair" (which I currently fill). The existence of the position is itself a signal of the importance that NWC and the National Defense University of which it is a part place on information related topics. The goal of the position is to cultivate senior leaders who appreciate and incorporate information strategy into their foreign policy programs, through discrete activities in and beyond the curriculum.

These have included developing courses that model an integrated understanding of the information landscape and activities through their organization, for example by considering both communication content and technologies together, or teaching information disciplines in the military (such as Military Information Support Operations) and public diplomacy in the same course, so that students are exposed to a range of activities. The classroom environment and strategic focus also give them the opportunity to critically examine both alignments and contradictory impulses inherent in these related, but distinct, information enterprises.

2. *Institute a formal process for networking and consultation about communication and information issues between government and non-government professionals.* As the cases in this chapter demonstrate, information management, communication, and non-state actors' power in the international system are intertwined: Non-state actors are gaining power in part because they have access to the means of mass communication. In many instances, the United States views the power of non-state actors to communication as a threat to its ability to control information flows and content. For their part, these actors are often equally persuaded that the government seeks either to thwart or to co-opt their ability to communicate.

Neither's paranoia is entirely justified, and both could be alleviated by the development of a professional network dedicated specifically to increasing information management, and communication collaboration between state and non-state actors. The communications network would seek to include representatives from NGOs, private firms, sub-national governments, and others, all committed to helping each other improve the flow and content of information between them, on behalf of better governance. Such a network is also a low-cost way to start building resident expertise about information management and communication in the government at low cost, and without relying on contractors or the private sector as a crutch.

3. *Improve flow of information from the State Department field to Washington.* Most discussions of communications or information flows in the foreign policy context revolve around how the United States can better communicate with others. Yet this is irrelevant if the activity is not based on a clear understanding of those with whom the government aims to communicate. Perhaps it is time to attend to the perennial observation within and beyond the State Department that Washington often ignores notes from the field about how American actions are being perceived, or how to improve them. This is especially so as the intelligence agencies, to which the National Security Council typically turns for regional information, become more entrenched in collection of this information via technologies that are useful for producing either specific information, or broad patterns, but not necessarily the kind of regional nuance which is required to produce nuanced communications and policies.

4. *Continue and Expand cooperation between Departments of State and Defense, through programs such as the Global Security Contingency Fund (GSCF).* The GSCF is a four-year pilot program begun in 2012 to encourage the Departments of State and Defense to work together. The current fund is dedicated rather narrowly to "improving U.S. efforts to enable foreign military and security forces to better combat terrorism and other threats," by providing State and Defense a mechanism for jointly providing training and rule of law programs. [15] The

---

[15] Nina Serafino, "Global Security Contingency Fund: Summary and Issue Overview," *Congressional Research Service Report*, R42641, January 22, 2013, 2.

GSCF grew, however, out of more ambitious proposals for mechanisms to generate interagency collaboration in foreign policy planning and execution. The still experimental program appears to be a qualified success, although there are charges that such cooperation is irrelevant in the absence of an overarching strategy for security assistance, and whether either Department is disadvantaged by the other's participation. Nevertheless, cooperative mechanisms are crucial in a substantive way because they provide the best possible means for constructing whole-of-government foreign policy practices that take into account, and plan for, both instrumental and communicative aspects of various activities. Such activities would be usefully advised, as permissible given information-sharing constraints, by the professional network of state and non-state communications professionals proposed in the previous point above.

5. *Reform the Office of the Undersecretary of Public Diplomacy and Public Affairs to reflect a role as whole-of-government manager.* A recommendation that today seems radical but may not seem so at some point in the future would be to restructure the way in which public diplomacy and public affairs are administered. Communications and engagement activities should, ideally, be highlighted and consciously executed from within every government agency. The U.S. Department of Agriculture engages in extensive public diplomacy through its Trade and Scientific Exchange programs. The Department of Defense engages in public diplomacy routinely through military exercises with its allies. It is unfortunate but true that the presence of an office dedicated to public diplomacy at the State Department conceptually reinforces the idea that communication and engagement are severable functions from the rest of policy making and execution, thus keeping it isolated and subordinate to functions considered more germane. We should consider ways of elevating the office to a level from which its holder could serve as coordinator and

manager of the many public diplomacy activities that occur across the U.S. government.

This would, however, require elimination of the office in its current shape.

U.S. Strategy Toward Iran: Confrontation or Grand Bargain?

Glenn E. Robinson

Introduction

For more than three decades, Iran has represented the most persistent strategic headache for American policy-makers. Other issues have come and gone since the Iranian revolution and the taking hostage of U.S. embassy personnel in 1979. The Soviet Union collapsed, along with the Cold War rationale for the containment of Communism; Eastern Europe turned from foe to friend; troubled and unstable Latin American dictatorships have been replaced, mostly by democracies, while Arab dictators have taken a serious hit; the rise of China has proved an economic boon to the world, while its strategic challenges to the U.S. have remained minor; apartheid in South Africa has been replaced by multi-racial democracy. Throughout the world during the past thirty-five years, the circle of friends and allies of the United States has grown, and American military and economic power remains unrivaled. Terrorism by non-state actors persists, but only at the level of deadly nuisance, not as a strategic threat.

The Islamic Republic of Iran, by contrast, has been a constant thorn in the side of the United States during the entire post-1979 period, although to a greater or lesser degree depending on the era. The fact that Iran sits abreast of the most strategically important region in the world – the Persian Gulf – makes it a country that cannot be ignored. That the U.S. has fought three wars on Iran's borders during this period further underlines its strategic centrality.

The U.S. and Iran will likely face a "moment of truth" in the next decade, driven in part by Iran's apparent quest for a nuclear weapons capability. At whatever point Iran is successful in this endeavor, the two states will likely either engage in conflict or set out a Grand Bargain that each side can live with. The primary purpose of this essay is to sketch out the history of the strategic dance the U.S. and Iran have engaged in and to suggest strategic choices each party faces in the coming era.

Historical Background: Why 1953 Still Matters

Prior to World War II, Iran was of little strategic interest to the United States. American oil companies had become active in the region – primarily on the Arabian Peninsula – with the discovery of large petroleum deposits early in the twentieth century. But Iran was very much in the British sphere of influence for the first half of the twentieth century, and less a target of specific American strategic interests. In the nineteenth and early twentieth centuries, Britain and Russia were the major foreign powers involved in Iran's affairs. As part of their "settlement" of the Great Game that centered on Afghanistan, Britain and Russia divided Iran into southern and northern spheres of influence. Russia was dominant in northern Iran, which is closest to its border, until the Russian revolution compelled Moscow to step back, momentarily, from its imperial ambitions. Britain's sphere was in the oil-rich south, which also allowed for British control of a continuous stretch of territory from Burma in Southeast Asia to Egypt on the African continent. Iran was in the middle of this vast and continuous strategic empire, which, by the 1920s, included the lands today known as Pakistan, (parts of) Afghanistan, India, Bangladesh and Burma (Myanmar) to the east, and Iraq, all of the Arabian Peninsula, Jordan, Israel and Egypt to the west. Russia returned to Iran during and after World War II, and helped set up a temporary puppet Kurdish state in northwestern Iran.

As Britain began to withdraw from its vast empire following the war, the balance of its interests in Iran began to shift from strategic and geopolitical to economic. The Anglo Iranian Oil Company (AIOC) — today's British Petroleum — became the main driver of British policy toward Iran during this period.

In the early 1950s, American and British interests in Iran coincided with the rise of Iranian nationalism and the coming to power of Mohammed Mossadegh, a charismatic Anglophile from an elite Iranian family. Mossadegh, who was educated in Europe, greatly admired the rule of law in Britain and the constraints on monarchical power that had evolved. He, too, wanted a monarch who reigned but did not rule in Iran, and he fiercely opposed European (primarily British) interference in Iranian affairs, which interference he argued had been historically empowered by the Iranian monarchy. Mossadegh was elected prime minister in 1951 and confirmed by the young Shah. Three days into his term, and citing AIOC's intransigence in renegotiating a more equitable oil deal, Mossadegh nationalized AIOC's assets in Iran, a move that was wildly popular in Iran, but viewed with concern in London and Washington.

Mossadegh's actions represented the beginning of a wave of nationalizations in the Middle East, including that of the Suez Canal in Egypt, in 1956, and the oil industry throughout the region in the subsequent two decades. But as the pioneers of nationalization, Mossadegh and Iran were subject to harsh sanctions by the west. By 1953, the sanctions had taken a toll, and there were important defections from Mossadegh's political coalition, all of which lent an air of growing instability. Concerned in part by Cold War calculations because of the proximity of the Soviet Union (USSR) to Iran and the strength of the Communist (Tudeh) party in Iran, but driven primarily by the economic concerns of British and American oil companies, Washington and London allied with elements of the Iranian military to overthrow Mossadegh and reinstate the Shah (who had lost a political stare-down with the prime minister).

The August 1953 coup, known as Operation Ajax, was heralded by American intelligence officials as a model of what was possible in the Middle East and elsewhere during the Cold War. It also represented the watershed moment when the U.S. eclipsed Britain as Iran's most important foreign patron, a state of affairs that continued for the following twenty-five years. The coup (or "counter-coup," as one of its authors, Kermit Roosevelt, liked to call it) and the subsequent close embrace of the Shah by Washington represent the basis of anti-Americanism in Iran, especially by those who came to power in 1979. The events of 1953, particularly the political narrative of those events in the minds of many Iranians, are still very much alive in Iranian political culture today.

From the White Revolution to Twin Pillars

Iran under the Shah was a reliable client state for the U.S. in the years following the coup, especially under a friendly Eisenhower administration. However, the election of John F. Kennedy in 1961 brought pressure from Washington for the Shah to liberalize the political system in Iran. The Shah's response was a set of far-reaching reforms known as the White Revolution. Among other things, land reform measures antagonized many members of the Iranian clergy, or *ulama*, and their landed aristocratic backers, and prompted protests among seminary students in Qom in 1963 (helped along by a little known cleric by the name of Ruhollah Khomeini). A separate measure, a year later, that granted U.S. personnel legal immunity in Iran was likewise greeted with protests; for leading these protests, Khomeini was exiled to Iraq.

Iran's place in American geo-strategic thinking changed with the Vietnam War. The policy of sending American troops directly to any hotspot as part of the Global Containment Strategy was losing support as a result of the quagmire in Vietnam, and a new policy emerged to arm and support regional powers who had coterminous interests with the United States. This policy was formally announced as the "Nixon Doctrine" of 1970, with its Persian Gulf manifestation seen in the Twin Pillars policy.[1] Iran and Saudi Arabia represented the two "pillars" around which the U.S. would construct an indirect policy toward Gulf security and stability. These two major oil countries were also in a position to purchase significant U.S. non-nuclear weaponry as part of the implementation of the Twin Pillars policy. Indeed, the first oil price increases by OPEC in the early 1970s were quietly supported by the Nixon administration as a means to give Iran and Saudi Arabia greater resources to enhance their military capabilities as the new policemen of the region.[2]

The first test of the Twin Pillars policy came in the form of Iranian intervention in Oman to protect the pro-West regime of Sultan Qaboos and help suppress the long-simmering Dhofar rebellion in southwestern Oman. While Iranian troops did not fare particularly well, the Dhofar rebellion was successfully put down. Iran had set down a strategic marker

---

[1] This geo-strategic shift in American policy also led to the strategic embrace of Israel by Washington, something that had not been done in the 1950s or 1960s.

[2] Needless to say, the oil embargo of the U.S. by OPEC to protest the U.S. military resupply of Israel during the 1973 Arab-Israeli war, and its accompanying sharp increase in the price of crude oil, was not foreseen by Kissinger and Nixon.

that it was willing to militarily intervene in Gulf countries to protect its interests and those of the U.S. and its allies. Twin Pillars and the strategy of indirect U.S. engagement through regional powers, instead of direct intervention, had its first success.

Exporting Iran's Islamic Revolution

The 1979 Iranian revolution turned the American strategic calculation in the Persian Gulf on its head, particularly given the virulent anti-Americanism that accompanied the revolution. The Twin Pillars policy was now dead, although Saudi Arabia remained a close strategic ally of the U.S. Indeed, the Iranian revolution frightened the Saudis, compelling them into an even closer strategic embrace of the United States. U.S. listening posts in northern Iran were likewise lost, diminishing American signal intelligence capabilities vis-à-vis the Soviet Union. Iran's capture of the U.S. Embassy and the holding hostage of embassy personnel—an act of war—highlighted an American inability to shape events in Iran and the region. It was the hostage crisis, dragging on for 444 days, that produced high levels of anti-Iranian sentiment in the U.S. and made any sort of strategic political compromise with Iran largely impossible for decades (even assuming a willing Iranian partner).

More important than these discrete events, the Iranian revolution produced a regime that was both actively hostile to American interests in the region and determined to export its Islamic revolution to the wider Middle East. Anti-Americanism immediately became a central component of regime ideology, notably with regard to foreign policy. Basing its stance on the events of 1953 and afterwards, the Iranian leadership viewed American meddling in the region as the primary source of its problems, accusing the U.S. of keeping the Muslim world down for its own imperial ambitions. This worldview was captured in the name for the U.S. that the regime used in its propaganda: *shaytan-i bezurg*, or the Great Satan. Israel was viewed as an extension of U.S. imperialism in the region and was given the moniker of *shaytan-i kucheck*, or Little Satan.

The primary foreign policy goal of the revolutionary Iranian regime was to drive the U.S. out of the region and undermine its allies. Perhaps the best example of how this ideology played out was the creation of the "Resistance Front," or a regional coalition of anti-American allies, with Iran at its head. The resistance, of course, was to the perceived American goal of controlling the Persian Gulf and the larger region, and included resistance to Zionism, that is, Israel. Iran began a surprisingly durable alliance with Syria in 1980, shortly after Iraq invaded Iran. Even though Syria was run by the secular Ba'th party, Iran saw its leadership as quintessentially Shi'a, given the "Alawi background of most top leaders of the state" ("Alawi Islam" is a folk religion with Shi'a origins). Iran has not been able to sign up any other state in the "Resistance Front," but does count several important non-state actors – especially Hizbullah in Lebanon – as part of its strategic orbit.

Closely related to this ideology was the export of Iran's Islamic revolution to other places in the Middle East. Leaders of social revolutions always see their own ideology of change in far more universal terms than their neighbors do. France spread the ideals of its own revolution of 1789 throughout much of Europe during the Napoleonic wars, believing that notions of citizenship, liberty, and an egalitarian polity belonged to the world, not just to France. Russian revolutionaries felt the same way about their own brand of Marxism-Leninism, and actively tried, for decades, to export it around the world. Notions of "American Exceptionalism" are essentially an expression of American revolutionary ideology often used to justify U.S. interventions around the world. Iran is no different in this regard: its leaders believe that their brand of Islamic revolution belongs to Muslims everywhere, and that it is not limited to Iran or even the Shi'a world.

In the euphoria of the first few years of the revolution, Iran actively promoted its ideology in the region, even while war was forced on it by Iraq in September 1980. An Iranian hand was evident in protests in Bahrain in 1979-80, and a rhetorical war immediately broke out between Ayatullah Khomeini and the Saudi royal family. Khomeini's oft-repeated line that "there is no monarchy in Islam" was a thinly veiled attack on the legitimacy of the Saudi monarchy in Riyadh. Indeed, in response to this ideological challenge, the Saudi ruling family reformulated its title to emphasize that it was primarily "the protector of the two holy mosques" in Mecca and Medina, rather than a kingship *per se*. But Iran's biggest strategic achievement in the region came with Israel's invasion of Lebanon in 1982. Building on its new alliance with Damascus, Tehran sent its Revolutionary Guards to Lebanon to mobilize Lebanese Shi'a to fight Israel and promote an Islamic revolution in Lebanon (which was its original tag line, before the word "resistance" replaced "revolution"). Thus was Hizbullah born, with very strong Iranian roots. While Hizbullah has built its own socio-political base and remains popular among Lebanon's historically dispossessed Shi'a community, Iranian material support remains critical to Hizbullah's prosperity to this day.

Iran's export of its revolution has come in two waves. The first wave, primarily during the 1980s, was based more on revolutionary euphoria than on calculations of state interests (although those were never far away). The creation of Hizbullah was the major success during this period, while Iranian meddling in other countries—Saudi Arabia, Bahrain, Iraq, Palestine—was far less successful. The 1990s, preeminantly the period under the presidency of Ayatullah Khatami (1997-2005), were a period of internal focus, much of it revolving around recovering from the grinding war with Iraq (1980-1988) and responding to increasing demands for internal reform after years of revolutionary austerity.

Revolutionary hardliners in Iran pushed back against reform efforts, leading to the election of Mahmud Ahmadinejad to the presidency in 2005. Ahmadinejad oversaw a second wave of regional meddling, in part to divert attention from economic failures at home. The strategic bonanza for Iran was the U.S. -led regime change in Iraq, which put into place a regime and a political structure far more friendly to Iranian interests than the previous regime of Saddam Hussein had been. Iranian agents, material, and monies flooded into Iraq after 2003, especially as Iraq's civil war began to heat up in 2005. Today, Iran is the most important and influential external actor inside Iraqi politics, eclipsing the role the U.S. had played there previously.

During the Ahmadinejad period (2005-2013), Iran boosted its relationship with Hizbullah further, including a major increase in the shipment of rocketry to Hizbullah both before and after Iran's brief 2006 war with Israel. Iran also sought to play a similar role with Hamas, although that relationship soured after Hamas deserted the Assad regime in Damascus in 2012. There is some evidence as well that Iran has begun to play a role behind the scenes in support of the Shi'a Houthi rebellion in the Sa'da region of Yemen. The Bahraini regime also pointed its finger at Iran for the protests there during the Arab spring (2011-12), but no compelling evidence was provided this time around. As well, Iran (and Hizbullah) have committed extensive resources (of all kinds) to save their ally in Damascus.

It took France and Russia many decades to end the export of their revolutions, and America, in many ways, never stopped acting internationally in the name of universal ideals of liberty and freedom. Seen in this historical light, Iran may be a long way from ending efforts to export its revolution to the Muslim world, however much those ideals make up a thinly veiled excuse for the exercise of national power designed to serve national interests.

The Advent of Dual Containment

Following the 1979 revolution, U.S. policy toward Iran lacked an underlying strategic vision, as Washington was primarily reactive in its approach. The hostage crisis, along with a failed attempt to rescue the hostages, consumed the last days of the Carter administration. Holding a world strategic view that focused on the fight against Communism, the Reagan administration had no cognitive means to understand what had happened in Iran, as the revolution did not fit a Cold War paradigm. As a result, the Reagan administration never really came to terms with whether Iran was an implacable enemy (the reflagging of Kuwaiti tankers was designed with this theme in mind) or whether it still shared strategic interests with Tehran (e.g., the Iran-Contra affair). The collapse of the Berlin wall in 1989 and Iraq's invasion of Kuwait in 1990 diverted any attention the George H.W. Bush administration may have given to Iran.

However, the Iraq war of 1991 did fundamentally change U.S. policy toward the Persian Gulf more broadly, as it represented the introduction of a permanent American military presence in the Gulf. This military footprint on the Arabian Peninsula had some strategic benefits, but also caused blowback, primarily in the form of providing the emerging jihadi movement with a mobilization *cause celebre*: an American "occupation" (*ihtilal*) of Islam's heartland. Usama Bin Laden and other jihadi ideologues used this new American military presence in Arabia as rhetorical proof that the U.S. was out to dominate the Muslim world.

In the midst of strategic drift in the Persian Gulf, the Clinton administration formulated a new strategic doctrine of

"Dual Containment" that was flawed from its inception. Dual Containment argued for the simultaneous and direct containment of both a war-weakened Iraq and an emergent Iran, rather than the historical balancing outside powers had practiced between these two countries. Few other countries subscribed to this new and ambitious policy, which led to its gradual demise. Virtually no other country was interested in sanctions against Iran in the 1990s, especially while those against Iraq were both controversial and gradually weakening. Particularly given that its primary author was Martin Indyk, Dual Containment was seen by some critics as having more to do with satisfying Israel's strategic ambitions than realizing U.S. national interests. In any case, the U.S. was not willing to commit the level of resources that would have been needed to implement the policy of Dual Containment fully.

With the American invasion of Iraq in 2003, Dual Containment fell apart, ushering in a new era in U.S. engagement with the Gulf. The Iraq war also increased the sense of vulnerability in Tehran, leading to its promotion of its nuclear program.

The Iranian Nuclear Challenge

Iran has consistently denied that it is pursuing a nuclear weapons capability, insisting that its nuclear program is for acceptable civilian uses, notably energy and medical needs. Such uses are approved under the Nuclear Non-Proliferation Treaty (NPT), of which Iran is a signatory. Iran's nuclear energy program was started under the Shah, so it is not new, and Iran's supreme leaders since the revolution, Ayatullah Khomeini and Ayatullah Khamenei, have both issued *fatwas*, or religious opinions, that nuclear weapons are immoral and violate the precepts of Islam. In short, Iranian leaders may be telling the truth or, at the least, they have not yet decided to go all the way to a nuclear weapons capability.

But don't bet on it. From the strategic perspective of Tehran, having a nuclear weapons capability — either nuclear latency ("the Japan option") or an actual stockpile of weapons — makes good sense, for two main reasons. First, such a nuclear capability is the best insurance against foreign military intervention in Iran, and thus the best guarantor of the survival of the Islamic Republic. No nuclear weapons state has ever been overthrown by external powers, although Russia and South Africa went through significant internal changes. Iran fears U.S. designs of regime change in Tehran, because such statements were frequently made in Washington during the Bush years, because significant sanctions have been imposed, and, most importantly, because the U.S. has significant military capacity all around the region. Those capabilities include major military facilities in Afghanistan, Turkey, Kuwait, Qatar, Bahrain, UAE, and Oman, as well as facilities slightly farther afield, in Central Asia, Djibouti, and Diego Garcia. In short, Iran feels surrounded and under threat, and a nuclear weapons capability would be its best insurance policy that the U.S. will not attack. That is, nuclear weapons would provide Tehran with a substantial deterrence capability.

In addition to securing the regime by deterring the U.S. and other potential external foes, a nuclear weapons capability would provide significant prestige for Iran, as befits its popular sense of being the natural and legitimate regional power. In turn, that new status would give Iran even more cachet as the leader of the Islamic world. If Iran follows the pattern set by other proliferators, nuclear weapons might also compel Iran to act more cautiously with its newfound power, and greater levels of international responsibility would be expected of Iran by other members of this exclusive club. But the period between initial proliferation and a hardened retaliatory capability (assuming latency is not sufficient) also represents the most dangerous period for military conflict, as rivals — in this case Israel, most of all — would see the time to act as "now or never."

A Grand Strategic Bargain or Military Confrontation?

The U.S. and Iran are nearing a crossroads in their relationship. A choice is emerging between military confrontation over Iran's nuclear program and consecrating a deal — and perhaps a grand bargain — between the U.S. and Iran. Other actors, (especially Israel) and other crises (especially Syria) have the ability to wreak havoc on any potential strategic bargain.

A military strike by the U.S. has little chance of significant success. Only an actual occupation of Iran by ground troops could physically destroy all elements of the Iranian nuclear program and prevent its renewal. Such a possibility has virtually no public support in the United States and, in any case, it would prove enormously costly in blood and treasure. Iran is three times as big as Iraq, with far more troops and security forces than Baghdad enjoyed in the last decade of Saddam's rule. Repeated military airstrikes at suspected targets could likely set Iran's program back for a year or two, but it's hardly likely that they would end the program permanently. The nuclear program is popular domestically in Iran, and in the 2013 presidential election most candidates were trying to outbid each other in rhetorical support for it, although the winner, Hassan Rouhani has struck a conciliatory tone on the issue. For its part, Israel's capacity to strike a serious and permanent blow against Iran's nuclear program is significantly smaller than that of the U.S.

In short, there are few, if any, viable and appealing military options. If the Iranian regime is determined to possess a nuclear weapons option, especially at the level of nuclear latency, and if it is willing to pay the political and economic price via sanctions and an ongoing low intensity conflict (e.g. "stuxnet"[3]), there is little the U.S. can do to prevent it. Iran's choice to proliferate will be made in Tehran, not in Washington.

Given such a reality, a grand strategic bargain must be considered, even though both sides have many hardline opponents to such a deal. On the Iranian side, there are plenty of old revolutionaries—likely including Ayatullah Ali Khamenei—who have no interest in reaching any sort of strategic deal with the U.S.. Under current circumstances, those hardliners appear to hold the political upper hand inside Iran. The American side also has plenty of strategic rejectionists when it comes to dealing with Iran in a cooperative and mutually beneficial way.

What would a grand bargain between the U.S. and Iran look like? The core of any deal would be that Iran not push any nuclear weapons program beyond latency, and then keep it unannounced. Israel has never officially acknowledged its own nuclear weapons capacities (which go well beyond latency), so a precedent does exist. On the American side, public statements and policy would need to acknowledge that Iran has legitimate interests in the Persian Gulf and must play a role in securing its own interests. The Iranian state has no interest in instability in the Persian Gulf that would threaten its own oil (and, increasingly, gas) exports, still the lifeblood of its economy.

Recognition that Iran's revolution is not teetering on its last legs, and that any reform must come from within rather than from some externally generated "regime change" would

---

[3] According to a wide variety of published press reports, the U .S. and Israel jointly developed a computer worm, discovered in 2010, that targeted computer systems in Iran's uranium enrichment program, briefly disrupting centrifuge operations.

help promote the international respect the regime craves. By helping Iran become more of a status quo power that is focused on protecting its national interests (as opposed to a revolutionary resistance power), the U.S. and its allies will, at the same time, protect their own interests in Persian Gulf stability. Such a strategic approach makes a good deal of sense, but it is not at all clear, after decades of intense hostility, that either side can overcome its own domestic challenges and ideological bugaboos to consummate such a grand strategic bargain.

Charging Forward or Lagging Behind? The Current Status of International norms for Cyber Warfare

Brian Mazanec

Introduction

In the conclusion of his book, *The History of a Crime*, Victor Hugo wrote that "one resists the invasion of armies; one does not resist the invasion of ideas."[1] This statement—in reference to the ideals of the French revolution—alludes to the fact that ideas, when spread, can grow, shape, and dominate. One category of ideas is known as norms, which are shared expectations of appropriate behavior.[2] Norms exist at various levels and apply to different actors. In the international arena, these non-binding shared expectations can, to some degree, constrain and regulate the behavior of international actors and, in that sense, have a structural impact on the international system as a whole. For example, early in the age of nuclear weapons, Lt. General James Gavin expressed the contemporary wisdom when he said, "nuclear weapons will

---

[1] Victor Hugo, *The History of a Crime* (Kessinger Publishing, 2004).
[2] Peter Katzenstein, Alexander Wendt, and Ronald Jepperson, "Norms, Identity, and Culture in National Security." *The Culture of National Security: Norms and Identity in World Politics* (Columbia University Press, 1996), 54.

become conventional for several reasons, among them cost, effectiveness against enemy weapons, and ease of handling."[3] However, as the nuclear era advanced, a constraining norm developed that made states more reluctant to possess or use nuclear weapons—thus helping prevent their widespread diffusion and use. Just as constraining norms emerged for nuclear weapons in the mid-twentieth century and airpower weapons early in the twentieth century, constraining norms are beginning to develop for emerging cyber weapons – though, many believe that the growing international use of cyber weapons is outpacing the development of constraining norms.[4]

If constraining norms for cyber warfare are not keeping pace, where do we currently stand? This article attempts to answer this question by first examining the state practice of cyber warfare and recent efforts to cultivate international norms. It also reviews potential game changing developments that could alter the evolution of international norms. An assessment of the status of norms for cyber warfare is important because international security and U.S. national security may be enhanced by the emergence of constraining norms, similar to those that have developed in the past. Ultimately, this article points out that various permissive and constraining norms for cyber warfare are beginning to emerge through state practice and deliberate "norm cultivation" efforts as more and more actors begin to employ an increasing number of organizational platforms. While these initial efforts have at times fostered mutual exclusivity and even contradiction, they have also suggested a future norm regime may evolve with the following characteristics or principles:

---

[3] James M. Gavin, *War and Peace in the Space Age*. Harper Brothers, 1958.

[4] James Clapper, "Statement for the Record: Worldwide Threat Assessment of the U.S. Intelligence Community." Senate Select Committee on Intelligence, March 12, 2013.

first, limiting targets to military objectives and holding civilian activities harmless; second, a "no first use" of cyber weapons; and third, the application of existing laws of armed conflict (LOAC) to cyber warfare.

State Practice of Cyber Warfare

Before examining the current state practice of cyber warfare, it is important to define the term itself. The term lacks a universally agreed upon definition but it generally references Computer Network Exploitation (CNE) and Computer Network Attack (CNA), with the former being the more-frequent of the two and involving the use of computer networks to gather intelligence on an adversary.[5] CNA, by contrast and on the more violent end of the spectrum, is the use of computer networks to disrupt, deny, degrade, or destroy either the information resident in enemy computers and computer networks, or the computers and networks themselves. This understanding of cyber warfare – with a focus on CNA between state actors (directly or through plausibly-deniable non-state clients) – will be the focus of this article.

Despite its emerging-technology status, and a dearth of available information regarding the use of such of weapons by states,[6] cyber conflict has been categorized into three historical phases by researcher Jason Healey: "realization" in the 1980s; "takeoff" from 1998-2003; and "militarization" from 2003 to

---

[5] United States Government Accountability Office, *Defense Department Cyber Efforts: Definitions, Focal Point, and Methodology Needed for DOD to Develop Full-Spectrum Cyberspace Budget Estimates*, GAO-11-695R, July 29, 2011, 10.

[6] Garry Brown and Keira Poellet, "The Customary International Law of Cyberspace," *Strategic Studies Quarterly* (Fall 2012): 129-130.

the present.[7] Two of the main differences in each of Healey's phases are the increasing diffusion of capabilities among nations and improved and formalized organizational approaches to cyber conflict. Focusing on the militarization phase, James Lewis has maintained a rolling list of "significant cyber incidents" at the Center for Strategic and International Studies (CSIS) since 2006 and, as of July 2013, identified 153 hostile cyber operations.[8] While Lewis does not separate the operations by CNE and CNA, the vast majority of the incidents (137 of 153, or approximately 89%) appear to be CNE-style operations.[9]

While much of the hostile cyber activity to date is not true cyber warfare, but instead is CNE and cyber crime, we should not interpret this to mean that a normative taboo has emerged against the conduct of CNA-style cyber attacks.[10] Instead, it should be seen as evidence of how early we are in the cyber era (akin to the absence of strategic bombing in the first decade of the nineteenth century when the full use of the technology remained relatively immature): advanced cyber warfare is only now becoming possible, and robust target sets are just beginning to emerge as societies become more immersed in and dependent on the cyberspace medium. The relatively light use of CNA techniques might also be seen as evidence of caution in the absence of any firm norms, as states slowly test the limits of what the international community

---

[7] Jason Healey, *A Fierce Domain: Conflict in Cyberspace, 1986 to 2012* (The Atlantic Council and Cyber Conflict Studies Association, 2013), 18.

[8] James Lewis, "Significant Cyber Events since 2006," *Center for Strategic and International Studies*, July 11, 2013.
http://csis.org/publication/cyber-events-2006.

[9] Based on author's analysis of James Lewis' "Significant Cyber Events since 2006," *Center for Strategic and International Studies*, July 11, 2013. <http://csis.org/publication/cyber-events-2006>.

[10] Thomas Rid, "Cyber War Will Not Take Place," *Journal of Strategic Studies*, 35:1 (2011): 5-32.

deems acceptable behavior in this realm. Of the major CNA-style attacks that have occurred, at least seven are notable in that they may portend what constitutes future acceptable behavior in cyberspace. They are listed below in Table 1, along with the suspected sponsor, target, and effect of the attack.

Attack Name	Date	Target	Effect	Suspected Sponsor
Trans-Siberian Gas Pipeline	June 1982	Soviet gas pipeline (civilian target)	Massive explosion	United States
Estonia	April-May 2007	Commercial and governmental web services (civilian target)	Major denial of service	Russia
Syrian Air Defense System as part of Operation Orchard	September 2007	Military air defense system (military target)	Degradation of air defense capabilities allowing kinetic strike	Israel
Georgia	July 2008	Commercial and governmental web services (civilian target)	Major denial of service	Russia
Stuxnet	Late 2009-2010, possibly as early as 2007	Iranian centrifuges (military target)	Physical destruction of Iranian centrifuges	United States
Saudi-Aramco	August 2012	State-owned commercial enterprise (civilian target)	Large-scale destruction of data and attempted physical disruption of oil production	Iran
Operation Ababil	September 2012-March 2013	Large financial institutions (civilian target)	Major denial of service	Iran

Figure 1: Selected CNA-style Cyber Attacks

The seven CNA-style attacks listed above collectively provide useful insight into the emergence of international norms through the customary practice of cyber warfare. There are three main observations or "take-aways" from these attacks. First, the majority of the attacks (or five of seven) were aimed at civilian targets, showing that a constraining norm limiting attacks to explicitly military targets or objectives has not yet taken form. Second, to the extent attacks did strike exclusively military targets, they were suspected to have been launched by Western nations (the United States and Israel). This seems to indicate that there may be competing, in some cases more permissive, norms regarding cyber warfare depending on the political bloc the nation is associated with — which is consistent with the expected competitive environment in the early days of norm emergence as outlined by norm evolution theory. Third, experience with cyber warfare is currently limited. No known deaths or casualties have yet resulted from cyber attacks, and the physical damage caused, while impacting strategically significant items such as Iranian centrifuges or Soviet gas pipelines, has not been particularly widespread or severe. While the current absence of massively disruptive cyber attacks is likely due to the existence of underdeveloped capabilities and not a constraining norm, the lack of such attacks nevertheless can be seen as a welcome reprieve — as it may allow the time necessary for a constraining norm to emerge.

Deliberate Norm Cultivation

While the preceding review of state practice makes it apparent that few, if any, normative constraints governing cyber warfare exist, increased attention and discussion — among other things — has helped spurn various efforts to reach a consensus for codifying emerging norms for cyber warfare. Norm evolution theory — which helps explain how norms emerge and develop — indicates that norm emergence is more likely to occur when key actors are intimately involved, specifically norm entrepreneurs with organizational platforms and key states acting as norm leaders. The two primary intergovernmental bodies and organizational platforms (and sub-platforms) currently promoting emerging norms for cyber warfare are the United Nations (UN) and the North Atlantic Treaty Organization (NATO), with Russia leading efforts at the former and the United States leading efforts at the latter organization. Other key multilateral efforts exist and are encouraging the development of cyber norms, including the London Conference on Cyberspace (and subsequent conferences) and numerous academic cyber norm workshops.

Within the UN, the main focus on cyber warfare has occurred in the UN General Assembly's First Committee (Disarmament and International Security Committee) as well as various subsidiary organs or specialized agencies — particularly the International Telecommunications Union, UN Institute of Disarmament Research, and the Counter-Terrorism Implementation Task Force working group.[11] While some discussions occurred in the early 1990s, a serious focus on cyber warfare did not really begin until 1998 when the Russian representatives introduced a resolution in the First Committee entitled "Developments in the field of information and telecommunications in the context of security," thereby beginning a process aimed at establishing "cyber arms control" in a manner similar to that which produced the Chemical Weapons Convention and the Nuclear Nonproliferation Treaty.[12]

If ultimately embraced and accepted, the Russian proposal would prohibit offensive cyber weapons and ban "cyberterrorism," a move many interpret as also aimed at

---

[11] Focus on other aspects of cyber security, such as cyber crime and cyber espionage, have occurred in other UN organizations such as the Second Committee and the Economic and Social Council (ECOSOC), however these efforts fall outside the scope of this article and focus on a different category of hostile cyber operations.

[12] Jeffrey Carr, *Inside Cyber Warfare: Mapping the Cyber Underworld* (O'Reilly, December 2009), 34.

prohibiting free speech and repressing potential political opposition to Moscow.[13] Russia's intentions have thus been interpreted as not only disingenuous but also as an attempt to undermine U.S. cyber superiority. Regardless of its underlying intentions, Moscow nevertheless continues to serve as the lead norm entrepreneur on this cyber arms control effort in the UN with Washington resisting any change.[14] Indeed, the United States has frequently defended its position by stating that a "cyberterrorism" ban would be impractical and unenforceable. Moreover, Washington laments, the broad scope of such a ban risks infringement on norms regarding civil liberties and the freedom of expression,[15] and has alternatively signaled a belief that existing protocols and legal constructs could be adapted and applied to cyber activities. In the midst of this internal UN debate, three key candidate norms have emerged for cyber warfare: 1) a complete prohibition on cyber weapons as part of cyber arms control, 2) a prohibition on first-use of cyber weapons, and 3) an obligation among states to police and prevent cyber attacks by non-state actors in their territory.

The UN efforts broke new ground in 2013 when the Group of Government Experts affirmed that "the application of norms derived from existing international law" was relevant to cyber warfare and "essential to reduce risks to international peace, security and stability."[16] This development seems to

---

[13] Tim Maurer, "Cyber Norm Emergence at The United Nations: An Analysis of the Activities At the UN Regarding Cyber-Security," *Harvard Kennedy School Belfer Center for Science and International Affairs* (September 2011): 17.

[14] Ibid.

[15] Ibid., 17.

[16] United Nations General Assembly. *A/68/98: Report of the Group of Governmental Experts on Developments in the Field of Information and Telecommunications in the Context of International Security,* June 24, 2013, 2-3.

---

lend credence to Washington's longstanding belief that existing international law and agreements regarding the use of force are sufficient to address the new challenge of cyber warfare. The Group of Government Experts went on to recommend an additional study to promote shared understanding regarding how existing international law and norms can apply to state behavior in cyberspace despite the unique characteristics of cyber warfare, noting also—in a possible nod to the Russian position—that "additional norms could be developed over time."[17] Yet efforts continue to be complicated and delayed by the lack of agreement on key terms and concepts, such as whether or not propaganda and information warfare are part of cyber warfare.

As noted, NATO has also served as a main intergovernmental body and organizational platform for promoting emerging cyber warfare norms. Following the major cyber attacks on Estonia in 2007 and Georgia in 2008 (the former a NATO member, the latter aspiring to be one), NATO began to focus more seriously on the issue.[18] In 2008, NATO established the NATO Cooperative Cyber Defence Centre of Excellence (NATO CCD COE.)[19] in Tallinn, Estonia (the epicenter of a 2007 cyber attack) with the sponsorship of 11 NATO members. It is focused on enhancing NATO's cyber defense through research, education, and consulting. For example, in 2012 the organization published a *National Cyber Security Framework Manual* to help member nations better develop national policies for cyber defense.[20]

NATO's commitment to addressing cyber warfare also extends beyond this center of excellence. In November 2010,

---

[17]Ibid., 3.

[18] Spencer Ackerman, "NATO Doesn't Yet Know How to Protect Its Networks," *Wired.com*, February 1, 2012.

[19] Alexander Klimburg, *National Cyber Security Framework Manual* (NATO CCD C OE Publication, 2012), 4.

[20] Ibid.

NATO adopted a new Strategic Concept, which recognized that cyber warfare "can reach a threshold that threatens national and Euro-Atlantic prosperity, security and stability."[21] In general, NATO, led by the United States, has approached cyber warfare from a perspective that seeks to apply the existing LOAC to cyber attacks rather than pursue new and more comprehensive restrictions like those proposed by Russia in the UN. NATO's most important activity in this effort was the development the *Tallinn Manual on the International Law Applicable to Cyber Warfare*.[22]

The Tallinn Manual, which does not reflect official NATO opinion but rather the personal opinion of its authors (an "international group of experts"), was sponsored by the NATO CCD COE and three organizations acting as observers: NATO, U.S. Cyber Command (CYBERCOM), and the International Committee of the Red Cross.[23] It does, however, reflect the main positions of the U.S. government,[24] as articulated in a September 2012 speech by State Department legal advisor Harold Koh.[25] Indeed, the 2011 *U.S. International*

---

[21] North Atlantic Treaty Organization. *Active Engagement, Modern Defence. Strategic Concept for the Defence and Security of the Members of the North Atlantic Treaty Organisation, adopted by Heads of State and Government at the NATO in Lisbon*, November 19-20, 2010, paragraph 12.
<http://www.nato.int/strategic-concept/pdf/Strat_Concept_web_en.pdf>.

[22] International Group of Experts, Schmitt, Michael, N., editor. *Tallinn Manual on The International Law Applicable to Cyber Warfare* (Cambridge University Press, 2013).

[23] Atlantic Council. "Fact Sheet: The Tallinn Manual on the International Law Applicable to Cyber Warfare," March 28, 2013.
<http://www.atlanticcouncil.org/events/past-events/tallinn-manual-launch-defines-legal-groundwork-for-cyber-warfare>.

[24] Schmitt, Michael N. "International Law in Cyberspace: The Koh Speech and Tallinn Manual Juxtaposed," *Harvard International Law Journal*, 54 (December 2012): 14.

[25] Ibid.

Strategy for Cyberspace clearly proclaimed that the "long-standing international norms guiding state behavior—in times of peace and conflict—also apply in cyberspace."[26]An independent yet similar effort led by Israeli Colonel Sharon Afek in early 2014 reached similar conclusions.[27]

Despite the official position by the NATO leadership in support of applying LOAC to cyber warfare, a complete consensus within the organization about what such application means remains elusive, even within the same member nations in some cases. For example, the U.S. supports a fairly broad definition of military objectives to include both "war-sustaining" and "war-fighting" objectives, leaving to subjective interpretation a large number of potential targets.[28] By contrast, other NATO members support limiting the definition of military objectives to just "war-fighting" targets.

Overall, media response to the Tallinn Manual has varied, with some misinterpreting and twisting its conclusions to justify the "killing [of] hackers."[29] However, the manual represents a significant step for developing an emerging cyber warfare norm linked to the existing war fighting norms as codified in the LOAC. Today all major powers, except China,

---

[26] United States. *International Strategy for Cyberspace: Prosperity, Security, and Openness in a Networked World* (Washington, D.C., May 2011), 9.

[27] Gili Cohen, "Israeli expert seeks ethics code for cyber warfare," *Haaretz*, January 20, 2014. <http://www.haaretz.com/news/diplomacy-defense/1.569450>.

[28] Michael N. Schmitt, "International Law in Cyberspace: The Koh Speech and Tallinn Manual Juxtaposed," *Harvard International Law Journal*, 54 (December 2012): 27.

[29] For example, see Russia Today. "NATO cyberwar directive declares hackers military targets," March 19, 2013. < http://rt.com/usa/nato-publishes-cyberwar-guidelines-502/>; and Souppouris, Aaron. "Killing hackers is justified in cyber warfare, says NATO-commissioned report," *The Verge*, March 21, 2013. <http://www.theverge.com/2013/3/21/4130740/tallin-manual-on-the-international-law-applicable-to-cyber-warfare>.

agree that major aspects—if not all—of the LOAC apply to cyber warfare.[30] And other individual nations have begun to assume the roles of norm entrepreneurs and norm leaders for organizing ad-hoc multilateral forums to, among other things, discuss norms for cyber warfare.

These additional actors—motivated by a variety of factors and employing a range of mechanisms—have promoted norms through a variety of organizational platforms and through the practice of general observance and routine, increasing the likelihood of norm emergence reaching a tipping point of critical mass, as predicted by norm evolution theory. Candidate norms and the related organizational platforms and associated actors are identified in Table 2 below:

Candidate Norm	Organizational Platform(s)	Entrepreneur(s)/Leader(s)
Targeting civilian and commercial objectives is acceptable	N/A—State Practice, Doctrine/Strategy	Russia (?), China(?), Iran,
Total prohibition on cyber weapons and cyber warfare	UN First Committee,	Russia, China
No first use of cyber weapons	UN First Committee, International Telecommunications Union	Russia, China
Responsibility to prevent third-party cyber attacks from a state's territory	International Telecommunications Union, London/Budapest/Seoul Conferences	Russia, China, U.S., UK, South Korea, NATO
Cyber confidence building measures are necessary to prevent misunderstanding	UN Government Group of Experts, ICT4Peace, World Summit on the Information Society, MIT Cyber Norm Workshops, NATO	Russia, China, U.S., UK, South Korea
Existing LOAC apply to cyber warfare (including limiting targets to narrow military objectives)	UN Government Group of Experts, NATO, London/Budapest/Seoul Conferences, State Practice (for limiting targets to military objectives)	U.S., UK, Germany, NATO, Israel, Russia

Figure 2: Emerging Candidate Norms for Cyber Warfare

---

[30] Roger Hurwitz, "An Augmented Summary of The Harvard, MIT and U. of Toronto Cyber Norms Workshop," May 2012, 12. < http://citizenlab.org/cybernorms/augmented-summary.pdf>.

Although building consensus for various norms is a sign of progress, many challenges remain. Colonel Afek, a former deputy military advocate general in the Israel government, highlighted some of these challenges when he said the international community "faces a complex and challenging period in which we can expect both a cyber arms race with the participation of state and non-state entities, and a massive battle between East and West over the character of the future legal regime."[31]

Potential "Game Changing" Developments That Could Impact the Future of Norms for Cyber Warfare

In addition to examining the current status of constraining norms for cyber warfare based on state practice and deliberate norm cultivation, it is also worth examining the possibility of other significant developments which could have a disruptive impact and unexpectedly influence norm evolution. Specifically, the most noteworthy potential developments include the introduction of revolutionary technology, a rise of non-state cyber actors, and the launching of a major strategic cyber attack. These game changing developments are summarized below in Table 3.

Scenario	Description
Introduction of revolutionary cyber technology	Introduction by one or more actors of revolutionary new cyber technology, which immediately renders current encryption or cyber defenses obsolete.
Rise of non-state cyber actors	Significant cyber attack capabilities proliferate and a range of non-state actors (corporations, hacktivists, terrorists, etc.) increasingly engage in cyber warfare, becoming the dominant cyber actors and blurring attribution and the role of states.
Major strategic cyber attack(s)	A catastrophic attack or series of attacks aimed at civilian targets (power grid, infrastructure, etc.) occurs, leading to physical destruction and loss of life.

Figure 3: "Game Changing" Developments Which Could Impact the Future of Cyber Warfare

---

[31] Gili Cohen, "Israeli expert seeks ethics code for cyber warfare," *Haaretz*, January 20, 2014. <http://www.haaretz.com/news/diplomacy-defense/1.569450>.

The first potential game-changing development impacting future norm evolution would be the sudden arrival of revolutionary cyber technologies. These could be in the form of a breakthrough in quantum computing, giving one state a massive advantage and allowing it to penetrate and attack well-defended targets and advanced cryptologic systems. Gret Tallant, a manager at Lockheed Martin who is working on quantum computing, has said that "computationally, quantum computing is the equivalent of the Wright Brothers at Kitty Hawk; it has the potential to be a turning point in our history."[32] Lockheed's Quantum Computing Center recently upgraded to a 512-qubit machine and the National Security Agency (NSA) allegedly has a $79.7 million research program focused on these machines,[33] although some assert that the recent rate of technological breakthroughs is beginning to slow.[34]

The development of malware that sonically transmits communications to "air gapped" devices would represent another potential revolutionary technological breakthrough (i.e., sending messages through acoustic waves between

---

[32] Lockheed Martin. "Speedy Qubits Lead the Quantum Evolution," October 28, 2013.
<http://www.lockheedmartin.com/us/news/features/2013/quantum.html?goback=%2Egde_4682795_member_5812625891389366275#%21>.

[33] Steven Rich, "NSA seeks to build quantum computer that could crack most types of encryption," *The Washington Post*, January 2, 2014.
<http://www.washingtonpost.com/world/national-security/nsa-seeks-to-build-quantum-computer-that-could-crack-most-types-of-encryption/2014/01/02/8fff297e-7195-11e3-8def-a33011492df2_story.html>.

[34] Don Clark, "Intel Explains Rare Moore's Law Stumble," *The Wall Street Journal*, November 21, 2013.
<http://blogs.wsj.com/digits/2013/11/21/intel-explains-rare-moores-law-stumble/>.

speakers and microphones).[35] Neuromorphic processing – or the development of adaptive computing technology based on the biological nervous system – offers a third potential avenue for a major cyber breakthrough,[36] with Qualcomm expected to make the first such processor commercially available later this year.[37] Any one of these breakthroughs – quantum computing, sonic malware, and neuromorphic processing – could upend the cyber balance of power and thus affect existing and prospective constraining cyber norms. Its abrupt arrival would impact norm evolution in profound and yet unknown ways as it almost certainly would alter states calculations of self-interest (state self-interest is a key variable identified by norm evolution theory for emerging-technology weapons).

The second potential game-changing development would be a rise in and increasing dominance of hostile non-state actors in cyberspace. Some individuals, such as futurist and defense expert Peter Singer, highlight that thus far terrorists and other hostile non-state actors have not engaged in cyber warfare and point out that other complexities and barriers prevent them from easily conducting such sophisticated attacks.[38] However, others such as Ralph Langner, an expert in

---

[35]Geoffrey Ingersoll, "U.S. Navy: Hackers Jumping The Air Gap Would Disrupt The World Balance Of Power," *Business Insider*, November 19, 2013. <http://www.businessinsider.com/navy-acoustic-hackers-could-halt-fleets-2013-11>.

[36] John Markoff, "Brainlike Computers, Learning From Experience," *The New York Times*, December 28, 2013.
<http://www.nytimes.com/2013/12/29/science/brainlike-computers-learning-from-experience.html>; Smith, Chris. "Brainlike processors coming from Qualcomm next year," *BGR.com*, December 30, 2013.
<http://bgr.com/2013/12/30/qualcomm-brain-like-processor-2014/>.

[37] Chris Smith, "Brainlike processors coming from Qualcomm next year," *BGR.com*, December 30, 2013. <http://bgr.com/2013/12/30/qualcomm-brain-like-processor-2014/>.

[38] P.W. Singer and Allan Friedman, *Cybersecurity and Cyberwar: What Everyone Needs to Know* (Oxford University Press, 2014), 96-99.

industrial control systems, has asserted that vast resources and intelligence capabilities needed to conduct an attack like Stuxnet may not be needed for future attacks on such "cyber-physical" systems.[39] Further, a recent National Intelligence Council (NIC) report identified a possible "tectonic shift" in the availability of capabilities, suggesting that lethal and disruptive technologies—and cyber weapons—previously only available to state-sponsored programs will soon be accessible to individuals and small groups.[40]

The NIC report explored the risks and plausibility of this scenario as well as the possibility of cyber mercenaries selling their expertise and services to terrorists interested in causing widespread economic and financial disruptions. [41] The scenario would involve a global diffusion of significant cyber attack capabilities and introduce them to non-state actors, due to, among other things, the multi-use nature of the technology, an increasingly low cost of entry, and a growing global reliance on IT-systems (thus providing an ever growing target set). The scenario also would almost certainly include corporations who are "hacking back," politically-motivated *hacktivists* (such as Anonymous), and nationalist groups with informal state affiliation. Perhaps an indicator of this non-state cyber threat already occurred in late 2013 when a Boeing vice president admitted to being "very concerned" about terrorists using malware to conduct attacks against aircraft due to the numerous Information Technology (IT) systems that openly

---

[39]Antone Gonsalves, "Stuxnet creators defined 21st century warfare," *Computer World*, November 21, 2013.
<http://news.idg.no/cw/art.cfm?id=D106D2FB-9CBD-E42D-6EA37EB5DE2701D3>.
[40]United States National Intelligence Council. *Global Trends 2030: Alternative Worlds* (December 2012), iii.
[41]Ibid., 68.

communicate with airport personnel and air traffic control during takeoff and landing.[42]

The path of norm evolution in such a technology-scattered scenario is uncertain. The increased number of cyber-empowered non-state actors might impair norm evolution simply because of the extreme proliferation of these capabilities, the likelihood of blurred attribution, and increased prospects of inadvertent escalation. The potential upside of the scenario—such as increased public pressure to establish constraining norms (an expectation developed from the history of norm development for other emerging-technology weapons)—could be negated by the limited and challenging application of constraining norms to non-state actors, who generally are not as likely to be influenced or constrained. While evidence indicates international norms do constrain and influence some armed non-state actors, the affected tend to be only those who "value their public reputation, moral authority, and source of legitimacy."[43] In practice therefore, norms only apply to some of the many potential non-state cyber actors and do not apply to ideologically-oriented groups such as Anonymous or al Qaida.[44]

Finally, a third potential game-changing development would be the occurrence of a major cyber attack or even a series of attacks on civilian targets. Such a scenario should not be deemed implausible as it could be perpetrated by either a

---

[42] Nick Collins, "Cyber terrorism is 'biggest threat to aircraft'," *The Telegraph*, December 27, 2013.
<http://www.telegraph.co.uk/finance/newsbysector/transport/105266 20/Cyber-terrorism-is-biggest-threat-to-aircraft.html>.

[43] Claudia Hofmann and Ulrich Schneckener, *Special Report: NGOs and Nonstate Armed Actors, Improving Compliance with International Norms* (United States Institute of Peace, July 2011), 11-12.

[44] Cedric Ryngaert, "Working Paper: Non-State Actors and International Humanitarian Law," *Katholieke Universiteit Leuven, Faculty of Law* (2008).

state or non-state actor. In March 2013, James Clapper, the Director of National Intelligence, testified that within the next two years the threat of a major cyber attack against the United States is real, would occur, and result in "long-term, wide-scale disruption of services, such as a regional power outage."[45] In 2014, Clapper testified that this threat is increasing as "malware and attack tradecraft proliferate."[46]

In 2010, the Economist envisioned the most extreme of major cyber attacks when it described "the almost instantaneous failure of the systems that keep the modern world turning. As computer networks collapse, factories and chemical plants explode, satellites spin out of control and the financial and power grids fail."[47] The targets of such an attack could include hospitals, Supervisory Control and Data Acquisition (SCADA) control systems for chemical or nuclear plants, water filtration systems, transportation systems such as air traffic management systems or subways, banking and financial systems, and the electrical grid itself.[48] Regarding the latter target, the potential consequences could be severe. In 2007, the National Academy of Sciences (NAS) estimated that a major cyber attack on the U.S. electrical grid could lead to "hundreds or even thousands of deaths" due to exposure to

---

[45] James Clapper, "Statement for the Record: Worldwide Threat Assessment of the U.S. Intelligence Community." Senate Select Committee on Intelligence, March 12, 2013.

[46] James Clapper. "Statement for the Record: Worldwide Threat Assessment of the U.S. Intelligence Community." Senate Select Committee on Intelligence, January 29, 2014. <http://online.wsj.com/public/resources/documents/DNIthreats2014.pdf >.

[47] *The Economist*. "Cyberwar," July 1, 2010. <http://www.economist.com/node/16481504>.

[48] FireEye Inc., *World War C: Understanding Nation-State Motives Behind Today's Advanced Cyber Threats* (2013), 20.

extreme temperatures.[49] A subsequent report on the electric grid's SCADA vulnerability dated May 2013 and released by Congressmen Edward Markey and Henry Waxman, added further credibility to NAS's estimate. The congressional report points out that most utilities are subject to numerous daily cyber attacks and yet they do not comply with the most robust cyber-security standards. The Markey-Waxman assessment further asserts that available spare transformers may not be adequate.[50] Doug Myers, chief information officer for Pepco, an electric company in the mid-Atlantic region, predicts that it isn't a question of if a cyber attack on the electrical grid happens, but when.[51] Further, a study from the U.S. Military Academy's Network Science Center indicated that cyber attackers can:

> cause blackouts by targeting a relative handful of small substations — the often-overlooked and poorly-defended parts of a power grid"…leading to a "chain reaction of power overloading known a cascading failure.[52]

The government is responding to this looming threat of major cyber attacks on civilian critical infrastructure, and hosted a massive public-private exercise called GridEx II in

---

[49] Lucas Kello, "The Meaning of the Cyber Revolution: Perils to Theory and Statecraft," *International Security*, 38:2 (Fall 2013): 23.

[50] Offices of U.S. Congressmen Markey and Waxman. "Electric Grid Vulnerability: Industry Responses Reveal Security Gaps," U.S. House of Representatives, May 21, 2013, 3.

[51] Yasmin Tadjdeh, "Fears of Devastating Cyber-Attacks on Electric Grid, Critical Infrastructure Grow," *National Defense Magazine*, October 2013, 24. <http://digital.nationaldefensemagazine.org/i/177663/26>.

[52] Paulo Shakarian, Hansheng Lei, and Roy Lindelauf, "Power Grid Defense Against Malicious Cascading Failure." *U.S. Military Academy*, <http://www.westpoint.edu/nsc/siteassets/sitepages/publications/power_grid_def.pdf>.

November 2013.[53] Less than two months later in January 2014, two indicators suggested that public awareness had increased: a survey of senior U.S. national security leaders identified cyber warfare as the most serious threat facing the United States, and a Pew Research Center poll highlighted cyber attacks as one of the top threats in the minds of the American public.[54] If nothing else, perhaps the demonstration of raw cyber power during GridEx II played a small part in enhancing greater awareness. Perhaps greater activity among norm leaders and entrepreneurs also will occur in the future as a result of GridEx II and other similar exercises and will eventually fuel and accelerate the development of constraining international norms.

Conclusion

Cyber warfare poses a real and growing threat, a threat that is growing faster than the development of constraining international norms — increasing the prospects for miscalculations and escalation.[55] This article highlights that while various permissive and constraining candidate norms

---

[53] Matthew Wald, "As Worries Over the Power Grid Rise, a Drill Will Simulate a Knockout Blow," *The New York Times*, August 16, 2013. <http://www.nytimes.com/2013/08/17/us/as-worries-over-the-power-grid-rise-a-drill-will-simulate-a-knockout-blow.html?_r=2&pagewanted=print&>.

[54] Zachary Fryer-Biggs, "Poll: Cyberwarfare is Top Threat Facing US," *DefenseNews*, January 5, 2014. <http://www.defensenews.com/article/20140105/DEFREG02/301050011/Poll-Cyberwarfare-Top-Threat-Facing-US?odyssey=nav%7Chead>; Bruce Stokes, "Extremists, cyber-attacks top Americans' security threat list," *Pew Research Center*, January 2, 2014. < http://www.pewresearch.org/fact-tank/2014/01/02/americans-see-extremists-cyber-attacks-as-major-threats-to-the-u-s/>.

[55] James Clapper, "Statement for the Record: Worldwide Threat Assessment of the U.S. Intelligence Community." Senate Select Committee on Intelligence, March 12, 2013.

for cyber warfare are beginning to emerge through state practice and deliberate norm cultivation efforts, many remain mutually exclusive and contradictory. Evolution of a single constraining norm or set of norms does not appear to be anywhere near a tipping point where adoption will accelerate and significantly impact state behavior. Nevertheless, among those candidate norms competing for a foothold are the expectation of "no first use" of cyber weapons, military target discrimination, and the application of existing LOAC to cyber warfare. Yet as technological advancement continues and policy makers debate both existing legal protocols and further innovations, only time will tell what constraining norms, if any, actually emerge or stay relevant.

Energy Security and American Foreign Policy: Looking to the Past to Think About the Future

Jason Brooks

Introduction

On the evening of November 25, 1973, President Richard Nixon addressed the nation from the White House Oval Office. President Nixon's concern that night was America's foreign energy dependence, and he argued that his reform objective could be summarized in a single word that captures the essential American character — independence. "In the last third of this century," he concluded, "our independence will depend on maintaining and achieving self sufficiency in energy...by the end of this decade, Americans will not have to rely on any source of energy beyond our own".[1]

Since Nixon's presidency, the notion that America can achieve energy independence has pervaded presidential Administrations and, yet, geological and technological constraints, an even greater reliance on fossil fuels, and the realities of U.S. National Security Strategy and the global energy market have thwarted every administrations reform agenda.

---

[1] Richard Nixon. Address to the Nation about National Energy Policy. November 25, 1973. Available at: http://www.presidency.ucsb.edu/ws/index.php?pid=4051. Last accessed October 25, 2013.

A Brief History of U.S. Energy (In)Security

1860 – 1970: The U.S. as the Global Producer

America was ground zero for the modern energy industry, and the U.S. has remained at the vanguard of this now global multi-billion dollar industry, which has been a key driver of the American economy and defense sector since the early twentieth century. What complicates this narrative is that the U.S. and the global economy have become dependent on energy resources from regions of the world that are politically unstable. As a consequence, being the *de facto* arbiter of global security, the United States has found itself embroiled in the mediation of conflict in hostile world regions, notably the Middle East.

The U.S. has not always been dependent on foreign oil, however. From the time Colonel William Drake completed the world's first drilled oil well—in Titusville, Pennsylvania, in 1859—until about 1970, America was self-reliant for its energy needs. After Colonel Drake's innovative breakthrough in oil extraction, the U.S. produced surplus oil, and exported it to the world. By the time World War I erupted, the U.S. was well established as the world's leading oil producer and exporter, accounting for more than two thirds of global production.[2] With the growth and diffusion of the Industrial Revolution and rapidly evolving military technological innovations—coupled with dramatically rising automobile ownership—growing demand for this newly abundant energy source, both at home and abroad, began to drain America's domestic reserves by the end of World War II.

Abroad, the advent of oil was revolutionizing military technology in the early twentieth century, especially in

---

[2] Daniel Yergin, *The Prize: The Epic Quest for Oil, Money & Power* (New York: Free Press, 2008 [1991]), 162.

Europe. In 1912, Winston Churchill, then First Lord of the Admiralty, convinced the British Parliament to approve the conversion of the British Navy to oil-fueled ships. This conversion would provide the British Navy with the fastest ships in the world and, as Churchill strategically calculated, would free up manpower from shoveling coal to manning guns.

During World War I, oil revolutionized warfare, not only on the high seas, but also on land and in the air. The British introduced the tank to battle in 1916, and by the end of the war the British and Americans had delivered more than 150,000 trucks, cars, and motorcycles and approximately 150,000 warplanes to the battlefield. The ability to break through enemy lines with the tank and move troops at great speed over longer distances with cars, trucks, and aircraft proved to be a decisive contribution to bringing the Great War to an end.[3]

By the end of the war, the U.S., noted one observer, "had become the oil granary for [Europe]; altogether, the United States was to satisfy 80 percent of the Allies' wartime requirement for petroleum."[4] And this wasn't the last time America's natural resources would power increasingly mechanized war in Europe.

In March 1941, following the outbreak of World War II, President Franklin Roosevelt instituted the Lend Lease program.[5] Chief among items to be lent was oil. However, the energy landscape had shifted since World War I. The U.S. could no longer produce adequate supplies to satiate domestic consumption *and* simultaneously support exports to European allies embroiled in war. American consumers, individual and

---

[3] The statistics on battlefield mechanization presented here can all be found in Yergin, *The Prize*, 140-156.

[4] Ibid., 162.

[5] Ibid., 353.

industrial users, were forced to ration their petroleum consumption, especially gasoline. Unfortunately, the end of war brought little relief for U.S. petroleum supplies.

The post-war recovery in America, Europe, and Japan fueled an economic boom that sustained high energy demand. The post-war tight energy supply problem was exacerbated when pessimistic forecasts of U.S. petroleum reserves precipitated fears of American supply exhaustion.

This sequence of events compelled the American energy industry to look abroad for additional resources that could bolster supply. With the prospect that the Middle East held vast oil reserves, American oil companies and political leaders sought exploration and production opportunities in the region. The industry's efforts were exemplified by Aramco's first ever American oil concession in the region—in Saudi Arabia. The political effort was exemplified by President Roosevelt's famous rendezvous with Saudi Arabia's King Abdul Aziz Ibn Saud, a meeting that took place aboard the USS *Quincy*, an American Destroyer, on Egypt's Great Bitter Lake.

During the early post-war period, American policy makers viewed dependence on foreign energy sources as a strategic benefit because they believed it allowed the U.S. to conserve its rapidly depleting domestic energy supply. However, this strategy soon lost appeal—both with the industry and with the political elite. As early as 1949, domestic producers began demanding import restrictions to protect the domestic energy market.[6] At the same time industry pressure was mounting, U.S. policy makers encountered the first hint of the national security implications of an over-reliance on foreign oil. Egypt's 1956 seizure of the Suez Canal—a strategic choke point in the global oil supply chain—shut off the major access route for Middle East oil transiting to European markets,

---

[6] Yergin, *The Prize*, 517.

producing a supply shortfall that temporarily caused global oil prices to spike upward. Concerns of foreign energy dependence became more acute in 1967 when Egypt closed the Suez in response to the Six Day War, consequently reducing global oil supplies and causing yet another global oil price spike.

Unfortunately, America's energy security margin tightened in the late 1960s and early 1970s, just as America reached its peak level of domestic oil production. The import restrictions established under President Eisenhower in the 1950s to placate domestic interests were relaxed, and between 1967 and 1973 U.S. oil imports nearly tripled, from 2.2 million to 6 million barrels per day.[7] The U.S. has thus remained a net energy importer since 1970.

1970 – Present: The U.S. as the Global Consumer

The decades from 1970 to present times have been scarred by periods of great turmoil in the global energy market, especially the oil market.

In an attempt to wrest some market control from the seven major western companies (the Seven Sisters) that had dominated the global oil industry since the 1930s, the developing world's major oil-producing countries created the Organization for Petroleum Exporting Countries (OPEC) in 1960.[8] OPEC's primary objective at inception was to create what its founders considered to be fair and stable prices, with stability in the global oil market being the key driving force.

However, as OPEC nations worked to establish their influence over the global oil market from the 1970s through

---

[7] Yergin, *The Prize,* 549.

[8] OPEC was founded at the Baghdad Conference in September 1960. The founding members were Iraq, Iran, Kuwait, Saudi Arabia, and Venezuela.

the 1990s, their efforts created uncertainty and turbulence in the global oil market.

The economic challenges of OPEC's rise were exacerbated by the organizations political wrangling with the west, unstable domestic politics in member states, infighting between member states, and ineptitude at managing stability in the global oil market. A string of OPEC related crises began with the 1973 Yom Kippur War and subsequent Arab Oil Embargo emplaced by OPEC member nations, followed by the 1979 Iranian Revolution, the 1980s global oil glut and subsequent price collapse[9], the Iran-Iraq War and, finally, the 1990 Gulf War.

The critical lessons of this history are that market stability is undermined by the constant churn of international politics and that oil crises are driven by temporary shortfalls in global supply, which generally have their roots in geopolitics.

The result of events in the decades between 1970 and the late 1990s was to harden in the minds of American policy makers the sentiment that foreign oil dependence created unwanted vulnerabilities.

Energy (or oil) Independence and Enhanced National Security

Energy Independence and the Public Discourse

Having faced the economic shocks produced by oil price crises, American policy makers since Richard Nixon have debated the perils of America's foreign energy dependence.

---

[9] Bassam Fattouh, "An Anatomy of the Crude Oil Pricing System," *Oxford Institute for Energy Studies* WPM 40 (January 2011), 18. Although the global glut undermined the bottom line of many producers, it ushered in the end of the OPEC-administered oil pricing system, finally leaving the free operation of the market to set prices.

American champions of energy independence contend that America stands to gain economic benefits including economic growth, an increase in jobs, and a reduced balance of payments deficit. On this point, I believe they are mostly right. Set against a greater geopolitical context, however, I hold a contrary view. It is this latter point, about geopolitics, that is central to this chapter.

The idea of energy independence often has been touted as a key part of the strategy to improve America's national security position because, in particular, it would allow the U.S. to alter its position in the political landscape of the Middle East. By this logic, if the U.S. were energy independent, it would not be beholden to despotic Middle East regimes, and it would have greater leverage over countries such as Iran and Saudi Arabia. In fact, the argument goes, energy independence could even facilitate a military withdrawal from the region.

Recent presidential candidate Mitt Romney echoed the enhanced national security theme when he asserted, "With the right policies in place, America can become an energy superpower—and we can end our expensive and dangerous dependence on OPEC." Accordingly, he believed that a benefit of his plan would have been that U.S. "National security [would be] strengthened by freedom from dependence on foreign energy supplies."[10] President Obama added his voice to the chorus in 2009 by saying that America's dependence on oil is one of the most serious threats our nation has faced.[11]

---

[10] Mitt Romney Campaign website, Issues, Energy, "Mitt's Plan." Available at: http://www.mittromney.com/issues/energy. Last accessed November 1, 2012.

[11] Remarks by the President on Jobs, Energy Independence, and Climate Change. East Room of the White House January 26, 2009. Available at: http://www.whitehouse.gov/blog/2009/01/26/peril-progress-environment. Last accessed October 20, 2012.

Congress has also weighed in on this debate relatively recently, with passage of the Energy Independence and Security Act of 2007 (P.L. 110-140) and consideration in 2010 and 2011 of the "Oil Independence for a Stronger America Act," a proposal put forth by a bipartisan group led by Senator Jeff Merkley (D-OR).

The movement to achieve greater energy independence gained further inspiration in 2012 with the release of the International Energy Agency's (IEA) *World Energy Outlook 2012*. This optimistic report projects that by 2020 the U.S. will become the world's leading global oil producer, and that by 2030 the U.S. will not only be nearly self-sufficient but also be a net exporter. If true, this turn of events might have important strategic implications. For example, as the IEA report contends, "This [tide turning] accelerates the switch in direction of international oil trade towards Asia, putting a focus on the security of the strategic routes that bring Middle East oil to Asian markets."[12]

A careful study of the circumstances, however, raises many points of concern. While energy independence has the potential to be a net economic gain for America, it would not change the fact that domestic energy prices will continue to be set on the global market and, therefore, continue to be vulnerable to the forces of international relations that have driven price crises in the past. But, more importantly, such energy independence would not likely improve America's national security position or alter the way it conducts international relations, especially in the Middle East.

---

[12] International Energy Agency, *World Energy Outlook 2012*, Executive Summary. Available at:
http://www.iea.org/publications/freepublications/publication/Englis h.pdf. Last accessed January 25, 2013. *There are many reasons to approach IEA reports with skepticism, but that discussion is left aside here. For an in depth discussion see Ann Florini, "The International Energy Agency in Global Energy Governance," *Global Policy* 2 (2011).

Such a conceptualization of energy's role in U.S. foreign policy and international affairs, in fact, is shortsighted. It is clearly based on a poor understanding of the global energy market and other various pressures affecting overall U.S. national security strategy.

To better understand the central critique of this chapter, it is necessary to draw on historical insights to understand U.S. national security strategy and how it has shaped U.S. foreign policy in the Middle East. As this framework of understanding is constructed, we must explore past and present U.S. Middle East policies and determine the extent to which, if at all, U.S. interests are guided by dependence on the region's resources. I will illustrate that even without dependence on Middle East energy resources, U.S. national security strategy — especially the maintenance of security alliances and international order — remains necessarily linked to Middle East political stability and the end of the Westphalian principle of sovereignty.

Historicizing U.S. National Security Strategy

The modern world of interconnected societies, economies, and politics had firmly taken shape by the end of the nineteenth century.[13] By that time, the Industrial Revolution had also woven the U.S. into the fabric of the international economy. In the early twentieth century, the shifting European balance of power drew the U.S. further into the international fold as a participant in World War I. Yet despite this growing international interdependence, cooperation on economic regulation languished in the 1920s and 1930s, in part because America's European allies and the American public rejected President Wilson's Fourteen Points. The lack of international cooperation created an international power

---

[13] C.A. Bayly, The Birth of the Modern World: 1780-1914 (Oxford: Blackwell, 2004).

vacuum, economically and politically, and this was a primary factor in the onset of the Great Depression. States turned to autarky in the wake of the Depression and Germany began to re-arm, building its economic power and military strength through a war-focused economy. Despite numerous diplomatic efforts, World War II engulfed Europe in 1939.

The lessons of the international power vacuum that fostered the Great Depression—and WWII—shattered the American isolationist paradigm.[14] The wars and economic crises of the first half of the twentieth century had made clear to U.S. policy makers that international events would in all future times have a significant impact on the peace and prosperity of the United States. Reflecting on his trip to the Yalta Peace Conference, a "reinvigorated" President Roosevelt exclaimed to the U.S. Congress that, "The structure of world peace cannot be the work of one man, or one party, or one nation. It cannot be just an American peace, or a British peace, or a Russian, a French, or a Chinese peace. It cannot be a peace of large Nations or of small Nations. It must be a peace which rests on the cooperative effort of the whole world."[15] Included in this cooperative effort, finally, was the United States of America.

Alongside President Roosevelt, prominent post-WWII policy makers, such as Dean Acheson, John Foster Dulles,

---

[14] By "isolationist paradigm" I am referring to the American tradition of isolationism (or unilateralism) as conceived by Walter McDougall. McDougall describes isolationism as synonymous with unilateralism, or an aversion to entangling alliances and enduring international leadership responsibilities. For an in-depth analysis of this idea, see Robert Tomes' "American Exceptionalism in the 21st Century" in this volume.

[15] Franklin D. Roosevelt, Address to Congress on the Yalta Conference. March 1, 1945. Available at: http://www.presidency.ucsb.edu/ws/index.php?pid=16591. Last accessed January 25, 2013.

George Kennan, and Paul Nitze, envisioned a new world order and a new American national security strategy. This new order would be based on the rule of law and codified in an international organization, the United Nations, which would keep international order through collective security. America's foreign policy strategy for sustaining this new world order was predicated on at least four guiding principles that have received relatively consistent bipartisan support ever since, and these principles continue to guide American foreign policy today.

American policy makers sought to sustain the new international order by using the United Nations to ensure that territorial change in the international system occurred through non-aggressive means, essentially making it a matter of principle to uphold the European-constructed Westphalian system of sovereign independent nation states.[16] The United States has remained committed to this strategic principle throughout the world, and the Middle East is no exception. In 1950, the U.S. government, led by President Eisenhower, signed the Tripartite Declaration along with the governments of Britain and France which, among other things, stated that "The three governments take the opportunity of declaring their deep interests in and their desire to promote the establishment and maintenance of peace and stability in the area [Middle East] and their unalterable opposition to the use of force or threat of force between any of the states in that area." In 1957, the U.S. Congress enshrined this principle in

---

[16] For the European origins of this state system, see Crawford Young, *The African Colonial State in Comparative Perspective* (New Haven: Yale University Press, 1994). For the American drive to sustain this system, see Jeremi Suri, *Liberty's Surest Guardian: American Nation-Building from the Founders to Obama* (New York: Free Press, 2011). This original principle of sovereignty, arguably, is in a state of flux as it has come under pressure from international initiatives such as the Responsibility to Protect (R2P).

law with passage of "a joint resolution known as the Eisenhower Doctrine declaring a vital U.S. national interest in the independence and integrity of the nations of the Middle East."[17]

In response to the Arab-Israeli Six Days War, President Lyndon B. Johnson reaffirmed U.S. commitment to the Westphalian-based principles when he remarked that, "Our position with regard to the present crisis rests on two fair and evenhanded principles of general application. The first is that we support the territorial integrity and political independence of all countries of the Middle East. We stand firmly against aggression there—by anyone and in any form—as we do elsewhere. This has been the policy of the United States under four Presidents—President Truman, President Eisenhower, President Kennedy and myself. It is a bipartisan policy which we have applied evenhandedly over the past twenty years." The second principle relates to "the right of the world community to the free use of international waters and waterways," a point addressed below in greater detail.[18]

Respect for the principle of non-aggression, and respect for territorial integrity in the Middle East, has carried over into the post-Cold War era. In response to the 1990 Iraqi invasion of Kuwait, President George H.W. Bush, addressing the nation from the Oval Office, said, "The acquisition of territory by force is unacceptable. No one, friend or foe should doubt our desire for peace, and no one should doubt our determination to confront aggression...my administration, as has been the

---

[17] Paul Wolfowitz, Memorandum for the Secretary of State, "U.S. Security Relations, Commitments, and Interests in the Persian Gulf," July 26, 1990. George Bush Presidential Records, National Security Council, Haass, Richard N. Files, Working Files, Iraq Pre 8/2/90 [4], George Bush Presidential Library.

[18] Lyndon B. Johnson, Remarks by the President, June 22, 1967. Lyndon B. Johnson Presidential Library, National Security File, National Security Council History, Middle East Crisis May 12 – June 19, 1967, Vol. 3.

case with every President from President Roosevelt to President Reagan, is committed to security and stability of the Persian Gulf."[19]

Second, post-WWII policy makers sought to sustain stability in the new international order by applying balance of power theories and strategies within key regions of the world, such as Europe and Asia, an approach that continues to shape events of today.[20] In 1945, this principle was most important on the European continent, where power shifts and their subsequent conflicts had twice pulled the international community into wars of unprecedented destruction. Yet the approach has been adopted and adhered to in other regions as well. There are several notable examples in the Middle East. During his 1980 State of the Union Address, President Jimmy Carter reaffirmed American commitment to the balance of power principle in the Middle East as he outlined what became known as the Carter Doctrine.[21] President Reagan's support for Iraq in the Iran-Iraq War, President George H.W. Bush's defense of Kuwait, and, more recently, U.S. concerns about Iran's nuclear development program all demonstrate an

---

[19] George H.W. Bush, "Address by the President to the Nation," The White House Office of the Press Secretary, August 8, 1990. George Bush Presidential Library, Haass, Richard N. Files, Presidential Meeting File, Kuwait Crisis 1990 [1].

[20] See George F. Kennan, *American Diplomacy* (Chicago: University of Chicago Press, 1984); Dean Acheson, *Present at the Creation: My Years in the State Department,* (New York: W.W. Norton and Company, 1969); NSC-68, "A Report to the President Pursuant to the President's Directive on January 31, 1950," Policy Planning Staff, U.S. Department of State (April 7, 1950); on John Foster Dulles see John Lewis Gaddis, *Strategies of Containment: A Critical Appraisal of American National Security Policy During the Cold War* (New York: Oxford University Press, 2005).

[21] Jimmy Carter, State of the Union Address 1980, January 23, 1980. Available at: http://www.jimmycarterlibrary.gov/documents/speeches/su80jec.phtml. Last accessed January 27, 2013.

American commitment to the balance of power principle in the region.[22] [23]

Third, post-WWII policy makers have advocated and fought for an open and cooperative international economy predicated on the principle of free trade and its corollary: the freedom of navigation. This reality is most visibly borne out in the global economic governance institutions that populate the international landscape today. The International Monetary Fund, the World Bank and the World Trade Organization all have their origins in the post-WWII peace settlement, and especially at the Bretton Woods conference. Rightly or wrongly, American policy makers rested much blame for the Great Depression and World War II on the collapse of international economic cooperation and the turn toward autarky that characterized the inter-war period.[24] The free trade principle, thus, is not simply an end in itself. Rather, it serves as an important mechanism for facilitating international cooperation. Part of President Roosevelt's motivation for meeting with King Ibn Saud aboard the *USS Quincy* was to secure acceptance of the United States' "Open Door" vision of international trade and commerce. President Roosevelt explained to King Ibn Saud that his "plans for the post-war world envisage a decline of spheres of influence in favor of the Open Door; that the United States hopes the door of Saudi Arabia will be open for her and for other nations, with no monopoly by anyone; for only by free exchange of

---

[22] George Bush and Brent Scowcroft, *A World Transformed* (New York: Alfred A. Knopf, Inc., 1998), 305.

[23] Interview with William Inboden, former Senior Director for Strategic Planning on the National Security Council Staff.

[24] Barry Eichengreen, Golden Fetters: The Gold Standard and the Great Depression, 1919-1939 (New York: Oxford University Press, 1995).

goods, services and opportunities can prosperity circulate to the advantage of free peoples." [25, 26]

Fourth, the promotion of democracy has been an enduring principle guiding American foreign policy. American efforts to promote democracy have been particularly prevalent in the Middle East throughout the years, by way of diplomatic channels and military force: from the State Department's 1960 Saudi Arabia policy assessment to the most recent engagements in Iraq and Afghanistan, the U.S. government has frequently forged and promoted policies designed to advance the ideals of democracy, universal suffrage, and social reform.[27]

The U.S. has yet other non-oil-related national security interests in the Middle East, some of which stem from the broader principles outlined above. For example, Weapons of Mass Destruction (WMD) non-proliferation is high on America's list of strategic interests, as this issue is inextricably linked to the maintenance of the balance of power. For a small country or a transnational group, the acquisition of nuclear weapons can decisively change its bargaining power relative to the U.S.[28]

Lest this analysis get carried away with a historically deterministic narrative, however, it is imperative to recognize that history is not linear. Punctuated moments in history can

---

[25] Thomas Lippman, "The Day FDR met Saudi Arabia's Ibn Saud," *The Link* 38:2 (2005): 11.

[26] Paul Wolfowitz, Memorandum for the Secretary of State, "U.S. Security Relations, Commitments, and Interests in the Persian Gulf," July 26, 1990. George Bush Presidential Records, National Security Council, Haass, Richard N. Files, Working Files, Iraq Pre 8/2/90 [4], George Bush Presidential Library.

[27] Cable, State 13312 0471320, to Lindis, February 16, 1966, #27, Country File, NSF Box 155, LBJ Library. From Ambassador Eilts.

[28] Interview with Francis J. Gavin. For bargaining dynamics and nuclear weapons, see Thomas Schelling, *Arms and Influence* (New Haven: Yale University Press, 1966).

compel nations such as the United States to re-conceptualize their world view and reconstruct the fundamental architecture of their national security strategy. World War I began pushing the U.S. in this direction, as evidenced by Woodrow Wilson's liberal internationalist world vision and the Fourteen Points framework (known popularly as Wilsonianism) that he promulgated at the Paris Peace Conference. WWII was a punctuated moment that finally pushed the U.S. to fundamentally change its national security strategy.

Considering that another punctuated moment may lie over the horizon or, as alluded to in Bill Natter's introduction to this book, may already have happened but not yet been realized, let us pretend for a moment that the U.S. is no longer dependent on Middle East oil or global oil prices, *and* that the U.S. no longer adheres to the guiding principles of its national security strategy that would otherwise keep it involved in the Middle East (i.e. balance of power, global trade, and WMD non-proliferation). The U.S. would still face a critical strategic imperative that draws it into the region. America's most important trade partners and security allies, particularly Japan and Western Europe, are heavily dependent on the Middle East for their energy resources.

Like the U.S., both Japan and members of the European Union remain vulnerable to unanticipated shifts in the global oil market. Cumulatively, the 27 countries of the EU import 20 percent of their oil from the Middle East, making the EU as dependent on that region as is the U.S.. Japan appears to be even more vulnerable, with oil imports from the Middle East totaling 75 percent of their oil consumption, and natural gas imports accounting for approximately 22 percent of their total gas consumption. And because Japan and the EU now represent two of the four largest economies in the world, global economic prosperity is, in large part, dependent on their respective economic performance.[29]

Even if the U.S. became independent of Middle East energy, and/or even isolated itself from the global energy market, it would still feel the effects of global energy shocks as they reverberated through major economies like those of Western Europe and Japan. Therefore, in our hypothetical scenario, as in reality, U.S. prosperity remains largely dependent on stability in the global oil market and, consequently, stability in the Middle East.

Conclusion

Reliance on foreign oil is not a uniquely American problem. It is a global problem. Likewise, insecurity in the Middle East is not just an American problem; it is a challenge facing all nations. That is to say, the great challenge of today is a global reliance on energy markets and an oil-rich Middle East region that is perennially embroiled in geopolitical conflict. As long as America is vulnerable to international commodity price fluctuations, and as long as America has a stake in all aspects of the international system, stability in the Middle East will—and should—remain a paramount American concern.

The current international system was largely thought of and constructed by the United States in the wake of WWII (although Woodrow Wilson advanced many of the ideas in various forms immediately after the First World War). Since

---

[29] European Commission, *Quarterly Report on European Gas Markets*, DG Energy Market Observatory for Energy
VOLUME 4, ISSUE 4: October 2011 – December 2011.
VOLUME 5, ISSUE 1: January 2012 – March 2012.
See also *The Economist*, July 14 - July 20, 2012, titled: "Come Back Kid: Rebuilding America's Economy," a 14-page Special Report on the Gas Bonanza.

then, the U.S. has served as the prominent international leader, investing enormous resources in the maintenance of the system to prevent a temporary breakdown or long-term systemic failure.

As long as the U.S. continues to fill the indispensable position of world leader, the nation will have a fundamental strategic interest in sustaining the commodity flows that fuel the world economy and the national economies of allies such as those in Western Europe and Japan. And, more importantly, it will continue to strive for the maintenance of an international order undergirded by western constructs conceived in places like Westphalia and Bretton Woods.

US Security Strategy for Latin America: An Opportunity to get it Right

Tom Carter

Introduction

On the afternoon of September 23, 2005, a team of FBI agents gathered near Hormigueros, in western Puerto Rico, and quietly approached the home of 72-year-old Filiberto Ojeda Rios. Although they didn't know it, the date was significant: September 23, 1868, had been the date of the *Grito de Lares* rebellion against Spanish occupiers. It was also the date chosen by Ojeda Rios, in 1990, to cut from his leg an electronic monitor while U.S. courts deliberated his role in a Wells Fargo robbery of $7 million several years earlier. By cutting off the bracelet on the *Grito de Lares* anniversary, Ojeda Rios was telling the world that he preferred a life on the run to the 55-year prison stint to which he ultimately would be sentenced — *in absentia*.

Some of the facts around the FBI's actions on that afternoon in 2005 remain under a Ruby Ridge-type cloud: whether or not Ojeda Rios fired first at the agents (if he fired at all) is an open question. What no one argues is that, at about 3:00 p.m., the agents arrived at the residence, and that nearly 24 hours later they finally entered the home to find Ojeda Rios dead of a single gunshot wound to the lung.

Lying lifeless on the floor was the mastermind of an estimated 120 terror attacks on U.S. soil by the groups that Ojeda Rios had led and founded — the *Boricua Popular Army*, better known as *Los Macheteros* and the FALN (Armed Forces of National Liberation of Puerto Rico). The most notable of their attacks was the 1974 explosion, which killed four people and wounded 50 others at the historic Fraunces Tavern restaurant in downtown New York City, less than a mile from the World Trade Center. This is the same Fraunces Tavern in which, in 1783, an independence-minded commander named George Washington bade goodbye to his own band of brothers after defeating British occupying forces.

Ojeda Rios's death may have closed the book on the most violent chapter of anti-U.S. political violence in the Americas. This, coupled with other recent milestones in the final chapter of the Cold War—the transfer of power from Fidel to Raul Castro in Cuba in July 2006, and the enormously significant death of Hugo Chavez in early 2013—signaled a new chapter of U.S. relations in this hemisphere. The security implications remain promising.

U.S. Security Strategy in Latin America – Executive Summary

In the pages ahead, we will develop the case for a peacetime expansion of economic and cultural ties, with Latin America as the cornerstone of U.S. security strategy. We will lay the groundwork via a brief exploration of geopolitical context—the end of Cold War footing in the Americas more than 20 years after it ended in Europe, coupled with the gradual softening of the defensive/assertive posture adopted by the United States subsequent to the September 11, 2001, terror attacks.

With the context properly defined, we can more closely look at key areas in which American policies could positively impact the political and security environment:

- Mexico- the primacy of the U.S.-Mexico relationship cannot be ignored. Of all of the "levers of influence" available to U.S. policy-makers, improving relations with Mexico at a political and cultural level is immediately attainable and has long-term implications;

- Immigration Policy — the hot button issue of the moment appears to be a U.S. domestic legislative issue, but it is more than that. It is blunt foreign policy message about America's future role in the world. As part and parcel of Immigration policy, we will look at the "security" component of border security;

- Brazil — the fastest rising power on the global stage represents a South American anchor to U.S. hemispheric strategy. Optimizing political, economic, and security relations with Brazil has compounding benefits from a security standpoint.

In a final segment, we will advocate for policy changes and recommendations that are both realistic and achievable in the near term.

The Cold War in the Americas, 1945 – 2013

In most of the world, the Cold War between the United States and the Soviet Union was territorial. One might summarize it as "Soviet expansionism meets U.S.-led containment efforts." In Latin America, however, the Cold War was less about territory and more about political power. Latin America is home to centuries of exploitation of the poor and landless by the wealthy and land-owning class — a fertile environment for Marxism to gain traction as an alternative to rightist oligarchy. In such an environment the Soviets could enjoy a disproportionate amount of influence by supporting groups whose land-reform platforms addressed legitimate complaints. Conversely, the dynamic repeatedly caused a poor light to shine on the United States, as Washington too often supported anti-Communists with questionable governing credentials and little regard for human rights.

In the 1970s Henry Kissinger, who saw the threat of Soviet expansion in the region as over-rated, described South America as a "dagger pointing at the heart of Antarctica." His *realpolitik* view—that there was no real security threat posed by Latin American communism,[1] did not sit well with President Nixon and others in the administration, who clung to the Dominoes Theory that if communism could gain a foothold in one country, other nearby countries would topple.

Against the backdrop of the all-or-nothing paranoia of the Cold War, and as U.S. interests in a Latin American country were threatened, intervention often followed:

- In Guatemala, the 1951 election of land-reformist Jacobo Arbenz Guzman was followed by a CIA-sponsored overthrow in 1954, and the resulting cycle of violence, oppression, and civil war lasted until 1996;
- In 1961, the U.S. launched the "Bay of Pigs" invasion aimed at toppling Castro and installing new leadership; thereafter Cuba became emblematic of the U.S. vs Communism dynamic;
- The U.S. facilitated the rise of and supported the post-Allende Chilean government of General Augusto Pinochet and waged covert wars against the communist governing parties in both Nicaragua and El Salvador during the 1980s. This also tarnished

---

[1] It should be noted that Kissinger, who just celebrated his 90th birthday, has been sporadically but persistently hounded for 30 years by those who felt that his involvement around the time of Chilean President Allende's election and subsequent expulsion in the early 1970s constituted criminal behavior.

President Reagan's legacy and ended the careers of several senior administration officials.[2]

The dissolution of the Soviet Union in 1991 ended the Cold War in Europe, but that sense of closure did not cross the Atlantic. When the Soviets began to reduce financial support to Cuba during the 1980s, this certainly undermined Cuba's ability to influence its hemispheric neighbors. Still, the internal left-right political dynamics of the region carried on unabated. The Soviet collapse was political, whereas the underlying issues driving leftist influence in the Americas were economic and social. Thus it was no accident that the violence perpetrated by the left-leaning Revolutionary Armed Forces of Colombia (FARC) and the National Liberation Army of Colombia (ELN) accelerated during the 1990s and into the early 2000s, or that a corresponding increase in violence involving the right-leaning United Self-Defense Forces of Colombia (AUC) occurred.[3] The social and economic

---

[2] Not all American interventions in the region were failures: U.S. troops arriving in the tiny Caribbean nation of Grenada in 1983 were received as heroes, and their actions bolstered President Reagan's credentials as a staunch anti-Communist. President George H.W. Bush's approval of *Operation Just Cause* in Panama in 1989 burnished his credentials as a leader who was not a "wimp." Two years later the Berlin Wall fell.

[3] Author's note: in 2000 and 2001, I led the U.S. Government effort to determine whether the AUC qualified as a Foreign Terrorist Organization (FTO). Resistance to this came from many quarters, because the AUC benefited from the concept that "the enemy of our enemy is my friend." It was the only organization at the time – pre-Uribe government – capable of fighting the FARC and the ELN using their own methods. This, however, was the problem – there was no discernible difference in the methods used by the AUC vs those used by the FARC and ELN, and the non-combatants were equally vulnerable to both sides. The declaration of the AUC's status as FTO was to be announced on September 11, 2001, by Colin Powell during his trip to Peru, where he was when the United States was attacked by al Qaeda.

precipitants of the conflict were truly self-sustaining and fairly independent of the global Cold War struggle.

The Role of Charm

In Europe and Asia, communist leaders were not known for their winning personalities, but in Latin America, the leaders on the left were more charismatic than those on the right and the leftists also demonstrated a talent for demonizing the United States. In their early days, Fidel Castro and Che Guevara set the standard for style and panache. Later, even as Castro brutally repressed all opposition in Cuba, he used humor to draw attention to particular American mis-deeds.

Today, as so many strategists focus their concerns on the Pacific Rim, many tend to forget the fierce anti-capitalist nature of the Marxist-inspired groups in South America. Journalists who braved the multi-hour journey into the jungles of southern Colombia to spend time with FARC leader Manuel "Sureshot" Marulanda Velez describe the steady arrival and nonchalant storage of millions of U.S. dollars in Hefty *Steel Sack* trash bags, from which $20 and $100 bills literally spilled out.[4] Insurgent leaders committed to their cause saw the money as a pathway to more weapons, more recruits, more camps in the jungle in which to hide hostages, and additional support for the world's most sophisticated kidnapping machine; they did not view the cash as a pathway to personal wealth.

Venezuelan President Hugo Chavez subsequently emerged as the epitome of the brazen, charming leader who could simultaneously underwrite heating oil for America's poor, and crush all opposition forces in Venezuela, and fund

---

[4] The result of a series of conversations with Colombian journalists in Bogota during 2002, 2003, and 2004.

Colombian terror groups on the border. Today, with the exception of a few stalwarts in Bolivia and Ecuador, the charismatic leaders who fiercely opposed "Yankee Imperialism" are gone. This provides an opportunity for the United States to espouse its values and virtues with greater impact.

Much as the events of 9/11/2001 abruptly marked the end of the 20th century in America, so, too, has the death of Chavez closed the chapter on a virulent breed of U.S. animosity south of America's border. From a security standpoint, a new phase has been entered, in which there are no serious people, not even the Castro brothers, who believe the U.S. is planning to *invade* Cuba. Similarly, Cuba's annual renewal on the U.S. list of "State Sponsors of Terrorism" stretches credibility to such an extent that it undermines the use of the list as a naming and shaming tool.[5] Panama is the most recent site of a serious American military intervention in the region – nearly 25 years ago – so it follows that an entire generation has now grown up in this hemisphere without the presence of armed U.S. intervention.

---

[5] Cuba was added to the U.S. State Department's list of "State Sponsors of Terrorism" in 1982. Inclusion on the list comes with a set of comprehensive unilateral sanctions, in addition to those already covered under the long-standing U.S. embargo of the Castro government. In recent years, the annual renewal of Cuba's inclusion uses carefully crafted language to indicate that Cuba offers ideological rather than tangible support to left-leaning terror organizations such as the FARC. Cuba has ceased meeting the definition of State Sponsor for at least a decade and remains on the list due to the lack of any political advantage to removing it from the list, a path which would require that the Administration take a series of steps which would then be approved by Congress. Neither process seems likely to take place during Communist control of Cuba.

The U.S. "War on Terror" and Latin America

Since the al Qaeda terror attacks of 2001, the United States has assumed a sustained, unilateral, defensive/assertive posture with no historical precedent. The shock and pain of 9/11 led to a driving "never again" principle, and so began the War on Terror (and several similar aliases) which has entailed great cost: economic, political, and human. Had a failed state in Latin America hosted al Qaeda, U.S. counter-terror operations in this hemisphere would certainly have followed. That it did not meant that the hemisphere fell mostly outside the conflict zone.[6] This is fortunate because, as mentioned, U.S. intervention within this hemisphere has a strong history for developing into a losing proposition for the administration that orders it.

It's the Economic Ties, Stupid!

As America begins slowly to loosen its security posture, Latin America is a natural environment in which to return to peacetime expansion of economic activity and cooperation. Enhancing hard power relationships – of the sort found in the furthering of military alliances, the establishment of naval ports of call, and an increased number of overseas deployments—is important, but robust economic ties are an equally effective deterrent to anti-U.S. activity.

---

[6] The Guantanamo detention facilities are a notable exception. Guantanamo, in this author's view, represents a failure of trust that U.S. domestic institutions can handle a small number of individual terrorists who, in many cases, might never even have been involved in terrorist activities. This failure of trust led officials to off-shore the problem to a wildly expensive facility, on a piece of disputed territory, on an island governed by a regime hostile to U.S. interests. The concept was sufficiently nonsensical to inspire then-candidate Barack Obama to set the closure of "Gitmo" as a campaign platform back in 2008.

A useful metric for the number of Free Trade Agreements (FTA) that the United States has negotiated with other countries is this: Of the 20 FTAs currently in place, 12 are in the Americas:

- Canada and Mexico under the North American FTA (NAFTA) (January 1994 effective);
- The Dominican Republic, El Salvador, Costa Rica, Guatemala, Honduras, and Nicaragua under the Central America FTA (CAFTA) and Dominican Republic Free Trade Act, or CAFTA-DR (effective dates 2005-2009, as each participant ratified);
- Chile under the United States – Chile Free Trade Agreement (January 2004 effective)
- Peru under the United States – Peru Free Trade Act (February 2009 effective);
- Colombia under the United States-Colombia Free Trade Act (May 2012 effective).

The remaining countries of the hemisphere were, at one point, tracking towards a hemispheric agreement—the Free Trade Area of the Americas, or FTAA—which aimed to expand NAFTA to all of the countries of the Americas and the Caribbean, except for Cuba. Negotiations lasted from 1994 until 2003, when they eventually collapsed. Contributing to the collapse was an inchoate but powerful anti-globalization movement in the late 1990s and early 2000s which notably disrupted a key summit meeting in Quebec in 2001. Well before the dramatic advances of the BRIC (Brazil, Russia, India, China) economies, Brazil and the United States had taken opposing sides during FTAA negotiations, with the U.S. seen as representing developed nations, and Brazil assuming a leadership position for developing nations.

The FTAA is moribund and unlikely to spring back to life, but the fact remains that free trade agreements have security as well as economic benefits. The mere act of negotiating complex agreements bilaterally and multilaterally over a period of years brings a heightened sense of linkage and understanding, and can pave the way to security-oriented agreements as well.

America must ask itself: What messages can it send to its strategic partners in the region to convey a commitment to their economic well-being? In this article we focus on two countries where the U.S. has existing opportunities to enhance bilateral ties and security: Mexico and Brazil.

The U.S. and Mexico 2013-14

For U.S. hemispheric security policy in 2013 and beyond, Mexico represents the top strategic interest. Even after examining the bilateral relationship from any angle — economic, social, military — Mexico remains primary in every respect.

Looking first through an economic lens: with one of the world's largest economies, Mexico currently ranks 13th on the World Bank GDP list and may ascend to tenth by the end of 2014, according to some forecasters. Mexico is also a top[7] U.S. trading partner, well behind Canada but roughly tied with China, such that the two countries are typically 2nd or 3rd ranked trading partners. Total U.S./Mexico trade volume for 2012 was $424 billion according the U.S. Census Bureau's revised figures for the year. In a typical month, the United States exports 17-22 billion dollars worth of goods to the neighbor immediately beyond its southern border.

From a social perspective, the depth of the U.S.-Mexico connection cannot be overstated. The great wave of Mexican emigration to the United States during recent decades has, like waves of other immigrant groups before (Irish, Italian,

---

[7] Or second-ranked, depending on the data source and time period. U.S. trade with Mexico and China is nearly equal.

German, Japanese, et alia), re-shaped American social fabric and culture. There is a strong Mexican influence in nearly every major U.S. city and in thousands of smaller cities and towns.

Why Does Bangladesh have a Bigger Military than Mexico?

Looking at Mexico through a military, or hard power, lens is also revealing. Americans – many of whom feel threatened by cheap Mexican labor – do not feel threatened by Mexico itself. There is a reason for this: Mexico believes that it has no foreign nation-state adversaries, and it has little ambition to impose itself upon other nations. At a constitutional level, Mexico repudiates the use of force to settle disputes and rejects interference by one nation in the affairs of another. With a total military personnel (active and reserve) of 343,000, Mexico ranks well behind such countries as Greece, Malaysia, Morocco, Bangladesh, and Finland. The strategic importance of this is not Mexico's military might, but the *absence* of it – Mexico has, to some degree, assigned its existential fate to that of the U.S. – trusting America not to invade and to prevent an invasion by others.

What the U.S. Can Do to Enhance Relations with Mexico

If the NAFTA-based U.S.-Mexican economic relationship is on solid footing (and it is), and there is no military threat by either party (there isn't), and the interwoven social fabric is a fact of life in both countries (it is), then what ability does the U.S. have to influence the longer term relationship?

In baseball terms, America could hit a first-base single with relative ease if Congress approved the *Transboundary Hydrocarbon Agreements* bill. The U.S. House of Representatives passed the bill on a bipartisan basis on June 27, 2013, and it now moves to the Senate for final passage.

The bill would effectively end more than thirty years of uncertainty over the rights to two large "donut holes" of disputed ocean; these lie outside the 200-mile sovereign limit, but they are entirely surrounded by U.S. or Mexican sovereign waters. The two areas comprise over 500 miles of the U.S./Mexico maritime border and are thought to hold billions of barrels of crude oil, though comprehensive seismic scans have not been undertaken. [8] The bill would appear to be mutually attractive; Pemex stands to benefit the most among Mexican entities, and U.S. oil companies will gain vital new reserves as well. The prolonged negotiations have been something of a model for setting up a bilateral mechanism so that both sides benefit and with plans in place to deal with almost any difference of opinion.

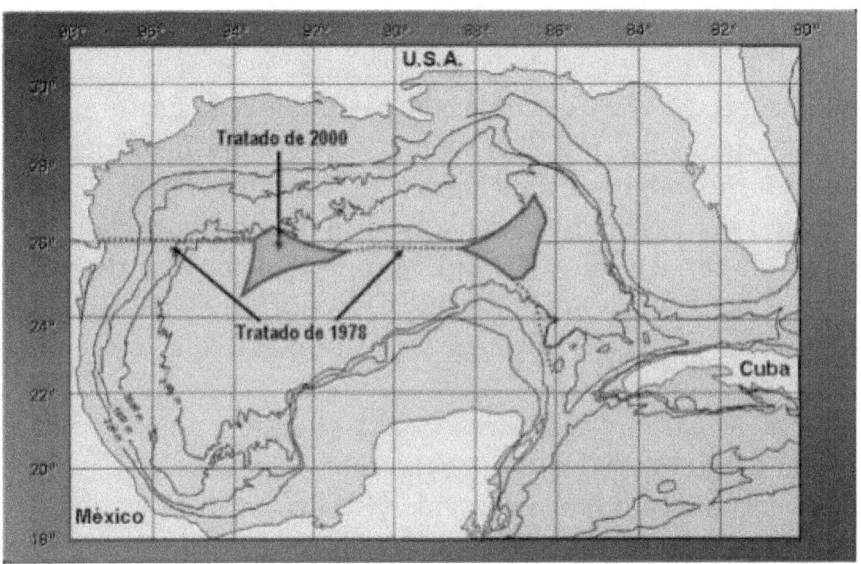

Figure 1: Disputed ocean zones

---

[8] Professor Duncan Wood has written the definitive paper on this topic, from which the map below is also derived. The full text can be found at http://www.wilsoncenter.org/sites/default/files/March_2012_Transbo undary_Oil_Agreement_0.pdf.

Mexico's Criminal State

Greater improvements in the relationship could be accomplished if the United States would help Mexico fight the cancer that weakens it: drug-fueled criminal violence. At this juncture, though, in the absence of greater political leadership in Mexico City, there is not much Washington can do. Looking at the Colombia precedent, political violence and insecurity were the norm until the Uribe presidency marshaled the political willpower to end it once and for all, at which point U.S. aid became a useful and necessary component of the effort. The current Mexican President has decided to "lower the temperature" of the conflict with powerful Mexican crime syndicates, moving away from efforts to confront them head-on and defeat them. This may turn out to be the strategy that works, or it may be a simple recognition that the state lacks the resources to win a head-to-head conflict. The Colombia comparison is only useful up to a point—the FARC and ELN were (or are) political entities that, even at the height of their power for brutality, clung to fairly classic Marxist-Leninist ideology. This meant that when they went too far, e.g. the 2002 kidnapping and six-year detention of presidential candidate Ingrid Betancourt, they risked losing important political patronage and support from left-leaning groups in Europe.

The Mexican syndicates do not operate under any such pretenses, seeking instead to increase "market share" of the criminalization of all economic activity in Mexico by any means necessary. The U.S. cannot unilaterally limit criminal violence in Mexico. However, if an Uribe-like decision is undertaken by Mexican President Enrique Pena Nieto, to pursue a military solution, the United States has the ability to help provide advanced military technology and expertise so that the fight is not lost or side-stepped for lack of firepower.

That stated, the "home run" of enhancing U.S.-Mexican relations is also the hot-button issue of the day.

U.S. Immigration Policy and Border "Security"

A common definition of terrorism is "political violence." Political violence stems from antipathy towards a government and/or its policies. Therefore, developing a positive external view of U.S. policies diminishes the likelihood of political violence and terrorism aimed at American citizens. One U.S. policy, in which all hemispheric neighbors have a direct stake, involves immigration.

On June 27, 2013, the U.S. Senate passed—by a vote of 68 to 32—a comprehensive immigration reform bill drafted by a bi-partisan Group of Eight Senators. The bill includes massive increases in funding for U.S./Mexican border security which, during the negotiation process, was considered a conservative quid pro quo for the approval of a path to citizenship for the estimated 11 million illegal immigrants currently living in the United States. The Senate bill then moved to the U.S. House of Representatives, where its fate is not yet known. Regardless of what the House does, the issues at stake are not going away. Indeed, the terms of the debate have become clear, and one of the assumptions is that the 2000-mile U.S.-Mexico border is not currently "secure." Secure from what, though? This is a question worth exploring. Do Americans believe that Mexico is poised to attack? Is an organized terror group making its way across the Rio Grande?

Figure 4: Security fence along the U.S.-Mexico Border

If we look at the U.S./Mexico border through the prism of political violence and terrorism, there is not much to support the need for increased security. None of the 9/11 attackers crossed the southern border, nor have any other high-profile terror attacks been linked to a crossing. The only high-profile terrorist to cross U.S. borders with deadly intent – Ahmed Ressam, aka Beni Noris – came across the Canadian, not Mexican, border—more than 13 years ago. And yet advocates for a secure southern border have not planned or called for a 3,000 mile security fence between the United States and Canada.

Border *control* is the more accurate term for what one calls border security in the context of the current debate. The increased spending to support U.S. Border Patrol efforts at the Mexican border are aimed at limiting the flow of illegal immigrants, both Mexican and otherwise. There is a valid argument for controlling this border in conjunction with measures—included in the pending U.S. legislation—which would allow the ebb and flow of temporary workers. Indeed, many of the estimated 11 million immigrants currently living in the shadow economy in the U.S. may return to their country of origin if their status becomes normalized.

What is Mexico's Position on the U.S. Immigration Legislation?

Absent from the immigration and border debate taking place within the U.S. Congress has been a clear articulation of Mexican interests. This would appear to be a golden opportunity for the Obama Administration to enhance bilateral relations: by seeking to articulate the views of the Mexican government as aligned with our own, and pivoting the discussion from domestic-only concerns to U.S./Mexico concerns. There is nothing in the current Senate version of the bill that would run counter to existing Mexican policy, certainly not enhanced border control. Mexican immigration laws, which underwent a comprehensive overhaul in 2011, have historically been much tougher than U.S. immigration laws. A more tightly controlled U.S. border discourages in-transit immigrants attempting to traverse Mexico from countries farther south, and it does not impinge upon Mexican sovereignty.

The U.S., Brazil, and Security Matters

Let's touch briefly on the world's seventh largest economic power—Brazil—and U.S. security policy. I was present at the Organization of American States (OAS) when, during a special session eight days after the 9/11 attacks, Brazil led the OAS effort approve a declaration that "an attack on one of us is an attack on all of us"—a bold message of solidarity. Since then, there have been substantial changes within both countries. During the 2001-2013 period, Brazil became an economic power-house and joined the modern Great Power club. Its prior identity—voice of the oppressed and developing -- has faded. The new identity—serious global player—comes with new responsibilities. Meanwhile, during the same period, the United States launched wars in Afghanistan and Iraq, invaded and provoked regime change in Libya, and hardened its overall security posture to an extent that no one could have predicted prior to 2002.

The Tri-Border Area – Still a Threat?

Viewed through an international security lens, an area of concern with Brazil is its position on the "Triple Frontera, Tri-Border Area," the commercial zone where the border is shared by Argentina and Paraguay. This area came under intense scrutiny as a possible staging ground for a series of brutal terror attacks in the 1990s: the bombing of the Israeli Embassy in Buenos Aries in 1992, which killed 29 people and wounded 242 others; and the Argentine Israelite Mutual Association (AMIA) bombing, which also took place in Buenos Aries in 1994, killing 85 people and injuring hundreds more. The governments of Argentina, Israel, and the United States investigated the Tri-Border Area extensively in the wake of the Buenos Aries attacks, and with renewed interest after the 9-11 attacks in the U.S. The area, home to large populations of Lebanese and Palestinian immigrant groups, is rumored to be the source of millions of dollars of cash remittances to Hezbollah and other sponsors of terrorism. Hard evidence of terrorist presence or financing has been elusive, however. [9]

---

[9] My own investigations in the area in 2002 took place over a whopping 48 hours, but even during that short period of time my summary conclusion was that there was actually very little going on there. The Muslim population seemed to more closely resemble the 2nd, 3rd, and 4th generation "turcos" who came from the Palestine area throughout the 20th century. My inclination was to believe the Tri-Border watchers who told me that the bad actors had fled the area in 1995-97 and not returned.

Brazil will once again face tremendous scrutiny when it hosts the 2016 summer Olympic Games, and the Tri-Border Area will once again be regarded with suspicion as a launch point, but Brazil has joined the ranks of Great Powers alongside the United States, Russia, China, and Japan. Brazil is evolving into a reliably internationalist entity, with a propensity to support the World Food Program and global peace-keeping missions, such as in Haiti and East Timor.

Brazil's Identity

As Brazil has surged forward economically into the global Top 10 nations, it makes a legitimate case that it, in addition to (or even instead of) India, should be considered for Permanent Representation in a modernized U.N. Security Council. In doing so, Brazil walks a fine line between acting like a mature global power, and holding on to its claim of representing "the little guy" of poor and developing nations. Looking at U.S. interests, one wonders whether the U.S. might leverage Brazil's growing internationalist inclinations to bring Brasilia further into U.S. and Western-led security-related efforts. For example, perhaps the time has come to work alongside Brazil to re-start the FTAA negotiations, with the U.S. and Brazil on the same page, or at least to take baby steps to build momentum for approving a more comprehensive FTAA.

Among economic indicators: Brazil is moving into the Top 10 U.S. trading partners, with roughly $100 billion in total bilateral trade. What is the risk to U.S. interests of an abrupt economic downturn in Brazil that might necessitate an international bail-out? In other words, has Brazil become "too big to fail?" A key factor that might contribute to such a collapse is the pervasive corruption that currently stunts direct foreign investment and hinders Brazil's competitiveness in international markets. A separate article might explore U.S.

efforts to step up anti-corruption assistance to reduce the "Brazil Cost" of doing business in that country.

A more assertive modern Brazil wants U.S. agriculture subsidies eliminated and reasonable guarantees for access to certain markets. Perhaps the U.S. could provide these in return for support of U.S. strategic objectives, both military and economic. A recent decision by the U.S. Air Force is to move forward with its order for 20 A-29 Super Tucano light air support vehicles made by Brazil's Embraer company, despite a vigorous lawsuit by domestic plane-maker Beechcraft, supports bilateralism.[10]

Summing Up – Policy Recommendations

In this article two major conflicts have been discussed – the Cold War and the U.S. War on Terror—in the context of enhancing U.S. security in the Americas. A case has been made for focusing U.S. efforts on optimizing economic and cultural relationships in the region, and for paying special attention to Mexico. Concrete recommendations for enhancing U.S. security policy in the region might include the following:

- Codify a U.S. policy of non-intervention in this region. Every passing year without unilateral U.S. intervention in the region increases trade, mutual respect and cooperation, and security. This is reality – the U.S. should look for a forum in which to put this forward as

---

[10] Brazil's size and complexity now yield more topics for further exploration than can be covered in this article. Separate and dedicated articles might address Brazilian "exceptionalism" and regional influence, asking whether these exert more power and influence in the southern cone than does the United States. Another topic to explore is China's role in the region: to what extent should the U.S. be concerned with Brazil's ties with the Chinese Navy?

a statement of principle and then make it a "talking point" within every bilateral statement hemisphere-wide;

- Develop a U.S.-Mexico bilateral message on comprehensive U.S. immigration reform. The administrations of both countries put forth statements expressing mutual support of the pending U.S. legislation. The facts on the ground support a case for action: the United States hosts 11 million illegal immigrants, most of whom are from neighboring countries to the south, and those 11 million people have upwards of 50 million extended relationships. Improving the respective livelihoods of the 11 million helps send a message of respect to 50 million more;
- Approve the *Transboundary Hydrocarbon Agreements* bill. This legislative action should be non-controversial and it should be accomplished during the first possible legislative session;
- Wind down the detention facilities in Guantanamo Bay. On-shoring this operation will show trust in U.S. institutions which have functioned well under one Constitution for more than 220 years, and which do not require extra-territorial and expensive facilities in order to be more effective;
- Maintain a steady pace of high level visits to the countries of the region: the President's May 2013 trip to Mexico and Costa Rica, and the Vice President's swing through South America, are welcome examples;
- Strengthen existing — and establish new — mutual security pacts, and increase joint military training opportunities and exercises;
- Promote investment and trade agreements and rejuvenate FTAA negotiations.

The Cold War is over. The U.S. War on Terror is moving into a new and perhaps a more non-military or non-kinetic phase. The United States has always benefited from fabulous geography: friendly neighbors to the north and south, wide oceans to the east and west. The security buffer that surrounds this country can be expanded hemispherically through the steps advocated here.

Part III: Potential Policies and Consequences

Future Implications for the U.S. Nuclear Posture and Nuclear Deterrence

John J. Klein

Abstract

The U.S. nuclear posture and the future role of nuclear deterrence are topics that continue to be hotly debated. This situation will continue because of changes in the international security environment and the pressure to find reductions within the U.S. defense budget. Regardless of claims to the contrary, nuclear deterrence remains critical in ensuring future peace and stability.

Introduction

Since the use of the first atomic bombs during World War II, nuclear weapons have been inextricably linked with U.S. national security policy. Nuclear weapons are a critical part of U.S. strategies to deter would-be aggressors.[1] Additionally,

---

[1] While nuclear deterrence tends to be focused on deterring state nuclear powers, under certain situations, it may be possible to deter non-state actors as well. John J. Klein, "Deterring and Dissuading Nuclear Terrorism," JOURNAL OF STRATEGIC SECURITY, 5 (2012): 15-30; available at http://scholarcommons.usf.edu/jss/vol5/iss1/6.

* The views expressed in this article are solely those of the author and do not necessarily reflect those of Analytic Services or those of the United States Government.

the U.S. promise of extending deterrence to partners and allies has limited the proliferation of nuclear weapons; this, in turn, promotes peace and stability in the international community.

Despite a record of success with nuclear deterrence, some policy makers and security experts continue to argue that the current U.S. nuclear posture is out of balance with today's security threat and that nuclear deterrence is not what it used to be. In a 2007 Op-Ed in the Wall Street Journal, George Shultz, William Perry, Henry Kissinger, and Sam Nunn state that the country's reliance on nuclear deterrence is becoming "decreasingly effective."[2] In his April 2009 speech in Prague, President Obama highlighted current nuclear dangers, declaring that, to overcome grave and growing threats, the United States will "seek the peace and security of a world without nuclear weapons."[3] The debate continues to unfold today. Many arms control advocates believe the world would be a better place without nuclear arms, and even supporters of nuclear weapons lament the high monetary costs associated with maintaining an effective arsenal.[4] The resulting discussions frequently focus on either reduction or all out elimination of these warheads.

Yet even though the international security environment is changing and fiscal pressures continue to increase, nuclear deterrence remains vital to efforts aimed at protecting and

---

[2] George Shultz, William Perry, Henry Kissinger, and Sam Nunn, "A World Free of Nuclear Weapons," *The Wall Street Journal*, January 4, 2007; available at
http://online.wsj.com/article/SB116787515251566636.html.

[3] President Barack Obama, remarks given in Hradcany Square, Prague, Czech Republic (April 5, 2009); available at
http://www.whitehouse.gov/the_press_office/Remarks-By-President-Barack-Obama-In-Prague-As-Delivered.

[4] George Perkovich et al., "Abolishing Nuclear Weapons: A Debate" (Carnegie Endowment for International Peace, February 13, 2009); available at http://carnegieendowment.org/2009/02/13/abolishing-nuclear-weapons-debate/4b0j.

promoting U.S. security interests around the globe. Given mounting security and fiscal challenges, it is, therefore, appropriate to discern recommendations regarding the future U.S. nuclear posture and the role of nuclear deterrence as part of a greater U.S. national security strategy.

Background and Recent Initiatives

The current debate between nuclear arms supporters and detractors centers on the specifics of existing treaties and periodic posture documents, such as the formal Nuclear Posture Reviews, put out by the Department of Defense (DoD).

Nuclear Posture Review

The most current U.S. Nuclear Posture Review (NPR), released in 2010, reaffirms existing strategic guidance and states that the primary role of the U.S. nuclear arsenal is to deter a nuclear attack on the United States, its allies, and partners.[5]* The NPR describes the following five policy objectives: preventing nuclear proliferation and nuclear terrorism; reducing the role of U.S. nuclear weapons in U.S. national security strategy; maintaining strategic deterrence and stability at reduced nuclear force levels; strengthening

---

[5] The Department of Defense, *Nuclear Posture Review Report* (Washington, D.C.: April 2010), vii. "The fundamental role of U.S. nuclear weapons, which will continue as long as nuclear weapons exist, is to deter nuclear attack on the United States, our allies, and partners." * The Editors note that Secretary Hagel ordered "comprehensive" internal and external reviews of the DoD nuclear enterprise in 2014. While comprehensive in name, the respective reviews were not critical assessments of the nation's nuclear posture in any strategic sense of the word and focused instead on training, testing, command oversight, mission performance, and funding. Ultimately, the both assumed a continuation of the current organizational make-up of the nuclear force and imbibed the findings and recommendations of the 2010 NPR."

regional deterrence and reassuring U.S. allies and partners; and sustaining a safe, secure, and effective nuclear arsenal.[6]

The 2010 NPR notes that as long as nuclear weapons exist, the United States will seek to deter potential adversaries and assure U.S. allies and other security partners with a credible and comprehensive security guarantee.[7] By maintaining a credible nuclear deterrent and reinforcing regional security architectures with missile defenses and other conventional military capabilities, Washington believes it can provide confidence to its non-nuclear allies while also discouraging any nuclear ambitions they may entertain. While the Obama administration has sought to reduce the number of warheads in the U.S. nuclear stockpile, its stated goal is to do so without affecting the reliability, efficacy, and deterrent effect of the entire arsenal.[8]

The 2010 NPR also states that the United States must continue to maintain stable strategic relationships with Russia and China. Correspondingly, the United States must further counter threats posed by any emerging nuclear-armed states, in order to protect the United States — along with its allies and partners — against nuclear threat or intimidation.[9] The NPR underscores the importance of the United States' "negative security assurance," by declaring that Washington will not use or threaten to use nuclear weapons against non-nuclear weapons states that are party to the Nuclear Non-Proliferation Treaty (NPT) and that are in compliance with established non-proliferation protocols.[10] This negative security assurance is

---

[6] Ibid., iii.

[7] Ibid.

[8] Executive Office of the President, *National Security Strategy* (Washington, D.C.: The White House, May 2010), 4. "We are reducing our nuclear arsenal and reliance on nuclear weapons, while ensuring the reliability and effectiveness of our deterrent."

[9] The Department of Defense, *Nuclear Posture Review Report*, 4.

[10] Ibid., viii.

intended to highlight the security benefits gained by adhering to, and fully complying with, the NPT, while also strengthening the current non-proliferation regime.

New Strategic Arms Reduction Treaty (New START)

Based upon the analysis conducted in support of the 2010 NPR, New START, signed in April 2010, limits Russia and the United States to fewer strategic nuclear weapons by 2018. New START includes three main points. First, it caps the number of deployed, long-range nuclear warheads on each side at 1,550, down from 2,200. Second, it establishes a combined limit of 800 deployed and non-deployed intercontinental ballistic missile (ICBM) launchers, submarine launched ballistic missile (SLBM) launchers, and heavy bombers equipped for nuclear armaments (the United States currently has about 850 deployed and Russia has an estimated 565) – and further caps at 700 the number of nuclear launchers allowed to be in deployable status at any given time.[11] Finally, it reestablishes a system in which each country monitors the other's arsenal.

Under New START, the verification regime includes relevant parts of START I as well as new provisions to cover items not previously monitored. The United States and Russia will each continue to depend on satellite surveillance, or National Technical Means (NTM), to monitor the other's strategic forces. With respect to Russian mobile ICBMs, all new missiles are subject to the treaty as soon as they leave a production facility, and each missile and bomber will carry a unique identifier. Russia must notify the United States 48 hours before a new solid-fueled ICBM or SLBM leaves its production facility and when it arrives at its destination,

---

[11] See the U.S. Department of State New START Web site for an overview of the Treaty, available at
http://www.state.gov/t/avc/newstart/index.htm.

which will facilitate monitoring by NTM. Verification of treaty limits and conversion or elimination of delivery systems is carried out by NTM and 18 annual short-notice, on-site inspections. The verification regime allows ten on-site inspections of deployed warheads and deployed and non-deployed delivery systems at any land, air, and submarine base. It also allows eight on-site inspections at facilities that may hold only non-deployed delivery systems.[12]

New START has been criticized for several shortcomings. In particular, it is criticized for failing to address Russia's large arsenal of short range, tactical nuclear weapons. According to U.S. officials, Russia has a nearly 10-to-1 numeric advantage in this class.[13] As of 2012, the United States is reported to have approximately 760 tactical nuclear weapons, and Russia is estimated to have upwards of 6,000 in its arsenal.[14] During negotiations, Senators Joe Biden and John Kerry both

---

[12] "Treaty Between the United States of America and the Russian Federation on Measures for the Further Reduction and Limitation of Strategic Offensive Arms," Article VI, IX, X, XI, Protocol and Annexes; available at http://www.state.gov/t/avc/newstart/c44126.htm.

[13] Keith Payne, "Evaluating the U.S.-Russia Nuclear Deal," *The Wall Street Journal* (online), April 8, 2010; available at http://online.wsj.com/article/SB100014240527023037206045751695329 20779888.html.

[14] Amy F. Woolf, "Nonstrategic Nuclear Weapons," *CRS Report for Congress*, December 19, 2012; available at www.fas.org/sgp/crs/nuke/RL32572.pdf. The U.S. forward deploys B-61 tactical nuclear warheads in Europe under American military custody, but they are on hand for delivery by NATO or U.S. dual-capable aircraft (Ibid). The Russians are believed to use a variety of tactical nuclear weapons, such as rocket forces, artillery, air defense, frontal aviation, naval aviation, and ships and submarines, tailored to different military units. *See* Gunnar Arbman and Charles Thornton, "Russia's Tactical Nuclear Weapons, Part I: Background and Policy Issues,"
(Swedish Defence Research Agency, November 2003), 17; available at http://drum.lib.umd.edu/bitstream/1903/7912/1/thorntonrussia.pdf.

expressed concern that the Bush administration's 2002 Moscow Treaty did not limit Russian tactical nuclear forces.[15] Senator Jim Risch tried to insert language addressing the tactical nuclear weapons issue into the New START treaty preamble, but his effort was unsuccessful.[16]

Interestingly, Washington and Moscow have reversed their respective views on the role of tactical nuclear weapons in military strategy. During the Cold War, the United States and NATO initially viewed tactical nuclear weapons as crucial to thwart the Warsaw Pact's overwhelming conventional forces, an approach validated and required once the West abandoned any hope of countering the threat man-for-man or tank-for-tank. Instead, NATO would employ tactical nuclear weapons along the assumed axes of Soviet advance.[17] Today, Russia views tactical nuclear weapons as an inexpensive option and "equalizer" that compensates for its potential security and military shortfalls, while providing for defense against potential aggression by NATO, which it still views as an aggressive bloc. For these reasons, Russian leaders will likely be reluctant to agree to any reductions in the number of their tactical nuclear weapons during future arms control negotiations.[18]

---

[15] Payne, "Evaluating the U.S.-Russia Nuclear Deal."

[16] Walter Pincus, "Russian tactical nuclear weapons still an issue after START treaty ratification," *The Washington Post*, December 27, 2010; available at http://www.washingtonpost.com/wpdyn/content/article/2010/12/27/AR2010122702931.html.

[17] Tom Nichols, Douglas Stuart, and Jeffrey D. McCausland, eds. *Tactical Nuclear Weapons and NATO* (Strategic Studies Institute, April 2012), Preface, viii.

[18] Leonid Polyakov, "Aspects of the Current Russian Perspective on Tactical Nuclear Weapons," in Tom Nichols, Douglas Stuart, and Jeffrey D. McCausland, eds. *Tactical Nuclear Weapons and NATO* (Strategic Studies Institute, April 2012), 155-56.

Calls for an Even Smaller Nuclear Force

Despite the significant reductions in long-range arms secured in New START, many security and policy experts continue to advocate for even further cuts. In the updated 2012 U.S. military strategy, the Secretary of Defense notes, "*It is possible that our deterrence goals can be achieved with a smaller nuclear force,* which would reduce the number of nuclear weapons in our inventory as well as their role in U.S. national security strategy."[19]

The idea of further reducing the U.S. nuclear arsenal is echoed by arms control groups advocating for the total elimination of all nuclear weapons. In May 2012 one such group—Global Zero—called for eliminating the U.S. fleet of fixed, land-based nuclear ICBMs that make up one leg of the American nuclear triad. It also advocated that all U.S. tactical nuclear weapons be eliminated over the next ten years, ranking their strategic utility as practically nil.[20] Global Zero advocates include the former Vice Chairman of the Joint Chiefs of Staff, General James Cartwright, who has stated that U.S. nuclear deterrence could be guaranteed with 900 nuclear warheads, and with only half deployed at a time.[21] Cartwright goes on to state that steep reductions in the U.S. nuclear arsenal are needed if the United States wants to maintain

---

[19] The Secretary of Defense, *Sustaining U.S. Global Leadership: Priorities for 21st Century Defense* (Washington, D.C.: January 2012), 5. Italics are original emphasis.

[20] Global Zero U.S. Nuclear Policy Commission, *Global Zero U.S. Nuclear Policy Commission Report: Modernizing U.S. Nuclear Strategy, Force Structure and Posture* (Global Zero, May 2012), 7-8.

[21] Thom Shanker, "Former Commander of U.S. Nuclear Forces Call for Large Cut in Warheads," *The New York Times,* May 15, 2012; available at http://www.nytimes.com/2012/05/16/world/cartwright-key-retired-general-backs-large-us-nuclear-reduction.html.

credibility in urging restraint by other nuclear-aspirant powers such as India, Pakistan, and North Korea.[22]

Reductions in U.S. nuclear forces are also said to be needed because of the high cost to maintain and upgrade the arsenal. Such a proponent is Republican Senator Tom Coburn, who advocates further cuts in the U.S. nuclear arsenal, to achieve more than $79 billion in savings.[23] Official DoD estimates put U.S. spending levels for nuclear weapons at about $214 billion over the next ten years, or just above $20 billion a year.[24] Yet according to a study by the Stimson Center, the United States actually spends more than $30 billion annually. As fiscal cuts to the U.S. Defense budget loom, reducing spending on efforts to upgrade and maintain the nuclear arsenal is seen by some as good policy.[25]

Still, those advocating for deeper cuts in the nuclear arsenal, particularly Global Zero, have been criticized for short-sightedness and for failing fully to understand the role of nuclear deterrence. Referring to General Cartwright and the Global Zero nuclear policy report, General Norton Schwartz, Chief of Staff of the Air Force, is reported to have admonished, "I don't agree with his assessment nor the

---

[22] Ibid.

[23] Tom Coburn, "Back in Black" (accessed April 30, 2013), 14-15; available at http://www.coburn.senate.gov/public/index.cfm?a=Files.Serve&File_id=92a11aeb-a484-45d4-b02a-83071603accf.

[24] Gordon Adams, "Our Nukes Cost More Than You Think; Stimson Pegs Annual Nuke Spending at $13B," *AOL Defense,* June 18, 2012; available at http://defense.aol.com/2012/06/18/our-nukes-cost-more-than-you-think-stimson-pegs-annual-nuke-spe/.

[25] Editor, "The Bloated Nuclear Weapons Budget," *The New York Times,* October 29, 2011; available at http://www.nytimes.com/2011/10/30/opinion/sunday/the-bloated-nuclear-weapons-budget.html.

study."[26] Keith Payne of the National Institute of Public Policy has taken exception to the report's assessment that "Security is mainly a state of mind, not a physical condition," noting that states feel insecure when under real threat or attack.[27] Payne also counters Global Zero's assertion that allies can and will be more assured by U.S. non-nuclear forces than by the "nuclear umbrella,"[28] noting that much evidence exists to the contrary, because key allies—South Korea, Japan, and members of NATO—continue to stress the importance of the U.S. nuclear umbrella in maintaining security assurances and promoting regional stability.[29]

The Role and Limitations of Nuclear Deterrence

When considering the future role of deterrence in U.S. national security policy, it is important to understand what deterrence is and what it is not. In one of the most enduring definitions, deterrence is said to be "persuading a potential enemy that he should, in his own interest, avoid certain courses of activity."[30] As a subset of general deterrence, the concept of nuclear deterrence holds that a credible and potentially overwhelming use of nuclear weapons in response to an adversary's attack is sufficient to deter most potential

---

[26] Marcus Weisgerber, "USAF Chief Raps Report on Cutting Nuke Arsenal," *Defense News*, May 16, 2012; available at http://www.defensenews.com/article/20120516/DEFREG02/305160009/USAF-Chief-Raps-Report-Cutting-Nuke-Arsenal.

[27] Ibid. Keith B. Payne, "Zero Nuclear Sense: Is Reckless Disarmament the Plan for the Second Obama Term?" *The Washington Times*, May 29, 2012; available at http://www.washingtontimes.com/news/2012/may/29/zero-nuclear-sense/.

[28] Ibid.

[29] Ibid.

[30] Thomas Schelling, *The Strategy of Conflict* (Cambridge, MA: Harvard University Press, 1960), 9.

aggressors from employing nuclear weapons. The 2010 Nuclear Posture Report underscores this idea when it states: "the United States will continue to ensure that, in the calculations of any potential opponent, the perceived gains of attacking the United States or its allies and partners would be far outweighed by the unacceptable costs of the response."[31]

Yet strategist Colin S. Gray helps us begin to understand that deterrence theory also has its limitations. "Given that deterrence can only work, when it does, in the minds of enemy leaders," he writes, "it is their worldview, not ours, that must determine whether or not deterrence succeeds."[32] Therefore, it ultimately does not matter if U.S. national leaders, strategic planners, and defense analysts all agree that a potential adversary *should be* deterred by the U.S. nuclear posture. It only matters if a potential adversary's leadership *is* deterred.

Nuclear deterrence theory is even more complex than many might appreciate because at its heart lies a fundamental paradox. Nuclear deterrence is only successful if it directly averts the use of nuclear weapons, but a credible deterrence capability requires planning for the weapons' intended use. If employed, deterrence has failed. In short, nuclear deterrence is possible only by means of maintaining an effective and credible nuclear strike capability, as well as through efforts to implement planning necessary for its use against potential adversaries.

The task of American strategists — indeed all strategists — is complicated further because the concept of nuclear deterrence can be undermined in two additional and important ways. First, if an offensive nuclear capability is unilaterally reduced so that the leadership of a potential

---

[31] The Secretary of Defense, *The Nuclear Posture Review Report*, xi.
[32] Colin S. Gray, *National Security Dilemmas: Challenges & Opportunities* (Dulles, VA: Potomac Books, Inc., 2009), 56.

adversary believes it can "win" — or at least "not lose" — a nuclear exchange, then such an arsenal cannot be considered sufficient, and deterrence is undermined. Second, deterrence or, more specifically, extended deterrence, may be subverted if a leading nuclear power such as the United States fails to maintain a reliable and sufficiently-sized arsenal capable of providing a nuclear guarantee to its allies. With respect to the United States, an unreliable security guarantee would confound the nation's existing policy objectives by encouraging allies to pursue the development of their own nuclear programs independent of U.S. stockpiles. An increase in the number of nuclear-armed countries, consequently, would exacerbate proliferation concerns and possibly increase the likelihood of a terrorist organization's acquiring such weapons from one of the adolescent nuclear powers.

Deterrence works only if a credible threat of retaliatory force exists, and for the U.S. defense community, credibility is typically governed by what is known as the Law of Armed Conflict, an extension of that part of international law regulating the conduct of armed hostilities.[33] Of the ideas and principles contained in the Law of Armed Conflict, the two following principles are most germane to the idea of nuclear deterrence and any action in response to nuclear aggression: the principle of military necessity and that of lawful targeting. The principle of military necessity calls for using only that degree and kind of force required for the partial or complete submission of the enemy, while taking into consideration the minimum expenditure of time, life, and physical resources.[34] This principle is designed to limit the application of force to

---

[33] U.S. Joint Chiefs of Staff, *Department of Defense Dictionary of Military and Associated Terms*, Joint Publication 1-02 (Washington, D.C.: March, 23 1994), 215.

[34] U.S. Department of the Navy, *The Commander's Handbook on the Law of Naval Operations*, NWP 1-14M (Washington, D.C.: July 9, 1995), 6-5.

that required for carrying out lawful military purposes. Although the principle of military necessity recognizes that some collateral damage and incidental injury to civilians may occur when a legitimate military target is attacked, it does not excuse the wanton destruction of lives and property disproportionate to the military advantage to be gained.[35]

In contrast, the principle of lawful targeting is based on three underpinnings.[36] First, it stipulates that a belligerent's right to injure the enemy is not unlimited. Second, it states that the launching of attacks specifically against civilian populations is prohibited. And third, it posits that the identification and distinction of combatants must be made clear so as to spare as much as possible any injury to non-combatants. Consequently, and by extension, the principle of lawful targeting requires that all "reasonable precautions" be taken to ensure the targeting of only military objectives, so that damage to civilian objects (collateral damage) or death and injury to civilians (incidental injury) is avoided as much as possible.[37] Such considerations are fundamentally important to all U.S. nuclear force posture decisions.

Recommendations for the Future

There are several kinds of assessments and analytical techniques that could be used to suggest the "correct" number of warheads so that the U.S. can "ensure" deterrence, and these techniques are dependent on the informed preconceptions of perceived threats. While providing specifics on the type and number of nuclear weapons needed to ensure deterrence may imply a finite degree of certitude about the accuracy of any forthcoming analysis, more often than not

---

[35] Ibid. This concept is also referred to as the principle of proportionality.
[36] Ibid., 8-1. This also referred to as the principle of distinction.
[37] Ibid.

such analysis is simply a best (though educated) guess about the potential threat. In other words, it is based on assumptions about the strength and extent of competing arsenals, as well as assumptions about the risk tolerance of those holding leadership positions in the governments of potential adversaries. Furthermore, once made, such assumptions almost certainly would become outdated within a relatively short period of time. For these reasons, this analysis will not provide policymakers specific recommended numbers of nuclear warheads and associated delivery systems. In the aggregate, such uncertainties may help explain why the U.S. defense establishment has consistently displayed an inability to assess accurately the capabilities of potential adversaries or to predict future threats.[38]

Yet despite the level of uncertainty embedded in such strategic calculations as the required number of nuclear weapons, it remains possible to provide specific recommendations concerning the future U.S. nuclear posture and the role of nuclear deterrence in addressing future global security challenges. These recommendations are as follows:

Don't Seek the Minimum Number of Weapons

Policymakers should not seek to reduce the U.S. nuclear arsenal to the minimum required to achieve deterrence, because any determined minimum threshold could be based upon erroneous information, and/or the threat assessment could change after such a determination is made. Among some analysts, there is a frequent tendency to determine, through some chosen analytical process, the minimum number of nuclear warheads that the United States should maintain in order to ensure effective deterrence while still

---

[38] Richard Danzig, *Driving in the Dark: Ten Propositions About Prediction and National Security* (Washington, D.C.: Center for a New American Century, October 2011), 5.

meeting our extended deterrence obligations with allies and partners. For example, Global Zero's Nuclear Policy Commission has advocated for a "substantially decreased stockpile of nuclear weapons and delivery vehicles," resulting in only 450 immediately deployable warheads.[39]

Seeking a minimum threshold is a dangerous strategy. If U.S. national security leadership decided only to have a nuclear arsenal that was on par with or comparable to that of a potential adversary, then deterrence would be limited. As Henry Kissinger and Brent Scowcroft have astutely noted, "Strategic stability is not inherent [in a strategic posture] with low numbers of weapons; indeed, excessively low numbers could lead to a situation in which surprise attacks are conceivable."[40] Therefore, a potential adversary, based upon its own assessments, could determine it could actually "win" or even achieve a stalemate during a nuclear exchange with the United States. So reductions that set an arbitrary bottom threshold on nuclear capability might increase the likelihood of deterrence's failing. This is because the lower the threshold, the greater the chance for ambiguity or uncertainty about the true U.S. nuclear capability, which could cause an adversary to seek conflict.

Maintain a Range of Nuclear Response Options

In order to have a plausible nuclear deterrent—one that is able to deter a range of potential future threats—the United States must have a variety of nuclear weapons that are able to deliver both minor and severe military effect commensurate with the anticipated threat. Specifically, the U.S. nuclear arsenal should include an ample number of low-yield nuclear

---

[39] Global Zero U.S. Nuclear Policy Commission, *Global Zero U.S. Nuclear Policy Commission Report*, 6-7.

[40] Henry A. Kissinger and Brent Scowcroft, "Strategic Stability in Today's Nuclear World," *The Washington Post*, April 23, 2012.

weapons, so that the president is provided with the best range of potential response options following an adversary's attack. According to the Law of Armed Conflict, the application of the principle of military necessity to any potential U.S. nuclear reaction should not exceed the kind or degree of force needed to accomplish the military objective.[41] Additionally, applying the principle of lawful targeting means that a nuclear response should discriminate between military objectives and civilian objects in order to mitigate collateral damage and incidental injury.[42] For these reasons, smaller low-yield weapons may prove to be the preferred nuclear response option versus larger and potentially more indiscriminate nuclear warheads.

If an adversary detonated a low-yield nuclear weapon within the United States and a commensurate low-yield nuclear weapon was not readily available for a U.S. response to the attack, U.S. national leadership would need to weigh other options, such as employing a higher-yield nuclear weapon, or perhaps conventional weapons with a similar destructive effect. Both options pose challenges for policymakers. Using a significantly higher yield nuclear weapon might increase the possibility of conflict escalation, which may not be in the best interests of the United States. The employment of a higher-yield nuclear response option might also exceed the degree of force needed to accomplish the military objective and could, therefore, violate the Law of Armed Conflict regime. As for planning for and relying on a conventional response to a nuclear strike, U.S. policymakers would be required to consider how this might undermine allied perceptions of Washington's resolve, commitment to the idea of extended deterrence, and the strength of the American nuclear arsenal.

---

[41] U.S. Department of the Navy, The Commander's Handbook on the Law of Naval Operations, 6-5.
[42] Ibid., 8-1.

Maintaining a range of U.S. nuclear options also means providing for a variety of delivery vehicles such as those provided in the current triad system, with launch capabilities across the air, sea, and land environs. This goes against Global Zero proposals to eliminate all fixed, land-based intercontinental ballistic missiles (ICBMs), in part because of perceived risks associated with this leg of the nuclear triad. The argument of Global Zero advocates is based on assertions that the existence of ICBMs can produce ambiguous attack indications in the minds of potential adversaries and might trigger unnecessary nuclear retaliation.[43] Also, the fixed locations of ICBM launch sites are said to be inherently targetable and depend heavily on launch warning for survival.[44] Admittedly, fixed ICBM sites are indeed targetable and their projected overflight paths might induce a level of anxiety in some nations. However, such anxiety can be addressed through greater diplomatic coordination with affected nations, whose inherent vulnerability can be mitigated through advanced indications methods and warning and anti-missile defenses. Submarines or aircraft that launch nuclear weapons are also targetable and vulnerable, albeit less so. Yet their existence in the nuclear triad system improves the survivability of the entire arsenal vis-à-vis the concept of dispersal, an effective approach for complicating the targeting calculations of potential adversaries.

Address Russia's Tactical Nuclear Weapons

Tactical nuclear weapons were not addressed in New START, specifically Russia's substantial inventory of these shorter-range nuclear weapons. This was a mistake. Even though Moscow views tactical nuclear weapons as critical to

---

[43] Global Zero U.S. Nuclear Policy Commission, *Global Zero U.S. Nuclear Policy Commission Report*, 7.
[44] Ibid., 8.

their strategic defense, these weapons should be open to discussion, primarily because the differentiation between "strategic" and "tactical" is no longer as important as it was in the past. Previously, the distinction may have had significant merit, but the technological and geopolitical developments that have occurred over the past several decades suggest the need for a new approach. Colin Gray has correctly observed that military activity is inherently tactical, but he also points out that the consequence of all military activity is the realm of strategy.[45] This holds true regarding nuclear weapons. The use of nuclear weapons to achieve military objectives is tactical in nature, but the consequences and effects of their use should and must be considered strategic.

Consequently, future language in a new treaty with Russia or any other country should address all classes and types of nuclear weapons, including shorter-range or "tactical" nuclear weapons.[46] Nuclear deterrence concerns all types and sizes of nuclear weapons and delivery systems. Arms control efforts to limit the future nuclear arsenals should, therefore, address the full spectrum of a country's nuclear capability.

Summary and Conclusion

Because of the ongoing pressure to find savings within the U.S. defense budget, it is likely that the role and size of the U.S. nuclear arsenal will continue to be debated. This fiscal pressure may indeed lead to reductions in the nuclear arsenal

---

[45] Colin S. Gray, *Modern Strategy* (London: Oxford University Press, 1999), 18.

[46] Such an agreement may be seen as inconsequential to China, whose arsenal is not assessed to include any tactical or low-yield nukes. See Office of the Secretary of Defense, "Military and Security Developments Involving the People's Republic of China" (Washington, D.C.: August 2011) 34; available at http://www.defense.gov/pubs/pdfs/2011_CMPR_Final.pdf.

or to additional delays in efforts to modernize and maintain the arsenal. Regardless of the outcome of such discussions, however, a better understanding of the role of nuclear deterrence—and extended deterrence—as well as the implications of the Law of Armed Conflict regime, would allow for a more careful discernment of preferred actions regarding the future U.S. nuclear strategy posture, and it would guide our leaders to the proper employment of American nuclear arms.

A more careful assessment of, and approach to, the use of American nuclear weapons must avoid undue reductions in the size of the overall arsenal; maintain a range of nuclear response options, to include a capacity for responding with small-yield nuclear devices and those delivered via ICBMs or SLBMs; and insist on the inclusion of Russian tactical nuclear weapons during future treaty negotiations.

Maintaining effective deterrence and ensuring future non-use of nuclear arms is an expensive proposition, but the alternative of deterrence failing and a state-to-state nuclear exchange occurring is many times more costly and severe. The maintenance of a sufficient amount of nuclear capacity is necessary to ensure a strong deterrent capability and to provide an extended guarantee of security to American allies. Such a plan will require a substantial but necessary investment. Failure to provide for adequate financial resources now may prove to be both costly and devastating in the future. It would be prudent for the U.S. to provide adequate investments now to reduce such risk.

Radical Resourcing: The Force Structure Implications of 'The Sovereignty Solution'

James Hasik

There is much to find intriguing in *The Sovereignty Solution: A Commonsense Approach to Global Security* (Naval Institute Press, 2011). Edward Luttwak termed it "a perfectly sound alternative" to current American military activities. Former Air Force Secretary James Roche called it "a strong case for a U.S. strategy that leaves other countries alone to live as they wish." The esteemed Andrew Marshall and his Office of Net Assessment provided the initial sponsorship for the book's genesis, a summer-long seminar at the Naval Postgraduate School (NPS) in 2006. The authors — Anna Simons, professor of defense analysis at the NPS, and Joe McGraw and Duane Lauchengco, serving officers of the Green Berets — hardly fit the antiestablishment mold, but their message is radical. Following their earlier article (with two more collaborators), in the spring 2007 issue of *The American Interest*, this book views American military activity around the world, at least since the end of the Cold War, as excessively interventionist, overly concerned with the plight of peoples outside the United States, and financially unsustainable. In its place, they recommend a strategy based simply on defending the sovereignty of the United States against all comers, and to the utmost extent of national abilities.

While the authors do not quite state it this way, the essence of their strategy comes down to five points. Cede the initiative to potential enemies, and fight only when attacked. Disclaim responsibility for defending allies from local bullies, as other countries' sovereignty is their own problem. When attacked, fight intensely and without remorse, confident that relaxed rules of engagement will provide some "shock and awe" to local populations backing the wrong people. Continue fighting until those enemies surrender or die. And all the while, marshal a renewed sense of national unity, seemingly unseen since the 1940s, to ensure the commitment of all resources required for the big win.

Just how this last requirement is to be met is left largely unanswered in the book, which is where the problems begin. Considerations of the balance of power in international relations theory are also left wholly unaddressed, and indeed, this is where the problems of the book get worse. But the biggest problem is that the book's go-it-alone argument only breezily addresses what those required resources might be, claiming that existing B-52s with cruise missiles, some "light ground forces backed by a swarm of American aircraft" from carriers, those now-popular "shoot-to-kill drones," and some special forces should suffice for most contingencies (pp. 127–128). To be fair, the authors' imagined missiles are meant for substantive targets, as they pointedly eschew the antiseptic cruise missile diplomacy of the 1990s. They don't mean, as George W. Bush famously panned in September 2001, "to fire a $2 million missile at a $10 empty tent and hit a camel in the butt." Rather, they mean decisive action—such as invading Afghanistan.[1]

---

[1] Comments by George W. Bush in the Oval Office on September 13, 2001, to the federal senators from Virginia and New York, in Howard Fineman, "A President Finds His True Voice," *Newsweek*, 24 September 2001.

Thus I propose that we analyze exactly what those resource requirements would be. To begin, consider their notable example of how this strategy would work in practice: the recommended response to an attack on the United States by Hezbollah. In this scenario, dealing with the Party of God properly means eradicating it. In their view, the prescribed approach begins with an ultimatum to the Lebanese and Syrian governments, rather like Richard Armitage's famous alleged threat against Pakistan: interfere, and "be prepared to be bombed."[2] Next comes an American invasion of southern Lebanon, and the destruction of any fortification, house, or village from which the attack is resisted. Hezbollah's so-called asymmetric and hybrid strategy is thus to be exposed as nothing more than the stark weakness of an armed gang that cannot afford, or cannot obtain, premier league weapons. The assault continues up to the Israeli and Syrian borders, which are to be sealed either by friendly troops (from a "partner state") or simply more bombing.

It is an interesting strategy, to be sure, and while the authors preemptively try to evade the tag, it is one that gets discussed more often at Midwestern barbecues than at cocktail parties inside the Beltway. But for strategy to be taken seriously, it must be properly resourced, and in this particular case, it is the alleged financial bankruptcy of current strategy that prompted the authors to offer an alternative. If this "sovereignty solution" is worthy of serious discussion, its tenets must not lead to unworkable conditions. And if this "commonsense approach" is garnering increased interest, we should consider the likely results of each scenario: a pullback from most overseas garrisons and deployments, a concomitant resolution to deal with all transgressions brutally, and an accompanying relative shift back towards overwhelming

---

[2] Interview with General Pervez Musharraf, *60 Minutes*, CBS News, September 21, 2006.

firepower for dealing with enemies hiding in shadows. As the authors raise the issue of Hezbollah, we might base our response on this case.

To begin, how would American forces enter Lebanon? Unless they were crossing the Israeli border — an assumption largely ruled out by the Jeffersonian allergy to "entangling alliances" — they would need to cross the shore in an amphibious assault. Without such a plan, there could be no reasonable supposition of local basing. The amphibious shipping the U.S. Navy currently possesses is massive, certainly in comparison to that of any other navy, but it still can land the assault echelons of, at most, two brigades of Marines.[3] Whatever the authors' assurances regarding those "light ground forces," two brigades do not invade most foreign lands on their own, even with massive applications of aerial firepower. As evidenced by its performance in 2006, even Hezbollah may be tougher than that. In the words of the Winograd Commission, Hezbollah, "a semi-military organization of a few thousand men resisted, for a few weeks, the strongest army in the Middle East, which enjoyed full air superiority and size and technology advances."[4] Although it may be true that the 2001 Afghan model of American intervention may induce enemies to break and run, they do not submit until they're rooted out at bayonet point. And if we accept the authors' assertion (p. 128) that any decisive action will be necessarily of short duration, then presumably the fleet to carry the troops should not be built after the attack, as if today were 1942. Thus without overseas allies, a much

---

[3] Ronald O'Rourke, *Navy LPD-17 Amphibious Ship Procurement: Background, Issues, and Options for Congress*, RL34476, Congressional Research Service, (April 20, 2011), 2.

[4] "English Summary of the Winograd Commission Report," *The New York Times*. January 30, 2008. Retrieved January 20, 2014.

larger amphibious fleet than the U.S. currently possesses may be required.

On the other hand, if American forces really were sized for defeating opposition once it arose, and not for patrolling the planet, then the size of the U.S. land-based fighter aircraft force would appear excessive. No country, except for China or Russia, has an air force remotely approaching the size of the U.S. joint fleets. Until recently, two of the largest opposing air forces were those of Libya and Syria; the former proved completely useless in its fight against NATO, and the latter, for all the physical devastation it has wrought, has been unable to break the nascent Free Syrian Army. Almost all plausible opposing air forces around the world are either small or similarly incompetent, and the *Sovereignty* authors suggest that sort of opposition is nothing to fear. The authors assert that two American super-carriers could deal with most enemy air forces. Double that number, for still but a fraction of the Navy's fleet, and they may have a point. Clearly Hezbollah would require nothing more.

Still, for a comfortable margin in other wars, one or two more carriers may be useful, for the land-based fighters that require local bases, presumably, will be unavailable. The absence of reliable access to overseas airfields would thus demand a relative shift towards a large, long-range bomber fleet, to supplement the more proximate carrier air cover. Until the enemy's air defenses are reduced, the bombers (apart from the B-2s) would fight largely with standoff weapons; alternatively, they could be from the nascent Long-Range Strike Bomber program, if it does not prove to be prohibitively expensive. Either way, the B-52s and their successors would, afterwards, rain torrents of Joint Direct Attack Munitions — assuming that the Air Force remembers to buy enough.

And then, according to *Sovereignty Solution*, to storm ashore we would consider throwing in *additional surface combatants*. Never mind that for decades the Marine Corps has wanted the Navy to support it with seaborne heavy artillery. For the cost of only two F-35s, the Navy could buy a few dozen precision-guided five-inch rounds for every gun in the fleet. The rounds would still suffer from a destroyer gun's limited range—under 20 kilometers. Soon, though, the service will have such a real cruiser's gun, the 6.1-inch "Advanced Gun System," with rocket-boosted, precision-guided rounds that can hit targets 100 kilometers away. The only trouble is, the Navy is only buying a total of six of these (aboard just three *Zumwalt*-class ships). If the Marines are to be storming ashore more often, "draining the swamps" of terrorists,[5] felling those miscreant bands with heavy firepower, then firepower must be at the ready. With potentially longer transit times for land-based aircraft, probably necessitated by that retreat from overseas bases, fewer aircraft will be on station at any time, and longer gaps in coverage must be endured. So, for timely responses to calls for fire, the Navy might need to invest in some more guns—vice land-attack missiles.

This might best be accomplished with some new ships meant for shore bombardment, surface action and possibly submarine hunting— frigates that would be rather less expensive than destroyers optimized for air defense. As the weapon and sensors suites of ships like those of the Aegis-equipped classes generally account for about seventy percent of the construction cost, the unit cost of a new frigate might be comfortably lower than one might guess. Despite recent promising test results, the Navy cannot be sure that all this fancy hardware has been a good investment. Since 1967, in more than 220 incidents worldwide, only once has a warship anywhere downed a missile with another missile in combat—

---

[5] U.S. Deputy Secretary of Defense Paul Wolfowitz to NATO ministers in Brussels, in Ambrose Evans-Pritchard, "U.S asks NATO for help in 'draining the swamp' of global terrorism," *The Telegraph*, September 27, 2001.

and that was, suitably for our purposes, in 1991, when HMS *Gloucester* successfully intercepted an Iraqi cruise missile aimed at USS *Missouri* during the "Mighty Mo's" artillery engagement of troops ashore.[6] A U.S. Navy configured more for distant blockade, surface action, and forcible entry against violent fanatics might prove less expensive in the long run than one configured to ward off barrages of long-range Chinese missiles. But even if such a configuration would work, the authors of *Sovereignty Solution* talk hardly at all of China, seeming willing to let Taiwan and any other small besieged states go it alone.

Moreover, with no intention to lead a counterinsurgency effort, with its constant circulation of troops through such battle zones, a United States governed by a *Sovereignty Solution* strategy would require a much smaller regular army than it fields today. The U.S. fought North Korea in the 1950s with only seven divisions, largely infantry, and took on Iraq in 1991 with just six, though they were rather greater in size and largely mechanized. It was the fights against guerrillas in Viet Nam, Iraq, and Afghanistan that demanded yet larger commitments: those wars dragged on and troops needed to rotate home, their places taken by fresh battalions. Thus today's large force structure is really necessitated by, and designed to meet, commitment to long wars, not the short, decisive ones the authors want. Assuming that American wars would again be fewer and farther between, a much larger National Guard, mobilized when needed, would appear to be more nearly consistent with the authors' aims. Refresher training for well-drilled reservists, after all, requires a

---

6 Published data are available in Wayne P. Hughes, *Fleet Tactics and Coastal Combat* (Naval Institute Press, 2000), 152. Hughes has been updating his database over time, and he is yet to record a success. See Hughes, "Prediction," address to the Military Applications Society of INFORMS, Monterey, California, March 27, 2012.

comparatively shorter time commitment; the construction of fleets of ships and bombers does not ramp up as quickly.

For all these reasons, it is very difficult to say whether the *Sovereignty* strategy would be more or less costly in the mid-term. It could reasonably lead to a massive truncation of the F-35 program, at least U.S. purchases of its land-based variant, and perhaps a complete abandonment of the program. Unable to reach the United States, China's J-20 and Russia's PAK-FA fifth generation aircraft might be considered someone else's problem. As noted, the strategy could also reasonably and logically lead to as much as a fifty-percent decrease in the size of the U.S. Army. With three divisions already, the U.S. Marine Corps supplies, arguably, about half the troops that historically have been needed for large, high-intensity, overseas campaigns — and it is the Marines who make possible those forcible entries. On the other hand, a building program for a new and larger-sized bomber fleet would require a prompt start and sustained commitment, as well as the construction of many more assault ships.

All this does assume that there will be no lingering problems after the mission is accomplished, but even if that should happen, part-time National Guardsman are far less expensive than regulars – at least in theory and over the long term, if the political assumption of limited use is correct. Yet if decisive and complete action were demanded after every affront, American troops might still find themselves engaged in frequent land wars overseas. As the authors argue, routing Hezbollah from Lebanon and removing similar antagonists from the rest of planet Earth would probably end the problem.[7] Killing or capturing the senior leaders of these groups could make for a decisive end result. But it would not be cheap.

---

[7] *Sovereignty Solution*, 129.

In the breach, of course, none of these assumptions can be fully honored. That glorious Second World War for which Simons *et alia* pine was well decided, but it was hardly brief. Indeed, it began—and then lasted so long—precisely *because* political leaders and policymakers in both the United States and the United Kingdom initially hoped that a strategy that left "other countries alone to live as they wish" would succeed. In reality, the approach left fascist regimes to brutalize their own populations until the inward-focused attention turned outward, and the militant efforts crossed international borders. This is not to Nazify all cranky mullahs, but merely to observe that *some* security problems are best dealt with early, through collective security arrangements, before they grow in magnitude. In contrast, *Sovereignty Solution* unwisely ignores both the time-honored concept of the balance of power and the value of leadership within a coalition of the willing. The alliances it undermines should be mutually beneficial arrangements that lower the cost of defense for all participants. They are not always so, but that is no cause to jettison the concept.

So what if we tempered the concept, salvaging some of the flavor without all the stridency? Indeed, there are things to like in *The Sovereignty Solution*. The authors' frustrations are understandable: given the size and nature of the nation's public debt, American strategists must craft and adopt more effective and affordable policy options, in a manner consistent with fundamental national security interests. Are there, then, functions from which the United States might safely back off, while still maintaining a commitment to its treaty-bound partners? Absolutely, and the preceding analysis may yet apply.

To start, amphibious lift may not need to expand beyond the current plan, as the alliance structure—if properly maintained—should continue to provide a means of access for U.S. military action. Even the part of the U.S. Navy that is truly differentiating, the *Nimitz*-sized super-carriers, could gradually draw down in number if their services were not expected for 'peacetime' presence and policing, but rather as a reserve of mobile striking power in the event that Americans or their allies are attacked. With a margin for refits and reserves, eight or nine super-carriers could easily supply adequate air power in a pinch. Only six were sent by the United States to fight Saddam in 1991, a number more than adequate to meet the needs of the mission. This option and argument is even more sound if the Marine F-35B jump jet program remains fully funded and sustained. Aboard the fleet of *Wasp* and *America*-class amphibious ships, the F-35B could provide combatant commanders with additional strike options from the sea whenever an amphibious landing or the threat of one is not a priority. As even Simons, McGraw, and Lauchengco observe, these naval aviators bring overmatch to almost any opponent in the world. Indeed, U.S. naval aviation's fighter-bomber force is larger than the land-based air force of any other country in the world except for two — Russia and China. If the possibility of fighting the Russians is remote, the possibility of that fight outside the context of the NATO alliance is inconceivable. And if China is the opponent, the USAF's land-based fighter fleet has profound problems of access and range. In that context, a larger bomber fleet, whether penetrating or not, still makes more sense.

But one thing is certain: with lower ambitions to forcibly remake the world in its own image, the U.S. might be able to accept greater risk in its force planning, and budget for fewer ground troops in active-duty formations. Defense could profitably shift manpower from the regular army to the National Guard, and from the Marine Corps to its Reserve, as most of America's allies have their own ground forces for securing their frontiers. For when discretionary and warranted, overland intervention must be embarked upon only after sober thought and planning, providing the weeks and months necessary for summoning the militia to the colors for the serious work of war. It should be, as Simons and her co-authors would have it, a genuine last resort.

The Sovereignty Solution: Not Radical, But Measured

Many thanks to James Hasik for the seriousness with which he has taken *The Sovereignty Solution,* especially since the three of us who co-wrote the book are not sufficiently expert to say exactly what impact our strategy might have on the United States' long term force structure. I can — and will — offer a few ideas here. However, there are also a number of things I should clarify. Among them, we contend that the U.S. needs to adopt a foreign policy premised on strategic clarity and operational ambiguity. Consequently, *which* U.S. forces Washington would use to respond to violations of U.S. sovereignty — whether the Marines or U.S. Special Operations Forces, Naval or Air Force bombardment — should matter less than that domestic and international audiences alike understand they can count on there *being* a response.

Nor would that response be aimed to "shock and awe," as Hasik implies. Rather, its purpose would be to render our attackers inert, and to pummel any government that willingly harbors or gives shelter to them.

In the Sovereignty Rules world we describe, there is no ceding the initiative to anyone. Rather, as we co-authors take pains to point out, not only must we Americans be our own first responders, but there are no other first responders

Americans can count on. No other cavalry will ride to our rescue. That is one reason we advocate the adoption of something we call Standing Declarations of Preemption, as well as a revival of the use of Declarations of War. Under our rubric, once red lines have been drawn, they cannot be re-drawn, or erased, or fudged.

Nor do we suggest the U.S. become a punching bag for anyone. Just the opposite. Let some set of non-state actors launch another attack against the U.S., and whichever countries those individuals hail from would have a lot to answer for. *How* Washington would respond would offer a salutary demonstration effect to the world. But the U.S. would not be in the least arbitrary, or vengeful—just punishing.

Actually, six steps would be taken:

1) Our sovereignty is violated.
2) In the wake of an attack, Washington makes demands of the witting or unwitting government(s)/authorities it suspects, or knows, harbored our attackers. The demands are simple and public.
3) Those in authority reject Washington's demands, or drag their feet.
4) The president asks Congress—and the American people—for a Declaration of War.
5) Congress issues a Declaration of War.
6) Only at this point does the U.S. military tailor its means to achieve U.S. ends, which are to decimate those with whom we are at war. Our military forces will, to the best of their abilities, spare innocents.

But—and this is an important "but"—a whole suite of things, from the hollow deference currently accorded heads of state, to non-combatant status, to Just War theory would need to be rethought beyond just adoption of a new framework for international relations. Otherwise, as we point out in the book, cunning adversaries will continue to turn residential neighborhoods into armed camps, forcing U.S. forces to try to make impossible determinations between non-uniformed militants and militant "civilians."

I do not want to reprise all of the book's arguments here. In fact, one reason we wrote the book rather than just an article or op-ed is that a whole succession of American principles have been thrown under the bus since World War II. Most of these principles need to be resuscitated. Do we really romanticize the Second World War, as Hasik implies? I do not think so. But we do like a number of pre-World War II sentiments. For instance, if I had to offer a pithy version of where we stand on warfare, here is what I would say. Actually, it is what I *have* said since *The Sovereignty Solution*:

1) If you are not prepared to wipe out the enemy, why fight?
2) If you will not, or cannot, wipe out the enemy, death and destruction are the wrong foreign policy tools to use.
3) And if you are not willing to either inflict or take large numbers of casualties, the cause must not be sufficiently existential. So again, why fight?[1]

Somehow, policymakers and plenty of otherwise smart people in Washington, think tanks, war colleges, and elsewhere have succumbed to the notion that our forces need to be re-tailored to fight long, sneaky "wars amongst the people" even though we have never been good at this kind of warfare — and nothing in our recent past suggests we will become better at it.

---

[1] Anna Simons, "21st Century Cultures of War: Advantage Them," *The Philadelphia Papers*, Foreign Policy Research Institute, April 2013.

Instead, the kind of warfare that fits with Americans' strategic personality remains a John Wayne-type of combativeness: "I won't be wronged. I won't be insulted. I won't be laid a hand on. I don't do these things to other people, and I require the same from them." In other words, "Don't cross me, or else." As for what that "or else" requires: it is serious firepower.

In this sense, Hasik reads us correctly. Where he errs, however, is in ignoring some of our chapters or not following through with our logic. For instance, under the sovereignty rubric, the U.S. would never have invaded Afghanistan preparatory to a long occupation. We never would have engaged in nation-building. Instead, Mullah Omar and his Taliban government would have been delivered an ultimatum; something like, "Turn over Usama bin Laden and root out al Qaeda." Washington would have issued clear deadlines and benchmarks. Only if Mullah Omar refused to comply would the U.S. have sought to obliterate both his regime (the Taliban) and al Qaeda — with no promise to the people in Kandahar that we would help them re-build in the wake of their continued support for either entity.

In other words, in a "sovereignty rules" world, there is minimal need for boots on the ground, and no need for occupation. Or alternatively, as we suggest in the book's Epilogue, say some gutsy politician decided to apply the "sovereignty solution" in real time, *now*. In that case, given the security commitments Washington has made, U.S. forces would have to quarantine Afghanistan so that Afghans, and only Afghans, can sort out their differences. As it is, Washington should have adopted a scorpions-in-a-bottle approach to Afghanistan years ago, without the CIA or the ISI delivering sacks full of money or U.S. taxpayers funding aid-cum-welfare. Arguably, the longer our involvement has lasted, the more we have managed not only to undermine Afghans' ability to govern themselves, but also the more we have turned Afghanistan into a cockpit for regional and supra-regional trouble.

What kind of force structure *does* lend itself to erecting and maintaining quarantines? This should actually be a pressing 21st-century question, given the very real threat of pandemics, never mind the spillover effects when states implode. Imagine what the conversations about Syria might be like had the world's more capable militaries begun building quarantine capabilities a decade ago.

Surprisingly, Hasik fails to mention Syria. So I will. What — if anything — the U.S. should do about Syria (circa May 2013) begs the far stickier question: what do our allies want us to do? This, in turn, raises other uncomfortable questions, such as that of who in the region *is* an ally? And what do our alliances commit us to do? While the fact that no one in Washington seems able to answer these questions is itself highly revealing, it means that the Obama administration has plenty of wriggle room to continue to waffle publicly. It means that Syrian rebels are still stuck vying with each other, hoping for our help. And it means our putative friends — Turkey, Jordan, Israel, Saudi Arabia, Qatar, and the UAE — can probably count on our doing some covert or clandestine things, while American taxpayers and most elements in the U.S. military remain clueless as to what those things might consist of, or what they might embroil us in down the road.

At least thus far into the 21st century, most members of the public seem to want transparency to be considered a critical public good, though even the Founders way back in the 1780s understood the degree to which foreign entanglements — never mind secret foreign entanglements (Iran-Contra, anyone?) — could corrode democracy. No doubt that is one reason the Founders delegated to the Senate the responsibility to ratify all treaties. Did they envision "Coalitions of the Willing?" Hardly. Rather, the whole point to treaties is to put everyone on notice: "we the people" of the United States of

America have entered into a full partnership with Country X. Mutual defense is a major commitment. It is also deadly serious business. But that is also precisely why such arrangements should only be bilateral and why they need to be publicly debated before they are agreed to. We explain all of this in the book. Thus when Hasik hones in on our hypothetical example of Hezbollah's violating U.S. sovereignty, it is not clear that Israel would not already be a U.S. ally, in which case we would not operate against Hezbollah *without* Israeli assistance. Would we, therefore, need to bypass Israel to conduct an amphibious landing in Lebanon? That seems doubtful.

I do agree with Hasik that self-defense in a Sovereignty Rules world calls for a much more robust U.S. Air Force and Navy, and that we should want to invest in the ability to pummel people into surrendering from stand-off distances. Again, I am not sure why Hasik thinks Marines would need to storm ashore, or why he thinks the Navy would need to develop forcible entry capabilities. Would we need a Navy that could blockade and quarantine? Absolutely.

Similarly, I do not see the connection between what we advocate in the book—many fewer, shorter, but much more decisive engagements (should they even have to occur)—and a much larger National Guard. To me, this hardly jibes. But, where I worry that Hasik does even more damage to our argument is in suggesting that "decisive and complete action" would be "demanded after every affront."

This description is flat out wrong. Let me try to explain. First, *The Sovereignty Solution* marries "don't tread on me" to "to each his own." Under our rubric, the U.S. government would get out of the business of telling other people how to arrange their lives. For instance, if most Afghan men and women want women to wear burqas, it would no longer be up to the U.S. government to convince them otherwise. If populations in Muslim countries choose to abide by sharia law, that is their prerogative. In other words, push what all liberals say they respect — namely, others' cultures — to its logical conclusion, and what does a true respect for others' cultures mean? That we stop hectoring other people to become more like us.

Now, imagine this was one of the two major planks of U.S. foreign policy. Would that not remove the crosshairs from our back? Would not fewer people feel affronted by us? Or, flip this around. *Why* would jihadists still want to come gunning for us?

Secondly, we make a very sharp distinction throughout the book between deeds and words, or, as we write at one point:

> Warning people to stop doing things we don't like — with no ability to punish them — makes no more sense than urging people to rise up without being able to protect them when their government then cracks down. Essentially, talk is cheap. Having said that, we Americans who laud free speech should never want to license other governments to stifle speech, even if it is hate speech. Better that people be able to vent than explode. Or, to invoke something American parents used to instill in American children: "sticks and stones may break my bones, but names can never hurt me."[2]

In other words, we co-authors distinguish between words and deeds because it is deeds, not words, that mark violations of sovereignty. Affronts, insults, name-calling — all of those would likely diminish once Washington stops proselytizing the American way of life abroad. But, even if words are hurled, so what? At the same time, as a mature actor on the world stage, it is imperative that *our* deeds and words be congruent, since this is the only way to guarantee that Washington will act in accordance with what the U.S. can do,

---

[2] Anna Simons, Joe McGraw, and Duane Lauchengco, *The Sovereignty Solution: A Commonsense Approach to Global Security* (Annapolis, MD: Naval Institute Press, 2011), 123.

and does not promise, threaten, or bluster to achieve things we cannot.

This brings me back to the use of force—which should only be used against named opponents under a Declaration of War (or a Standing Declaration of Preemption). Again, the aim whenever force is used would be to force an opponent to disarm and to acknowledge defeat. Or, to put none too fine a point on it: either the enemy concedes, or we do.

I am not sure this would entail exactly the kinds of changes to our force structure that Hasik envisions, but I certainly welcome the debate. And no question, "strategic clarity, operational ambiguity" *would* liberate DoD to re-think the military's division of labor, its manning, and its resourcing. Indeed, as Hasik points out, given the financial unsustainability of Washington's current approach, now would be the time to assess just how little something like the "sovereignty solution" would cost in comparison to other options. Though to make a truly fair comparison would also require taking into account the cost of everything from combat soldiers' long-term mental health to the rents in our social fabric when we Americans cannot agree on something that should be as straightforward as the question of who is an enemy combatant.

This is also why we co-authors advocate reinvigorating citizens' sense of what it means to be American. Much like General (ret.) McChrystal has recently advocated, we see the value in universal national service. But the book strives to make an even deeper point: at a minimum, we Americans need to understand what makes the U.S. so exceptional, we Americans need to understand what is required to preserve that exceptionalism, and we need to stop trying to foist our way of life on others. Indeed, only if we adopt a "we'll be us, you be you" attitude are we likely to be able to live more securely in the world so that it will no longer be up to the U.S.

military to either police the planet or re-build others' nations for them.[3]

In sum, by liberating others to follow their own path, we would be liberating ourselves. Nor would this require a retreat into isolationism. The opposite is true. For the first time in more than a century, we could re-separate U.S. national security from so-called American national interests. As it is, there is no "national" interest apart from security. Just try to name one. I guarantee you that whatever industry you might mention — oil, for instance — would provoke competitors (e.g. coal, or alternative energy) to disagree. But for that argument, you would have to take a look at pages 98-99 of our book.

All told, we offer 161 pages of text (and 67 pages of additional endnotes). *The Sovereignty Solution* is a relatively short read. And I'd like to thank James Hasik for giving me the opportunity to recommend it.

---

[3] As General, and then President, Eisenhower described the American way of life, it entails "freedom of choice for individuals, democratic procedures for government, and private enterprise for the economy" (John Lewis Gaddis, *Strategies of Containment: A Critical Appraisal of American National Security Policy During the Cold War*, 2nd ed. (Oxford University Press, 2005), p. 133). Nothing in such a definition requires that our exceptionalism be extended abroad, or that American companies, to do business abroad, need to turn others into individuated democratic capitalists. But likewise, preserving the American way of life here at home does not *require* that businesses be as aggressively far-flung as they are. The nature of their globalized profiteering — and whether they conduct themselves responsibly or not — is also up to them, and should never be allowed to imperil the rest of us.

Part IV: Empowering the Practitioner

The Sound of One Hand Clapping: The Expeditionary Imperative of Interagency Integration

Jesse Pruett

Two hands clap and there is a sound. What is the sound of one hand?

— Hakuin Ekaku

Introduction

When the civilian and military elements of the United States government work together effectively each element complements the other, just as when two hands combine to produce a clap. The value of an integrated, whole-of-government approach to foreign relations can be understood as such a reciprocal display. By contrast, when interagency mechanisms fail, the result is awkward—similar to the sound of one hand clapping, a silence that serves as an ominous metaphor for the future of U.S. foreign policy. In the movement towards an interagency ideal, analysts, who have identified significant shortcomings, continue to focus on the reform of interagency institutions and frameworks writ large. This focus is a necessary component of the way forward, but it minimizes the significant body of knowledge gained at operational and tactical levels. The U.S. foreign policy community must work to adequately recognize true field experience and better capture its defining characteristics or risk losing the fundamental piece of any comprehensive interagency solution: its on-the-ground application.

The Expeditionary Interagency

Since 9/11, personnel from a variety of organizations of the U.S. government have found themselves thrust together in environments characterized by austerity and the pervasive threat of violence. When such intra-governmental groups form and are assigned to insecure environments abroad as an "expeditionary interagency," a team effort is born. An interagency team may be assembled around any number of focal points, such as energy policy, counterterrorism, or counternarcotics. However, the most challenging and perhaps most relevant configuration is centered on the civil-military nexus of the "3-Ds" of defense, diplomacy, and development, as manifest in the context of a conflict or crisis. These expeditionary interagency teams form the pioneering edge of U.S. foreign policy and serve as a prototype for the future projection of U.S. interests into the nontraditional foreign engagements that have emerged since the end of the Cold War.

For more than ten years, observers have analyzed the performance of the most prominent manifestation of this team concept, the provincial reconstruction team (PRT), which collocates members of the U.S. government's key expeditionary agencies in selected locations throughout Afghanistan and Iraq. Now that U.S. military involvement in Iraq is negligible, and coalition forces in Afghanistan are also headed for the exit, it may be tempting to dismiss these constructs as relics of an uncomfortable era. Perhaps it will be enough to walk away from Afghanistan and Iraq with at least one clear lesson learned: to avoid such large-scale and complex enterprises. A focus on this view, however, minimizes what may be the most critical and far-reaching national security implication to emerge from these two conflicts, which is that institutions, frameworks, and policies are important, but the integration of national power is only as effective as its ultimate application.

While the ambitious attempt to transform nations under the banner of the Global War on Terrorism is probably not a sufficient template for the future of U.S. foreign policy, the debate remains over how, exactly, this future will be defined. There are elements of the post-9/11 world that provide additional context to the definition, including the rise of non-state actors, the impact of low-technology responses to conventional military might, and a greater parity among most national powers as the bipolar era fades deeper into history.

Responding to these realities, the U.S. is adjusting the way it approaches its relations with other nations. Rather than a sudden and dramatic pivot, this adjustment is a response to gradual shifts in the global reality foreshadowed at the close of World War II, but only recently solidified through U.S. experiences in Iraq and Afghanistan. Largely due to these developments, interagency dexterity has become an imperative component of an effective foreign policy tool kit.

The True Imperative

One interpretation of this imperative is to focus on organization and policy reforms to help produce more talented bureaucratic operatives with a greater ability to successfully navigate the labyrinthine corridors of Washington, D.C. The problem is defined in executive branch, national-security-apparatus terms, and many of the remedies enacted thus far carry this top-down perspective.

Bureaucratic skills are vital to the long-term health of any interagency system. However, the ultimate and most pressing foreign policy imperative of the day is the need to cultivate a new class of practitioner, one who effectively pursues U.S. interests abroad through a complementary integration of talent represented from a variety of the federal government's many institutions. Few reform efforts pay sufficient attention to the significant progress made in the ranks by those who have ventured abroad in response to their nation's call.

To realize the full benefit of the application of their specific expertise, government organizations must evolve from the organic, bottom-up influence of these expeditionary veterans. Therefore, there may be value in revisiting some of the fundamental arguments that frame the current debate and refocusing the lens on areas where success or failure has been evident, either in spite of, or perhaps *because* of, insufficient institutional support mechanisms. This may provide useful context to inform potential personnel management reform proposals.

The Policy Realm

Influenced by realities encountered during operations in Somalia, Haiti, and the Balkans, the Clinton Administration recognized the changing global landscape and the requirement for corresponding reform. In 1997, the Administration issued Presidential Decision Directive 56, which identified that, "While agencies of government have developed independent capacities to respond to complex emergencies, military and civilian agencies should operate in a synchronized manner through effective interagency management and the use of special mechanisms to coordinate agency efforts."[1]

---

[1] "Managing Complex Contingency Operations," Presidential Decision Directive/National Security Council 56, May 1997, http://www.fas.org/irp/offdocs/pdd56.htm, accessed on April 09, 2012.

Since that time, many government initiatives have been launched to codify and catalyze the interagency system and its application. Some of these are presented in Figure 1.

Government Initiated Interagency Initiatives and Guiding Documents

Following are just some of the more significant documents and initiatives (along with the sponsoring branch or agency) which capture the efforts of government to improve the interagency reality. This list is illustrative of the many efforts undertaken, but is not exhaustive. *DoS and DoD actions are treated as independent of the executive

1997 Presidential Decision Directive (PDD) 56 "Managing Complex Contingency Operations" (Executive)

2001 National Security Presidential Directive (NSPD) 01 "Organization of the National Security Council System" (Executive)

2004 The Office of the Coordinator for Reconstruction and Stabilization (S/CRS) (State)

2005 National Security Presidential Directive (NSPD) 44 "Management of Interagency Efforts Concerning Reconstruction and Stabilization" (Executive)

2005 Department of Defense Directive (DODD) 3000.05 "Military Support to Security, Stabilization, Transition and Reconstruction" (Defense)

2006 Joint Publication (JP) 3-08, *Interagency, Intergovernmental Organization, and Nongovernmental Organization Coordination During Joint Operations, Volumes I and II* (Defense)

2006-2010 Section 1207: Security and Stabilization Assistance Funds (State from Defense from Legislative)

2007 National Security Professional Development (NSPD) Program (Executive)

2007 National Security Executive Leadership Seminar (NSELS) (State)

2007 Interagency Management System (Executive via National Security Council)

2008 *The Reconstruction and Stabilization Civilian Management Act (Title XVI of Public Law 110-447)* (Legislative)

2008 *National Security Professionals Act* (Legislative)

2008 Civilian Response Corps (Executive via State)

2008 & 2010 Project on National Security Reform (PNSR) Studies (Legislative mandate to Defense)

2009 Department of Defense Instruction (DODI) 3000.05 "Stability Operations" (Defense)

2009 Department of Defense Directive 1404.10 "Civilian Expeditionary Workforce" (Defense)

2010 The First Quadrennial Diplomacy and Development Review (QDDR) (State)

2010 *Interagency National Security Professional Education, Administration, and Development System Act (INSPEAD)* (Legislative)

2010 Complex Crisis Fund (USAID via Legislative)

2011 NSPD "2.0" (Executive)

2011 Joint Publication (JP) 3-08, *Interorganizational Coordination During Joint Operations* (Defense)

2011 *Interagency Personnel Rotation Act* (Legislative)

Figure 1: Government-Initiated Initiatives and Guiding Documents

The aggregate result of this collective effort is uninspiring. A 2008 House Armed Services Committee study declared, "Although efforts have been made over the last seven years attempting to improve interagency coordination and cooperation, the government has not gone far enough or fast enough to support the people in the field or accomplish the nation's mission."[2] As recently as March 2012, Senators John McCain and Tom Coburn highlighted persistent weaknesses in these interagency efforts in a letter to Defense Secretary Leon Panetta, stating, "The Department of Defense's efforts in [the stabilization, reconstruction, and humanitarian assistance] space are similar to State and USAID (United States Agency for International Development) efforts, so interagency coordination is vital....But each of these agencies have failed to successfully monitor and evaluate their own humanitarian efforts—much less coordinate activities. GAO [Government Accountability Office] finds that information-sharing among them has been particularly problematic."[3]

So what is to be done? Foreign policy journals frequently analyze the causes of interagency cooperation and integration and also suggest roadmaps to achieving the whole-of-government ideal.[4] Think tanks, scholars, and officials have offered various top-down prescriptions to remedy the ailments of the system, ranging from a Goldwater/Nichols-type reform, to the creation of a new department-level umbrella organization, to the formation of regional interagency command centers modeled on the military's current combatant command structures. These approaches propose that the interagency system as a whole must be

---

[2] "Agency Stovepipes vs. Strategic Agility: Lessons We Need to Learn from Provincial Reconstruction Teams in Iraq and Afghanistan," Congressional Committee Report, United States House of Representatives, Committee on Armed Services, Subcommittee on Oversight and Investigations, Washington, D.C., 2008.

[3] John McCain and Tom Coburn, attachment in letter to Secretary of Defense Leon Panetta, March 19, 2012.

[4] Colonel Arthur D. Simons Center for the Study of Interagency Cooperation http://thesimonscenter.org/resources/interagency-bibliography, accessed on March 12, 2012. This Web site refers to more than 800 published works related to the issue of interagency cooperation.

fundamentally transformed in order to achieve the desired results. This leaves practitioners—those operating within the interagency reality—stuck looking upward, as hatchlings in the nest, waiting for the "solution" to be offered from above.

Looking Upward

While the observers noted herein tend to agree that a problem exists, there is less consensus or clarity as to its exact nature. Nevertheless, three interrelated observations are frequently made: (1) insufficient resources are typically made available for the civilian agencies, (2) an inadequate or outdated institutional structure exists, and (3) an unbalanced foreign affairs posture is in place. The consistency with which these observations appear in literature lends them some validity. However, organizations and practitioners must avoid the pitfall of waiting to be handed solutions to these concerns. Such solutions may ultimately prove elusive.

1. Insufficient resources: If Congress would only give "us" more of what they give "them," we would be fine. This view contends that there are too few people with too little funding in the civilian agencies, notably the Department of State and USAID. Too often this argument seems to hinge on civilian agencies' budgets and manpower, in direct relation to that of the Department of Defense (DoD). It is true that the disparities between the size and funding of DoD and any other expeditionary contributor are stark, even after accounting for natural economies of scale (no need for USAID naval fleets or State Department fighter squadrons). However, this distracts from the more critical reality that, in absolute terms, the demand for the expeditionary services of these organizations has increased, while staffing and budgets continue to remain stagnant. This despite the fact that at the highest levels the DoD has been a vocal supporter of State's role in the national security apparatus. In 2007, Secretary

Gates argued for "a dramatic increase in spending on the civilian instruments of national power."[5] And four years later, Secretary Panetta, appearing alongside Secretary of State Hillary Clinton at the National Defense University, reinforced the notion that "...our national security is our military power, our Defense Department, but it's also our diplomatic power and the State Department...[a resource that is] absolutely essential to our national security."[6]

However legitimate and accepted these claims may be, institutions and practitioners must remain mindful of two additional and significant constraining factors: (1) the federal budget line for Function 150 (international affairs) and related efforts may simply never be what advocates want it to be (as evidenced by the slight, below-the-rate-of-inflation increase requested in the State Department fiscal year 2013 budget request)[7], and (2) the scale of operations and simultaneity of Iraq and Afghanistan, which demanded such unachievable elasticity of the civilian agencies, are unlikely to be replicated in the future.

Given these realities and constraints, organizations may find value through capturing and internalizing the considerable in-the-field skills and efficiencies that have evolved over the past decade. For example, in testifying before the House Armed Services Committee in 2011, Principal

---

[5] Robert M. Gates, transcript of remarks, Landon Lecture, Kansas State University, November 26, 2007, http://www.defense.gov/speeches/speech.aspx?speechid=1199, accessed on November 17, 2011.

[6] Leon Panetta, transcript of remarks, National Defense University, Fort McNair, Washington, D.C., August 16, 2011, http://www.defense.gov/transcripts/transcript.aspx?transcriptid=4864, accessed on April 13, 2012.

[7] "Executive Budget Summary for Function 150 & Other International Programs Fiscal Year 2013," Department of State, <http://www.state.gov/s/d/rm /rls/ebs /2013/pdf/index.htm>, accessed on April 13, 2012.

Deputy Undersecretary of Defense for Policy Ryan Henry identified the disparity between the way the interagency works in the field and at headquarters, remarking, ". . . in the field, they can work interagency a lot of times much better than we can inside the beltway."[8] Many published reviews, audits, analyses, and reports include, along with their litany of suggested improvements, a fundamental agreement that, at the operational and tactical levels, personnel responded well, and achievement was evident. In one comprehensive assessment, reviewers from a Princeton University-sponsored effort concluded, ". . . PRTs have reported enough positive feedback to suggest that sponsoring countries should continue funding them and expending energy and resources toward their improvement."[9]

   2. **Inadequate structure: Existing institutions are anachronisms that cannot hope to find relevance in a modern world that is changing more rapidly than the institutions' ability to adapt.** In this view, the fundamental problems facing the interagency are structural: organizations themselves are unable to support a true interagency approach because of outdated mandates as well as inherent flaws in the organizations' construction. The interagency field has produced a spectrum of ideas, but there are no real, sweeping

---

[8] "Provincial Reconstruction Teams: A Case for Interagency National Security Reform," Hearing No. 110–115, United States House of Representatives, Committee on Armed Services, Subcommittee on Oversight and Investigations, Washington, D.C., February 16, 2008, p. 16.

[9] Nima Abbaszadeh, Mark Crow, Marianne El-Khoury, Jonathan Gandomi, David Kuwayama, Christopher MacPherson, Meghan Nutting, Nealin Parker, and Taya Weiss, "Provincial Reconstruction Teams: Lessons and Recommendations," Woodrow Wilson School Graduate Workshop on Provincial Reconstruction Teams, Princeton University, Princeton, N.J., January 2008, http://wws.princeton.edu/research/pwreports_f07/wws591b.pdf, 4, accessed on October 19, 2011.

reform measures being seriously considered by the senior levels of the executive or legislative branches. Absent an entirely new architecture, the creation of new offices and positions only promotes a myth that things are moving in the right direction. Instead, some of these efforts may actually exacerbate the problem, as pointed out by researchers Craig Cohen and Noam Unger: "Creating additional offices and institutions that have the appeal of 'signature initiatives' is more politically viable than broad institutional reform, even though this often compounds the problems of fragmentation and dilution of America's civilian tools of power."[10] As one author puts it, "Calls for institutional reform can sometimes feel like moving around [or rearranging] the deckchairs on the Titanic..."[11]

One prime example of the limitations of structural remedies is the State Department's experiment with its Office of the Coordinator for Reconstruction and Stabilization (S/CRS). Created in 2004, the department never really achieved the critical mass necessary to fulfill its role effectively. Three years into the effort Norah Bensahel and Anne M. Moisan argued in *Joint Forces Quarterly* that S/CRS was "...too weak to become an effective interagency lead for stabilization and reconstruction operations, and the causes of its weakness seem unlikely to be rectified soon. It is faced with limited interagency authority, resources, and capabilities."[12]

---

[10] Craig Cohen and Noam Unger, "Surveying the Civilian Reform Landscape," Stanley Foundation Project Brief, 2008, <http://www.stanleyfoundation.org/publications /other/Unger_CohenPB608.pdf >, p. 2, accessed on April 9, 2012.

[11] Ernest J Wilson III, "Hard Power, Soft Power, Smart Power," *The Annals of the American Academy of Political and Social Science*, No. 616, March 2008, 118.

[12] Nora Bensahel and Anne M. Moisan, "Repairing the Interagency Process," *Joint Forces Quarterly*, No. 44, 1st Quarter 2007, p. 107,

Its functions were subsumed into the new Bureau of Conflict and Stabilization Operations (CSO) in 2011. It remains to be seen whether CSO will enjoy greater success than did its predecessor, but there are encouraging signs that it is more aligned with expeditionary realities. According to the State Department's fiscal year 2013 Executive Budget Summary, "The restructuring was designed to make the bureau more agile and expeditionary, with a greater emphasis on creating a flexible response capacity with a smaller staff. This will produce greater deployment capacity, but with significantly less overhead."[13] While encouraging, the situation also calls for more creative approaches at operational levels and below.

3. Foreign policy imbalance: Those in uniform hold disproportionate influence in foreign policy decision-making and resource allocation, leading to a dangerous civil-military imbalance and projecting a dominant (and perhaps dangerous) military "face" on our international engagements. This observation holds that the interagency effort cannot advance because the military is too powerful to be an equal partner. A fundamental tenet of this position is the presumed distinction between military and civilian areas of responsibility, and the corollary belief that the military might increasingly encroach on traditionally civilian areas of responsibility. Given the nature and realities on the ground in such contingencies, however, the practical application of such efforts is more complex.

Since the end of World War II, U.S. military involvement in traditional civilian domains, such as governance, economic development, and rule of law, has usually followed in the shadow of armed conflict, when external civilian institutions

---

http://www.ndu.edu /press /JointForceQuarterly.html, accessed on October 19, 2011.

[13] Executive Budget Summary, 39.

were unable or unwilling to establish the necessary support mechanisms within an affected country. A contemporary demonstration of this occurred in 2003, when a series of car bombs in Iraq targeted the headquarters of both the United Nations and the International Committee of the Red Cross. As a result of the violence, most agencies were marginalized. They retreated to neighboring countries, were sequestered behind fortified locations (as the supporting security apparatus had yet to be installed), or they abandoned the effort altogether. This dilution of civilian-support capacity and a corresponding increase in the support requirements of the populace created a gap. The military, as unprepared and untrained for this mission as it was, became the default "best" choice to fill the void.

These incidents in Iraq proved to be pivotal. In their aftermath, the civil-military interagency construct evolved from an important, but perhaps unnecessary or occasional, aspiration into a fundamental and vital implementation tool for successfully addressing crisis and conflict situations abroad.

Ironically, an alternative view has evolved as civilians, too, have adapted in response to changes in the world — in many cases moving toward what traditionally has been within the sole purview of the military profession. One report by the Center for a New American Security identified a significant demand for State Department and USAID participation in "operations abroad that respond to conflicts and humanitarian and natural disasters," stating also that "requirements for these types of operations will likely continue well into the future."[14] Another study, from the Center for Complex

---

[14] Nora Bensahel and Patrick M. Cronin, "America's Civilian Operations Abroad: Understanding Past and Future Requirements," The Center for a New American Security, January 2012, http://www.cnas.org/civilian, accessed on April 09, 2012.

Operations (CCO), evaluated numerous complex operations from the last century and concluded that, in fact, it is the U.S. military that has traditionally occupied this space, noting that civilians are the new players.[15] Still, despite the expanded roles of civilians, it is precisely because of the military's role in the complex operations of Afghanistan and Iraq that much of the operationally-based (vice budgetary-based) claim of military intrusion into the civilian sphere has occurred.

However, the debate itself is a bit of a red herring, as the nature of an increased civil-military partnership in the field is now an established reality. But the debate does help illustrate the interagency imperative, which has come about largely due to the dissolution of traditional "black and white" divisions of responsibility and a corresponding increase in "gray space," which is neither entirely military nor entirely civilian in scope. To facilitate mission execution within these gray spaces, agencies have had to modify their mandates. The military has embraced stability operations as a core mission, one "given priority comparable to combat operations and [to] be explicitly addressed and integrated across all DoD activities."[16] Civilian agencies themselves respond through making "conflict prevention and response a core mission," as highlighted in the Quadrennial Diplomacy and Development Review.[17] Thus, seemingly, with the representatives of defense, diplomacy, and development deliberately adopting

---

[15] "PRT Lessons Learned Project Progress Report," Center for Complex Operations, June 2011.

[16] "Military Support for Stability, Security, Transition, and Reconstruction (SSTR) Operations," Department of Defense (DoD) Directive 3000.05, Washington, D.C., November 28, 2005, fhp.osd.mil/intlhealth/pdfs/DoDD3000.05.pdf, accessed on April 9, 2012.

[17] "Leading Through Civilian Power," The First Quadrennial Diplomacy and Development Review, Department of State, Washington, D.C., December 2010, www.state.gov/documents/organization/153108.pdf, accessed on April 09, 2012.

overlapping missions, the expeditionary arena will continue to feature the nexus of civilian and military actors as the expectation rather than the exception.

The Lines of Sight

Efforts aimed at producing meaningful institutional and policy reform are worth developing further, in order to facilitate synchronicity among all elements of national power and to implement long-term solutions. Yet while a sweeping, wholesale, and top-down reform effort may be required to provide the needed fix for a disconnected interagency community, the lack of results delivered so far, and the necessities created by the operational environment, have encouraged significant and substantial in-the-field adjustments. It would be wise to allow these to inform and shape future success.

Looking Back

Do Iraq and Afghanistan matter? Some consider the experiences of the past decade an aberration, and these observers suggest that Iraq and Afghanistan have little to teach us because we shall not pass this way again. Gordon Adams of the Stimson Center provides a voice to this perspective when he states, "operations in Iraq and Afghanistan are not the best guidelines for future reform in the interagency space. Interagency needs of the future cannot be extrapolated from these cases because future commitments likely will not be the result of a sizeable deployment of military forces."[18]

---

[18] Gordon Adams, "Interagency National Security Reform: The Road Ahead," Subcommittee on Oversight and Investigations of the House Armed Services Committee Testimony, June 9, 2010, 5.

Yet to dismiss the experience and lessons of recent contingencies, either because of their scale or because of the significant military role, misses two key points: (1) these conflicts do not represent single monolithic experiences and are, rather, collections of microcosmic and interconnected experiences; and (2) these micro experiences absolutely do contribute relevant guidelines for the future of interagency activities in the field.

The current expeditionary interagency class has already emerged from the forge of two of the most intricate, complex, and longest-lasting conflicts encountered by the U.S. It carries with it the scars of failure, but also the blueprints for triumph in the face of conflict and chaos.

One RAND study identifies the experiences of the post 9/11 period as particularly fertile for producing ground-level interagency lessons, stating:

> It is striking that lessons learned and best practices in this area have emanated mostly from the field rather than at the national command level in Washington (or at NATO-Brussels). More often than not, lessons with the greatest utility for the future have emerged from what individual commands, missions, units, and individuals have done in practice in order to complete their assignments and achieve their broader goals. This has led to innovation and cooperation across institutional bureaucratic, and cultural boundaries, both military and civilian, and between U.S. government entities, international institutions, and nongovernmental organizations.[19]

The next generation of interagency structures may emerge in a variety of formats and configurations. However they are

---

[19] Robert Hunter, Edward Gnehm, and George Joulwan, *Integrating Instruments of Power and Influence: Lessons Learned and Best Practices*, RAND Corporation, Santa Monica, 2008, p. vii, <http://www.rand.org/pubs/conf. proceedings /CF251.html>, accessed on November 14, 2011.

constructed, they will share many of the same characteristics and will need to overcome many of the same challenges as those encountered during the various PRT efforts in Iraq and Afghanistan.

A new tradecraft. The changing face of the new expeditionary interagency is, as Secretary Clinton described in a Town Hall meeting in 2012, "...deployed...to hotspots in more than thirty countries around the world...often in some of the most remote and least governed places on earth. They can be found camped alongside special forces, sleeping under mosquito nets in campsites hacked out of the jungle by machete, eating MREs [meals, ready to eat], hitching rides in the back of pickups to meet with local leaders—not the common image of a diplomat. But they are among the hundreds of State and USAID employees practicing a tradecraft that now lives at the intersection of diplomacy, development, and security."[20] Clearly, professionals in the future can build upon the lessons provided from the past decade of innovative field experience.

The CCO, the United States Institute for Peace, the U.S. Army Center for Lessons Learned, and the Arthur D. Simons Center for the Study of Interagency Cooperation are just a few organizations that have conducted in-depth research and published reviews and collections of lessons for operational and tactical (or team) field units. Understanding the challenges, responses, and results of these team experiences may allow organizations to identify additional mechanisms to accelerate seemingly glacial institutional changes over the years.

---

[20] Secretary Hillary Clinton, transcript of remarks, Town Hall Meeting on the Quadrennial Diplomacy and Development Review, January 26, 2012 <http://www.state.gov /secretary/rm/2012/01/182613.htm>, accessed on April 13, 2012.

Looking Around

Existing templates. PRTs provide a wealth of tangible lessons, but other contemporary examples of the expeditionary interagency may provide insights as well. Non-DoD organizations have been addressing interagency issues for some time, usually coalescing around specific problems such as counterterrorism or counternarcotics. While the general lesson to be learned from these enterprises (as well as from the more directly salient PRT experiences) is that the interagency can function effectively at the point of impact, more valuable insight is gained by examining how they have achieved such effectiveness.

Joint Interagency Task Force-South (JIATF-South) leverages the skills and abilities of a spectrum of agencies and directs them toward the shared goal of counternarcotics. The JIATF-South model is not a direct corollary to the expeditionary interagency discussed here but its positive attributes are obvious. Its model "has earned a reputation as the 'gold standard' and 'crown jewel' of interagency cooperation and intelligence fusion."[21] JIATF-South's establishment, maturation process, and current construct, as well as its emphasis on cultivating the interagency team provide an instructive example.

The Special Operations Forces (SOF) community provides another example. SOF offers accessible interagency training, sponsors informative interagency reference handbooks, and draws from lessons learned in less explored areas (such as the Philippines and Colombia) to inform future operations and

---

[21] Evan Munsing and Christopher J. Lamb, "Joint Interagency Task Force-South: The Best Known, Least Understood Interagency Success," *Strategic Perspectives, No. 5*, Institute for National Strategic Studies, National Defense University Press, Washington, D.C., June 2011, 4. http://www.ndu.edu/inss/index.cfm ?secID=100&pageID =8&type=section, accessed on October 19, 2011.

planning. A review of SOF methodologies thus can provide valuable insight about the military approach to "teaming" and can demonstrate tangible lessons for the potential application or adaptation across the interagency spectrum.

In each of these representative cases, the relevant organizations have documented and analyzed their own development and identified critical aspects of their evolution. The processes themselves are as informative as the results of these processes. An honestly introspective organization, at any level, thereby allows its partners a level of insight that fosters the trust and understanding fundamental to sustained, future interagency success.

"Left of boom." The term "left-of-boom" is instructive. In the fight against improvised explosive devices, one measure of progress is how effective U.S. countermeasures are at moving from reacting to the explosion ("the boom") to getting "left-of-boom" (before the explosion), either through identifying the device before it explodes or, ideally, interdicting the supporting network fundamental to the device so that its placement is prevented. Applying this mindset to the interagency scenario, field personnel must get "left-of-boom" to gain interactive, face-to-face exposure to the organizational cultures they will encounter prior to deployment.

To address this, current pre-deployment training incorporates, to varying degrees, a mix of civil-military components. The two-week Afghanistan pre-deployment training plan for USAID personnel includes a four-hour block of civil-military coordination (although aspects of the civil-military relationship are infused throughout the curriculum). Likewise, the sister pre-deployment training sites of Camp Atterbury (DoD) and Muscatatuck (State Department) in Indiana serve multiple roles as training grounds for military and civilian personnel preparing to deploy to Afghanistan.

Current policy level reform efforts consider the need for civil-military exposure through advocacy of rotational assignments, and institutions tend to explore shared training environments to effect positive change. Indeed, some of these have already begun to bring diverse agency audiences together for instruction. But until these or similar initiatives become ingrained and expanded to affect a more comprehensive set of expeditionary professionals, operational leaders will be forced to create their own ad hoc solutions. They may adopt a passive stance and wait for Assistant Deputy Secretaries to pen Memoranda of Understanding before addressing the deficiency. Alternatively, they may proactively seek out remedies through informal partnerships with their field counterparts in other agencies (as indeed they have). These remedies can include attending organizational functions and seminars, providing capability briefings to targeted groups of partner agencies, and sending either observers or participants to training courses and exercises.[22] The training offered indeed may be valuable in its own right, but the intrinsic value is enhanced exponentially because of greater interagency exposure for the participants and the development of personal relationships.

New Horizons. Creative leaders also can leverage opportunities abroad to train and interact in real-world circumstances free from the pressure or scrutiny of a combat or crisis zone. Such scenarios can safely expose the interagency practitioner to more austere—and thus more realistic—environments. In this way, personnel can gradually improve skills before the deeper test of conflict or crisis emerges.

---

[22] See John Dyson, "Navigating Interagency Education and Training Courses," *Interagency Journal*, Vol. I, Issue I, Fall 2010, <http://thesimonscenter.org/iaj-1-1-fall-2010>, accessed on April 15, 2012.

Operation New Horizons, an ongoing set of actual U.S. military operations in the Latin American and Caribbean regions, is one example of greater civil-military collaboration and integration. A typical New Horizons mission might find an Army National Guard unit drilling drinking wells, Air Force light construction units working on bridges or roads, or military police units conducting training with indigenous forces in neglected areas of nations such as Nicaragua or Haiti. Additional coordination between the expeditionary elements of the State Department, USAID, and the Department of Agriculture can increase the value of the opportunity, providing technical expertise to joint events and expanding the interagency fluency of all involved.

Looking Ahead

Intercultural competence. Individual organizations have rhythms and personalities all their own. Regardless of institutional specifics, it is critical that the very real existence of such cultures be not simply recognized, but highlighted, and their impact explored.

Foreign culture, in general, is already a clear focus for the primary expeditionary agencies. Military personnel preparing for service as members of a PRT participate in a number of various pre-deployment classes and receive exposure to the language, customs, and other distinguishing characteristics of a destination country. Likewise, the State Department's Foreign Service Institute provides similar training to Foreign Service Officers. In both cases, personnel deploying today receive a far greater level of cultural preparation than earlier expeditionary pioneers. Consideration must be given to ensure that these programs continue to develop and deliver a consistent message to the varied audiences.

Yet such training addresses only one facet of the total requirement. Successful expeditionary interagency practitioners recognize the fundamental requirement to develop at least a familiarization with, and, ideally, eventual mastery of, not just the national cultures they will encounter, but also the cultures of the partner-agencies that comprise the team. Dr. Milton J. Bennett, founding director of The Intercultural Communication Institute, agrees and refers to this as "intercultural competence."[23] To be sure, instilling and sustaining such competence in support of expeditionary deployments would help usher U.S. foreign policy into the role now demanded by the contemporary environment.

Conclusion

The nature and form of the post-9/11 expeditionary interagency community has emerged from the unique situations in Afghanistan and Iraq. While it is unlikely that the landscape for expeditionary interagency teams in the future will encounter the same scale of military involvement, they should be expected to feature a significant, if limited, military component. The fundamental lessons derived from the employment of expeditionary interagency teams in Afghanistan and Iraq provide the richest vein of insight into the difficulties that future interagency constructs may face. The experiences of the PRTs provided a laboratory to explore the inherent realities of the expeditionary interagency and have done so in circumstances likely more difficult than future manifestations are anticipated to encounter.

A multitude of reform efforts designed to establish a responsive and relevant set of interagency support mechanisms have been initiated by the policymaking community. Someday these reforms may deliver the ideal

---

[23] Milton J. Bennett, "Becoming Interculturally Competent," in J.S. Wurzel (ed.), *Toward Multiculturalism: A Reader in Multicultural Education,* Intercultural Resource Corporation, Newton, 2004.

resources, structures, and balance to facilitate the seamless integration of interagency efforts. Until then, agencies, their mid-level leaders, and individual personnel can and should pursue an agenda of increased interagency competency and intercultural fluency. To this end, the reform-minded should consider **looking back** to the hard-earned lessons of the PRTs in order to identify the critical factors most relevant to the role of their respective organizations. They should consider **looking around** at the successes of other contemporary interagency endeavors and for opportunities to prepare personnel for more peaceful interagency experiences outside the intensity of conflict or crisis. Finally, the recognition that significant achievements were generated in the absence of ideal conditions should catalyze the expeditionary offices of relevant agencies to **look forward** and foster an organizational climate that is more conducive to expeditionary and interagency culture. Harnessing the combined perspectives from such examinations can enable agencies to take positive action that is not dependent on high-level reform measures.

Protecting Soft Networks: Time for a Global Partner Protection Program?

Steve Miska

Military units deployed to combat zones employ force protection measures to make patrols and bases difficult — or "hard" — targets for the enemy to strike. The art of force protection involves shifting patrol patterns, along with random security measures at gates and perimeters, in addition to many other techniques — all with the intent of making it difficult for an adversary to identify likely patterns and gaps for exploitation. Those skilled in the art of security, such as the U.S. Secret Service, the military, and private security firms, constantly use predictive scenario drills to identify or "game out" potential points of weakness on patrols and on bases, and often frustrate attempted enemy attacks in the process. While this protects U.S. men and women in uniform, it leaves many people on whom they rely increasingly vulnerable.

As a result, enemies coerce, harm, and intimidate civilians, precisely because they are "softer," meaning more exposed and less risky targets to attack. Because insurgents, terrorists, and militia fight from positions of weakness, they view soft targets as optimal victims to assault. While the strategy of targeting "soft networks"[1] is time tested and well-

---

[1] "Soft networks" refer to non-military, indigenous partners in counterinsurgency and counterterrorism operations. Many times soft

documented, Western military forces in Afghanistan and Iraq seemed caught off guard when insurgents targeted unprotected interpreters and other local nationals who were commuting to work in personal vehicles or on foot.

But why the surprise? Weaker opponents routinely pursue soft objectives as a default strategy when confronting superior or well-protected military forces. And when unable to threaten local partners directly, the weaker opponent resorts to pressuring family members or perhaps even friends of these locals, creating a stifling effect on the stronger force by indirectly breeding insecurity within the ranks of the soft network. While this reality has too often caught the U.S. military off guard in Iraq and Afghanistan, personnel serving in non-government organizations (NGOs), media agencies, and domestic law enforcement communities have often implemented pro-active protection measures. Given the likelihood of more irregular warfare and combined interagency missions in the future,[2] national security leaders should pro-actively weave matters of local agent protection into their strategic architectures. To that end, a global witness protection program would strengthen U.S. national security by improving the United States' ability to disrupt criminal, terrorist, and insurgent networks.

If a country with a strong rule of law, such as the United States, requires federal and state witness protection, then surely national security agencies could utilize similar tools when operating in less developed overseas environments during counterterrorism (CT) or counterinsurgency (COIN) operations. For more than four decades, the United States, through the U.S. Marshals Service, has employed domestic

---

networks include interpreters, local business contractors, politicians, local police, and others, to include their families.

[2] Secretary of Defense Robert M. Gates, "Helping Others Defend Themselves," *Foreign Affairs* (May/June 2010).

witness security to insulate key witnesses and their families (i.e. soft networks) in cases against organized gangs, criminals, and other malign actors. Domestic efforts have not been limited to just the federal level. States such as Massachusetts,[3] California, Colorado, and many others administer their own programs to supplement national efforts. Examining best practices from the domestic witness security landscape thus illuminates protection principles and programs that could yield benefits to COIN and CT operations overseas.

America's Case: Managing Organized Crime & Gangs

U.S. Federal Witness Security

The Organized Crime Control Act of 1970 authorized the establishment of the federal witness security program, and since 1971 U.S. Marshals have relocated more than 8,500 witnesses and 9,900 associated family members.[4] In addition, the U.S. Attorney General has the authority to provide "competitive grants to eligible state, tribal, and local prosecutors to establish and maintain certain protection and witness assistance programs," and to create a forum to share best practices with operators in the field.[5] When it comes to domestic policy, U.S. legislators and law enforcement officials therefore understand the need to protect soft networks. They see such programs as "enhanced security measures" that make witnesses "more likely to cooperate with police and prosecutors in identifying criminals and testifying against

---

[3] Deval L. Patrick, "An Overview of Cases in Fiscal Year 2007," The Commonwealth of Massachusetts Witness Protection Program (October 2007), 1-27.

[4] U.S. Marshal's Service at http://www.usmarshals.gov/witsec/ accessed on July 11, 2013.

[5] U.S. House of Representatives, 111th Congress, Report 111-138, "Witness Security and Protection Grant Program Act of 2009," Report to accompany H.R. 1741, (June 8, 2009), 1-7.

them."[6] Together, the federal witness security program and complementary state-level programs work side by side, bolstering the entire domestic law enforcement community and protecting soft networks in dynamic ways.

Many states provide identity protection and witness assistance measures short of relocation and complete identity change. While states do provide relocation in extreme cases, law enforcement agencies maintain a diverse portfolio of options, allowing for case-by-case flexibility and tailored protective services. For example, in cases involving domestic violence, sexual assault, or stalking, New Hampshire provides victims with alternate addresses for all forms of identification, including a driver's license, and for those required for health care and other government services.[7] After experiencing initial implementation problems, Colorado chose to enhance its program and re-sensitize law enforcement agencies once leaders learned of a general ignorance of the policies among agency personnel. To generate better situational awareness, the state mandated training for law enforcement professionals and created a witness risk assessment tool.[8] Elsewhere, as in California, state initiatives more closely mirror the federal program and offer complete identity changes and comprehensive relocation services when needed.[9] Across the United States, most law enforcement enterprises prioritize

---

[6] Ibid.

[7] Department of Justice, New Hampshire, "Address Confidentiality Program," accessed 23 November 2010 at http://www.doj.nh.gov/victim/addressfaq.html.

[8] Lisa Ryckman, "Colorado's Witness Protection Program Under Scrutiny," *The Rocky Mountain News*, (July 28, 2008).

[9] Office of the Attorney General of California, "California Witness Relocation and Assistance Program: Annual Report to the Legislature 2009-2010," California Department of Justice, accessed June 19, 2013, at http://ag.ca.gov/cms_attachments/press/pdfs/n2062_calwrap_annual _report_to_the_legislature_09-10_final.pdf, 1-6.

witness protection—33 states administer confidentiality programs,[10] and nearly every state allocates at least some resources to help its witnesses.

Overseas Applications

Because the U.S. Departments of Defense and State could benefit from more policy options overseas, the United States leadership should consider extending to foreign interventions the same policy flexibility enjoyed by domestic law enforcement personnel. Insurgents continue to target U.S. soft networks abroad, much as gangs and mafia target key witnesses domestically. And, as in domestic police operations, military professionals require flexible policies to enable identity protection and limited relocation alternatives. Sadly, the Special Immigrant VISA (SIV) has been the only policy implemented by the U.S. to protect soft networks during the Iraq and Afghanistan conflicts. Originally set to expire the end of 2013 before receiving an extension,[11] the SIV initially proved inadequate—it failed to address the full extent of the problem.

---

[10] Stalking Resource Center, "Address Confidentiality Program," The National Center for Victims of Crime, accessed June 19, 2013, at www.victimsofcrime.org.

[11] The 2014 National Defense Authorization Act (NDAA) added provisions to extend the SIV. However, the NDAA authorized the issuance of 2,500 immigrant visas after January 1, 2014 to qualified principal applicants. The NDAA does not include a date by which these visas must be issued, so consular officers have the authority to issue visas under this program until all 2,500 numbers have been used worldwide. The Iraqi SIV program will end after all visas have been issued. See http://iraq.usembassy.gov/siv-special.html for more details.

Too Little, Too Late: The U.S. Special Immigrant VISA

In 2006, the U.S. Congress began to take action to ameliorate the suffering of millions of refugees and internally displaced persons (IDPs) within Iraq and in nearby countries. Much of the impetus for action came from those for whom "soft network trust" was integral for operational success, mainly those uniformed and civilian personnel who worked closely with Iraqi subject matter experts during COIN operations during the conflict. Diplomats, journalists, and military leaders all developed close working relationships with Iraqi locals. Branded as collaborators, these Iraqi locals sacrificed a great deal to work with the U.S.-led coalition: insurgents repeatedly threatened and attacked them and their families; hundreds lost their lives; and thousands more became IDPs as a result of militia and insurgent intimidation.[12] Despite the critical role these individuals played in operational successes, the overall U.S. response to protect them has proven to be lukewarm.

Rather than pro-actively formulating policy in advance of operations in Iraq and Afghanistan, the U.S. enacted an ad hoc policy long after local loyalists' lives were already placed at risk.[13] Furthermore, section 1059 of the National Defense Authorization Act for Fiscal Year (FY) 2006, provided SIV eligibility to as many as 50 Iraqi and Afghan translators

---

[12] The CIA World Factbook estimated that, in 2007, two million Iraqi refugees were displaced to Jordan and Syria, while another 2.4 million were displaced internally 7. The UNHCR estimated that 300,000 internally displaced persons spontaneously returned home between 2008 and 2009 ,as conditions improved, yet former U.S. government employees, "collaborators," were still being threatened. For an example, see Associated Press, "27 Killed, Including U.S. Army Translator In Iraq: Interpreter for U.S. Army Gunned Down by Son, Nephew After Refusing to Quit his Job," (June 18, 2010).

[13] George Packer, "Betrayed," *The New Yorker* (March 26, 2007).

working for the U.S. government. This number represented only a fraction of the total demand. At the time the legislation passed, the U.S. military alone employed thousands of interpreters, with thousands more additional contractors employed by other federal departments in support of logistics and other key tasks. Public Law 110-36, subsequently enacted with President Bush's signature on June 15, 2007, amended section 1059 by expanding the total number of beneficiaries to 500 per year for FY2007 and FY2008. If an interpreter met the requirements, one of which was working with a U.S. unit for at least twelve months, he or she could apply for a SIV. Still, the process remained cumbersome, difficult to understand, and a challenging bureaucratic labyrinth to navigate. Importantly, the initiative provided assistance to only interpreters, while doing nothing to assist others who helped the U.S. effort in other capacities. Nor did the expansion provide relief for those who could not meet the basic immigration requirements for gaining entry into the United States.[14] If a local partner did not meet such eligibility requirements, he or she simply had no further options. Despite the existence of an official American military COIN doctrine stating that units should rely on indigenous subject matter experts to achieve mission success,[15] the U.S. government implemented only one policy—the SIV initiative—to protect all its partners abroad. That policy proved to be—and remains—insufficient in most cases. U.S. practitioners need more tools.

Other western countries struggled with this issue as well. The British displayed similarly lackluster behavior in Iraq. The Danish example served as the only bright spot in that

---

[14] Spencer S. Hsu and Robin Wright, "Crocker Blasts Refugee Process," *Washington Post* (September 17, 2007).

[15] FM 3-24/MCWP 3-33.5 *Counterinsurgency*, Headquarters U.S. Army (December 15, 2006); See Appendix C: Linguist Support.

campaign, as Denmark evacuated all 200 interpreters, support staff, and their families in 2007 when ultimately departing the "land between two rivers."[16] Given the smaller scope of the Danish enterprise, the leaders in Copenhagen could afford such an extreme relocation solution. By contrast, a similar move by the United States almost certainly would have undermined future operations in Iraq and caused political and social turmoil at home. Furthermore, the size of the U.S. soft network in need of relocation would have removed vast numbers of young, educated Iraqis — just the type needed (and desired by the U.S.) to remain and help rebuild. Any future policy must therefore require flexibility and balance.

The SIV: Lessons Learned

The Iraq SIV case demonstrates and presents several conclusions, all of which the U.S. must consider for future contingencies. First and foremost, American adversaries will continue to think strategically about soft networks. As in the cases of the Viet Cong during the Vietnam conflict, the French underground during the German occupation of World War II, or the American patriots during the Revolutionary War, the weaker opponent always has an incentive to target soft networks critical to the greater power's strategy. In contemporary times, we need look no further than present-day Iraq where Islamic State fighters have targeted those previously allied with U.S.-led coalition forces.

Second, the Iraq SIV case further revealed the limits placed on operational flexibility due to a perennial American weakness in-theater: a failure to strategically protect soft networks. U.S. leadership belatedly perceived this vulnerability and enacted an unsatisfactory piece of legislation in 2007 — four years after the beginning of hostilities. Even

---

[16] Gelu Sulugiuc, "Denmark airlifts 200 Iraqi translators and relatives," *Reuters* (July 20, 2007).

then, the program proved inadequate: tens of thousands of people applied and only a small percentage were admitted. Moreover, of the Iraqis accepted for relocation, many experienced significant assimilation challenges, making it virtually impossible for them to build meaningful lives for themselves and their families in the United States. The SIV fell short, in both scope and character, for military and civilian needs in the field, and, importantly, for the closest of U.S. partners—partners the U.S. promised (implicitly, at least) to protect.

Finally, the Iraq SIV case also unveils the pitfalls of ceding the initiative to an adversary. Had Washington anticipated such attacks earlier, U.S. operators might have effectively pre-empted enemy strikes, better protected local partners, and enhanced the U.S. position on the ground, both during the conflict and in preparation for reconstruction. Overall, lessons learned from the SIV example suggests the following: an effective policy in the future requires flexibility and balance, providing not just relocation to United States as an option, but also temporary local relocation as well. In addition, proactive identity protection must begin at the outset of U.S. operations.

Policy Recommendations: *Implementing a Global Partner Protection Program*

The Importance of Identity Protection

In order to counter threats to soft networks, the United States should promote greater awareness among the ranks of its government personnel through a number of concurrent efforts focused on additional training and the development of policies aimed at enhancing operational flexibility. The implementation of policies similar to those found in domestic witness security initiatives that protect individual identities (including temporary and local relocation programs) could effectively arm national security professionals with tools to insulate indigenous partners more effectively.

To achieve this, leaders must first generate awareness about the issue within national security departments and agencies. Pre-deployment training and risk assessment tools similar to those used in Colorado, and the sharing of best practices from the entire U.S. domestic law enforcement community, almost certainly would help national security agents improve operations. Too many soldiers, Marines, diplomats, and other practitioners fail to anticipate enemy threats or attacks against local allies. The problem is recognized too late, usually after experiencing the loss of a key partner. Because this threat remains all too real, U.S. national security agencies must begin to develop long term measures to sustain soft networks abroad and create a culture of awareness that not only anticipates the potential threat to local partners but also mitigates the risk enough to ensure mission viability.

Operators also need measures short of relocation, especially at the earliest stages of local network development. The use of aliases, false or alternative addresses for work or home, disguises, and other measures can thwart the actions of insurgents and other adversaries and maintain an agent's[17] safety and thus usefulness in the field. All of these measures should be considered to help form a new set of standard operating procedures.

---

[17] The author uses the term "agent" to refer to interpreters and other local nationals employed within a soft network. The term comes from agency theory, which examines incentives between principals and agents. In most examples, a military leader is the principal and an interpreter or other local national contractor is the agent.

Guiding Principles for Relocation

Operators must weigh the stress of relocation against the threats in the field. Relocation may be the best option, despite the heavy financial and emotional costs involved with uprooting individuals and their families. If relocation becomes necessary, some attempt to limit the extent of social and physical displacement should occur. As some researchers point out, a move can be "a profoundly disorienting and destabilizing personal experience, which leaves a legacy of people trying to come to terms with their displaced lives."[18] A relocated individual experiences immense internal conflict when he or she is required to live in a fabricated existence. Behavioral scientist Fred Montanino explains, "Lying to ensure their secrecy poses a personal, moral conflict to the witnesses and places them in an antithetical position with regard to social structure."[19] Sponsors, therefore, must seek to minimize such disruption, while balancing the risks of exposure to the witness or local agent. The following guiding principles should be considered:

1 – Seek local and/or temporary solutions first. By moving an individual to another location within his or her native country, logistics remain relatively simple. More importantly, a local or temporary move can mitigate both the individual's emotional disruption and the operator's concern about the identified country's potential "brain drain." Depending on the nature of the new environment, the agent may also be able to maintain the same identity. Alternatively if the environment is too dangerous, the operator could alter the informant's identity, disguise his or her employment, or provide similar

---

[18] Nicholas R. Fyfe and Heather McKay, "Witness Intimidation, Forced Migration and Resettlement: A British Case Study," *Transactions of the Institute of British Geographers*, New Series, Vol. 25, No. 1 (2000), 77-90.

[19] Fred Montanino, "Protecting the Federal Witness," *The American Behavioral Scientist*, Vol. 27, No. 4 (March/April 1984), 510.

protective measures to the informant's family. NGOs and media organizations have employed such tactics—especially temporary moves—to good effect.[20]

2 – Regional Relocation. If relocation in the immediate area is impractical, a relocation further away, yet in the same region, may be the next best option (preferably to a place with a similar culture and language). In Somalia, for example, an international NGO deemed threats too great for their indigenous partners in-country (in provinces such as Puntland and Somaliland), and the organization successfully relocated local nationals to Kenya and Uganda.[21]

Field operatives may opt for either a temporary or permanent regional relocation, depending on the nature of the threat and the individual circumstances of the person in question. For temporary relocations, a tourist visa for the agent may suffice, saving him or her from the process of seeking refugee status or asylum. The option of a tourist visa is not a panacea, however, as some countries may view it as an attempt to skirt normal immigration protocols and deny approval. Sponsors must exercise caution and properly understand the legal status of the relocated agent in a new country, as some countries do not open their gates to refugees. The viability of the relocation option depends on the specific circumstances of the move, as well as whether or not the newly identified host country has signed the 1951 United Nations Convention on Refugees.[22] During the recent Iraq conflict, most Iraqis with the means to flee migrated to Jordan or Syria, nations with similar language and culture. Yet, upon

---

[20] Author interviews and personal experience. Identities of organizations and individuals are anonymous to protect from potential threat.

[21] Author interview, February 13, 2011. Identities protected by nondisclosure agreement.

[22] United Nations High Commission on Refugees, "The 1951 Refugee Convention," accessed December 7, 2010, at http://www.unhcr.org/pages/49da0e466.html.

arrival, large numbers of them faced daunting conditions[23] and many have since returned to Iraq, placing them at risk once again. For policymakers, therefore, flexibility remains paramount, as individual circumstances require nuanced and tailored responses. If a local threat persists, intensifies, or expands across the region, an extreme relocation may be not only warranted, but necessary.

3 – Extreme Relocation. If the local agent faces immediate danger, and if relocation to a nearby country is not feasible, then an extreme relocation might provide the best amount of safety. This is where the SIV can play a valuable role in the policy toolkit. For example, an Iraqi veteran of the 1980-88 Iran-Iraq War who has more recently provided interpreter assistance to American forces might not be safe in many Middle East countries due to the presence of Iranian assassins across the region. According to press reports, Iranian agents killed scores of Iraqi Air Force pilots during the U.S. post-1991 occupation of Iraq.[24] It is therefore reasonable to assume that other "revenge killings" could take place elsewhere.

It is critical to remember that extreme relocation often involves significant social upheaval for the individual (and his or her family) and results in an awkward or difficult assimilation, not dissimilar to the plight of some relocated witnesses in U.S. domestic protection programs. One observer of domestic efforts notes, "Protected witnesses and their immediate (nuclear) family members must end social

---

[23] Elizabeth Ferris, "The Looming Crisis: Displacement and Security in Iraq: Policy Paper Number 5," Brookings Institution (August 2008); The International Rescue Committee "A Tough Road Home: Uprooted Iraqis in Jordan, Syria, and Iraq" *A Report of the IRC Commission on Iraqi Refugees* (February 2010).

[24] ABC News Baghdad Staff, "Wikileaks Exposes Iran's Secret Revenge on Iraqi Pilots For 1980s War: Iran Has Hunted Down and Killed 182 Iraqi Pilots Who Fought in Iran-Iraq War," *ABC News International* (December 6, 2010).

existence in the context in which they have known it."[25] If Americans relocating within the U.S. indeed experience social and psychological setbacks upon relocation, it should come as no surprise that many Iraqis relocated to the U.S. endured substantial cultural challenges, requiring additional assimilation assistance from sponsors.[26] Given such dynamics, the SIV initiative should be seen not as a cure-all but rather as an important option and perhaps as a last resort. In conjunction with other approaches, therefore, a variation of the SIV initiative should remain one of the many cost-effective instruments in the CT and COIN policy toolbox — an option that can be adjusted and teamed with other mitigation techniques.

Cost Implications

If the extent of the federal and state domestic witness protection effort is any indication, a similar initiative for global applications should require relatively moderate investment. The federal program, for example, costs only $30 million per year, or $150 million from FY2010-2014, as estimated by the Congressional Budget Office.[27] Funding requirements for state-level initiatives also appear modest. In Massachusetts, annual expenses for the program amounted to approximately $500,000 for nearly sixty individual cases in 2007,[28] and California spends under $5 million a year[29] to

---

[25] Montanino, 505.

[26] The International Rescue Committee, "Iraqi Refugees in the United States: In Dire Straits," *A Report of the IRC Commission on Iraqi Refugees* (June 2009); Kirk Semple, "Iraqi Immigrants Face Lonely Struggle in U.S.," *The New York Times* (August 13, 2009).

[27] U.S. House of Representatives, "Witness Security and Protection Grant Program Act of 2009," 5.

[28] Patrick, "An Overview of Cases in Fiscal Year 2007," 9.

effectively insulate soft networks from gangs and other violent actors. As of 2010, California's program had protected 1,482 witnesses, 2,272 family members, and 2,433 defendants.[30] Modest in spending but robust in results, similar policies and programs could enhance U.S. operational effectiveness in the international arena.

Although a global witness protection program may require a greater financial commitment in initial investments, it should prove to be relatively inexpensive in the long run. The total military and diplomatic cost associated with recent U.S. overseas engagements in Iraq and Afghanistan stands as incontrovertible proof. The Pentagon's total allocation for war from 2001-2011, in current dollars, amounts to more than $1.406 trillion according to one estimate,[31] and this does not account for the billions of dollars the U.S. might continue to spend on stabilization and reconstruction. Setting aside just a small fraction of this spending for a witness protection initiative during the same period could have achieved great effect, possibly resulting in the transformation of some coalition efforts and perhaps developing soft networks in such a way to enable future (and unforeseen) policy initiatives. Moreover, providing modest expenditures for protecting soft networks can produce huge dividends as U.S.-led COIN and CT campaigns shift emphasis and transform into rule of law development and institution-building initiatives elsewhere around the globe.

[29] Department of Finance, "2012-13 Final Budget Summary," State of California, accessed June 19, 2013, at http://www.documents.dgs.ca.gov/osp/GovernorsBudget/pdf/Governors_Budget_2012-2013.pdf, 58.

[30] Attorney General of California, "California Witness Relocation and Assistance Program," 2.

[31] "Costs of War," Brown University, accessed July 11, 2013, at http://costsofwar.org/article/economic-cost-summary.

Conclusion

As the U.S. adapts and pursues methods to counter malign actors abroad, it must continue to apply creative techniques to counter criminal and terrorist activities. A global partner protection program is an example of such creativity: it promises to not only establish mutual trust and stronger cultural ties between America and partner nations, but also offers comfort to those allied with and contributing to the implementation of U.S. foreign policy goals. Such an approach almost certainly bolsters U.S. influence in vexing regions of the world and pays dividends at both the micro and macro levels of COIN and CT operations. The insulation of those supporting U.S. efforts deepens relationships and networks, and creates a greater capacity for future campaigns.

A global protection program also enhances America's international standing as it provides a moral underpinning to U.S. operations: those who have contributed will be protected. Too many critical partners of the United States have been left to defend themselves upon the departure of American and other allied forces, many of whom continue to face significant security threats and have few options other than to vie for one of the rare immigration visas available under the existing SIV program. [32] The expansion of the SIV initiative would be a step in the right direction. However, the U.S. could significantly improve its operational flexibility and effectiveness with a more comprehensive approach, one including a full set of relocation and identity protection options. A global partner protection program would help achieve this critically

---

[32] Alana Goodman, "The Abandoned Afghan translator of Medal of Honor recipient Dakota Meyer caught in bureaucratic limbo," accessed August 16, 2013, at http://freebeacon.com/the-abandoned/ about a heroic interpreter and his sponsor's inability to get him through the SIV process.

important end state and should be considered by senior policy makers. Rather than perpetuate America's post-9/11 image as a fortress few can enter, a comprehensive set of policy options would portray an America that extends protection to friends and partners wherever they reside.

Acknowledgement: I would like to thank Roslyn Warren, a master's student at Georgetown University and the National Security and Joint Warfare research assistant at Marine Corps War College, for her generous assistance. Roslyn's research helped update this piece, specifically with respect to current state level witness security programs.

Non-Material Factors and Taking the Soldier Seriously: Five Clarifications in Military Technological Innovation

Nina A. Kollars

Military innovation is central to determining and sustaining military power. Yet for so fundamental an aspect of power, military innovation remains tragically misconceived. Senior decision makers arrogate far too much weight to cutting-edge technology and not enough to users and the practical aspect of warfare. Consider the story of the Reffye Mitrailleuse—the first rapid-fire weapon to see actual battle. Napoleon brought this revolutionary gun to the battlefield as standard equipment for the first time during the Franco-Prussian War, and by modern standards it should have been a decisive factor in battle. The problem was that the Mitrailleuse was a machine without an established mode of practice. Not even Napoleon's own commanders understood what they should do with it. Rather than moving it to the forefront as an anti-personnel gun, they held it to the back as artillery—as if it were a field cannon. The effect proved to be notably underwhelming, and would remain so on battlefields for more than a century.[1] For military historians the lesson is important: the promise of any technology is revealed not at the point of

---

[1] Larry H. Addington, *The Patterns of War since the Eighteenth Century*, 2nd ed. (Bloomington: Indiana University Press, 1994), 98.

invention but in its successful application.

This means that innovation is, at its foundation, change in "how" war is practiced — or how material factors are applied during warfare — rather than change in "what" material is available and fielded. Recognizing this distinction suggests something quite radical: that the ultimate arbiter of innovation is the soldier who uses technology and executes missions. This means that we must move beyond the material and instead uncover the non-material factors associated with bringing about a real transformation. Unfortunately, this is not where most people place an emphasis during contemporary conversations about military innovation.

Policymakers and industry researchers have long labored under a conceptual cloud as regards the factors that induce effective military innovation. These misconceptions reinforce a materialist imbalance and bias against the practical art of application in meeting military objectives. It is a top-down bias favoring material solutions over non-material factors in war. This essay seeks to correct this imbalance and suggests a path forward for bringing the user (i.e. the soldier) back into the conversation.

This essay offers a synthesis of research that is well-established, but which is distributed across academic disciplines. In fact, understanding innovation is difficult partially because of the lack of a centralized disciplinary home. Innovation research is dispersed across the fields of history, philosophy, business, sociology, and the hard sciences. The aim here is not to provide a comprehensive recovery of innovation research across the academic disciplines, but to place special emphasis on user-centered research that may determine an organization's success or failure to innovate. While this essay will likely preach to many of the already converted, it is the author's interpretation that the predominant narrative of innovation remains elitist and materials-oriented. The purpose of this essay is to elevate and extend the conversation and to invite honest and open consideration of the merits of taking the user more seriously.

Overall, the points presented reveal that innovation is simultaneously far more complex and far more common than generally presumed. I accept that the points, as presented, are made artificially independent, and that they build upon one another rather than maintaining their own autonomy. I merely divide them out to make them explicit and clear. I conclude the essay with an invitation to scholars and practitioners to consider that true innovation is larger than the invention and/or recombination of cutting-edge military machines. Rather, I assert that mature attempts at major military innovation must pay due diligence to the contributions and practices of individual soldiers, sailors, airmen, and Marines. This means accepting that, as we entertain our fantasies about the next supposedly revolutionary innovation, we must keep in mind that the user will be the agent who will adapt and employ its ultimate use.

1. *Inventions are what we create, but they are not innovation*

Although machines are the material means through which innovations become possible, until such creations are put into practice they are not true innovation; they are simply inventions.[2] While novel inventions can enable innovation, they do not necessarily produce it. Innovation is a change in how something is done—whether it is in the way cars are constructed and driven, the way in which communication occurs between humans, or the way in which a room is lit. Inventions, alternately, are the combination (or recombination) of objects in new and novel ways. Invention is

---

[2] On Invention and Innovation see: Yale Brozen, "Invention, Innovation, and Imitation," *The American Economic Review* 41, no. 2 (1951). W. Ruttan Vernon, "Usher and Schumpeter on Invention, Innovation, and Technological Change," *The Quarterly Journal of Economics* 73, no. 4 (1959).

the act of producing an object—physical or virtual, as in the case of computer programming—and new inventions often bring about innovation. Consider the examples of the telephone and the light bulb as truly transformative inventions. One fundamentally altered how people communicate from a distance; the other provided an artificial source of light and forever changed societies in profound ways.

Yet confusion persists. Too many people still tend to mistake new technologies for innovation, and perhaps the vernacular use of the term causes much of this confusion. When the concept of innovation is considered, we tend to think of nuclear weapons and Oppenheimer, Tesla, Bill Gates, and iPods. But innovation is much more.

The post-Gulf War literature of the 1990s referencing the Revolution in Military Affairs (RMA) confused technology thrusts for innovation. The RMA movement envisioned a type of warfare based almost entirely on a technological revolution whereby an adversary would be overwhelmed with the might of machines in the air, land, and sea domains simultaneously. It promised full-spectrum dominance—low cost, low casualty, and quick paths to victory.[3] It also never happened. The RMA ultimately proved to be unrealized. The history of its failure is riddled with cost overruns and bureaucratic wrangling, but no small part of it was the result of the conflation of the invention and innovation concepts.

The cancellation of the Army's Future Combat Systems (FCS) suffered from this same misconception. FCS, according to RAND, "was compromised by an overreliance on assumptions that the acquisition community could develop and integrate items using both evolutionary and unknown revolutionary technologies." Translation: the Army neglected

---

[3] Eliot Cohen, "Change and Transformation in Military Affairs," *Journal of Strategic Studies* 27, no. 3 (2004).

to adequately consider employment concepts, integration, and human factors and instead hoped the technology and machinery would take care of itself. Post-mortem reviewers at RAND made an appeal for "earlier, more rigorous analysis of technological forecasts, assumptions, and operational environments" and "sound technical feasibility analysis" as a prerequisite for future programs to succeed.[4]

The fervor in favor of technological advancement over innovation can also be seen throughout the contemporary emphasis on robotics. There is no shortage of conversation about how these machines are revolutionary and "changing the face of war."[5] Few have stopped to look at the actual conduct of war on the ground, which, as Joshua Davis points out, is a far more complicated picture of innovation: "What I discovered was something entirely different from the shiny picture of techno-supremacy touted by the proponents of the [Secretary] Rumsfeld doctrine. I found an unsung corps of geeks improvising as they went, cobbling together a remarkable system from a hodgepodge of military-built networking technology, off-the-shelf gear, miles of Ethernet cable, and commercial software."[6]

---

[4] Christopher G. Pernin et al., eds., *Lesson from the Army's Future Combat Systems Program* (Washington, D.C.: Rand, 2012).

[5] David Axe and Steve Olexa, *War Bots: U.S. Military Robots Are Transforming War in Iraq, Afghanistan and the Future* (Ann Arbor, Michigan: Nimble Books, LLC, 2008), P.W. Singer, *Wired for War : The Robotics Revolution and Conflict in the Twenty-First Century* (New York: Penguin Press, 2009), Joel Garreau, "Bots on the Ground," *Washington Post*, May 6, 2007.

[6] Joshua Davis, "If We Run Out of Batteries, This War Is Screwed," *Wired*, June 2003.

2. Military innovation is change in the practice of war – and change is hard

Military technological innovation is the successful and formal incorporation of a particular constellation of technologies that alters the practice of warfare. Not all military innovations are major, but all innovations lead to a change in how war is practiced. Practices, however, do not shift easily or completely but rather gradually and partially – if at all. A process of exploration and learning is required to incorporate technological invention into practice. True innovation rarely occurs in a model characterized by a one-way transfer of tactics and technologies to practitioners. Rather, innovation requires two-way communication, because the user is the final arbiter of how it shapes battlefield practices, regardless of a technology's design maturity or sophistication.

Changing how organizations achieve their objectives is not as simple as replacing one technology for another. The intent and efforts of planners are often undermined by the habits of users. Engineers and scientists can do their best to anticipate the contextualized lives of soldiers, but the majority of engineers and scientists will never actually practice war. Erik von Hippel of the Massachusetts Institute of Technology (MIT) calls this phenomenon "information asymmetry." This is a condition where the perspective of the designer and the perspective of the user are almost always two different things and each one has a unique idea of how to achieve an objective. This is particularly true of military weaponry.[7]

If true innovation is going to occur, the role and nature of the user must be understood and respected, but querying soldiers is insufficient. Bringing soldier practices into line with emerging technologies cannot be reduced to something as simple as getting "feedback." Emerging programs must study

---

[7] Eric von Hippel, *The Sources of Innovation* (New York: Oxford University Press, 1988).

the practitioners themselves and honestly critique whether these technologies align in a reasonable and manageable manner with the current conduct of warfare. Will the technologies actually assist the user, making him or her more efficient? Or will they simply add layers to previously established routines? Due consideration of the soldier's state of mind — perspective, experience, behavior — must be part of the calculus for bringing about military innovation. We should no longer simply assume that soldiers are passive recipients of training and technology. The practitioners of war are contextually embodied living creatures with both professional and private habits and routines.

In practice this may require the interdisciplinary analytical skills of anthropologists, sociologists, oral historians, and psychologists. Perhaps, through interdisciplinary collaboration, we can better understand the complexity of the soldier experience and the challenges of adjusting to new technology. At a minimum, a comprehensive and unified program of interviews with soldiers recently returned from the field could capture vital information. Beyond this, there exists an impressive collection of historical transcripts stored at the Center for Army Lessons Learned (CALL), the Defense Technical Information Center (DTIC) and the National Archives. But it is not enough. These sources can serve as a starting point for truly understanding soldier practices, how they evolve, and how they spread across the battlefield. But their use must be strengthened, along with dozens of other "lessons learned" programs throughout the Department of Defense (DoD), to promote greater interdisciplinary collaboration and avoid monocular analyses of innovation. The innovation phenomenon is so hard to study precisely because it is the product of social, cognitive, and physical interactions. This is the true challenge at hand.

In terms of technological acquisition in pursuit of true innovation, a smoother transition of invention to the field can occur by embracing the concept of familiar design. Soldiers are already accustomed to powerful civilian technologies: GPS systems, smartphones, video games, and laptops. It is for this reason that some remote-controlled robotic systems are modeled after the Xbox video gaming controller and other familiar formats.[8] Soldiers in the field have a pre-existing fluency with that format of control.[9]

Of course, the presumption that the soldier always knows best is also a flawed notion. Nevertheless, understanding the soldier, his environment, and whatever challenges he may face is a clear and decisive factor standing between a failed effort and successful military innovation.

3. Users are Inventors and Innovators, too (Often better than DARPA scientists)

Military innovation researchers are increasingly discovering what historians have long known about soldiers in the field: they are remarkable at invention and innovation.[10] Though systematic scientific assessments have proven elusive,

---

[8] Axe and Olexa, *War Bots*, 12. There is a secondary debate in philosophy and the dehumanization of war that speaks directly to this sort of design.

[9] This solution isn't exactly problem-free. Ethicists worry about the physical connection between the rise of first-person shooter video games, and its expression in weapons design. Serious consideration of whether familiarity with technologies regularly used in virtual worlds degrades the gravity of a soldier's consideration of the effects of their button-pushing needs consideration. The paradigm that presents itself through game controllers could just as easily communicate problematic assumptions about the conduct of war through the new technology. "Joysticks Transform U.S. Warfare in Afghanistan," *UAV News*, no. 9 (October, 2011), available at: http://www.spacewar.com/reports/Joysticks_transform_US_warfare_in_Afghanistan_999.html. Last accessed October 5, 2013.

[10] See: Ralf W. Zimmermann, "GI Ingenuity Unleashed in Iraq," *Defense Watch Forum* 2004.

extensive documentation of the ingenuity of soldiers exists.[11] The *Rome Plow*, the *delayed-fire rifle*, and the *mason jar grenade*, for instance, are hallowed historical examples.[12]

A few contemporary examples are just as fascinating. When Army Captain Jonathan Springer was not performing his duties in Afghanistan's Pech River Valley, he was in his bunk creating a software application for his smartphone, which he subsequently named "Tactical NAV." Tactical NAV combined his phone's compass, camera, and GPS system into

---

[11] See: James Jay Carafano, *GI Ingenuity : Improvisation, Technology, and Winning World War II* (Westport, Conn.: Praeger Security International, 2006).

[12] Lance Corporal Scurry created the delayed-fire rifle while in the trenches at the World War I Battle of Gallipoli. As the Anzac forces attempted to retreat from their trenches they feared the attack of the Turks. As the soldiers contemplated their escape, Lance Corporal Scurry took his Enfield rifle, some strings, two tins, and a bit of water. He attached the string to the trigger and then to the lower tin. He filled the upper tin with water. Just before they departed the trench they could punch a hole in the upper tin. As the water dripped into the lower tin it eventually created enough pull on the trigger to let off a round. See: C.E.W. Bean, *The Story of Anzac from 4 May, 1915, to the Evacuation of the Gallipoli Peninsula, Australia in the War of 1914-1918.*, vol. II (Canberra: Australian War Memorial, 1941).

The tank "rhino" or Rome plow of Normandy was the brainchild of Sergeant Curtis G. Cullin who, pitted against the impenetrable hedgerows, and inspired by a soldier named Roberts, welded a long tusk-shaped piece of a nearby roadblock to a Sherman tank that would push through and split the hedge. Michael D. Doubler ed., *Busting the Bocage*, U.S. Army Command and General Staff College, Combat Studies Institute (Fort Leavenworth: Library of Congress, 1955).

Along a more morbid line was the mason jar grenade, originally fashioned in the Korean war, but widely used in the Vietnam intervention. The design was simple enough: pull the pin on the grenade, nestle it in the mason jar so that the grenade's spoon remained depressed, then drop the jar from the helicopter. When the glass broke, the grenade would eventually detonate. See: Tommy Franks, *American Soldier*, 1st ed., (New York: Regan Books, 2004), 143.

a single application. Tactical NAV also had 'compass lock,' allowing the phone's camera to capture the location coordinates of what it could "see."[13] Springer successfully called in an artillery strike on a position using his new app — the strike was authorized, the use of the new technology not as much.[14] For our purposes, however, the net result is that, for $5.99, directing artillery fire with an iPhone is now possible.

The "Rhino" improvised explosive device (IED) detonation system also began as a rapid field solution in Iraq. Not to be confused with its similarly titled WWII predecessor (the Rome Plow was also known as the Rhino), this Rhino was designed to protect soldiers from roadside bombs. The problem was a particular type of IED — one detonated by a source of heat. As an anti-vehicle weapon, a heat-detonated IED is particularly effective because vehicle engines are positioned directly in front of the driver, thus often triggering a fatal blow to operators. In an effort to counter such effectiveness, Army doctrine emphasized traditional sweep detection methods. But soldiers became unsettled by such an approach. In an effort to innovate, they conducted commercial on-line research, gathered long poles, wiring, glow plugs, and ammunition boxes. The glow plug was wired to the engine's battery and placed in the box, and mounted on the long pole in front of the vehicle. By design, the resulting "hot box"

---

[13] Dominic Adams, "Local Soldier's App Helps Fight in Afghanistan, Directs Artillery for the 101st," *The Journal Gazette*, no. 6 (March, 2011). Available at: http://www.journalgazette.net/apps/pbcs.dll/article?AID=/20110306/LOCAL12/303069921/-1/LOCAL11&asid=06b57d0d. Last Accessed October 5, 2013.

[14] Dave Howard, "U.S. Soldier Makes App for Tracking Down Taliban Fighters," *BBC*, 2011. Available at: http://www.bbc.co.uk/newsbeat/13928538. Last accessed October 5, 2013.

would detonate an IED in front of, rather than underneath, an oncoming vehicle. This particular invention is remarkable not simply for its ingenuity, but also for its non-traditional use of non-military items and exploitation of both public and commercial resources via the internet. Ironically, Specialist Hurst of the 206th Transportation Group in Iraq initiated this effort by posting requests on public chat forums accessible to the U.S. public, asking commercial repair shops to send used glow plugs to construct and maintain the Rhino prototype.[15]

Irrespective of the specific era or context of a fight, soldiers adapt tactics and technologies to suit the circumstances of their specific environment. This kind of technological tinkering is thus a common, yet seldom researched, component of the battlefield. Therefore, additional research aimed at enhancing soldier-inspired innovation is not only essential but also useful.[16]

The thread of research most commonly associated with capturing user inventiveness is called User-Innovation Theory (UIT). But this is a misnomer. Despite its name, UIT places a greater emphasis on invention than on an actual change in practice—innovation. User-innovation theorists study the networks of associations, the diffusion or spread of ideas, and the conditions under which user-initiated invention is likely to happen.[17] Their point of emphasis is that people enjoy contributing to problem-solving enterprises, and will actively

---

[15] Black Cloud Diesel, "Military Man Needs Used Glow Plugs." Available at:: http://www.competitiondiesel.com/forums/archive/index.php/t-15921.html. Last accessed November 12, 2013.

[16] Theo Farrell, "Improving in War: Military Adaptation and the British in Helmand Province, Afghanistan, 2006," *Journal of Strategic Studies* 33, no. 4 (2010).

[17] Eric von Hippel, "Horizontal Innovation Networks—By and For Users," *Industrial and Corporate Change* 16, no. 2 (2007).

look for ways to engage in the activity—even without financial motivators.[18]

Despite its bias toward invention, user-innovation efforts have a positive role and can be performed individually or in a collaborative "wiki-style" group setting. User-innovators tend to produce their own niche solutions for needs that are unmet by available products.[19] As the number of individuals creating networks via the internet has increased, more collaborative approaches have proliferated. The rise in the number of cooperative and collaborative group problem-solving efforts (generally referred to as "crowd sourcing") has revealed that the introduction of multiple perspectives to a single question can often produce new and potentially more effective solutions.[20]

The Defense Advanced Research Projects Agency (DARPA) is just beginning to take user innovation and collaborative problem solving seriously. In 2012, DARPA opened an "app" marketplace for soldiers to download and test new applications on their Android phones.[21] The program provides direct avenues for collaboration between experienced designers of applications and soldiers with needs and insight.[22] Program manager Dr. Mari Maeda wants to

---

[18] Karim R. Lakhani and Robert G. Wolf, "Why Hackers Do What They Do: Understanding Motivation and Effort in Free/Open Source Software Projects," *SSRN eLibrary* (2003).

[19] Eric von Hippel, "Democratizing Innovation: The Evolving Phenomenon of User Innovation," *International Journal of Innovation Science* 1, no. 1 (2009).

[20] Paul Boutin, "Crowdsourcing: Consumers as Creators," *Business Week*, July 13, 2006.

[21] Henry Kenyon, "Dod's Move to Android Started with Darpa Apps Program," *Government Computer News*, January 31, 2012.

[22] "The Transformative Apps program will develop a diverse array of militarily-relevant software applications ("apps") using an innovative new development and acquisition process. A military apps marketplace will be created to enable rapid innovation to meet user needs based on a

---

"...empower the soldiers." She says she wants "to give them the vote. Let them figure out what would be useful to them."[23] The site incorporates individual development toolkits and online specialists to facilitate the production of user-specific solutions.[24]

The most convincing cases that have bubbled up from individual soldier initiatives are web-based forums with names like Company Command, Platoon Leader, and CAVNET.[25] Each is an information-sharing site initially pushed by soldiers in search of ways to communicate more effectively. Company Command (CC) was the brainchild of two men serving as company commanders in Hawaii in 2000. Captains Nate Allen and Tony Burgess noticed their soldiers often had no forum through which to share ideas, lessons, and

---

direct collaboration between a vibrant and highly competitive development community and involved communities of end-users. The program will address all the challenges--technical, business and operational--to make the new capabilities available for use in the field. The objectives are to transition the resulting systems to end-users in the Services and to foster a new model for rapidly and effectively acquiring, introducing, maintaining, and enhancing software." Mari Maeda, "Darpa: Transformative Apps Program." Available at : http://www.darpa.mil/Our_Work/I2O/Programs/Transformative_Apps.aspx. Last accessed November 12, 2013.

[23] Maryann Lawlor, "Apps Advance Onto the Frontline," *SIGNAL*, no. 5, (October 2010). Available at: http://www.afcea.org/signal/articles/templates/Signal_Article_Template.asp?articleid=2426&zoneid=302. Last accessed October 10, 2013.

[24] MaryAnn Lawlor, "Web 2.0 Military Style," *SIGNAL*, March 2008. Available at: http://www.afcea.org/signal/articles/templates/Signal_Article_Template.asp?articleid=1527&zoneid=228. Last accessed January 5, 2014.

[25] CAVNET is more of an abbreviation than an acronym (CAV for cavalry and NET for Internet). CAVNET was the brainchild of Peter Chiarelli. For more, see: William Matthews, "Helping Info Flow Freely: Insurgents Outdo U.S. Military, Says U.S. 3-Star," *Defense News*, January 28, 2008.

---

challenges.[26] Working outside Army protocol, they created companycommand.com or "CC." CC was a forum for young captains to share ideas and pass on best practices. A year later, finding some success but aware that soldiers of lower rank needed help, too, they created platoonleader.org or "PL" — a site for young lieutenants to source, find, and share command tips. In 2004, a third web-based community, CAVNET, was established online. Unlike CC and PL, CAVNET was a direct outcome of soldiers living and working in Iraq. Major Patrick Michaelis created CAVNET on the military's secure classified internet connection based on a faith in Web interfaces for providing an adaptive advantage vis-à-vis real-time updates on tactics, techniques, and procedures (TTPs).[27] Although the effectiveness of these projects is mixed, each serves as an example of the desire and potential for soldiers to solve their own problems.

Taking users seriously may also mean giving users more responsibility and control. This shifts the point of emphasis for DoD leadership from one of "creating" inventions that have innovative potential to "harnessing" the natural by-products of soldier tinkering. Because it is clear that many solutions are produced while soldiers are down range, DoD leadership should consider a more formal program for placing innovation analysts with troops in theater. During Operation Iraqi Freedom, Army Transportation historian Richard Killblane was assigned to do just this. His research revealed a massive amount of soldier invention in transportation units. Spurred by the IED problem in an uncertain environment

---

[26] Kelly Jones, "Taking the Guidon Interview," Company Command Forum. Available at:
http://cc.army.mil/aboutccl/contentFiles/TakingTheGuidonInterview_KellyJones.pdf. Last accessed Decemer 5, 2013.

[27] *Frontline*, "Innovating and Improvising." Available at:
http://www.pbs.org/wgbh/pages/frontline/shows/company/lessons/. Last accessed January 5, 2014.

with no secure rear area, Killblane documented the development and ubiquitous rise of the gun trucks in Iraq, an impromptu invention designed and implemented in the field to provide an offensive solution to transportation vulnerability.[28]

4. Adaptation is a necessary component of military innovation, and organizations can be structured to harness it

Adaptation is a form of innovation that is introduced through reactive impulse. Whether performed at the user-level or at the point of production, adaptation is the act of defining an unmet need and finding an immediate solution to an unmet and immediate need.[29] Although there is a tendency to see adaptation as being something distinct from the innovation process, the vast majority of inventions do not bring about innovation without adaptation. A new technology or concept is rarely fully capable of application without some modification. While testing and simulations attempt to iron out the bugs, nothing replicates the current fight quite like the current fight. In essence, adaptation is a necessary component of war. As James Russell argues, innovation is a dialectical process of experimentation, adaptation, and modification.[30]

If we accept the premise that adaptation is a necessary component of the innovation process, then serious

---

[28] Dean Dominique, "Gun Trucks: A Vietnam Innovation Returns," *Army Logistician* 38, no. 1 (2006).

[29] Significant work on adaptation is represented in psychology, history of technology (particularly the Social Construction of Technology theorists), business management, information technology, and the natural sciences. For more on SCOT, see: Wiebe E. Bijker, Thomas Parke Hughes, and T. J. Pinch, *The Social Construction of Technological Systems : New Directions in the Sociology and History of Technology*, 1st MIT Press paperback ed. (Cambridge: MIT Press, 1989).

[30] J. A. Russell, "Innovation in War: Counterinsurgency Operations in Anbar and Ninewa Provinces, Iraq, 2005-2007," *Journal of Strategic Studies* 33, no. 4 (2010).

organizational implications arise. One way to approach this is to create a specific organization for innovation, not unlike the establishment of the Limited Warfare Laboratory (LWL) during the Vietnam conflict. The LWL's mission and purpose was to implement a faster connection from technological idea to finalized project. The LWL was set up to be an "R&D organization working directly with troops in the field."[31] The lab worked as an information-gathering organization that studied how soldiers used and adapted their technology. The organization's mandate emphasized that "Producing hardware on a quick-reaction basis was a revolutionary approach to material problems. The degree of emphasis placed by LWL on maintaining close liaison with the field fostered the development of an intense interest in the welfare of the individual soldier."[32] Rather than developing technology independently, the LWL focused on the incremental adaptation process already taking place in the field in order more successfully to usher along the innovation process. By the end of the organization's seven-year lifespan, it developed a catalog of hundreds of individual technologies that were in a constant process of adjustment.

Contemporary examples of the LWL-approach appear in the form of rapid acquisition initiatives, such as Lawrence Livermore National Laboratory's ASK armor kit, the creation of the Joint IED Defeat Organization (JIEDDO), and the Mine-Resistant Ambush Protected (MRAP) initiative to harden the soft-skinned Army transport vehicle, or HMMWV. These initiatives all share the adaptive perspective on the process of innovation. Although in 2011 Ashton Carter called for the

---

[31] J.E. Mortland et al., eds., *U.S. Army Land Warfare Laboratory* Volume I, Project Report, Appendix A. Documentation," U.S. Department of Commerce, Battelle Columbus Laboratories (Columbus, OH: National Technical Information Service, 1974).
[32] Ibid, 2.

establishment of a permanent rapid acquisition program while serving as the Under Secretary of Defense for Acquisition (USD/AT&L), the lack of a serious organizational analysis and historical review has hindered the effort. Perhaps a more thorough review of past efforts such as LWL would help assess, navigate, recommend, and construct a more effective field-level support activity to inspire adaptation and innovation.[33]

Another potential path not exclusive to, but perhaps better suited for, periods of peace, is the effort to harness and formalize user insight within and throughout government pre-acquisition and development cycles. In some circles, the concept of human systems integration (HSI) has received a great deal of attention. HSI studies the incorporation of new technologies into organizations.[34] It holds the user as central to the success of any technology, and it takes into account that the successful implementation of new practices calls for persistent feedback between how leaders want the technology to be used and how users are actually going to use it. This is often referred to as a spiral model of development, or the mutual adaptation process.[35] Several contemporary initiatives reinforce this mode of thinking and these deserve more attention. Examples include a series of experiments sponsored several times each year by the Naval Postgraduate School (NPS), the Office of the USD/AT&L, and U.S. Special Operations Command (USSOCOM); the annual "Trident Spectre" event hosted by Naval Special Warfare personnel; an

---

[33] *Technology and Logistics Testimony on Department of Defense Acquisition in the Fiscal Year 2012 Budget Before the House Appropriations Subcommittee on Defense,* 113th Congress, (April 13, 2011, The Honorable Dr. Ashton B. Carter, Under Secretary of Defense for Acquisition).

[34] See: Harold R. Booher, *Handbook of Human Systems Integration* (Hoboken, NJ: Wiley-Interscience, 2003).

[35] Dorothy Leonard-Barton, "Implementation As Mutual Adaptation," *Research Policy* 17, no. 1988 (1988).

HSI curriculum and graduate program at NPS; and the establishment of an Innovation Center at USSOCOM. Other examples include the various (albeit limited) research, equipping, and prototyping initiatives at the Army Research Laboratories, within the Office of the USD (AT&L), and at the Army's Training and Doctrine Command, or TRADOC (such as the Army's Rapid Equipping Force, or REF).[36]

5. Inventions must be designed to enable adaptation. If this fact is not accepted, soldiers will ignore and work around new technology proposals

The non-material nature of innovation does not mean that the importance of machines should be ignored. On the contrary, policy makers should be more rational about the effects material factors have on soldiers, and vice versa. Materially then, one way to harness the naturally creative tendencies of users is to design technology with an eye toward enabling simple adjustment and play. To make this happen, two things are required. The first is openness. By openness, I mean designing material solutions that can be adjusted and tinkered with by the soldier. Machines can be designed such that user-inspired invention and innovation are encouraged. In computer-science and business, this is sometimes called the open source model.[37] Overall, machines exist on a spectrum of "openness" and "closedness," the latter often referred to as

---

[36] The Naval Postgraduate School in Monterey, CA, established a graduate certificate program in Human Systems Integration (HSI) to study personnel training and fatigue, human factors, human-machine interface and weapons systems design. Yet the program has received uneven support over the years from the leadership of the Navy and thus has achieved mixed results. http://www.nps.edu/or/hsi/.

[37] To date, the literature does not specify a difference between spiral development and individually produced solutions but, given the continued development of user toolkits, it is clear that entirely user-produced solutions can be an outcome of this design approach.

"black-boxing."[38] "Openness" permits soldier tinkering while "black-boxing" prohibits it. In order to enhance the capability of the warfighter, openness and adaptability can be designed into machines themselves.

A completely open technology requires a great deal of time and effort to reconstruct and such a product is thus impractical to the soldier. A more practical approach involves the use of toolkits and modularity.[39] Toolkits are an increasing feature in engineering and first became popular in the 1980s. As electronic circuit designers grew tired of trying to understand every possible permutation of customer needs (i.e. when prediction essentially became too costly), designers shifted tactics: they opted to design the system so that the user could adjust it on his or her own. This yielded the toolkit, a function not unlike a set of plastic Legos — the small, exploitable children's toy capable of nearly-infinite rearrangement. Toolkits reduced a user's need to know software code in order to operate and adapt, allowing the use of simpler building blocks to create unique solutions.[40]

Modularity proved to be an even simpler enabler for invention and innovation. Modularity is a time-honored engineering practice that provides single components of capabilities for mixing and matching onto a single base.[41]

---

[38] For more on black box see: Christer Karlsson, Rajesh Nellore, and Klas Soderquist, "Black Box Engineering: Redefining the Role of Product Specifications," *Journal of Product Innovation Management* 15, no. 6 (1998).

[39] There is often ambiguity regarding the distinction between user toolkits and modular design. In general, especially in currently published work on user innovation and machine design, the words modular and toolkit are used interchangeably. I maintain that there is a distinction, by degree if not in kind. See, for example: Kenyon, "Dod's Move to Android Started with Darpa Apps Program."

[40] Ibid.

[41] Modular designs likely took on particular importance in electronics design as portable power sources proliferated. See: Eric S. Hintz,

Modular designs exist more near the closed end of the design spectrum (see figure below), with clearly delineated parts and a limited degree of rearrangement, not unlike that found in the popular "Mr. Potatohead" children's toy (a plaything with different configurations of arms, legs, eyes, and noses that produce near-infinite variations on the same base).

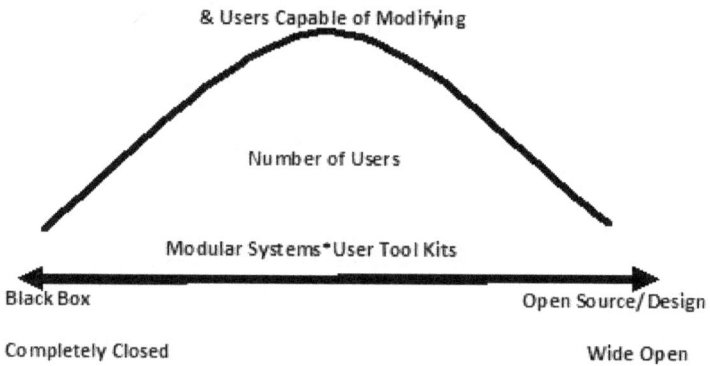

Range of Open and Black Box Designs

& Users Capable of Modifying

Number of Users

Modular Systems*User Tool Kits

Black Box — Open Source/Design

Completely Closed — Wide Open

Most of the weapons industry has shifted to some degree of modularity or open design. Most vehicle armor is now designed to be modular.[42] Most personal body armor systems are also modular. After the early lessons of Afghanistan and Iraq, soldiers grew tired of juggling awkward technologies and choosing to use or leave behind such protection. The transition to modular systems eased this friction point.[43] The Navy's Littoral Combat Ship, or LCS—its newest class—utilizes modular mission packages to meet various threat

"Portable Power: Inventor Samuel Ruben and the Birth of Duracell," *Technology and Culture* 50, no. 1 (2008).

[42] Dominique, "Gun Trucks: A Vietnam Innovation Returns."

[43] Kenneth P. Horn, Rand Corporation, and Center Arroyo, *Lightening Body Armor : Arroyo Support to the Army Response to Section 125 of the National Defense Authorization Act for Fiscal Year 2011* (Santa Monica, CA: RAND, 2012).

scenarios. And efforts continue to work on more creative solutions. Black Diamond Advanced Technology, for example, has been immensely successful with its line of modular-based wearable tactical computers.[44]

Pushing designs that better enable user-tinkering provides an additional advantage: increasing the likelihood of innovation. When a technology is delivered with few application restrictions, the likelihood of its use is increased. This also results in an exponentially better budgetary "bang for the buck" for public investments. Of perhaps greater concern, however, is that soldiers tend to adapt and sometimes break equipment. Indeed, in the absence of openness and user-friendly designs, breakage and non-use may become more common.

The push for greater modularity and openness in design remains challenged, however, by at least one important practical aspect and persistent reality of the acquisition system. Because most modular approaches exist *within* a particular contract award or contractor team, rather than among and across all programmatic efforts, systems primarily work only with other components from the same manufacturer, and not necessarily between them. This hinders interoperability and, in some cases, creates additional "bridging" requirements that lead to patchwork or translation software and even greater cost increases. Despite repeated attempts and efforts from Congressional and DoD leadership, further coordination is necessary to force industry suppliers to agree to a common standard of ports, electronic lexicon, and connections, such that contractors produce systems that are more interoperable across individual contracts.

---

[44] Black Diamond, "Advancements in Wearable Computing Solutions Aid Jtac Missions," (Tempe, AZ: BDAT, 2011).

Summary

Innovation is the successful change in practices often performed and achieved through the adaptation of material technologies. However, changing human practices is complex, and efforts to effect this change require a deep contextual knowledge of the user. Users are inherently creative and likely to invent their own solutions when given the opportunity. Organizations are unique in their own way and yet can be structured to harness the inventive behavior of users. Designers, too, can harness soldier creativity by designing machines to enable technological tinkering. And while the emergent picture for policymakers might somewhat diminish hopes that complex innovation programs can prove successful, it should also encourage further research into the wellspring of soldier insight and creativity. Either way, beginning here starts with a real-world perspective that is often underappreciated.

Securing a tighter relationship between scholars and practitioners is a good first step towards a more user-based approach in military innovation. A greater commitment to analysis and historical research about operations certainly would be worthwhile, including the placement in theater of analysts familiar with the paths of user-innovation. At a minimum, scholars and practitioners must increase the frequency of conversations with one another in order to open more in-depth dialogue about the practicality of current projects, their applicability to the current fight, and lessons about the future. Such conversations can also facilitate better understanding of how to harness knowledge and ideas developed in the field. Exploration of these paths will not be unprecedented or misguided. Much has been written in business literature on flat organizations and their capacity for innovation.[45] Much has also been documented about firms that have successfully developed innovative feedback channels from the top of the organization down to the factory floor.[46]

Second and third lines of effort for the DoD is further emphasis on openness and interoperability across acquisition contracts, as this will at least provide users with the freedom to tinker and solve problems locally until macro-level solutions can be found across the enterprise. In many cases the answer might be to refuse to buy from producers who fail to comply. Permitting contractors to constrain flexibility of design in order to maintain a dominant market niche is a behavior we can no longer accept. In some cases, this may mean turning to commercially available and disposable solutions until traditional contractors can figure out how to make the transition (if at all).

The user is the final arbiter of the success of any innovation. This means that the non-material factors of innovation should be the first consideration in any contract, organizational transformation, or calculus of military power. The system must be modified to emphasize usability, interoperability, and flexibility. These are the new characteristics of the realm. A reluctance to understand these

---

[45] David J. Teece, "Firm Organization, Industrial Structure, and Technological Innovation," *Journal of Economic Behavior & Organization* 31, no. 2 (1996), Jeffrey G. Covin and Dennis P. Slevin, "The Influence of Organization Structure on the Utility of an Entrepreneurial Top Management Style," *Journal of Management Studies* 25, no. 3 (1988).

[46] The literature is decidedly vast. For examples see: Brian Shaw, "Innovation and New Product Development in the UK Medical Equipment Industry," *International Journal of Technology Management* 15, no. 3 (1998), Nikolaus Franke and Frank Piller, "Value Creation by Toolkits for User Innovation and Design: The Case of the Watch Market," *Journal of Product Innovation Management* 21, no. 6 (2004), Shneiderman Ben, "Creating Creativity: User Interfaces for Supporting Innovation," *ACM Trans. Comput.-Hum. Interact.* 7, no. 1 (2000).

important and fundamental tenets of innovation has led to wasteful spending and, arguably, it has put lives at risk.

Part V: Great Power Strategy

Thinking Three-Dimensionally About American Defense

John Arquilla

There is a distinct rhythm to the production of high-level official reports that bear upon the protection of the Republic. Two main forms, the national security strategy and the presidential guidance, tend to bloom anew in the wake or on the cusp of high-level political change. A third — the latest thinking of senior Pentagon leaders, in and out of uniform — appears every four years, off years in the presidential cycle: the quadrennial defense review (QDR). A fourth type of report often follows, the national military strategy, which offers a more distilled version of the QDR. All four forms admirably exposit, and in unison tend to restate in significantly overlapping manner, the goals of the United States. These aims tend to remain highly consistent over time in their emphasis on ensuring American military supremacy, the cultivation of like-thinking allies, the deterrence and/or defeat of all manner of enemies, and the need to undertake all actions in a cost-effective fashion.

The large body of academic, policy-institute, and think-tank analyses of these reports tends, in the main, to accept their basic premises — though sharp, articulate critiques do occasionally surface. Andrew Bacevich, for example, has emerged as one of our country's most important challengers to the twin notions of maintaining American military preponderance in every corner of the globe, and relentlessly pressuring others to become more democratic. In many respects, Bacevich has restored to respectability key concepts introduced by Charles Beard in the years leading up to American involvement in World War II. Beard's ideas about nonintervention may have been inadequate for coping with the threats posed by Nazi Germany and Imperial Japan. But Bacevich has made a strong argument in support of Beard's central theme—the pursuit of good relations with the world while remaining reluctant to militarize American foreign policy—that is particularly timely today. As Bacevich sees things, "[t]he proper aim of American statecraft is not to redeem humankind or to prescribe some specific world order, not to police the planet by force of arms..." but rather "to create at home a 'more perfect union'."[1]

Those who contribute to each of the four types of recurring official reports emphasize, repeatedly, that they are "strategy-driven," yet it is hard to identify specific guidance in any of them. For example, one document readily, if vaguely, admits: "[i]n some areas, meeting emerging challenges will call for the development of wholly new concepts of operations."[2] There is no attempt to identify which "areas" demand such changes or what "new concepts" might be developed. In another instance, there is, across the board, an expressed sense of the need to counter China's rise by redirecting the U.S. military to "pivot to the Asia-Pacific." But once again there is little or no indication of the specific manner in which such a Pacific shift might be pursued—and there is no clue that there was ever any debate about the propriety of refocusing our strategic

---

1 Andrew Bacevich, *Washington Rules: America's Path to Permanent War* (New York: Henry Holt and Company, 2010), 237. Charles Beard, *A Foreign Policy for America* (Boston: The Atlantic Monthly Press, 1940) clearly exposits this historian's ideas.
2 *Quadrennial Defense Review Report, 2010* (Washington, DC: Government Printing Office, 2010), 41.

emphasis. Indeed, in addition to being short on identifying the means by which our ends should be pursued, none of these documents reflects the existence of *alternative approaches* in thinking about the American response to the rise of China. These all seem to have been "boiled away" in the report-writing process, leaving the Academy, the policy institute, and the think tank to take up the cudgels, if they dare, in the face of this strategic *fait accompli*.

With these concerns in mind, I want to make one simple request of those who devote their lives and efforts to our security: Be more specific. By focusing on the security problems of our time in a more detailed fashion—even when engaging in "strategic" thinking—the paths to improving our prospects in a hard, riotous world may be more clearly discerned. Such specificity need not become bogged down in policy minutiae; but it is an absolute imperative to reason and report in a less vague manner—especially when it comes to the military aspects of grand strategy. Political aims can be neatly summarized by the goal of encouraging the spread of democracy. Likewise, economic aims are well encapsulated by the notion of opening up more of the world system to free trade. But the military domain requires deeper exploration, for asserting one's need for preponderant power simply begs the question of how this goal is to be pursued.

A three-dimensional strategic framework – with historical examples

To assist in the specification process as it applies to military and security affairs, I suggest that a strategic framework properly drafted should begin with the identification of key issue areas. In our case today, and throughout the long history of the great powers, ancient and modern, I see that three fundamental questions have always recurred: Where should the military be positioned? What is the right size for the standing forces? And which technological advances should impel innovation and reform? These are the generic questions that have guided military affairs through time. Issues about when to fight, and whether or how to engage in irregular warfare—from dealing with ancient raiders to modern insurgents and terrorists—have always been present as well. Such considerations have often informed and guided thinking about the "big three" issues in focus here: where forces are to be based; the numbers required to achieve overall aims; and the tools to be acquired and practices to be employed in the field.

Each of these three fundamental areas of emphasis implies a kind of directional movement. The disposition of forces is lateral, like the x-axis in geometry. Sizing has more a vertical feel, like the y-axis. New technologies may take militaries off into generally uncharted, fresh territory, like a diagonal z-axis. Taken together, these axes form a three-dimensional "strategic space" in which they can interact. For example, the emergence of a new technology may allow for wider spatial movement (i.e., along the x-axis) than ever before. This edge in mobility, when coupled with advances in weaponry—occurring along the diagonal z-axis—might then allow much smaller forces (a y-axis nuance) to achieve great things. A strategic phenomenon of this sort arose in the 16th century when the marriage of heavy guns and long-range sailing ships first propelled Europeans to global dominance.[3]

The very existence of this sort of three-dimensional interrelationship of key strategic factors does not imply that simple awareness of them will lead to the identification of correct policy paths. The late Roman Empire, for example, provides a remarkably clear case of catastrophic failure, despite its leaders' awareness of all three dimensions. For

---

[3] This period is covered in some detail in Jared Diamond's *Guns, Germs, and Steel* (New York: W.W. Norton, 1999). Carlo Cipolla, in his *Guns, Sails, and Empires* (New York: Pantheon Books, 1965), identified the gun-and-sail nexus decades earlier.

example, in the 3rd century C.E., Emperor Diocletian felt that, in order to maintain all territory currently under Roman control, the size of the standing army had to be increased by almost half, from 350,000 to a bit over 500,000.[4] This proved unsustainable over time, and in the 4th century Emperor Constantine reduced the overall size of legionary forces, stripped frontier garrisons down to a network of lightly-manned, defensible strong points, and relied on a mobile, centrally deployed strike force of about 100,000 legionaries to come to the rescue.

Good roads made swift movement possible, but infantry were still infantry, and needed to lighten their loads if they were to move faster. So Emperor Gratian decided to have the legionaries discard their heavy body armor. The result was a series of bloody, unmitigated disasters for Roman field armies. Edward Gibbon summed up the catastrophe well: "the Goths, the Huns and the Alani...excelled in the management of missile weapons; they easily overwhelmed the naked and trembling legions."[5]

In effect, the Roman strategy at this troubled time relied on shifts in the x (spatial deployment) and y (force size) axes that improved territorial "coverage" and troop mobility. But Roman military leaders made an oddly backward-looking choice on the z (technological) axis—removing body armor—that indicated a failure to understand the effects of increasingly accurate missile weapons on unarmored infantry. For Gibbon, this was the main cause of the fall of the Empire in the West.

---

[4] The figures are rough estimates, and there is debate among historians about exact numbers. But the consensus view is that Diocletian greatly increased the size of the force. See a summary of this discourse in Arther Ferrill, *The Fall of the Roman Empire: The Military Explanation* (London: Thames and Hudson, 1986), 42-4.

[5] Edward Gibbon, *The History of the Decline and Fall of the Roman Empire*, edited by J.B. Bury, (New York: The Heritage Press, 1946), Vol. II, 853.

In the East, however, Byzantium survived the fall of Rome by a thousand years, all the while employing a very similar defense-in-depth concept. How is it that the Eastern Empire prospered with this approach, where the West had relied upon it and fallen? The key lies in Byzantine attention given to the z-axis. Yes, there were smaller numbers of troops garrisoning fortified outposts on the frontiers, whose job was to give the alarm in the case of an invasion and hold out until help came. The help itself was centrally located, as in the Roman case. But the difference was that the "quick reaction force" was made up almost entirely of heavy cavalry—i.e., armored men *and* armored horses—who came with a range of missile and shock weapons, and a "swarming" doctrine for employing them in assault waves. In his magisterial study of Byzantine grand strategy, Edward Luttwak sums up the field manual prepared by Emperor Constantine VII as designed "instead of trying to preclude incursions—too hard to do—enemy columns [were] to be trapped" by infantry holding key passes while the heavy cavalry moved in for the kill.[6]

Other historical examples of the military affairs of great powers fit this "*xyz* framework" for strategic thinking as well, the most notable being the British Empire in the half-century running from the end of the American Civil War in 1865— perhaps the first true modern war—to the outbreak of World War I in 1914. Industrialization was quickening during this period, and British holdings were scattered all over the world. The Royal Navy was by far the largest among all nations, and was distributed between home waters and the world's other oceans and seas in ways that ensured its continued preponderance. The British Army was small, but even early in this period it was well armed with Maxim guns, which proved

---

[6] Edward Luttwak, *The Grand Strategy of the Byzantine Empire* (Cambridge: The Harvard University Press, 2009), 343.

crucially important in conflicts with tribal irregulars in many settings.[7]

Further, the Army could be projected to any point in the world thanks to the sea control sustained by the navy. The army was also easily expandable, with any increased numbers being just as deployable, too, as can be seen by the Empire's ability to send over half a million troops to southern Africa during the Boer War (1899-1902). Thus in its heyday the British Empire had forces capable of: global coverage (the x-axis); rapidly scaling up in size (the y-axis); and utilizing the most advanced technologies—at sea, steam propulsion and, eventually, big-gun battleships, and on land machine guns and high-explosive artillery (the z-axis).

But during this same period it grew clear that technological advances were threatening to impose on the Royal Navy what Bernard Brodie called "a sharp narrowing of its range of action."[8] Steam vessels needed to refuel and refit; and even colonial bases could not support great naval striking forces in sustained ways against serious opposition. This limitation served to ease and enable the rise of competing naval powers like Japan, Germany—even the United States—so British maritime strategists shifted along the x-axis, drawing more of the fleet to home waters, from which it could surge out in time of war.

It was a move like Emperor Constantine's centralization of Roman legionary strike forces. On the y-axis, though, the Royal Navy, while remaining fairly steady in absolute size, was losing its leadership position when counted against the growing battle fleets of all other navies. Britain had just over

---

[7] As C.E. Calwell noted in his class *Small Wars* (London: H.M.S.O., 1906), 440, "Maxims, which can be easily handled and used, have done excellent service in East Africa, Matabililand, and in the campaigns on the North West frontier of India."

[8] Bernard Brodie, *Sea Power in the Machine Age* (Princeton: Princeton University Press, 1943), 11.

60% of the world's capital warships in 1890, a percentage that dropped to 40% by 1900. Still, Britain's naval strength was maintained at just enough of a margin that it remained greater than the next two leading powers combined.[9] As for the army, it rapidly downsized in the wake of the Boer War, presumably ready to scale up once again as needed.

The foregoing approach consisted of accepting more risk on the x- and y-axes, respectively, by bringing the navy home and sharply reducing the size of the standing army. This would have been quite reasonable had the British been attentive to and skillful in meeting the demands of the more technologically oriented z-axis. But they were not. The Royal Navy had two decades to contemplate the possibility of submarine warfare before the onslaught of the German Kaiser's U-boats, yet the British went into the Great War with no reliable means of detecting submerged vessels. The all-big-gun battleship ("dreadnought") technology was indeed experimented with, though not in an entirely productive way. Naval architects were drawn to an innovative "battle cruiser" concept that featured as much firepower as and more speed than dreadnoughts, but less defensive armor. Thus the battle cruisers tended to blow up when hit in battle.[10] These failures on the z-axis of sea power nearly lost the British the war. Further steps toward defeat were taken by the army's inability to comprehend that machine guns and high-explosive artillery — so valuable in colonial wars — meant that attacking in massed infantry formations was suicidal in a conventional

---

9 This was the so-called "two-power rule." On the declining British share of global sea power during this period, see G.T. Modelski and W.R. Thompson, *Seapower in Global Politics* (Seattle: University of Washington Press, 1988), 76.

10 Robert Massie chronicled British pre-war naval deficiencies in his *Dreadnought* (New York: Random House, 1991) and wartime consequences in his *Castles of Steel* (New York: Random House, 2003).

war.[11] All in all, the British neglect of the z-axis came very close to causing a catastrophe.

American experience during a key period

At this point, it is useful to inquire into the American performance in the three-dimensional "strategic space" introduced herein. A good analytic point of departure would be the forty years from the end of the Korean War to a few years after Operation Desert Storm (1953-1993). This was a time when Americans of all political stripes embraced the apparent need to "contain" communist expansion on a global basis and, after the fall of the Soviet Union at the end of 1991, to keep some form of "global order."[12] On the x-axis, having to do with the spatial disposition of forces, the major sustained overseas commitment was to NATO: a fairly steady quarter-million troops were kept in Germany, with another 100,000 spread around the rest of Western Europe and the Mediterranean. About 100,000 service members were regularly deployed to East Asia during this period as well, divided between Korea and Japan. Numbers in Asia spiked during the Vietnam War (1965-1973), to which over half a million troops were sent by 1968 — though very significant drawdowns were swiftly made, to 150,000 by 1971, with complete withdrawal by 1973. There was a similar overseas spike in 1991-92, a time during which some 500,000 American service members deployed to the Persian Gulf region.[13]

---

[11] See Alan Clark's classic indictment of British military leadership during World War I, *The Donkeys* (London: Pimlico, [1961]1991).

[12] Gallup surveys during this period indicate a relatively steady two-thirds of Americans — sometimes slightly more, sometimes slightly less — supported "taking an active part in world affairs." Even in the wake of withdrawal from Vietnam (early in 1973), the figure stood at 66% support for continued engagement as a world leader.

[13] These data were all derived from *The Statistical Abstracts of the United States*.

On the *y*-axis, pursuit of American strategic interests at the outset of this period (1953) entailed maintenance of a military aggregating about 3.5 million on active duty in all services. Both the U.S. Navy and Air Force, it must be noted, had unquestioned pre-eminence among the world powers — much like the position of the Royal Navy at the 19th century zenith of the British Empire. But after direct American involvement in the Vietnam War ended in 1973, the number of active duty service members dropped by 40% to a little over two million, and conscription was ended. In the years immediately following the Soviet Union's collapse at the end of 1991, a further reduction of almost a third took place, bringing the active forces down to 1.4 million — just about where the number stands today.[14]

If the geographical dispositions and force-size dimensions of the U.S. military during this period seem to have followed sensible patterns of movement, the more technical domain, the *z*-axis, is where leaders drifted far off course. In the 1950s, atomic weapons provided a seeming fix to the problem of defending Europe from afar. This was the era of the "New Look," and of the "pentomic division," when smaller standing forces, it was argued, would win thanks to a capacity for mounting nuclear assaults against the enemy. The only problem with this strategy was that the Soviets could fight in a similar way, and would likely win out in a massive attritional struggle of this sort, given their superior numbers. So, nuclear deterrence would remain robust, even if conventional war broke out. As General Maxwell Taylor put matters at the time, the New Look "prepares for one improbable type of war,

---

[14] Figures for total active duty service members were also derived from *The Statistical Abstracts of the United States.*

while leaving the United States weak in its ability to meet the most probable type of threat."[15]

Analyzing Strategy in Three Dimensions
Example: From The New Look to Flexible Response for NATO

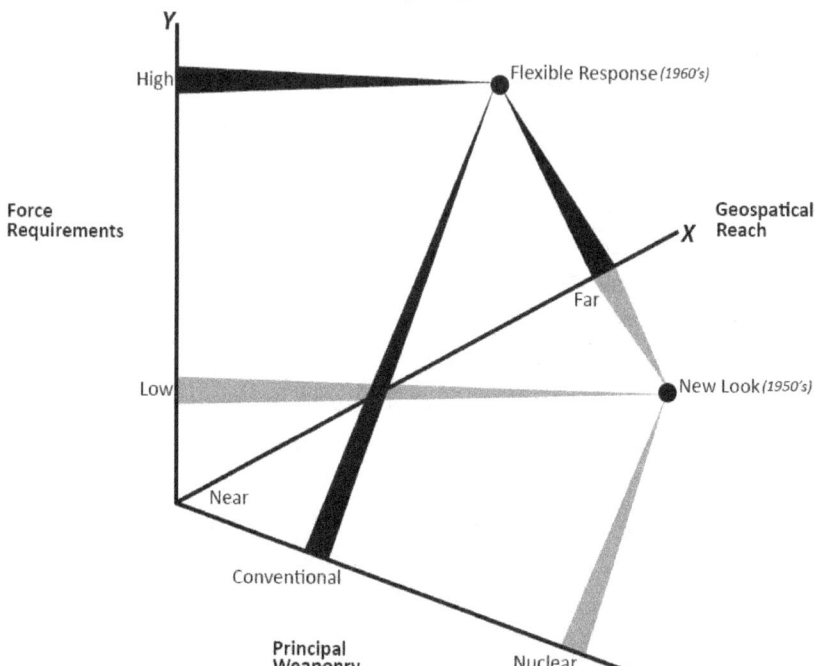

Taylor and those aligned with his critique eventually prevailed, and the nuclear mania—which even included for a while a doctrine of "massive retaliation" against *any* act of military aggression, no matter how small—subsided.[16] Thus the 1960s saw a renaissance of conventional warfighting capabilities, allowing U.S. forces to respond "flexibly" (i.e., in

---

[15] Maxwell Taylor, *The Uncertain Trumpet* (New York: Harper & Brothers, Publishers, 1959), 40-41.

[16] Of massive retaliation, Thomas Schelling noted in his *Arms and Influence* (New Haven: Yale University Press, 1966), 190, that it was a doctrine "in decline almost from its enunciation in 1954."

non-nuclear ways) to Soviet aggression. But yet another technology fetish emerged, this one having to do with the widespread use of helicopters that were intended to "vertically envelop" any and all foes. This became the "big bet" on the z-axis that the U.S. military laid down in Vietnam—and lost with, given the choppers' lack of stealth and vulnerability to ground fire. Well over four thousand were brought down during the war. Historian Michael Maclear's haunting query lingers: "Perhaps the greatest question mark is whether the helicopter 'came of age' in Vietnam."[17] In the wake of Vietnam, there was renewed emphasis on European security, and once again the Pentagon sought a solution heavily dependent on the technological z-axis: precision-guided munitions (PGMs). The long-feared war in the Fulda Gap never happened; but PGMs were nevertheless made and, for the first time in military history, posed the prospect of firing at great range with deadly accuracy. These weapons, never used against the Red Army, soon proved their worth in Operation Desert Storm, helping to win an exceptionally lop-sided victory in the field against the Iraqis. And this was the technology that was taken into the new millennium with high hopes of success against any sort of adversary, large or small, conventional or irregular.

The post-9/11 era: Practice first, theory next

The early auguries were good. In the opening phase of Operation Enduring Freedom in Afghanistan late in 2001, just eleven Special Forces A-teams—less than 200 sets of boots on the ground, but aided by precision strikes from the air—drove the Taliban and al Qaeda from power. Yes, the A-teams rode with indigenous allies. They were nevertheless still quite

---

[17] Michael Maclear, *The Ten Thousand Day War: Vietnam, 1945-1975* (New York: St. Martin's Press, 1981), 205. Maclear pegs helicopter losses at 4,865.

outnumbered; and the soldiers of the Northern Alliance were the same ones who had just lost 95% of the country *to* the Taliban. The difference clearly came in the form of the Special Forces A-teams' ability to actualize the great potential of American air power by guiding and coordinating close support. Military historian Stephen Biddle has observed, "air strikes were directed mostly by commandos whose methods, equipment, and centrality to the outcome were *unprecedented.*"[18]

But instead of a continued string of special-operations-oriented, tech-led triumphs, the invasion of Iraq in 2003 quickly lapsed into a long slog against insurgents. And after years of quiescence, the Taliban, perhaps having learned some lessons from the Iraqi example, mounted their own guerrilla campaign. In both cases, the numbers of U.S. forces deployed were quite substantial, with nearly 200,000 in Iraq and about half that, at the peak, in Afghanistan. In Iraq the tide was turned when a physical network of small yet highly-effective outposts was established, and complemented by a "social network" that grew from efforts to separate and turn insurgents away from al Qaeda. Once this movement began, the violence soon dropped by about 90%. This was not a turnaround that could be attributed simply to the addition of 28,000 troops in a "surge." Nor were the roughly 400,000 troops that General Eric Shinseki once called for needed to achieve this result.[19] In Afghanistan, forces have already drawn down to less than 50,000, and most of these will leave by the end of 2014. The current "stay behind" troop level being considered for Afghanistan is in the 10,000-range, a low

---

[18] Stephen Biddle, *Afghanistan and the Future of Warfare: Implications for Army and Defense Policy* (Carlisle, PA: Strategic Studies Institute, 2002), p. 6. Emphasis added.

[19] General Shinseki first called for this large number of troops in his testimony before the Senate Armed Services Committee on February 25, 2003.

number that some analysts think might still be too high, politically.[20]

In both Iraq and Afghanistan, insurgents will likely continue to ply their trade, even if at reduced levels. And American presence, though small on the ground in Afghanistan—and very light in Iraq, even if invited to return—will linger indefinitely and be supported by the reach and power that come with continued U.S. air and naval superiority. Thus, on the x-axis, it may be that there is a way to maintain a global disposition of forces—not just in south and southwest Asia—so long as those deployed forward are kept in small numbers. The ability to receive near-immediate support from air and naval assets, and the capacity for swift reinforcement, give the x-axis (spatial dimension) much of the flavor of the long-lived Byzantine grand strategy mentioned earlier. As to the disposition of air and naval assets, in the information age there is little sign of the "narrowed range" effect that Bernard Brodie observed came with industrialization.

If all's well on the x-axis, the same may not be true when it comes to the force sizing issues highlighted by the y-axis. The clearest lesson of the past decade is that the U.S. military has a problem "scaling down" to wage smaller wars. Afghanistan started small, but senior American leaders eventually chose to shift to a "big unit" approach that achieved insufficient results against dogged enemy resistance. In Iraq, on the other hand, the campaign began on a large scale, but made real progress only when a small percentage of troops were allocated to the network of outposts in Anbar Province. Even when the forces needed to support this initiative are counted, they totaled less than a fifth of the overall occupation force. The clear challenge on the y-axis is to allow smaller units of action to emerge.

---

[20] See Phil Stewart, "For Obama, Could 10,000 Troops in Afghanistan Be Too Many?" *Reuters,* November 26, 2012.

To some extent, the Army's shift from an emphasis on divisions to brigade combat teams (BCTs) reflects an awareness of the need to scale down—and the persistence of division-level organizational structures makes clear that the ability to "scale up" to a larger conflict, as needed, is also retained. The last Quadrennial Defense Review called for increasing the number of BCTs to 73, counting both active and reserve components – a substantial increase in the number in place a decade ago.[21] This would be a very positive development were the numbers of BCTs to continue to grow. But the increase in the number of BCTs has now apparently been reversed in favor having a smaller number of them that possess heavier (i.e., more armor and artillery) elements.[22]

In an era of straitened economic conditions, it is clear today, as it was to Constantine so long ago, that standing forces must decline in numbers. This too is a y-axis issue; but if indeed the appropriate unit of action is now smaller—but scalable upward—then reduced active forces, complemented by Reserve and Guard units, form the way ahead. This is the direction in which the Obama administration is headed; the only question is how much to reduce the standing forces. The answer is directly related to the level of effectiveness of smaller formations of land, air, and naval forces—which is the domain of the z-axis.

As noted earlier, the U.S. military experience along this technological axis has, oddly, not been very good overall during the past sixty years. The belief in the New Look, so dependent on nuclear weapons to revolutionize warfare, proved illusory. The heli-borne "vertical envelopment" concept of operations led to disaster in Vietnam. Precision-guided munitions seemed at least to have come into their

---

[21] *Quadrennial Defense Review Report*, 2010, 46.

[22] Tony Capaccio, "Army to Cut Twelve Combat Brigades by 2017 in Postwar Move," *Bloomberg News*, June 25, 2013.

own—but did little to strategically defeat irregular foes in Iraq and Afghanistan. In Iraq, the greatest gains came from small units of infantryman working from outposts with friendly Iraqis. In Afghanistan, the use of PGMs in a counter-leadership-targeting mode against al Qaeda may have missed the point that, "in a network, everybody is No. 3." Replacements abound.

Nevertheless, the tele-operated system—aerial drones being at center stage currently—seems to be the technology of the moment. But drone strikes unfold at too slow a pace to debilitate networks, and the drones themselves may have trouble surviving in any but the most permissive of combat environments. My concern is that this technology, too, will suffer the fate of preceding z-axis favorites. Indeed, the spread of al Qaeda's influence and the violence it has fomented in Mali, Libya, Somalia, Syria, even Iraq—to which the network has returned in our wake—augur ill, and should caution us against over-reliance on drones.

Still, there may be a way to proceed along the z-axis, at a slightly different angle, that can provide a real opportunity for meaningful progress. Where previous technological emphases have largely been on weapons systems, the great z-axis opportunity today—and tomorrow—lies in information systems. For it is by improved sensing that enemies, especially irregular ones, will be found. Better guidance systems will give weapons the ability to strike against either conventional armies or insurgent or terrorist cells with greater accuracy at ever increasing range. And the ubiquitous networking of information flows will empower forces in the field, at sea, and in the air to outmaneuver even the nimblest adversaries. If the United States wishes to maintain global strategic leadership with smaller forces, this is the only affordable way to do so.

Conclusion

It seems, in the end, that the z-axis may be the first among equals, over and above the spatial and quantitative axes. Had the Romans gotten the z-axis right in ancient times, they might not have fallen quite so hard. The Byzantines did get the technological solution of the time right. Their empire outlasted Rome by a thousand years. The British, at the zenith of imperial power, went astray on the technological axis. They were not conquered, but paid far too high a price in blood and treasure during the world wars, and then saw their empire collapse. Americans, a most technologically oriented people, have, ironically, had real and sometimes severe problems finding the right way ahead with the technologies of war. For the U.S. military, it is high time to focus on the z-axis in ways that identify lasting future solutions.

With all the foregoing in mind, I close with a second request to add to my initial one about seeking greater specificity in the preparation of the key national security documents: Is it possible, instead of following the well-worn path of the impending Quadrennial Defense Review process, to break pattern—just this time—and also prepare a three-dimensional strategic review that integrates the spatial, quantitative, and technological factors that will ultimately determine our fate and, necessarily, the fate of much of the world? I hope so.

ABOUT THE CONTRIBUTORS

John Arquilla

John Arquilla, Ph.D., is professor of defense analysis at the Naval Postgraduate School, where he has taught in the special operations curriculum since 1993. He also serves as director of the Information Operations Center. His teaching interests revolve around the history of irregular warfare, terrorism, and the implications of the information age for society and security. He earned his degrees in international relations from Rosary College (BA 1975) and Stanford University (MA 1989, PhD 1991).

Best known for his concept of "netwar" (i.e., the distinct manner in which those organized into networks fight), Dr. Arquilla is author of more than one hundred articles in both leading academic journals and more general publications such as *The Atlantic Monthly*, *Wired*, and *The New Republic*. His books include: *Dubious Battles: Aggression Defeat and the International System* (1992); *From Troy to Entebbe: Special Operations in Ancient & Modern Times* (1996); *In Athena's Camp* (1997); *Networks and Netwars: The Future of Terror, Crime and Militancy* (2001); *The Reagan Imprint: Ideas in American Foreign Policy from the Collapse of Communism to the War on Terror* (2006); *Worst Enemy: The Reluctant Transformation of the American Military* (2008); *Insurgents, Raiders, and Bandits* (2011); and *Afghan Endgames* (2012).

Jason Brooks

Jason Brooks is a former Marine, Iraq veteran, and graduate of the Lyndon B. Johnson School of Public Affairs where he earned a Master of Global Policy Studies. At the LBJ School, Jason specialized in History, Strategy and Statecraft with an emphasis on the geopolitics of energy. He also served as

Fellow for the Next Generation Project Texas, was the first recipient of the Elspeth Rostow Public Service Fellowship, and helped develop and publish the U.S. Army War College's first ever outsourced international strategic crisis negotiation exercise.

In the Marine Corps, Jason served one tour in East and Southeast Asia, including a 30 day detachment training Republic of Korea (ROK) Marines in helicopter operations. During his two tours in Iraq, Jason was awarded two Navy and Marine Corps Achievement medals for distinguished leadership and was awarded five Air Medals for his participation as an Aerial Gunner in combat support flight operations. After the LBJ School, Jason served as a Presidential Management Fellow for the U.S. Forest Service in Seattle, WA. He currently works as a Business Analyst for SunPower Corporation, a global solar energy provider. He is an Associate Director and member of CENSA. Jason lives in Austin, TX with his wife and son.

Tom Carter

Tom Carter's Latin America experience includes roles as Policy Director for the Western Hemisphere in the State Department's Office of Counter-Terrorism. In this capacity he directed policy initiatives to combat terror groups in Colombia (FARC, ELN, AUC) and in in the Tri-Border Region; he initiated first-ever U.S. financial support for Anti-Kidnapping programs managed by the Colombian National Police; he led the U.S. effort to declare the AUC as a Foreign Terrorist Organization. Previously, assigned to the U.S. Embassy in Managua, Nicaragua, he managed a counter-narcotics program aimed at stemming the flow of U.S.-bound cocaine; concurrently, he served as the U.S. Human Rights Officer within the Embassy staff, monitoring and reporting on Human Rights abuse cases in the aftermath of the Nicaraguan civil conflict. During his final years as a U.S. diplomat, Tom served as a Delegate to the United Nations with special responsibilities in Haiti: he authored two Haiti-focused Security Council Resolutions authorizing 10,000 UN Peacekeepers on the island. He earned a B.S. in Foreign Service from Georgetown University's School of Foreign Service (1988), an M.P.A. from Harvard (1992), and lives in New York City with his wife and seven children.

Major General Paul D. Eaton

Major General Paul D. Eaton served more than 30 years in the United States Army, including combat and post-combat assignments in Iraq, Bosnia, and Somalia. As a major general he was assigned to Iraq from 2003 to 2004 as Commanding General of the Coalition Military Assistance Training Team (CMATT), where he designed, manned, trained and equipped the Iraqi armed forces for the Iraqi Ministry of Defense and the security forces for the Interior Ministry. Prior to that assignment, he commanded the Army's Infantry Center and was Chief of Infantry for the Army. Eaton has appeared on a number of news and commentary programs including Face the Nation, Hardball and all major networks. During the 2008 campaign season, he advised candidates for both congressional and presidential campaigns. He holds a bachelor's degree from West Point and a master's in French Political Science from Middlebury College. He is married to PJ, has two sons and a daughter, all soldiers.

Sebastian L. v. Gorka

Sebastian L. v. Gorka, Ph.D. currently serves as the Major General Matthew C. Horner Distinguished Chair of Military Theory at Marine Corps University and is the National Security Affairs Editor for Breitbart.com . Previously he was

Associate Dean of Congressional Affairs and Relations to the Special Operations Community at National Defense University.

A graduate of the University of London and former Kokkalis Fellow at Harvard's J. F. Kennedy School of Government, he is an Associate Fellow with SOCOM's Joint Special Operations University and an Adjunct Professor with Georgetown University. A member of CENSA, he is also a regular instructor with the Special Warfare Center and School in Fort Bragg and for the FBI's Counterterrorism Division. Dr. Gorka has testified before Congress and briefed the CIA , ODNI, and NCTC.

Seb served as an adviser to the Department of Defense in the renewal of its Irregular Warfare Joint Operating Concept and is contributing co-editor, with the late COL Nick Pratt (USMC ret.) and Dr. Christopher Harmon, of *Toward a Grand Strategy Against Terrorism* (McGraw Hil). His special area of interest is the strategic culture and ideology of Global Jihadism and the proper use of Grand Strategy. He welcomes comments at seb.gorka@gmail.com.

James Hasik

James Hasik is a William Powers Fellow at the University of Texas at Austin, where he is a Ph.D. student in public policy at the Lyndon B. Johnson School of Public Affairs. He also serves as a non-resident senior fellow in the Brent Scowcroft Center for International Security at the Atlantic Council of the United States. At the Atlantic Council Mr. Hasik also serves as the editor and primary author of *The Defense Industrialist* blog. Jim holds an MBA in business economics from the University of Chicago and a BA in history and physics from Duke

University. He is a member of CENSA, the US Naval Institute, and the National Defense Industries Association (NDIA).

David C. Hendrickson

David C. Hendrickson has taught at Colorado College since 1983, and was chair of the Political Science department from 2000 to 2003. The author of seven books, Hendrickson received a Ph.D. in Political Science from Johns Hopkins University (Baltimore) and teaches courses in American foreign policy and international relations. Past publications include *Union, Nation, or Empire: The American Debate over International Relations, 1789-1941* (2009) and *Peace Pact: The Lost World of the American Founding* (2003), both published by the University Press of Kansas.

John J. Klein

John J. Klein, Ph.D., is a Senior Analyst at ANSER in Arlington, Virginia. He holds a Ph.D. in politics, with a strategic studies focus, from the University of Reading and a master's in national security and strategic studies from the U.S. Naval War College, where he was a Mahan Scholar. He previously served as a Federal Executive Fellow at the Brookings Institution in its Foreign Policy Studies program. A member of CENSA, John has served as a Countering WMD Planner for the last four years, and writes frequently on national policy, military strategy, and the implications of the Law of Armed Conflict. The author may be reached at: john.klein@anser.org.

Nina A. Kollars

Nina A. Kollars, Ph.D., is an Assistant Professor of Government at Franklin and Marshall College. She holds a B.A. from the College of St. Benedict (1996), an M.A. from George Washington University (2003), and a Ph.D. from Ohio

State (2012). Nina's scholarship examines the innovative practices of U.S. soldiers in war, and organizational responses to that creativity. Specifically, she traces technological and tactical modifications that fall outside military guidelines and whether those new practices and technologies become incorporated into doctrine. Her second passion is teaching and developing new techniques that emphasize active-learning processes. Prior to her Ph.D., she worked as an analyst at the Federal Research Division of the Library of Congress, a researcher for the World Bank, and has authored several reports on terrorism. Dr. Kollars' newest project looks at DoD's emphasis on user-innovation models as a new direction for weapons development. She is a member of CENSA.

Guermantes Lailari

Guermantes Lailari is currently a Senior Subject Matter Expert at the Human Geo Group, LLC. He is a retired USAF officer, specializing in counterterrorism, irregular warfare, counter-radicalization, and the Middle East. He has lived, studied, and worked in the Middle East and North Africa for almost nine years and similarly in Europe for six years. He directed the Middle East Orientation Course and the Dynamics of International Terrorism Course at the USAF Special Operations School, and served as an US Air Force Attaché in the Middle East. He holds advanced degrees in International Relations and Strategic Intelligence, and has begun his doctoral studies in Public Policy at George Mason University. He recently wrote chapters in books on the Israeli-Hezbollah War in *Influence Warfare* (James J. F. Forest (ed), Praeger Security International, 2009) and Islamic Hybrid Warfare in *Hybrid Warfare and Transnational Threats* (CENSA, 2011). Mr. Lailari is a member of CENSA.

Oriana Skylar Mastro

Oriana Skylar Mastro, Ph.D., is an assistant professor of security studies at the Edmund A. Walsh School of Foreign Service at Georgetown University where her research focuses on Chinese military and security policy, Asia-Pacific security issues, war termination, and coercive diplomacy. She is also in the United States Air Force Reserve, for which she works as an Asia-Pacific strategist at the Pentagon. Oriana has been a fellow in the Asia-Pacific Security program at the Center for a New American Security (CNAS), a University of Virginia Miller Center National Fellow, and a Center for Strategic and International Studies (CSIS) Pacific Forum Sasakawa Peace Fellow. Additionally, she has worked on China policy issues at the Carnegie Endowment for International Peace, RAND Corporation, U.S. Pacific Command, and Project 2049, and has also testified for the U.S.-China Economic and Security Review Commission.

Highly proficient in Mandarin, Oriana worked at a Chinese valve-manufacturing firm in Beijing as a translator and has made appearances on a Chinese-language debate show. She holds a B.A. in East Asian Studies from Stanford University, both an M.A. and Ph.D in Politics from Princeton University, and is a member of CENSA.

Brian Mazanec

Brian M. Mazanec earned his PhD from George Mason University's Department of Public and International Affairs in May 2014. He also holds a B.A. in political science from the University of Richmond and a M.S. in defense and strategic studies from Missouri State University's Department of Defense and Strategic Studies. Brian's academic research has published in various journals, such as *Comparative Strategy*, the *National Cybersecurity Institute Journal*, *Politics and the Life*

Sciences, and the *Journal of International Security Affairs*. His work has also been presented at international conferences and used as part of the curriculum in the U.S. Army War College's Department of Military Strategy, Planning and Operations. He is an adjunct professor at George Mason University and a senior defense analyst with the U.S. government. Brian can be reached at brianmazanec@gmail.com.

Aaron Eitan Meyer

Aaron Eitan Meyer is a practicing attorney, consultant, analyst, researcher, and public speaker. He is legal correspondent for the Terror Finance Blog, an advisory board member for the digital advocacy group Act for Israel, and a member of the Internet Corporation for Assigned Names and Numbers' Noncommercial Users Constituency. He has previously served as a research director for a lawfare organization, and as assistant director of the Legal Project at the Middle East Forum. In addition to one book to date, he has written or coauthored a number of articles, memoranda and blog entries on a wide variety of subjects, including lawfare, Middle East history, Zionism, terrorism, international and comparative law, World War II General Orde Charles Wingate, and various legal filings. He received his B.A. from New School University, where his studies focused on Middle East history and politics; and his J.D. from Touro College Jacob D. Fuchsberg Law Center, during which time he received awards for his coursework in Cybercrime, American Legal History and Holocaust, Genocide and the Law.

Keith W. Mines

Keith Mines is a career Foreign Service Officer currently serving as Political Counselor at the U.S. Embassy in Tel Aviv. Prior to this he was U.S. Senior Civilian Representative in Mazar-e Sharif, Afghanistan and has also served in San

Salvador, Port-au-Prince, Washington, D.C. (Brazil Desk), Budapest, Ottawa, and Mexico City. In addition, Mr. Mines ran the U.S. Field Office in Darfur in 2007; served as Governance Coordinator in the Al Anbar Province of Iraq from 2003-2004; was Economic and Commercial Counselor in the U.S. Embassy in Kabul in 2002; and Executive Assistant to the Special Representative of the U.N. Secretary General in the UNOSOM II peacekeeping mission in Somalia in 1994. Prior to joining the Foreign Service, Mr. Mines was a U.S. Army Special Forces Officer with service in Grenada, Central America, and North Carolina. He was educated at Brigham Young University and Georgetown University, where he studied history and diplomacy. A member of CENSA and a native of Colorado, Mr. Mines is married to the former Cecile McGuire of New York City; they have four children.

Steve Miska

Colonel Miska is currently the Lieutenant General Robert Eichelberger Army Chair at the Marine Corps War College, Marine Corps University at Quantico. He recently left the White House as a Director for Iraq on the National Security Staff, focusing on security aspects of the Iraq portfolio. Previously, he completed a Counterterrorism Fellowship at the College of International Security Affairs at National Defense University (NDU). He commanded a battalion from 2008-2010 in the 172nd Infantry Brigade stationed in Germany and deployed to Babil, Diwaniyah, and Najaf Provinces in Iraq as the Task Force 1-2 Commander, working closely with interagency Provincial Reconstruction Teams. His previous deployments to Iraq include fourteen months in Baghdad from 2006-2007 during the "Surge" where he commanded Task Force Justice and served as Deputy Brigade Commander for the Dagger Brigade, and a year in Tikrit from 2004-2005 where he served as the Task Force 1-18 Operations Officer. He has served in airborne infantry assignments in the 82nd Airborne Division at Fort Bragg, North Carolina, and the 1st Battalion, 508th Parachute Infantry Regiment in the Republic of Panama.

Steve was commissioned an Infantry officer in 1990 from the United States Military Academy (USMA) at West Point, earned a Masters degree in Business Administration from Cornell University from 1997-1999, and subsequently taught economics as an Assistant Professor at USMA West Point from 1999-2001. He also earned a Master of Arts in Strategic Security Studies from NDU in 2011, writing a thesis on protecting soft networks (indigenous allies like interpreters and other local nationals) during counterinsurgency operations. A member of CENSA, Colonel Miska has published several articles and currently continues his research on protecting soft networks.

William H. Natter, III

Bill Natter is a Director on the Board at CENSA and currently serves as a consultant to both government and commercial organizations. During the course of his career he has worked on a variety of national security issues related to science and technology (S&T), intelligence, terrorism, special programs, and special operations. He has served as the Deputy Under Secretary of the Navy, a position from which he managed the Department of the Navy's involvement in the 2010 Quadrennial Defense Review. He served as a senior staff member on the House Armed Services Committee for more than 11 years, with specific duties requiring oversight of U.S. Special Operations Command and various research and development (and especially S&T) programs. From 1994-1998, Bill served as the military legislative assistant (MLA) to Rep. Ike Skelton (D-MO), a position from which he focused on inter-agency matters, the NATO intervention in Bosnia-

Herzegovina, U.S. long-range strike options, and terrorism. And prior to his service as MLA, he helped oversee DoD's Small Business Innovation Research program while a staff member on the House Small Business Committee. Bill's accomplishments and awards include a B.A. in Political Science/International Affairs from the Colorado College, and the Distinguished Public Service Award from the Department of the Navy for work on strategic matters. In 2011, he served as co-editor of *Hybrid Warfare and Transnational Threats* (CENSA).

Jesse Pruett

Jesse P. Pruett is the recipient of the 2012 Samuel L. Sharp Award for Creative Work in International Relations at the Graduate Level from the School of International Service at American University. He is a veteran of nearly 20 years of military and government service, including four tours to Afghanistan and Iraq. He served on two Provincial Reconstruction Teams and as a PRT advisor at the Multi-National Division level. Additionally, he has served abroad in Nicaragua, El Salvador, and Bosnia. He is a member of CENSA and a Distinguished Member of the U.S. Army Civil Affairs Corps. Mr. Pruett currently supports the Department of the Army Staff at the Pentagon. He resides in Alexandria, Virginia, and continues to serve as a United States Army Reserve Paratrooper. A version of the essay included in *American Strategy and Purpose* was first presented as part of the Interagency Essay Series on the Web site for the Simons Center for the Study of Interagency Cooperation.

Glenn E. Robinson

Glenn E. Robinson, Ph.D., is an expert on Middle East affairs and an award-winning teacher, serving as professor at the Naval Postgraduate School in Monterey, California, and affiliated faculty member at the Center for Middle East Studies at the University of California, Berkeley. On three occasions he has been recognized for his outstanding teaching, twice by the Naval Postgraduate School and once by Berkeley. He has lived and studied in a number of countries and institutions in the Middle East, including as a Fulbright scholar at the University of Jordan, the Hebrew University of Jerusalem, the American University in Cairo, Yarmouk University in Jordan, and as an exchange student to Iran in 1978. He has published and lectured widely on Islamic fundamentalism, the Arab-Israeli conflict, and related challenges facing the Middle East. Glenn received his PhD from Berkeley in 1992 and has been teaching at NPS since 1991.

Anna Simons

Anna Simons, Ph.D., is a Professor of Defense Analysis at the U.S. Naval Postgraduate School (NPS), joining the faculty in 1998. Prior to teaching at NPS, she was an assistant and then associate professor of anthropology at the University of California at Los Angeles, as well as chair of the Masters in African Area Studies Program. At NPS, she teaches courses in the anthropology of conflict, military advising, low intensity conflict in Africa, and political anthropology. Anna is the author of *Networks of Dissolution: Somalia Undone and The Company They Keep: Life Inside the U.S. Army Special Forces.* She has written extensively about intervention, conflict, and the military from an anthropological perspective for a wide range of publications, such as *The American Interest, The National Interest, Orbis, Third World Quarterly, and Parameters.* Dr. Simons holds an A.B. from Harvard College and a Ph.D. in social anthropology from Harvard University.

The Honorable Mac Thornberry

Congressman Mac Thornberry currently serves as the Vice Chairman of the House Armed Services Committee (HASC), and also leads the HASC Subcommittee on Intelligence, Emerging Threats, and Capabilities. Widely recognized for his work on various strategic and terrorism-related issues, Mr. Thornberry has concurrently served on the House Permanent Select Committee on Intelligence for several years. Long recognized for championing transformative causes and new threats such as those related to cyber and ideological extremism, Congressman Thornberry is, according to the National Journal, "well-regarded in both parties for his thoughtfulness." Mr. Thornberry has represented the 13th congressional district of Texas since 1994. See more at http://thornberry.house.gov/biography/nationalsecuritybio. htm#sthash.vpKLddJP.dpuf .

Robert R. Tomes

Robert R. Tomes, Ph.D., is a Director on the Board at CENSA, President of the MapStory Foundation, and a consultant to government and commercial organizations through Liminal Leadership, LLC. His work has appeared in *Survival, Armed Forces & Society, Parameters, The Naval War College Review, Policy Studies, Defence Studies, Military Review, Defense & Security Analysis, Small Wars & Insurgencies,* and *The Small Wars Journal.* An adjunct professor of security studies at Georgetown University, he is the author of *US Defense Strategy from Vietnam to Operation Iraqi Freedom: US Military Innovation and the New American Way of War* (Routledge), co-editor of *Human Geography: Socio-Cultural Dynamics and Global Security* (USGIF Press), and co-editor of *Hybrid Warfare and Transnational Threats* (CENSA) and *Crossroads Africa* (CENSA). Robert received his Ph.D. in Government and Politics from the University of Maryland, College Park.

Ali Wyne

Ali Wyne is a researcher at Harvard University's Belfer Center for Science and International Affairs. He graduated from the Massachusetts Institute of Technology in 2008 with bachelor's degrees in Management Science and Political Science, and, as a senior, received the Institute's highest honor for students, the Karl Taylor Compton Prize. Prior to joining the Belfer Center, Ali was a Junior Fellow in the China Program (now the Asia Program) at the Carnegie Endowment for International Peace. Ali is a member of Chatham House, the International Institute for Strategic Studies, CENSA, and Young Professionals in Foreign Policy. He also serves as a discussant at Bloggingheads.tv, as a Next America Fellow at the Center for Strategic and International Studies, and as a contributing analyst for Wikistrat. He is a co-author, along with Graham Allison and Robert Blackwill, of Lee Kuan Yew: *The Grand Master's Insights on China, the United States, and the World* (Cambridge, MA: MIT Press, 2013).

Amy Zalman

Amy Zalman, Ph.D., is the CEO and President of the World Future Society, the world's oldest and largest membership organization dedicated to empowering futurists and igniting dialogue about the future. Prior to assuming her current position, she served as the Department of Defense Information Integration Chair and Professor of National Security at the National War College. From 2007 – 2012, Dr. Zalman worked at Science Applications International Corporation (SAIC, now Leidos), a Washington DC-based science and technology firm, where she developed new market strategies and basic research projects in the government strategic communications sector. Dr. Zalman is the founder of Strategic Narrative (http://strategic-narrative.net), which helps governments and the private sector use insights from storytelling to guide strategy and communications. Dr. Zalman also serves on the steering committee of the National Defense University Foresight Initiative, the Board of Directors of CENSA, the Influence Advisory Panel, and the Senior Information Operations Advisory Council and the Public Diplomacy Council; a former Fulbright scholar, she is also a professional member of the World Future Society, and a former research fellow at the EastWest Institute. She holds a Ph.D. in Middle Eastern Studies from New York University, a Masters Degree of Fine Arts from Cornell University and a Bachelors Degree from Columbia University. She is also proficient in Arabic and Hebrew.

ABOUT CENSA

The Council for Emerging National Security Affairs is a non-partisan, nonprofit research organization established in 1999. Its mission is to contribute to the ongoing dialogue shaping national security policy through formal discussion series, graduate level teaching programs, and collaborative research projects leading to publications of lasting quality. CENSA's activities draw upon the talents of its mid0career membership, a diverse, international group of public sector foreign policy specialists, military officers, private sector professionals, and accomplished academics.

www.censa.net

CENSA

COUNCIL FOR EMERGING NATIONAL SECURITY AFFAIRS

www.ingramcontent.com/pod-product-compliance
Lightning Source LLC
Chambersburg PA
CBHW060611290526
45793CB00001B/2